OLD LONDON

Westminster to St. James's

THE
'VILLAGE LONDON'
SERIES
from
THE ALDERMAN PRESS

THE VILLAGE LONDON SERIES

Other titles already published in hard back are:

VILLAGE LONDON Volume I
VILLAGE LONDON Volume II
LONDON RECOLLECTED Volume I
LONDON RECOLLECTED Volume II
LONDON RECOLLECTED Volume III
LONDON RECOLLECTED Volume IV
LONDON RECOLLECTED Volume V
LONDON RECOLLECTED Volume VI
VILLAGE LONDON ATLAS

Other titles already published in paperback:

VILLAGE LONDON Pt. 1 West and North
VILLAGE LONDON Pt. 2 North and East
VILLAGE LONDON Pt. 3 South-East
VILLAGE LONDON Pt. 4 South-West

OLD FLEET STREET
CHEAPSIDE AND ST. PAUL'S
THE TOWER AND EAST END
SHOREDITCH to SMITHFIELD
CHARTERHOUSE to HOLBORN
STRAND to SOHO
COVENT GARDEN and the THAMES to WHITEHALL
WESTMINSTER to ST. JAMES'S
HAYMARKET to MAYFAIR
HYDE PARK to BLOOMSBURY

The above ten titles are extracts from the hardback edition of London Recollected.

OLD LONDON

Westminster to St. James's
by
EDWARD WALFORD

THE ALDERMAN PRESS

British Library Cataloguing in Publication Data

Walford, Edward, *1823–1897*
    Old London: Westminster to St James's.
    1. London, history
    I. Title
    942.1

ISBN 0-946619-36-0

This edition published 1989

The Village Press Ltd.,
7d Keats Parade,
Church Street,
Edmonton,
London N9 9DP

Printed and bound in Great Britain
by Redwood Burn Ltd, Yeoman Way,
Trowbridge, Wiltshire

CONTENTS.

CONTENTS.

CONTENTS.

LIST OF ILLUSTRATIONS.

LONDON.

CHAPTER I.

WESTMINSTER.—A SURVEY OF THE CITY: MILLBANK, AND ITS NEIGHBOURHOOD.

> "London, thou comprehensive word
> What joy thy streets and squares afford!
> And think not thy admirer rallies
> If he should add, thy "lanes and alleys."
> *P. Egan, "Tom and Jerry."*

Millbank—Inigo Jones and Ben Jonson—Great College Street—Little College Street—Barton and Cowley Streets—Abingdon Street—Thomas Telford, the Engineer—Wood Street—John Carter, F.S.A.—North Street—Elliston, the Actor—Peterborough House—"High Livings"—Annual Procession of Stage Coaches—The Manor of Neyte—The Church of St. John the Evangelist—Lord Grosvenor's Residence—Fanciful Style of Street-naming—Vine Street—Vineyards in the Olden Times—Horseferry Road—Escape of Queen Mary of Modena—Flight of King James—The Great Seal of England thrown into the Thames—A Lucky Ferryman—Vauxhall Regatta—Works of the Gas Light and Coke Company—The "White Horse and Bower"—Page Street—Millbank Prison—Vauxhall Bridge—Holy Trinity Church—Vauxhall Bridge Road—Residence of Cardinal Manning—A New Cathedral—Vincent Square—Church of St. Mary the Virgin—Rochester Row—Emery Hill's Almshouses—St. Stephen's Church—Tothill Fields Prison—The Old Bridewell—Grey-Coat School—Strutton Ground—Dacre Street.

"THE old City of Westminster proper, with its venerable Abbey, and its gloomy and narrow streets, once the residence of peers, courtiers, and poets, constitutes perhaps the most interesting district of the great metropolis."

So writes Mr. J. H. Jesse, in his pleasant and interesting work on "London." Let us then endeavour to show our readers a few of the chief points of interest which lie around the Abbey. As lately as the reign of Elizabeth, the Middlesex shore opposite to Lambeth was a mere low and marshy tract of land, almost wholly free from buildings, except the Abbey and Palace, and some few public edifices which adjoined them and had grown up under their shadow. The region now known as Millbank was so called from a mill on the bank of the river which occupied the site on which stood Peterborough House, delineated in Hollar's "View of London." This house was pulled down and rebuilt about the year 1735, by the then head of the Grosvenor family, shortly after his marriage with Miss Davis, the heiress of Ebury Manor, by which he acquired the property now known as Belgravia; the Grosvenors continued to occupy it as their town mansion till early in the present century, when they removed to their present house in Upper Grosvenor Street. In St. John's Church, Westminster, between the Abbey and their former home, is one proof of their connection with the parish, in the shape of a panel recording the fact of King George and Queen Charlotte, in 1800, standing there as sponsors at the baptism of "Thomas, second son of Viscount Belgrave," who succeeded whilst still young to the Earldom of Wilton.

But the neighbourhood of which we write has still more ancient associations. Late in life, when he had quarrelled with Inigo Jones, with the Court, and the City, who had been his friends and patrons, we find Ben Jonson living almost under the shadow of Westminster Abbey, "in the house under which you pass," says Aubrey, "to go out of the churchyard into the old Palace." At this time he, whose "mountain belly," "prodigious waist," and stooping back, are familiar to all readers of his works, was suffering from the double misfortune of the palsy and of poverty, from the latter of which he was rescued to some extent by the Earl of Newcastle. Here, probably, he died (his death occurred in August, 1637); and he was buried in the Abbey hard by, where it is a tradition that "Jack Young," happening to pass by, gave a stonemason eighteen pence to carve on the pavement where he lay, the well-known words, "O rare Ben Jonson!"

Immediately to the south of the Abbey precincts is Great College Street, which runs westward from Abingdon Street to Tufton Street. It was formerly known simply as the "Dead Wall," from the wall built by Abbot Litlington round the Infirmary Garden, which once extended, in a semi-circular form, from the place where it now ends in College Street, to the Gate House. Gibbon's aunt, Mrs. Porter, "the affectionate guardian of his tender years," lived in College Street, where for some time she kept a boarding-house for the town boys of Westminster School.

Beyond is Little College Street, which, in the reign of Queen Anne, rejoiced in the name of Piper's Ground, and consisted of "a few houses built, the rest lying waste." Wealthy and well-born families, and even bishops, lived about its neighbourhood. From his house in College Court, in May, 1703, Edward Jones, Bishop of St. Asaph, was borne to his grave in the chancel of St. Margaret's Church.

Barton Street and Cowley Street, both of which branch out of College Street, are stated to have been built by Barton Booth, the actor, whom we have mentioned as a Westminster schoolboy under Dr. Busby. To the former street Booth gave his own Christian name, and to the latter that of his favourite poet, who also, as we have already seen, was an "old Westminster." There is a large old house at the end of Cowley Street, having a fine double staircase; indeed, there are fine staircases, and other marks of aristocratic occupation, in many of the houses round about this spot.

Abingdon Street, which forms the connecting link between Old Palace Yard and Millbank, was, at the commencement of the last century, known as Lindsay Lane, down the narrow length of which the lumbersome state carriage and eight heavily-caparisoned horses were driven into the court-yard of Lindsay House (at the south-west end of the thoroughfare), afterwards the residence of the Earl of Abingdon, and subsequently that of the Earl of Carnarvon, in order to be turned round to take up the King when he went to open Parliament.

At No. 24 in this street, in September, 1834, died, at an advanced age, Thomas Telford, the engineer. He was buried in the Abbey.

Wood Street, the thoroughfare extending from the south end of Abingdon Street to Tufton Street, was described, in 1720, as "very narrow, being old boarded hovels, ready to fall." Here resided John Carter, Esq., F.S.A., the distinguished author of "Specimens of Ancient Sculpture and Painting." He first became known to the public by his etchings engraved in the "Sepulchral Monuments," and other valuable antiquarian works. He died in September, 1817. In North Street, which leads from Wood Street to Smith Square, resided Mr. R. W. Elliston, the celebrated actor of his day, and some time manager of Drury Lane and the Olympic Theatres.

Millbank is described by Strype as "a very long place, which beginneth by Lindsay House, or, rather, by the Old Palace Yard, and runneth up into Peterborough (afterwards Grosvenor) House, which is the farthest house. The part from against College Street unto the Horseferry hath a good row of buildings on the east side, next to the Thames, which is most taken up with large wood-mongers' yards and brewhouses. The north side is but ordinary, except one or two houses by the end of College Street; and that part beyond the Horseferry hath a very good row of houses, much inhabited by gentry, by reason of the pleasant situation and prospect of the Thames. The Earl of Peterborough's house hath a large court-yard before it, and a fine garden behind it, but its situation is but bleak in the winter, and not over-healthful, as being so near the low meadows on the south and west parts."

Pennant speaks of Millbank not as a "very long place," or a district, but as a single mansion. He says it is "the last dwelling in Westminster," and describes it as "a large house, which took its name from a mill which once occupied its site." He says that it was purchased from the Mordaunts, Earls of Peterborough, by the ancestor of Sir Robert Grosvenor, whose hospitality he had often experienced as a boy. In the plan of London by Hollar, the site is marked as Peterborough House, and was owned by that family till, at least, the middle of the eighteenth century, though occa-sionally let to wealthy merchants. The wall round the garden, with an outer footpath along the river-side, was not removed till about 1810. The Earl of Wilton, brother of the late marquis, and uncle of the Duke of Westminster, was born here, and baptised, as we have said, in the adjoining church of St. John the Evangelist.

It was whilst living here, in 1735, that Charles, third Earl of Peterborough, married, as his second wife, Mrs. Anastasia Robinson, the celebrated singer. His lordship died the same year, after which the house was rebuilt by the Grosvenor family.

The mansion—or its occupant—at this time became the subject of a joke in Joe Miller's "Jest Book," under the head of "High Living," which will bear re-telling:—"Peterborough House, which is the very last in London, one way, being rebuilt, a gentleman asked another who lived in it. His friend told him Sir Robert Grosvenor. 'I don't know,' said the first, 'what estate Sir Robert has, but he ought to have a very good one; for nobody lives beyond him in the whole town.'"

As Congreve was being rowed in a wherry up the Thames, at Millbank, the boatman remarked that, owing to its bad foundation, Peterborough House had sunk a story. "No, friend," said he, "I rather believe it is a story raised."

Holywell Street, erected on the grounds of Peter-borough House, was so called after an estate belong-ing to Lord Grosvenor, in Flintshire.

The Government contractor, Mr. Vidler, lived in a house which had been built in the middle of Millbank by a Sir John Crosse, and to it, as Mr. Mackenzie Walcott informs us, the mail-coaches, before the unromantic days of railroads, used to be driven in annual procession, upon the King's birth-day, from Lombard Street. At noon the cavalcade set out—the horses belonging to the different mails being decked out with new harness, the guards and coachmen decorated with beautiful nosegays, and the postboys in scarlet jackets on horseback in advance. The king's birthday, in 1790, was the occasion of the first of these processions, when sixteen set out with plated harness and hammer-cloths of scarlet and gold.

In the Clause Rolls, 28 Henry VIII., is a grant wherein is mentioned "the manor of Neyte, with the precinct of water called the Mote of the said manor." Some buildings which afterwards occu-pied the site were known as the "Neat Houses." Stowe mentions them as "a parcel of houses most seated on the banks of the Thames, and inhabited by gardeners." John, fifth son of Richard, Duke of York, was born at the Manor House of Neyte, in 1448; and Edward VI., in his first year, granted the "House of Neyte" to Sir Anthony Brown. Pepys mentions going to take his amusement in these "Neat gardens;" and, if we may believe the *Domestic Intelligencer* of August 5th, 1679, "the mother of Nell Gwyn fell into the water near this spot, by accident, and was drowned."

In Smith Square, which lies between Wood Street and Romney Street, is a singular building, which a stranger would never be likely to take for a church, and yet it *is* a church—that of St. John the Evan-gelist; and it is one of the fifty churches built in and about the metropolis in the reign of Queen Anne. The Act of Parliament under which this church was built is commemorated by Tickell in his "Epistles" thus:—

"The pious Town sees fifty churches rise."

Its architect was not Vanbrugh, as is often stated, but a Mr. Archer, who certainly seems to have defied all the rules of architecture, loading the heavy structure with still heavier ornamenta-tion, by building at each of the four angles a stone tower and a pinnacle of ugliness that passes description. In front is a portico supported by

Doric columns, and the same order is continued, after a fashion, in pilasters round the building. It has, also, on the north and south sides other porticos, supported by massive stone pillars. Over the communion-table is a painted window, representing the "Descent from the Cross." The author of "A New Review of the Public Buildings," &c., published in 1736, speaks of "the new church with the four towers at Westminster" as an ornament to the city, and deeply regrets that a vista was not opened from Old Palace Yard, so as to bring its "beauty" fairly into view! Some idea of the writer's taste may be formed when our readers learn that he proposed, as a further improvement, to dwarf the said four towers, "cutting them off in the middle, like those of Babel!"

Lord Grosvenor lived at Millbank till the beginning of the present century; his house stood near the river, and had a pretty garden attached to it. Pennant, the antiquary, used to visit his lordship there, as he tells us in his work on London. At that time the locality was a fashionable resort on Sundays, and the bank of the river was edged with pollard oaks, presenting a view almost as rural as that which we now see at Fulham or Putney.

Marsham Street, Earl Street, and Romney Street, in this immediate neighbourhood, were all named after the owner of the property, Charles Marsham, Earl of Romney. Of the same fanciful style of naming streets we have already given an instance in our account of "George," "Villiers," "Duke," and "Buckingham" Streets, close by Charing Cross. Nearly the whole of one side of Earl Street is occupied by the Westminster Brewery, and the other side by Messrs. Hadfield's marble works and gallery of sculpture, which were established here in 1804.

Vine Street—the old name of Romney Street—which we pass on our right, recalls the time when, as was the case also at Smithfield, in Hatton Garden, and in St. Giles's, there was here a flourishing vineyard. "There was a garden," says Stow, "they called the Vine Garden, because perhaps vines anciently were there nourished, and wine made." Under date of 1565, in the Overseers' Book, a rate is made for "the Vyne Garden," and "Myll," next to Bowling Alley. In the first year of Edward VI., as we learn from Brayley's "History," payment was made to "Rich. Wolward, keeper of the King's house at Westminster, j mark to repair the King's vineyard there." In that reign the place appears to have been inclosed with houses and other buildings. "With a parcel of ground called the Mill-bank, valued at 58s., it was given by Edward VI., in the third year of his reign, to Joanna Smith, in consideration of service."

Churchill, the satirist, was born in this street in the year 1731. He writes :—

"Famed Vine Street,
Where Heaven, the kindest wish of man to grant,
Gave me an old house and a kinder aunt !"

The aunt, however, so far as we know, left him no memorial of her kindness, in recompense for the immortality which he has bestowed upon her.

It is enough to make the mouth of one bred in the country to water when one reads of a Vine Street near Piccadilly Circus, and another in the heart of Westminster, and remembers that these names were not given and written up in irony and mockery, but point to the fact that vineyards, most probably the property of the Abbot of Westminster, did once exist on the slopes which existed near the Abbey. As Mr. Matthew Browne remarks in "Chaucer's England :"—"It is not difficult for a man who wanders as far as he can into the heart of the purlieus of Westminster Abbey, to imagine in that old garden there, with the well in the midst, that the Abbot's orchery and vinery are close at hand somewhere, with a pond fringed by fallen leaves blown off the beeches, and peopled with delicious fish—so strong is the sense that comes over you of shade and monastic stillness." It need, however, be no matter of surprise to find that even in Westminster there were vineyards, where wine was squeezed from the juice of grapes grown on the spot. At Beaulieu Abbey, near Southampton, there are fields still known as the Vineyards ; and the late Lord Montagu, who died in 1845, had in his cellar brandy made from the vines grown on that estate. In Barnaby Googe's "Four Books of Husbandry," published in 1578, we find several remarks on the former growth of vineyards in England. The author quaintly adds, "There hath, moreover, good experience of late years been made by two noble and honourable barons of this realm—the Lord Cobham and the Lord Willyams — who had both growing about their houses as good wines as are in many parts of France." Stow also mentions an old MS. roll, in his time extant in the Gate House of Windsor Castle, in which was to be seen the yearly account of the charges of the planting of vines that, in the time of Richard II., "grew in great plenty in the Little Park, and also of the wine itself, whereof some part was spent in the King's house." If this was certainly the case at Windsor, there is no reason to doubt that the vine may have grown and flourished in vineyards on the southern slopes that looked down what was St. James's Park ; indeed, a plot of ground in that park in the last century was called "the King's Vineyard."

Horseferry Road, which we may be supposed to have reached, leads to that part of the river between Westminster and Lambeth, where was the only horse-ferry allowed on the Thames in London. The ferry was granted by patent to the Archbishop of Canterbury; and the ferry-boat station on the Lambeth side was near the palace-gate. On the opening of Westminster Bridge the ferry practically ceased, and compensation, amounting to upwards of £2,200, was granted to the see of Canterbury; but, as we learn from a work styled "Select Views of London and its Environs," published in 1805, the ferry was still in use in the early part of the present century, though its traffic was sadly diminished. Indeed, it may be said to have continued more or less as a ferry, down to the building of Lambeth Bridge, in 1862. This bridge, which is constructed of iron, on the suspension principle, has three spans of 280 feet. As our readers may perhaps feel interested in learning what were the rates charged at the horse-ferry, we here give them:—For a man and horse, 2s.; horse and chaise, 1s.; coach and two horses, 1s. 6d.; coach and four horses, 2s.; coach and six horses, 2s. 6d.; a laden cart, 2s. 6d.; cart or wagon, 2s. Mr. Mackenzie Walcott tells us that close to the ferry a wooden house was built for a small guard, which was posted here at the time of the Commonwealth.

Here, on the shore of the dark wintry waters, on the 9th of December, 1688, Mary of Modena, the ill-starred consort of James II., having quitted Whitehall for the last time, stepped into the boat that was to convey her across the river to Lambeth. Passing through the Privy Gardens into the street, the Queen with her infant son, his two nurses, and two male attendants, got into a coach, and threading her way through the narrow lanes which surrounded the east and south of the old Abbey precincts, drove to the horse-ferry, where a boat awaited her. "The night was wet and stormy, and so dark," writes St. Victor, in his "Narrative of the Escape of the Queen of England," "that when we got into the boat we could not see each other, though we were closely seated, for the boat was very small." Thus, literally "with only one frail plank between her and eternity," did the Queen cross the swollen waters, her tender infant of six months old in her arms, with no better attendants than his nurses, and having no other escort than the Count de Lauzun and the writer (St. Victor), who confessed that he felt an extreme terror at the peril to which he saw personages of their importance exposed, and that his only reliance was in the mercy of God, "by whose especial providence,"

he says, "we were preserved, and arrived at our destination. Our passage," he adds, "was rendered very difficult and dangerous by the violence of the wind and the heavy and incessant rain. When we reached the opposite side of the Thames, . . . the coach was still at the inn." Thither St. Victor ran to hasten it, leaving Lauzun to protect the Queen. Her Majesty meantime withdrew herself and her little company under the walls of Lambeth Old Church, without any other shelter from the wind and bitter cold. The child fortunately slept through it all; the coach was soon found, and the party arrived safely at Gravesend, where a yacht was ready to convey them to the coast of France. History tells us that they reached Calais without further disaster, and that they never set eyes on the shores of England again.

A curious print of the time represents the boat in which the Queen effected her escape as in no little danger, and the two gentlemen as assisting the rowers, who are labouring against wind and tide. The Queen herself is seated by the steersman, enveloped in a large cloak, with a hood drawn over her head: her attitude is expressive of melancholy; and she appears most anxious to conceal the little prince, who is asleep on her bosom, partially shrouded among the ample folds of her drapery. The other two females betray alarm. The engraving is rudely executed, and printed on coarse paper; but the design is not without merit, being bold and original in its conception and full of expression. It was probably intended as an appeal to the sympathies of the humbler classes on behalf of the royal fugitives.

Two evenings after the departure of his Queen and Consort, King James quitted Whitehall, and took at the horse-ferry a little boat with a single pair of oars, with which he crossed over to Vauxhall, where horses awaited him. He took with him the Great Seal of England, doubtless with the idea that he might have to use it when safe in France; but, induced by some motive or other, he threw it into the river while crossing. He effected his escape as far as Feversham, where he was recognised, and whence he was brought back to Whitehall. A few days later, however, the Prince of Orange ordered his Dutch guards from St. James's Palace to enter Whitehall, and the King was compelled to depart. He dropped down the river in his barge as far as Gravesend, whence, as history tells us, he effected his escape to the shores of France. On the last night that he slept at Whitehall, when he was about to retire to bed, "Lord Craven came to tell him that the Dutch guards, horse and foot, were marching through the park in order of battle, in order to take possession of White-hall. The stout old earl, though in his eightieth year, professed his determination rather to be cut to pieces at his post than to resign his post at Whitehall to the Dutch. But this bloodshed the King forbade, knowing that it would be useless. The English guards reluctantly gave place to the foreigners, by whom they were superseded, and the next day the King left Whitehall for the last time."

Probably the last person of consequence who crossed the river here was the Princess Augusta of Saxe-Gotha, on Tuesday, April 27, 1736, on her way to be married to the Prince of Wales, the father of George III.

It sounds strange to hear that there was a Horse-ferry and Vauxhall Regatta as recently as 1840, but it is nevertheless true. In Colburn's "Calendar of Amusements" we read that "the arrangements.

MILLBANK ABOUT 1800. (*See page* 3.)

His subsequent sojourn and his death at St. Ger-main-en-Laye, near Paris, are matters known to every reader of English history.

The Great Seal, we may add, was afterwards re-covered, in a net cast at random by some poor fishermen, who delivered it into the hands of the Lords of the Council.

Mr. Mackenzie Walcott, in his amusing manner, tells us how that "very early one morning, while the watermen were dreaming of fares when they should have been at the river-side, the Duke of Marlborough with his hounds desired to cross. By good fortune one Wharton chanced to be at hand, and the duke rewarded him by obtaining a grant of the 'Ferry house' for him : the present owner is a descendant of Wharton."

made by the parochial authorities and others of the parish of St. John's, in getting up this regatta, are deserving of every encomium. The prizes, which bring into competition the watermen of Vauxhall and Westminster Horseferry, are really worth con-tending for — viz., two excellent wherries, and various sums of money. A steamer is engaged for the accommodation of the subscribers."

The works belonging to the Gas Light and Coke Company, which occupy a considerable space of ground between Peter Street and Horseferry Road, stand partly on the site of what was, at the begin-ning of the present century, the residence of a market-gardener, known as the "Bower" ale-house and tea-gardens—a name still perpetuated in that of the adjacent public-house—"The White Horse

THE OLD HORSEFERRY ABOUT 1800.

and Bower," in the Horseferry Road. These gas-works (one of the three earliest stations established by the first gas company in the metropolis, which received its charter of incorporation in 1812) owe their origin to the enterprise of a Mr. Winsor, the same who, on the evening of the King's birthday, in 1807, made a brilliant display of gas along the wall between the Mall and St. James's Park. It may be worth while to note here that the general lighting of the metropolis with gas began on Christmas Day, 1814. Branch establishments in connection with these gas-works have since been erected further westward, and more recently a larger establishment has been opened at Beckton, North Woolwich. There are also branches at Silvertown, Bromley, Bow Common Lane, Great Cambridge Street (Hackney Road), Haggerston, Nine Elms, Kensal Green, King's Cross, Fulham, &c.

The only other buildings in Horseferry Road which we need mention are the small Roman Catholic Chapel of St. Mary, served by the Jesuit Fathers (see *post*, p. 41) ; a Wesleyan Chapel ; the Westminster Training College for Schoolmasters and Practising Schools ; and the Westminster Mortuary and Coroner's Court, a substantial and well-designed structure which stands on ground presented by the Duke of Westminster, and dates from 1893.

Page Street, a clean and broad thoroughfare running parallel with Horseferry Road, presents a striking contrast to most of the streets and lanes which surround it. The graveyard belonging to St. John's Church occupies the greater part of one side ; it is railed in from the street, and with its surrounding trees, and level surface of turf, appears like an oasis in the wilderness. Its conversion into a public recreation ground has proved to be an immense boon to the children of this crowded neighbourhood.

A short distance from Page Street, with its frowning gateway overlooking the river, was Millbank Prison, formerly called the Penitentiary. In 1799 a plan was formed of penitentiary confinement calculated to reform offenders, and an Act of Parliament was drawn up under the direction of Sir William Blackstone, according to the suggestions of Mr. Howard, the prison philanthropist. Fifteen years after another Act was passed for carrying out the design, and a contract was entered into with Mr. Jeremy Bentham, the economist and philanthropist. It was intended as a realisation of a plan which Bentham had put forward on paper, and which he called " The Panopticon, or Inspection House," in recommendation of which scheme he published a work under that title, addressed to Mr. Pitt. The latter, though a strong Tory, entered keenly into the views of the great social reformer, but the obstinacy of George III. prevented any experiment being made in the direction of the "separate system" in London for more than twenty years. Charles Knight tells us that the cost of the site was £12,000, and that of the building exceeded half a million, or about £500 for each cell. So it seems that felons are rather expensive luxuries for the country.

In the "Picture of London," published in the reign of George III., we read that this prison was established "for the punishment of offenders of secondary turpitude, usually punished by transportation for a term of years, since the disputes began which terminated in the separation from this country of the American States. The plan for colonising New South Wales led to a general system of expatriation to the antipodes ; which, as applied to definite periods, was cruel and unjust, because the wretched objects were generally precluded from the power of returning, however short might be the intended period of their punishment ! A strong and affecting memorial of the sheriffs of London led, however, to several Parliamentary notices and remonstrances against this indiscriminate mode of transportation, which was, in nearly all cases, *in effect*, for life ; and in consequence, this place of punishment and reform was projected at Millbank, and no culprits are, we understand, in future to be sent to New South Wales, except in those enormous cases that justify irrevocable transportation."

The building stood on ground purchased of the Marquis of Salisbury ; and although the Parliamentary grant for its erection was made as far back as 1799, it was not completed till 1821. It was a mass of brickwork, which, in its ground-plan, resembled a wheel, the governor's house occupying a circle in the centre, from which radiated six piles of buildings, terminating externally in circular towers with conical roofs, which gave to the prison the aspect of a fortress. The ground on which it stood is raised but little above the river, and was at one time considered unhealthy. It was the largest prison in London, and contained accommodation for about 1,100 prisoners. Every convict sentenced to penal servitude in Great Britain was sent to Millbank for a term previous to the sentence being carried into effect. The external walls formed an irregular octagon, and enclosed an area of eighteen acres of ground, and within that space the various ranges of buildings were so constructed that the governor, from a room in the centre, was able to view every one of the rows of cells. The circular towers are connected by what may be termed curtains, which has the effect of giving the appearance of a multiplicity of sides to the building. It was first named "The Penitentiary," or "Penitentiary House for London and Middlesex," but in 1843 the name was altered, by Act of Parliament, to "Millbank Prison." Here Arthur Orton, the "claimant" of the Tichborne title and estates—the "unfortunate young nobleman doomed to languish in a prison," in the eyes of certain "fools and fanatics"—spent the first six months of his fourteen years of penal servitude.

A broad esplanade or embankment extends the whole length of the river front of Millbank Prison, and, with a broad and open thoroughfare called Ponsonby Street, leads to the foot of Vauxhall Bridge.

Vauxhall Bridge was at first called "Regent" Bridge, probably from the circumstance that the first stone on the Middlesex side was laid by Lord Dundas, as proxy for the Prince Regent (George IV.). The works were commenced in May, 1811. The first stone of the abutment on the Surrey side was laid in September, 1813, by Prince Charles of Brunswick, eldest son of the Duke of Brunswick, the same who fell soon afterwards on the field of Waterloo. The bridge was finished in August, 1816. It was built from the designs of Mr. James Walker, and cost about £300,000. The iron superstructure, consisting of nine equal arches, each seventy-eight feet in span, is supported on eight rusticated stone piers, built on a foundation of wooden framing cased with stone. The length of the bridge is about 800 feet. The proximity of the bridge to the once famous gardens of Vauxhall, and the facility it was likely to afford to visitors, led to the original name being soon changed to Vauxhall. As we have now lost the gardens for ever, it is pleasant —to quote the words of Mr. Charles Knight—" to have some memorial of the spot made so familiar to us by the writings of our great men."

In Bessborough Gardens, at the foot of Vauxhall Bridge, is the beautiful church of the Holy Trinity, which was built at the expense of the Rev. W. H. E. Bentinck, Archdeacon and Prebendary of Westminster; the first stone of it was laid by Mrs. Bentinck, in November, 1849. The ground on which the church is built was given by Mr. Thomas Cubitt, M.P.; and the building—which is in the "Early Decorated" style of architecture of the time of Edward I. and II.—was erected from the designs of Mr. John L. Pearson, at a cost of about £10,000. The church can accommodate about 850 worshippers. It consists of a lofty nave, transepts, chancel, and a vestibule at the north-east corner of the chancel. The tower has a double-lighted belfry, windows and pinnacles at the corner, crocketed at the angle; and on the top of the tower is a spire rising to the height of about 200 feet.

Vauxhall Bridge Road, which extends from the Bridge and Bessborough Gardens to the western end of Victoria Street, may be regarded as forming the termination of Westminster in this direction. A large house on the eastern side of it, formerly built as a club and library for the Guards, was bought about the year 1870, by the Roman Catholic body, in order to form a residence for the "Archbishop of Westminster" for the time being, and shortly afterwards Cardinal Manning took up his abode in it. The rooms are large and lofty, but, in spite of some fine pictures of Roman Catholic prelates which grace its walls, the house has anything but a palatial appearance. Not far off, and between Rochester Row and Victoria Street, it is ultimately intended to erect the Westminster Cathedral of the future; but many centuries must elapse before it equals in historic interest the venerable Abbey hard by. Its plan is that of a lofty Gothic structure of the Decorated or Edwardian style, with nave, chancel, transepts, side chapels, tower, and lofty spire.

It may, perhaps, appear strange to think of finding a Regent Street in the purlieus of Westminster; nevertheless there is one, and in passing through it, one may, of course, look in vain for such fashionable establishments as those which meet the eye in the street which most persons know by that name. Crossing Regent Street at right angles is Vincent Street, and by this latter turning we enter Vincent Square, a large space of ground covering about ten acres, which once formed part of Tothill Fields, of which we shall have more to say in our next chapter. In 1810, this plot of land was marked out as a playground for the Westminster scholars, the sum of £3 being paid for a plough and a team of horses to drive deep furrows round the site, and £2 4s. more for the digging of a trench at the north-east end, to prevent carts from passing over it, as it was then open and unfenced. Further sums were paid for levelling the surface for cricket, and for railing the ten acres in, and fixing gates. It was named after the learned Dean Vincent, who then presided over the Abbey Church.

The church of St. Mary the Virgin, in this square, was built from the designs of Mr. Edward Blore, and was consecrated in October, 1837. The Dean and Chapter gave the ground, and also granted a site for schools which have since been erected, for the accommodation of 600 children.

Rochester Row, running parallel with Vincent Square on its north side, is so called after the bishopric of that name, which was held conjointly with the deanery of Westminster by Dolben, Sprat, Atterbury, Bradford, Wilcocks, Pearce, Thomas, and Horsley. George III., it is said, condoled with Dr. Vincent on the separation of the see and the deanery. Many others of the neighbouring streets are named from clergymen connected with Westminster, as Carey and Page Streets, from the head-masters of St. Peter's College ; Fynes Street, from Dr. Fynes-Clinton, of St. Margaret's ; and Douglas Street, from the Rev. Prebendary Douglas.

On the north side of Rochester Row are Emery Hill's almshouses, founded in 1708, to provide homes for twelve poor persons, and also the Rev. James Palmer's almshouses, to be homes for a like number of poor persons. The latter were founded in 1656, and re-erected in 1881-2.

Opposite these almshouses is St. Stephen's Church, which was erected and endowed about the year 1847, by Miss (now Baroness) Burdett-Coutts. It is from the designs of Mr. Benjamin Ferrey. It is built in the Decorated Gothic style of the fourteenth century, with a tower and spire on the northern side, nearly 200 feet high. The church, which is most richly decorated and picturesque, will hold about 1,000 worshippers. On the south side of the west front is a group of schools attached to the church, which afford accommodation for about 400 children ; together with a parsonage, or presbytery, a portion of which forms a tower surmounted by a quaint, foreign-looking louvre.

In Francis Street, an out-of-the-way thoroughfare on the north side of Rochester Row, and only a few yards from the new and noble thoroughfare of Victoria Street, is a building of more interest, perhaps, to the criminal classes than to Londoners in general, called Tothill Fields Prison, or Bridewell, as it used to be termed. It stands out of sight, being screened from view on almost every side by new mansions taller than itself, justifying the saying of Jeremy Bentham, to the effect that " if a place could exist of which it could be said that it was in no neighbourhood, that place would be Tothill Fields."

The old Bridewell occupied the plot of ground adjoining the north side of the Green-Coat School site, on the west side of Artillery Place, and leading into Victoria Street ; so that, as this same school, or " St. Margaret's Hospital," as it was formerly called, was dedicated as far back as the year 1633, to the relief of the poor fatherless children of St. Margaret's parish, it is probable that the hospital, or "abiding house," for the poor, and its next-door

neighbour, the Bridewell, or " house of correction," for the compulsory employment of able-bodied but indolent paupers, were originally joint parish institutions—the one for granting relief to the industrious poor, and the other for punishing the idle. Hence these twin establishments—the one erected under James I., and the other under Charles I.— were probably among the first institutions raised for carrying out the provisions of the first Poor Law, enacted in 1601.

The Bridewell itself, which Sir Richard Steele mentions as existing in Tothill Fields at the beginning of the eighteenth century, was erected nearly a hundred years earlier, namely, in 1618, as may be seen from an inscription let into the wall of the House of Correction. "This ancient prison," says the London chronicles, "was altered and enlarged in the year 1655;" and "in corroboration of the statement," writes the author of "The Great World of London," "we find in the garden surrounding the present building the stone frame, or skeleton, as it were, of the old prison gateway, in shape like the Greek letter Π, standing by itself as a memorial at the back of Bridewell." This cromlech-like relic is covered with ivy, and looks at first more like some piece of imitation ruin-work than the remains of a prison portal, for the doorway is so primitive in character (being not more than five feet ten inches high and three feet wide) that it seems hardly bigger than the entrance to a cottage ; nevertheless, an inscription painted on the lintel assures us that it was " The Gateway, or Principal Entrance, to Tothill Fields Prison ; erected 1665 ; taken down and removed to this site A.D. 1836." Colonel Despard was imprisoned in the former Bridewell in 1803.

Although originally designed as a Bridewell for *vagrants*, Tothill Fields was converted, we are told, in the reign of Queen Anne, into a gaol for the confinement of criminals also ; and Howard, writing towards the end of the last century (1777), describes it as being "remarkably well managed" at that period, holding up its enlightened and careful keeper, one George Smith, as "a model to other governors." In 1826, however, the erection of a new prison was decided upon, and an Act for that purpose obtained. Then a different site was chosen, and eight acres of land on the western side of the Green-Coat School, and near the Vauxhall Bridge Road, were purchased for £16,000. The designs were furnished by Mr. Robert Abraham, and the building, which cost £186,000, was completed and opened for the reception of prisoners in the year 1834 ; soon after which the old prison was pulled down, and the relics already described transferred to the new one, as we have said, in 1836.

The new prison, which will accommodate about 900 prisoners in all, is situate on the southern side of Victoria Street. It is a solid and even handsome structure, and one of great extent as well as strength. "Seen from Victoria Street," says one London topographer—though, by the bye, it is in no way visible in that direction—"it resembles a substantial fortress." The main entrance is on the Vauxhall side of the building in Francis Street, and the doorway here is formed of massive granite blocks, and immense iron gates, ornamented above with portcullis work. "Viewed from this point," the author of "London Prisons" describes the exterior (though there is nothing but a huge dead wall and the prison gateway to be seen) as being "the very ideal of a national prison—vast, airy, light, and yet inexorably safe."

The building is said to be one of the finest specimens of brickwork in the metropolis, and consists of three distinct prisons, each constructed alike, on Bentham's "panopticon" plan, in the form of a half-wheel, i.e., with a series of detached wings, radiating, spoke-fashion, from a central lodge, or "argus," as such places were formerly styled. One of such lodges is situate, midway, in each of the three sides of the spacious turfed and planted court-yard ; so that the outline of the ground-plan of these three distinct, half-wheel-like prisons resembles the ace of clubs, with the court-yard forming an open square in the centre.

The building is good in its sanitary conditions, and the death-rate is said to be lower than that of most prisons in the kingdom.

On the face of the building is a memorial stone, with the inscription recording the original purpose of its erection :—" Here are several sorts of Work for the Poor of this Parish of St. Margaret, Westminster, as also the County, according to LAW, and for such as will beg and live Idle in this City and Liberty of Westminster, Anno 1655." From this it will be seen that it was originally intended as a Bridewell or House of Correction, and a place of "penitentiary amendment" of such vagrants and "sturdy beggars," and "valiant rogues" as objected to work for their living. In fact, it was meant to be a sort of penal establishment in connection with the Poor House, and, like it, maintained at the expense of the City.

Mr. Hepworth Dixon finds fault with this building as ill planned, and a "costly blunder;" and possibly such may be the case. Down to 1850 it had been appropriated to the reception of all classes of convicted prisoners, but from and after

that date it has been set apart for convicted female prisoners, and for males below seventeen years old.

Speaking of Tothill Fields Prison, the witty author of the "Town Spy," published in 1725, quaintly remarks : " In the fields of this parish stands a famous factory for hemp, which is wrought with greater industry than ordinary, because the manufacturers enjoy the fruits of their own labour, a number of English gentlemen having here a restraint put upon their liberties."

The names of the various courts and alleys to the south of this prison still serve to keep in remembrance the once rural character of the locality : here is Willow Walk ; close by are Pool Place, and Pond Place, and so on. Here, also, are two lofty brick buildings, which will at once attract attention : one is the hospital for the Grenadier Guards, which was erected about the year 1860, on a vacant plot of ground between Rochester Row and Francis Street ; the other rejoices in the name of the Guards' Industrial Home. Close by the latter is the large and spacious building already mentioned as the residence of Cardinal Manning.

At the east end of Rochester Row, facing Grey-Coat Place, is the Grey-Coat School, or Hospital, so named from the colour of the clothing worn by its inmates. It was founded in the year 1698, for the education of seventy poor boys and forty poor girls. The hospital presents a considerable frontage towards Grey-Coat Place, from which it is separated by a large court-yard. It is composed of a central building, ornamented with a clock, turret, and bell, above the royal arms of Queen Anne, with the motto "Semper eadem," flanked by a figure on either side, dressed in the former costume of the children. The south side, which looks out upon an open garden and spacious detached play-grounds (the whole surrounded by an extensive wall), contains the school-rooms. Above is a wainscoted dining-hall, used also for the private prayers of the inmates of the hospital. The dormitories occupy the whole attic storey. In the board-room—a noble panelled apartment—are portraits of the royal foundress, Queen Anne ; Dr. Compton, Bishop of London ; Dr. Smalridge, Bishop of Bristol ; and those of other former governors. In July, 1875, the first distribution of prizes to the children was made by the Duke of Buccleuch, who congratulated the children and visitors upon the successful working of the school under the new scheme. The number of children had increased from twenty-eight to upwards of one hundred.

In Strutton Ground, not far from Grey-Coat

Place, was formerly a house named "the Million Gardens," where, in 1718, tickets were to be purchased for a lottery of plate, as we learn from the *Weekly Journal*. "The name, in reality," observes Mr. Larwood in his "History of Sign Boards," "refers to the Melon Gardens, a fruit which was often pronounced as 'Million' in the seventeenth and eighteenth centuries."

Strutton (or, as it ought more properly to be

the other side, at the entry into Tothill Field, Stourton House, which Giles, the last Lord Dacre, purchased and built anew; whose lady and wife, Anne, left money to build a hospital for twenty poor men and so many children, which hospital," the old historian adds, "her executors have now begun in the field adjoining." This institution is now known as Dacre's Almshouses, or Emmanuel Hospital, and stands in Hopkins' Row, at the

THE GREYCOAT SCHOOL. *From an Original Sketch.* (*See page* 11.)

called, Stourton) Ground perpetuates the name of the Lords Stourton, whose town-house, surrounded by fair garden-grounds, once stood here. The mansion became afterwards the residence of the Lords Dacre. Opposite to Stourton House, in the days of the Stuarts, stood the residence of Lord Grey de Wilton. Both these houses are shown in Norden's Map of London in 1603.

A little to the north of the district which we have been describing is, or rather was, Tothill Street, for it is now all but swept away. According to honest John Stow, it "runneth" from the west gate of the old Palace at Westminster, which gate, as we know, formerly stood at the entrance to Dean's Yard. "Herein," as Stow informs us, "is a house of the Lord Grey of Wilton; and on

back of York Street. The house of the Lords Dacre is, or was in the year 1856, still standing in Dacre Street, leading out of the Broadway, and its gardens occupied the site of what is now termed Strutton Ground—not a very elegant variation of the name Stourton.

In an old map of Westminster, bearing date 1776, the City of Westminster seems limited within its south-western boundary to that ancient causeway, the Horseferry Road. Beyond this, toward Pimlico and Chelsea, spread the open fields, with but here and there scattered buildings. Ponds and marshy ground appear at the western end of Rochester Row, and patches of garden-ground distinguish the cultivated from the generally waste character of the soil. On the site of the present gas-works was Eldrick's Nursery, which supplied the district with fruit and flowering shrubs, as the Abbey vineyard had supplied the monks in the olden time with many a vintage, and the site of which, as we have shown above, might be traced in the thoroughfare till a recent date known as Vine Street.

It will be seen from these remarks that it has been often said that Westminster proper—the trian-

recently, more almshouses, more charity schools, and more prisons, more ancient mansions, and more costermongers' hovels, more thieves' dens and low public houses, than in any other part of the metropolis of equal extent.

It has been sarcastically, but perhaps not undeservedly, remarked, that the City of Westminster is, and has long been, the centre of dissipation of the whole empire; and such perhaps it may be,

THE "FIVE HOUSES." *From an Engraving published in* 1796. (*See page* 14.)

gular slip of the metropolis which lies between the Thames, St. James's Park, and the Vauxhall Bridge Road—can boast at once of some of the noblest and the meanest structures to be found throughout London; the grand old Abbey contrasting with the filthy and squalid Duck Lane almost as strongly as do the new Houses of Parliament and the Palace of which they form a part with the slums about the Broadway, which well nigh equal the dingy tenements which till lately stood about the Almonry, now almost absorbed into the Westminster Palace Hotel. But such is really the case. In Westminster we have the contrast between rich and poor as marked as in St. Giles's and St. James's; for almost within a stone's throw of the seat of the great Legislature of England there are, or were till

for the region to the north of Pall Mall has been, ever since the institution of "clubs," the headquarters of luxury; while a visit to the purlieus of Westminster proper—to the south of the Abbey and Victoria Street—would serve to convince the most incredulous that dissipation does not belong to the upper classes exclusively. Here, however, as in other parts of the great metropolis, recent years have witnessed vast improvements. The building of Victoria Street, and the demolition of old buildings for the construction of the Metropolitan District Railway, necessitated the removal of some of the worst neighbourhoods of Westminster. Still, in the district bordering on the river, the general aspect of the dwellings is to a great extent unchanged.

CHAPTER II.

WESTMINSTER.—TOTHILL FIELDS AND NEIGHBOURHOOD.

"No mead so fit
For courtly joust or tourney brave."—*Cavalier Song.*

Origin of the Word "Tothill"—Punishment of Necromancers—Grant of a Market and Fair to be held in "Tuthill"—Burials in Tothill Fields —The "Five Houses" or "Seven Chimneys"—The Pest-house—The "Maze" and Public Recreation Ground—The "Butts"—Trial by Wager of Battle—The Last "Affair of Honour"—"Masked Highwaymen in Tothill Fields"—Tothill Fields in the time of Charles I.— Westminster Fair—St. Edward's Fair—Tothill Street—Strutton Ground—Southern, the Dramatic Poet—Drinking-houses in the Olden Time—The Old Swan-yard—The "Cock" Tavern—Royal Aquarium and Summer and Winter Garden—Old and New Pye Streets—The Broadway—Westminster Town Hall—York Street—Van Dun's Almshouses—Westminster Panorama—Milton's Residence—Emmanuel Hospital—Westminster Chapel—The Infirmary—James Street—Richard Glover—William Gifford.

THE origin of the word "Tot-hill" is probably the "toot," or beacon hill, from the Welch word "twt," a spring or rising; and the name was probably given to this district from a beacon placed here, as the highest spot in and around the flat region of Westminster. The antiquary, Mr. Wykeham Archer, however, derives the name from Teut, the chief divinity of the Druids, and the equivalent of Thoth, the Egyptian Mercury, adding that the "Tot," "Teut," "Tut," or "Thoth" Hill, often, by the way, styled "Tuttle" and "Tut-hill," was the spot on which solemn proclamations were made to the people. Another derivation may also be suggested. The Normans, as we happen to know, often spoke of these parts as "Thorny Island, *et tout la champ*." What more easy than the corruption of these two words into "Tuttle?" It should, however, be stated that in Rocque's Map (1746), "Toote Hill" is marked at a bend in the Horseferry Road. "Toot," also, in one of its varied forms, is not an uncommon prefix to the names of other places in different parts of England, as, *Tot*nes, *Tot*ham, *Tut*bury, *Too*ting, *Tot*tenham, &c.; and it may be added that all these are places of considerable elevation compared with the surrounding parts.

"Tothill Fields," says Mr. Archer, in his "Vestiges of Old London," "were, within three centuries, part of a marshy tract of land lying between Millbank and Westminster Abbey, and on which stood a few scattered buildings, some of them the residences of noble personages." They must have witnessed some extraordinary scenes in the Middle Ages. Here necromancers were punished by the destruction of their instruments; for we read that, in the reign of Edward III., a man was taken "practising with a dead man's head, and brought to the bar at the King's Bench, where, after abjuration of his art, his trinkets were taken from him, carried to Tothill, and burned before his face." And, again, in the time of Richard I., Raulf Wigtoft, chaplain to Geoffrey, Archbishop of York, "had provided a girdle and ring, cunningly intoxicated. wherewith

he meant to have destroyed Simon (the Dean of York) and others; but his messenger was intercepted, and his girdle and ring burned at this place before the people."

These fields, according to Stow, in the reign of Henry III., formed part of a manor in Westminster, belonging to "John Mansell, the King's counsellor and priest, who did invite to a stately dinner (at his house at Totehill) the kings and queens of England and Scotland, with divers courtiers and citizens, and whereof there was such a multitude that seven hundred messes of meat did not serve for the first dinner." By an Act passed in the same reign, 34 Henry III., the Abbot of Westminster obtained "leave to keepe a markett in the Tuthill every Munday, and a faire every yeare, for three days." Here, in 1236, "royal solemnities and goodly jousts were held" after the coronation of Queen Eleanor, consort of Henry III. Two centuries afterwards, the fields in the neighbourhood were used for appeals by combat; and Stow describes "a combate that was appointed to have been fought" the 18th of June, "in Trinity Terme, 1571," for a "certain manour or demaine lands," in the Isle of Harty, "adjoining to the Isle of Sheppey, in Kent," and for which "it was thought good," says the historian, that "the Court should sit in Tuthill Fields, where was prepared one plot of ground, one and twenty yardes square, double railed, for the combate, without the West Square." In the time of Nicholas Culpepper, the author of the well-known "Herbal," these fields were famous for their parsley. In 1651 (August 25th) "the trained bands of London, Westminster," &c., to the number of 14,000, we are told, "drew out into Tuttle Fields." Here, too, were built the "Five Houses," or "Seven Chimneys," as pest-houses for victims to the plague, and in 1665 many of those who had fallen victims to that direful scourge were buried here. Under date of July 18, 1665, Samuel Pepys writes in his "Diary:"—"I was much troubled this day to hear at Westminster how the officers do bury the dead in the open Tuttle Fields, pretending want of room elsewhere; whereas the New Chapel churchyard was walled in at the publick charge in the last plague-time, merely for want of room, and now none but such as are able to pay dear for it can be buried there." Here, a short while previously, some "1,200 Scotch prisoners, taken at the battle of Worcester," were interred; for in the accounts of the churchwardens of St. Margaret's, Westminster, there is the payment of "thirty shillings for sixty-seven loads of soil laid on the graves of Tothill Fields, wherein," it is added, "the Scotch prisoners are buried." Some of the Scotch were "driven like a herd of swine," says Heath's "Chronicle," "through Westminster to Tuthill Fields," and there sold to several merchants, and sent to the island of Barbadoes.

The "Five Houses," if we may trust the *Builder*, retained much of their primitive appearance in 1832. "With the moss and lichens growing on the roofs and walls, and their generally old-fashioned quaintness, a very small stretch of the imagination removed the buildings which had surrounded them even then, and brought them once more into the open ground. They marked the site of a battery and breastwork when the fortifications around the cities of London and Westminster were hurriedly thrown up in 1642, by an order of Parliament. This battery is marked as about midway between the Chelsea Road and the bank of the river opposite Vauxhall."

The Pest Houses were built by Lord Craven as a lazaretto for the reception of the victims of the Great Plague which preceded the Fire of London. We have already mentioned this nobleman in our account of Craven House, Drury Lane; and it deserves to be recorded to his credit that at that awful season he was not satisfied with building this hospital, but that he sheltered many of the sufferers by that disease who had no residences except in the doomed city, remaining himself on the spot, "with the same coolness with which he had fought the battles of his mistress, the Queen of Bohemia," in order to maintain order and to mitigate the horrors of the scene.

These "pest-houses" consisted of a row of red-brick buildings, and were erected at a cost of £250. At the beginning of the last century they were made into almshouses for twenty-four aged married people. Some remains of them are—or were recently—to be seen near Vauxhall Bridge Road.

"Many a torch or lanthorn-lighted group of mysterious-looking figures have borne the litter of the stricken to this then solitary spot, not so much with hope of recovery, as from fear of spreading the dire infection by retaining them within the frighted and unhealthy town." In connection with the surrounding fields, there are several incidents recorded illustrative of the days of old. Prior to the Statutes of Restraint, they were considered to be within the limits of the sanctuary of the Abbey.

In the seventeenth century the people used to resort to a "Maze" in these same Tothill Fields, which, according to an old writer, was "much frequented in the summer-time, in fair afternoons," the fields being described as "of great use, pleasure, and recreation," to the King's Scholars and neighbours. And Sir Richard Steele, writing in "The Tatler," in 1709, says, "Here was a military garden, a bridewell, and, as I have heard tell, a racecourse." A bear-garden, kept by one William Wells, stood upon the site of the present Vincent Square during the reign of Queen Anne. Mr. Mackenzie Walcott says that, as lately as 1793, there was a famous bear-garden in these fields; and near Willow Walk resided one Haverfield, a noted highwayman, who kept two bears in his rooms as myrmidons. Willow Walk was formerly noted for its "monster" tea-gardens. Bull-baiting occasionally took place here as recently as 1820; and the three days' fair, held in honour of St. Edward, was not finally discontinued till some time afterwards.

Upon the spot now occupied by Artillery Place, the men of Westminster used to practise at the "butts," which were provided by the parish in the year 1579, in obedience to an ordinance of Queen Elizabeth. In the beginning of the last century it is described as a large inclosure, "made use of by those who delight in military exercises." The butts were a large mound of turf, and at them the volunteers used to shoot. They were close to the "Five Chimneys." The ground was inclosed within a ditch, and a "shooting-house" was provided for shelter and retirement. The actual butts were removed before the battle of Waterloo, and the name of "The Butts" has almost perished from the memory of the present generation, here as elsewhere.

"The open Tothill Fields, as they were called," observes a writer in the *Builder*, "existed in this state till 1810, with a group of lonely cottages standing in their midst, when the note of preparation for an altered site might have been heard in the construction of the iron bridge at Vauxhall. Dr. Vincent had already inclosed a portion of the fields for the square which bears his name, and the Westminster Gas and Coke Company removed their offices, and commenced their new buildings in the Horseferry Road, on the site of the before-mentioned nursery. In 1830, the Vauxhall Road was not entirely built upon, and bits of the hedgerow were still to be seen. Patches of greensward might as yet be observed beneath the litter of old iron, which Andrew Mann so liberally spread over any plot of waste ground; and the site of the present South Belgravia remained open market-garden ground, intersected by bridle-paths, for some ten years subsequently. The present Warwick Street, uniting Westminster with Chelsea, occupies the precise site of the 'Willow Walk.'"

Tothill Fields, in the days of trial by wager of battle, was the place where the judges sat in all the majesty of their official robes, wigs, and gold chains, as arbiters of these encounters—one of the last remnants of the barbarous laws of another age. It is related that in 1441 such a one occurred in a combat between "two theves." The "pælour" (appellant) is described to have "hadde the felde and victory within three strokes." This absurdity was not formally set aside until 1819, when an Act of Parliament was passed forbidding all such trials both in civil and criminal matters.

Tothill Fields was also, in the seventeenth century, a celebrated duelling-ground; the last "affair of honour" fought there, of which we have any account, took place, it is said, in 1711, when a Kentish gentleman, Sir Cholmley Dering, was killed by a Mr. Richard Thornhill—the fools fighting with pistols so near that the muzzles touched each other.

There is extant a curious etching, by Hollar, of Tothill Fields as they were in the time of Charles I. They appear to be a dead level, broken only by a clump of trees in the centre, forming a sort of maze. The foreground is broken by a row of slight terraces, not unlike the "butts;" and some ladies are promenading leisurely, dressed in the fashionable costume of the day.

In an able article on this interesting locality, a writer in the *Builder*, of January, 1875, observes: —"The solitary character of this tract of land, spreading out to the Chelsea Road, beyond which lay the 'Five Fields' extending to Knightsbridge, is illustrated by an incident not uncommon to the neighbourhood at a period when the highwayman would lie in ambush for the belated pedestrian, or for the chaise, which in this instance is conveying not the most loyal subjects of George II. from one of those political meetings when the 'mug-house riots' were at their height. Such was the disturbed condition of society at this period, that two witnesses were sufficient for the immediate arrest of any party suspected of harbouring either Romish priest, or other of proven Jacobite politics, and great abuses were consequent upon this hasty legislation. The panic created by the rumoured march

of the Highlanders, with the numerous party of the disaffected in London, kept the alarmed citizens wakeful in their beds; for the Highlanders were feared as a terrible race, and possibly no anticipated result had been surrounded with greater doubt and uncertainty, but that the energy of the King, backed as it was by the commercial interests of the Londoners, threw the balance in favour of the new dynasty. In the summer of 1745, two adherents of the House of Stuart—one a young officer in the Pretender's army—had hired a chaise to convey them from Westminster to the then remote village of Chelsea. To avoid the rioting in the town, they had taken a route across the less-disturbed fields. They had not proceeded very far, however, before two well-mounted men made their appearance, and so suddenly that had they risen out of the earth it could not have surprised them more. Both men wore masks; and whilst one of them stopped the postboy, the other rode up to the window of the chaise, and scrutinised the occupants within. The post-boy spoke in too low a tone to be heard by the travellers, but whatever might have been the nature of the conversation, it was sufficiently talismanic to relieve the party of their apprehensions. Making a sign to his companion, both men turned their horses' heads in the direction of the town, and the post-boy proceeded on his journey. Upon reaching their destination, they asked the 'boy' who his rather suspicious-looking friends were, to which he gave no answer, but upon being pressed again on the subject, said, 'It's not much matter who they are, but they belong to those who don't care to meddle with Prince Charley's boys!' The mystery seemed now greater than before, and further inquiry might only have involved further difficulty. It was evident the post-boy knew too much, but in what manner he had become acquainted with their political bias it was impossible for them to conceive. Treating the matter, however, as a joke, and paying the boy handsomely, the matter ended, but their anxiety only terminated by their quitting London for the North. The widow of one of these gentlemen died in 1824, at the advanced age of ninety-five years. After the amnesty, her husband, who fought at the battle of Culloden, had, in common with others, some curious restraints laid upon him, one of which was that he could not ride a horse of a higher value than £10 without forfeiture of it to any one who chose to avail himself of the prohibition." But this restraint was also imposed on all Roman Catholics in the seventeenth and the early part of the eighteenth century.

On that part of Tothill Fields which is now

covered by the Westminster House of Correction and some neighbouring streets, was held, in ancient times, Westminster Fair, locally named "St. Magdalen's," or "Magdalen's," from the day on which it was celebrated. Mr. Frost, in his "Old Showmen of London," tells us that it was established in 1257, under a charter granted by Henry III. to the Abbot and Canons of St. Peter's Church. From the same authority we learn that the three days to which it was originally limited were extended by favour of Edward III. to thirty-one; but the fair never proved a dangerous rival to that of St. Bartholomew's, in Smithfield, and gradually fell into discredit and disuse.

In the reign of Henry III., St. Edward's Fair, originally held in St. Margaret's Churchyard, was removed hither, and in 1302, the Abbot of Westminster was allowed to levy tolls upon all traders who sold their wares at the time, even within the precincts of the Palace. In 1628 was preserved in the muniment-room of St. Margaret's Church, King Henry III.'s patent to the Abbot of Westminster, giving him leave to keep a market in Tothill every Monday, and a fair every year for three days. The fair was held in Rochester Row, in the space between Emery Hill's Almshouses and the ground now occupied by the Church of St. Stephen the Martyr. The fair was in existence in 1819, but died away gradually, previously to the general suppression of fairs in 1840.

Tothill Street, which extends to the Broadway from the Broad Sanctuary, near the west front of the Abbey, is the most ancient street in Westminster. It was at one time inhabited by noblemen "and the flower of the gentry." Here the Bishop of Chester was residing in 1488, and in 1522 Lord Dudley rented a house here from the fraternity of St. Mary. Sir Andrew Dudley also lived and died here. At the north-west end of the street, in what is now called Strutton Ground, were the residences of Lord Dacre of the South and Lord Grey de Wilton, as stated in the previous chapter. In 1612 Sir George Carew died at Carew House in this street; and in a house near the Gate House, at one time towards the end of the last century, lived the famous Edmund Burke. Lincoln House was the office of the Revels, when Sir Henry Herbert was master in 1644-5. Southern, the dramatic poet, and author of "Oroonoko," for the last ten years of his life, resided in Tothill Street, where he died in the year 1746. The poet Gray, in a letter to Horace Walpole, dated Burnham, Bucks, 1737, says, "We have old Mr. Southern at a gentleman's house a little way off, who often comes to see us. He is now seventy years old, and has almost wholly lost his memory; but is as agreeable an old man as can be—at least I persuade myself so, when I look at him, and think of 'Isabella' and 'Oroonoko.'" He is said to have been wealthy, but very mean; he used to print tickets on his benefit nights, and press them for sale upon his aristocratic friends. Thomas Betterton, the actor, and friend of Pope, was born in this street.

In the reign of Elizabeth, there were houses on both sides of Tothill Street; those on the north side had large gardens reaching to St. James's Park, and those upon the south had likewise extensive grounds, extending as far as Orchard Street. Very few houses were then built in Petty France (now York Street); a few detached residences appear on the south side only of Orchard Street; and some villas in St. Anne's Lane, Pye Street, and Duck Lane, with gardens along a stream.

Most of the signs of the old inns of Westminster were either religious charges, or else the cognisances of sovereigns or of noblemen residing in the neighbourhood. Such were the "Salutation" (of the Blessed Virgin), in Barton Street; the "Maidenhead," or, more properly, the "Maiden's Head"—in other words, that of "Our Lady;" the "St. George and the Dragon," the "Swan," the "Antelope" (the badge of Henry V.), the "Sun" (that of Richard II.), and the "Blue Boar," the cognisance of the Veres, Earls of Oxford. The "Chequers," in Abingdon Street, was the bearing of the Earls of Arundel, who at one time were empowered by the king to grant licenses to public-houses. Hence the frequency of the "Chequers" as a sign, especially in Westminster, where it was constantly to be seen painted on the walls and door-posts of hostelries; and so the "needy knife-grinder" of Canning was neither the only nor the latest toper who has spent last night in this fair city "a drinking at the Chequers."

Swan Yard was so called after the old hostelry, noted as a resort for highwaymen, "The Swan with Two Necks." The latter word is, as most persons know, a corruption from "nicks"—the marks set upon the birds by the Lord Mayor, in his annual "swan-upping," or, as it is called, vulgarly, "swan-hopping," when he makes his yearly progress up the Thames to count the young cygnets and old swans within the civic jurisdiction.

One of the oldest taverns in the metropolis, bearing the sign of "The Cock," surrounding a quaint old inn-yard, stood till 1871, on the north side of Tothill Street. An ancient coat of arms, those of England and France carved in stone, discovered in this house, was walled up in the front of the building. "Tradition," writes Mr. Larwood in his "History of Sign-boards," "says that the work-men employed at the building of the east end of Westminster Abbey, in the reign of Henry VII., used to receive their wages here." Later, it enjoyed a reputation on quite another account, as having been the inn from which the first stage-coach to an inn of considerable importance, as its rafters and timbers were principally of cedar intermixed with oak. It was formerly entered by steps. The building exhibited traces of great antiquity, and appears at one time to have been a house of some pretensions. There was a curious hiding-

MILTON'S HOUSE. *From a Drawing by J. W. Archer.* (*See page* **22.**)

Oxford started, some two centuries ago. Those who knew the inn down to a very recent date say that in the back parlour there was a picture of a jolly and bluff-looking man in a red coat, who is said to have been its driver. The house was built so as to inclose a quaint and spacious inn-yard, much frequented by carriers, not unlike some of those still standing in Bishopsgate Street and the Borough. The house in all probability was in former times place on the staircase, which may have secreted either a "mass-priest" or else a highwayman in the days when both were in open hostility to the law of the land. In the house was also formerly a massive carving of Abraham about to offer his son Isaac; and another, in wood, representing the adoration of the Magi, said to have been kept in pledge, at some remote period, for an unpaid score. The cock may have been adopted as a

THE OLD "COCK TAVERN." *From an Original Drawing in the possession of J. G. Crace, Esq. (See page 17.)*

sign here on account of the vicinity of the Abbey, of which St. Peter was the patron, for in the Middle Ages a cock crowing on the top of a pillar was often one of the accessories in a picture of the Apostle. This certainly was a very unkind allusion for the saint, particularly when accompanied with such a sneering rhyme as that under the sign of the Red Cock in Amsterdam in 1682. On the one side was written :—

> " When the cock began to crow
> St. Peter began to cry."

On the reverse :—

> " The cock does not crow for nothing ;
> Ask St. Peter, he can tell you ! "

The " Cock and Tabard " in Tothill Street is described by Stow as having existed as far back as the reign of Edward III. He also says that at this tavern the workmen were paid during the building of the Abbey, when the wages of most of the artificers did not exceed one penny per day. On the demolition of the ancient inn, a new one bearing the sign of the " Cock " was built on the opposite side of the street. Shortly after its erection, while some draymen were in the act of placing a supply of porter in the cellars, it was discovered that an additional wedge was required, and accordingly one of the men looking round perceived a] e of oak, which had formed part of one of the girders of the ancient building. This, it was conceived, would answer the purpose, if it could be riven asunder, and this process was accordingly pursued. " Much to the amazement, however, of all present," we read in a newspaper account of the discovery, " in the course of the operation there suddenly emerged, from one of the mortise-holes or some other aperture, a considerable quantity of gold coins, consisting of forty-one rose nobles, and thirteen marks. The former coins were of the date of Edward III., the first reign in which gold coin was struck in this country. The marks were of the reign of Henry VII. and VIII." The whole of the coin is stated to have been in an admirable state of preservation.

The north side of Tothill Street is almost entirely taken up by the Royal Aquarium, and the Imperial Theatre, which forms its western extremity. The buildings occupy an irregular parallelogram of nearly three acres, extending from Princes Street to the corner of Dartmouth Street, and receding to the north nearly as far as the backs of the houses in Queen Street. The Aquarium, which was erected in 1875-6 from the designs of Mr. Bedborough, is in the Classical style, constructed of red brick and Portland stone, with an arched roof of glass, similar in general plan to that of the Crystal Palace, though widely different in its details. It is two storeys in height, and contains in the basement a great central tank of salt and fresh water, holding no less than 600,000 gallons. On the ground floor, at the eastern end, is a large vestibule, or ante-chamber, leading to the central hall, or promenade, and containing a series of table-tanks for the reception of the smaller fish, the zoophytes, sea-anemones, and the like. The Aquarium .is utilised for concerts and exhibitions.

New Tothill Street was in the last century called White Hart Street. In the New Way, not far from where the present Workhouse stands, resided the well-known Sir Robert Pye, from whom Old and New Pye Streets derive their names, and the husband of Anne Hampden, the "patriot's" daughter. The New Way Chapel stood, according to Hopwood's map of 1801, at the west end of the Great Almonry, opposite the entrance to Jeffery's Buildings from New Tothill Street : here the celebrated Calvinist, Romaine, used to preach, previous to his election as Lecturer of St. Dunstan's-in-the-West. " At this time," says Mr. Mackenzie Walcott, " Dr. Wilson, then Rector of St. Margaret's, was a suitor at Court for a bishopric ; and being asked by King George III., 'What news from his parish ?' he replied that there was 'that fellow Romaine, who had got a chapel in the New Way, and drew all his parishioners from the church.' The king quickly replied, ' Well, we will make a bishop of him ; that will silence him ! ' " During the last century, the Government rented the New Way Chapel from the Dean and Chapter, and the Guards attended divine service there for many years.

One side of the Broadway is now nearly occupied by the St. James's Park station on the Metropolitan District Railway. Here James I. granted a hay-market to be held for a certain number of years ; a further term was obtained by licence of Charles II., but it had expired long before 1730. In a survey made in 1722 mention is made of " the White Horse and Black Horse Inns, for the entertainment of man and horse ; there being none in the parish of St. Margaret, at Westminster, for stage-coaches, wagons, or carriers."

Dick Turpin, the notorious highwayman, it is said, lodged in an obscure court hard by, and used to set out from this place on his marauding expeditions, upon his famous mare, Black Bess, from which one of these taverns took its name.

Christ Church, in the Broadway, rebuilt in the Early Pointed style, from the designs of Mr. A. Poynter, in 1843, stands upon the site of a former edifice which was known as the New Chapel.

It consists of chancel, nave and aisles, and a lofty tower. Several of the windows are filled with stained glass, illustrative of the life of our Saviour. The New Chapel was erected upon a piece of waste ground belonging to the Dean and Chapter; its founder being Mr. George Darrell, Prebendary of St. Peter's, who, in the year 1631, bequeathed £400 to build it, provided it was used for "publick prayers on Sundays, Wednesdays, and Fridays, and for prayers and plain catechisings on Sunday afternoons." The bequest was insufficient to complete the building, and was therefore increased by voluntary subscriptions.

Archbishop Laud was a liberal contributor to this chapel, and in its churchyard was interred Sir William Waller, one of the heroes of the Parliamentary army, who died in 1668. In this burial-ground is a memorial of a parishioner, Margaret Pattens, who was buried here in 1739. Her portrait is preserved in St. Margaret's Workhouse, in which she died (as asserted) at the advanced age of 136 years.

In March, 1882, the foundation-stone of a new Town Hall, for the parishes of St. Margaret and St. John, was laid by Lady Burdett-Coutts, on a piece of ground in the rear of Christ Church. The building will be constructed of red brick and stone in the Renaissance style of architecture.

York Street, the thoroughfare running westward in continuation of the Broadway, was formerly known by the name of "Petty France." There were two districts in this locality with foreign names, says Widmore—"Petty Calais," where the wool-staplers principally resided; and "Petty France," where lived the French merchants, who came over to trade at the Staple. An Act of an interchange between the King and the Abbot of Westminster, in the reign of Henry VIII., mentions "a certain great messuage or tenement commonly called 'Pety Caleys,' and all messuages, houses, barns, stables, dove-houses, orchards, gardens, pools, fisheries, waters, ditches, lands, meadows, and pastures." The street received its present name, by a vote of the inhabitants, from Frederick, Duke of York, son of George II., who for some time had a residence among them.

Between Chapel Street and the narrow turning known as Ermin's or Hermit's Hill, stood until very recently a charitable institution—one of a similar character to many others in this neighbourhood—known as the Red Lion Almshouses, but more commonly as Van Dun's Almshouses. These houses contained, originally, twenty rooms, to be inhabited rent free by as many poor women. They were founded in the reign of Elizabeth, under whom and whose predecessors Van Dun officiated as Yeoman of the Guard. His monument in St. Margaret's, Westminster, has a good bust and the following inscription:—"Cornelius Van Dun lieth here, borne at Breda, in Brabant; soldier with King Henry at Turney, Yeoman of the Guard, and Vsher to King Henry, King Edward, Queen Mary, and Queen Elizabeth: of honest and vertuous life, a careful man for poore folke, who in the end of this towne did build for poore widowes twenty houses at his own cost." Round the figure is inscribed:—"Obijt anno Dom. 1577, buried the 4 of September, ætatis suæ 94."

The tenements founded by Van Dun were of the smallest and plainest description. Not being endowed, they were appropriated to the parish pensioners of St. Margaret's, Westminster. The site of these humble edifices was formerly called St. Hermit's Hill, probably from a cell or hermitage there situate. A chapel dedicated to St. Mary Magdalen is mentioned by Stow as standing near this spot, "wholly ruinated."

These almshouses retained much of their primitive character down to the year 1862; but the alterations in the neighbourhood since the building of the St. James's Park Station of the Metropolitan District Railway have at length swept them away. Stow, in his survey of London and Westminster, mentions them as standing upon "St. Hermit's" Hill; and in Rocque's map this hill is clearly marked as bordering on the fields. Even at the beginning of the last century this neighbourhood retained enough of its rural or suburban character for the churchyard of the New Chapel (now Christ Church) to be considered the "pleasantest about London and Westminster."

The author of the article in the *Builder* to which we have referred in the commencement of this chapter, observes that—"Some interest is awakened by the circumstance that the site on which these almshouses once stood was a spot sacred alike to the Briton, the Roman, and the Saxon. The 'Thoth' of the Egyptian," he argues, "is identical with the Hermes or Mercury of the Greek and Roman, as also with the Tuisco or Teut of the Saxon. The hill of 'Hermes' and the 'teut-hill' of the Saxon are the same; and the name which Stow gives it, and by which it seems to have been known, is a curious coincidence, since the transition from 'Hermes' to St. Hermit is not very difficult of solution. The mound once sacred to this tutelary divinity of merchants and wayfarers is now a heap of rubbish; the caduceus and petasus have taken refuge in the locomotive and telegraph hard by; but through the long vista of time perhaps this transition is not greater than the annual setting up of the May-pole on the neighbouring village green, or the wayside inn and cottages with their gardens yet in the remembrance of the octogenarian."

The Westminster Panorama, in York Street, was opened in 1881. The picture on view, representing the Battle of Waterloo, covers upwards of 22,000 feet of canvas, and was painted by M. Castellani.

The house No. 19 lately standing in York Street occupied the site of the residence of John Milton, the author of "Paradise Lost." Part of the grounds had long been walled up, and appropriated to the house formerly inhabited by Jeremy Bentham. The cotton willow-tree planted by the great poet has now entirely disappeared, and in the place of the garden workshops and other buildings have sprung up. It is evident that the original front of the house was that facing the Park. On that side Jeremy Bentham placed a small tablet, with the following inscription :—"Sacred to Milton, Prince of Poets." In the old wall which bounded the garden on the Park side, opposite the house, were the indications of a door, long built up, which was probably used by Milton in passing between his house and Whitehall during his intercourse with Cromwell in the capacity of Latin secretary. In the house itself, which was pulled down in 1881–2, the arrangement of the windows was entirely changed. It is probable that they formerly extended along the whole front, with sliding frames or lattices, divided by panelled spaces. The original panelling remained in the large room on the first floor. The upper rooms were small, and the staircase, which had not been altered, was steep and narrow. The ground floor seemed to have been comprised in one large room, as the original fireplace was evidently situated about the centre of the wall on the west side. This was probably the family room, or compromise between kitchen and parlour, so common to the economy of houses of respectable pretensions in the olden time. This distinguished house was, in later years, the residence of William Hazlitt, the critic and essayist.

An American paper of 1874 stated that the Historical Society of Pennsylvania has recently received from the Hon. Benjamin Rush an original baluster or newel-post from the stairway of the house formerly inhabited by John Milton, the poet, accompanied by a water-colour sketch of the building, with the following certificate from the hand of the celebrated English jurist, Jeremy Bentham :—"A.D. 1821, August 15. Sketch of a house for some time inhabited by John Milton. It is situated in Westminster, in the street then called Petty France, but on the occasion of the French Revolutionary War, newly named York Street, in horror of France and honour of the Duke of York. This sketch was this day taken from the garden attached to the residence of Jeremy Bentham, into which garden the house has a door, being, under the Dean and Chapter of Westminster, his property. From this house, August 14th, 1821, under the direction of the said Jeremy Bentham, was cut the balustrade pillar, composed of four twisted columns, presented by him, in company with this sketch, to his truly dear and highly-respected friend Richard Rush, Envoy Extraordinary to the United Kingdom of Great Britain and Ireland. Witness my hand, JEREMY BENTHAM."

In Little James Street is Emmanuel Hospital, known also by the name of Lady Dacre's Almshouses. It was founded and built in the year 1600, under the will of Ann, widow of Gregory Fiennes, Lord Dacre, for the support of ten men and ten women, as pensioners ; and also for ten boys and ten girls, with a master for the former and a mistress for the latter. The children, when educated and grown up, were formerly apprenticed to different trades. The buildings and gardens of the hospital occupy about three and a half acres. The original buildings becoming decayed, the present almshouses were erected in the reign of Queen Anne, the chapel in that of George II., and the schoolrooms in the present century. In 1873 the Endowed Schools Commission successfully carried a "scheme" for the "reform" of the schools attached to the hospital. This institution, therefore, was the first of the kind which the "reforming" tendencies of the age may be said to have touched. These schools afford a good middle-class education to sixty-three children, selected from Westminster, Chelsea, and the village of Hayes, near Uxbridge, and also from the City of London and Brandesburton, near Beverley, Yorkshire. All the children are fed, clothed, sheltered, and educated, free of all expense to their relatives. In the education of the girls domestic work has always occupied a prominent position.

The will of Lady Dacre, under which this hospital was established, has often been printed. The testatrix provides, after declaring that her husband in his lifetime, and herself, designed to erect a hospital for the poor in Westminster or its neighbourhood, that her executors, if she should not perform it before her decease, should cause to be erected "a neat and convenient house, with room of habitation for twenty poor folk and twenty poor children," and that it should be entitled "Emmanuel Hospital." She expresses her design to be "the relief of aged people, and the bringing up of children in virtue and good and laudable arts, whereby they may the better live in time to come by their own honest labour," and enjoins her executors to be humble suitors to the Queen for a charter of incorporation. Accordingly a charter was obtained in 1601, ordaining "the house in Tuttle Fields an hospital for the poor, under the name of Emmanuel Hospital," and appointing, after the decease of the last-surviving executor, the Lord Mayor and Aldermen of London governors in perpetuity. The terms of this charter, however, are somewhat peculiar and contradictory; whilst allowing the governors very direct authority in the management of the charity, it nevertheless entrusts the alms-people themselves with very considerable powers of self-government, and incorporates them as "a body corporate of themselves for ever." This corporation is authorised "to purchase land, to grant leases, to have a common seal, to sue and be sued," &c., to choose its own warden, and "to have the custody of all deeds, writings, and surplus moneys in the common chest provided in the chapel." Practically, by custom, long disuse, and by an Act of Parliament passed in 1794, this corporation is defunct, and the jurisdiction entirely in the hands of the aldermen as the governing body. The statutes of 1601 are interesting, as showing the kind of persons which, in the opinion of Lady Dacre's executors, ought to have preference as pensioners :—" 1. Decayed and distressed servants of Lady Dacre. 2. Former servants of this family who have grown poor, lame, or diseased 'in the service of their prince,' or 'without their own fault.' 3. Any poor, honest, godly people past labour. 4. Those born blind, or lamed, or disabled in the service of their prince. 5. Those brought down from riches to poverty without their own fault." The present inmates are entirely of the third class. It would appear from the founder's will that she did not contemplate a school, but rather a cluster of industrial houses, in which each of the aged pensioners, in return for shelter and support, should "bring up and instruct in virtue, and good and laudable acts," one child. But, "as the present poor people are not capable of instructing children, the governors were of opinion that some honest and industrious clergyman who has a wife should be nominated and appointed to read prayers twice a day in the chapel, and instruct the children." Accordingly the school was founded, and the first clerical master appointed in 1735. In 1793 the pensioners' allowance (originally £5 only, and subsequently £15) was increased to £18, and is now fixed at £20 per annum.

In 1794, the lease of the Brandesburton estate having fallen in, the governors obtained an Act of Parliament to "increase and extend the objects of the charity." Ten out-pensioners were added to the almshouse branch, and the benefits of the in-pensioners were increased by the addition of twenty chaldrons of coals to their annual pension. In 1821 the number of children was increased from twenty to forty, which number was finally raised to sixty, in 1845, when the new schools were erected. In 1846 the chapel was enlarged, by the addition of an apex on the west side, to serve the purpose of a chancel. Before this time there had been no means of celebrating the holy communion. The altar-piece was purchased at the taking down of the church of St. Benet Fink, near the Royal Exchange. The pulpit is of elaborately-carved oak, and apparently of the time of James I. Under an arch at the north end of the chapel is a small model of the tomb of the founder, Lady Dacre, in Chelsea Church.

Of the masters of the hospital the only man of eminence was the Rev. William Beloe, the translator of Herodotus, who retained the office from 1783 to 1808, when he was appointed Rector of Allhallows, London Wall, and Assistant Librarian in the British Museum.

The most valuable endowments of this ancient charity consist of the manorial estate of Brandes-burton, the greater part of which parish belongs to the " poor of Emmanuel Hospital." The aldermen of London, as "trustees of the poor of Emmanuel Hospital," have been liberal and popular landlords. In 1843 they rebuilt the Brandesburton Schools, which had already been founded and endowed by a Yorkshire lady in the reign of George I.

In 1869 was passed the "Endowed Schools' Act," bringing this and other hospital schools under the stern and reforming hands of the "Endowed Schools' Commission." In 1873 this commission carried in Parliament a "scheme" for the reconstruction of this hospital, and the separation of the schools from the almshouse branch of the charity. Under the provisions of this scheme the endowments of four hospital schools in Westminster were to be united under the management of one body of governors, viz., Emmanuel, St. Margaret's, Palmer's, and Emery Hill's hospitals. Out of these endowments it was proposed to establish three large middle-class schools, namely, a boarding-school, to be erected within twenty miles of London, and two day-schools in Westminster, each providing accommodation for 300 boys, of whom 200 in each should pay a small sum for their education, whilst the other 100 free places were to be reserved as scholarships and exhibitions for deserving candidates, principally for those belonging to the public elementary day-schools of Westminster and Chelsea. The governing body, or trustees, as at present constituted, consist of the Lord Mayor of London, the Aldermen, the Recorder, and nine elected inhabitants of Westminster. It may be added that the school will be as soon as possible removed into the country. The almshouse branch of the

best acoustical arrangements, were the main considerations. The chapel is constructed of brick, and, with its semicircular-headed windows and doorways, has an elegant appearance. The campanile, at the north-east corner, rises to a height of about 160 feet. The interior is commodious and admirably adapted for the purpose for which it was built. There are two galleries, the fronts of which are of open iron-work, supported on a wooden

VAN DUN'S ALMSHOUSES, 1820. (*See page* 21.)

hospital is not touched by the above scheme, and one-third of the revenues of the charity is henceforth set aside for its support.

The hospital forms three sides of a quadrangle, the fourth side, opening to the street, being enclosed with iron railings and gates. The chapel has an enriched pediment, and is in the centre of the west side of the building.

On the north side of Emmanuel Hospital, and at the corner of James Street and Castle Lane, is a Nonconformist edifice called Westminster Chapel, which was rebuilt in 1864, from the designs of Mr. W. F. Poulton. In an architectural sense it is an adaptation of the Lombardic style to the requirements of a building in which convenient accommodation for a large number of persons, and the

basement of such a height as to secure the advantages of an enclosed gallery front; the two ends of the chapel are semi-circular. The ceiling is flat in the centre and coved at the sides; the whole being divided into panels by moulded ribs, springing at the base of the cove from semi-detached stone columns, which divide the wall in bays of equal width round the whole chapel. The coved part of the ceiling is groined between each bay in order to admit of the windows being continued above the caps of the columns.

The Infirmary, out of which Westminster Hospital originated, stood formerly on the east side of Castle Lane.

James Street, which extends from York Street to Buckingham Gate, is so called from its vicinity to the Park.   On the west side of this street was formerly Tart Hall, built in 1638, by Nicholas Stone, for Alethea, Countess of Arundel, and belonging to the family of the Howards.   It was the residence of William, Viscount Stafford, who was beheaded, on the evidence of Titus Oates, in the

At No. 11 in this street lived the poet, Richard Glover, whose song of "Hosier's Ghost" roused the nation to a war with Spain.   Another distinguished writer who resided in James Street was William Gifford, editor of the *Quarterly Review* for the first fifteen years of its existence: he died

WENCESLAUS HOLLAR.   (*See page* 29.)

reign of Charles II.   Having been used for some time as a place of entertainment, it was demolished early in the last century.   The old gateway of Tart Hall, which stood till 1737, was not opened after the condemned nobleman passed under it for the last time.   According to Strype, the old hall was partly in the parish of St. Martin's-in-the-Fields, and partly in that of St. James's: we shall have more to say of it in a subsequent chapter.   At the garden wall, on the site of which now stands Stafford Row, a boy was whipped annually, in order to keep the parish bounds in remembrance.

here in 1826.   His early history is prefixed to his translation of "Juvenal."

A native of Devonshire, and eminently a self-made man, Gifford was a political writer and critic of no small influence in his lifetime.   His early life was spent as a cabin-boy on board a little coasting-vessel; but at the age of fifteen he was apprenticed to a shoemaker at Ashburton.   In spite of a neglected education, his talents showed themselves in a strong thirst for knowledge.   Mathematics at first were his favourite study; and he relates that, in want of paper, he used to hammer scraps of leather smooth, and work his problems on them with a blunt awl. Through the kindness of Mr. Cookesley and the Earl Grosvenor, the poor and friendless orphan was enabled ultimately to manifest his talents, and to gain admission into the most brilliant literary and political circles, members of which were Pitt, Canning, Lord Liverpool, and the Marquis Wellesley.

In James Street, at the house of Thomas Harley, occurred the secret interview between Harley and the Duke of Marlborough—who, we are informed, entered by the garden door at the back of the house looking into the Park—when Harley discovered the existence of the secret negotiations between the French King and the General, a discovery which placed Marlborough's life in the Minister's hands.

CHAPTER III.

WESTMINSTER.—KING STREET, GREAT GEORGE STREET, AND THE BROAD SANCTUARY.

"Urbs antiqua fuit."—Virg., "Æn.," i.

Ancient Gates in King Street—Distinguished Residents in King Street—Oliver Cromwell's Mother—A Strange Incident in the Life of Cromwell—King Charles on his Way to his Trial—The Plague—Ancient Hostelries and Coffee-houses—Death of Hollar, the Engraver—Delahay Street—Duke Street and its Distinguished Residents—Judge Jeffreys—Fludyer Street—Great George Street—Lying in State of Lord Byron's Body—Institution of Civil Engineers—National Portrait Gallery—Burial of Sheridan—The Buxton Memorial Drinking Fountain—Statue of George Canning—The Sessions House—Westminster Hospital—Training School and Home for Nurses—The National Society—Anecdote about Sir John Hawkins's "History of Music"—Her Majesty's Stationery Office—Parker Street—John Wilkes—The Westminster Crimean Memorial.

KING Street, which we have already mentioned incidentally in our notice of Whitehall, was the ancient thoroughfare between the regions of the Court and the Abbey. It runs parallel to its modern sister, Parliament Street, between it and the Park. King Street was formerly extremely, and, it would appear, even dangerously narrow. Pepys thus commemorates it in his "Diary," November 27, 1660:—"To Westminster Hall; and in King Street there being a great stop of coaches, there was a falling out between a drayman and my Lord of Chesterfield's coachman, and one of his footmen killed."

At the north end of this street was the Cock-pit Gate; at the south end, the High Gate, which is shown in one of Hollar's etchings. The latter Gate House, which was taken down in 1723, was occupied at one time by the Earl of Rochester. Part of the land in King Street, extending as far southward as the Bars, was conveyed by the Abbot of Westminster to King Henry VIII., when he was bent on enlarging Whitehall. After the burning of Whitehall Palace, it was resolved to make a broader street to the Abbey, and in course of time Parliament Street was formed, as we have already stated in a previous chapter. Although part of King Street still remains, it is as narrow as ever, though somewhat better paved, and latterly its length has been considerably curtailed at the northern end by the erection of the new India and Foreign Offices.

Narrow as it was, King Street was the residence of many distinguished personages, doubtless owing to its proximity to the Court and the Parliament House. In it lived Lord Howard of Effingham, the High Admiral who, Roman Catholic as he was, went forth to fight the cause of his country against the Spanish Armada. Here, too, Edmund Spenser, the author of "The Faery Queen," after his escape from the troubles in Ireland, spent the last few weeks of his life, and died in actual penury and even in want of bread. Such was the end of the man who had sung the praises of the great Elizabeth in higher than mere courtly strains. But his sad end is only another example of the fate that too often waits on poetic genius. "The breath had scarcely departed from his body when the great, the titled, and the powerful came forward to do honour to his memory and to shower laurels on his grave. His remains were carried in state from King Street to Westminster Abbey, the expenses of the funeral being defrayed by the great favourite of the Court, the Earl of Essex." "His hearse," writes Camden, "was attended by poets, and mournful elegies, and poems, with the pens that wrote them, were thrown into his tomb." And it may be added that Anne, the Countess of Dorset, erected the monument over his grave. "The armorial shield of the Spencers," justly observes Gibbon, "may be emblazoned with the triumphs of a Marlborough, but I exhort them to look upon the 'Faery Queen' as the brightest jewel in their coronet."

In King Street, too, resided that most graceful of the courtier poets of the time of Charles I., Thomas Carew, who wrote the masque of "Cœlum Britannicum" for that prince, and who was the friend and boon-companion of Ben Jonson and Sir

John Suckling, and the author of that charming song which begins :—

> " He that loves a rosy cheek,
> 　Or a coral lip admires."

Here, too, lived Charles, Lord Buckhurst, afterwards Earl of Dorset, the witty and accomplished courtier and poet, and the author of the famous song addressed to the gay ladies of Charles II.'s court, the first stanza of which runs thus :—

> "To all you ladies now on land
> 　We men at sea indite ;
> But first would have you understand
> 　How hard it is to write ;
> The Muses now, and Neptune, too,
> 　We must implore to write to you."

Here the Lord Protector assigned to his mother a suite of apartments, which she occupied until the day of her death, in 1654 : she was buried in Westminster Abbey. She was devotedly fond of her son, and lived in constant fear of hearing of his assassination ; indeed it is said, in Ludlow's "Memoirs," that she was quite unhappy if she did not see him twice a day, and never heard the report of a gun without calling out, "My son is shot." Mr. Noble, in his "Memoirs of the Cromwell Family," tells us that "she requested, when dying, to have a private funeral, and that her body might not be deposited in the Abbey ; but that, instead of fulfilling her request, the Protector conveyed her remains, with great solemnity, and attended with many hundred torches, though it was daylight, and interred them in the dormitory of our English monarchs, in a manner suitable to those of the mother of a person of his then rank." He adds that, "the needless ceremonies and great expense to which the Protector put the public in thus burying her gave great offence to the Republicans."

It would have been well for her if her wish had been granted, for, at the Restoration, Mrs. Cromwell's body was taken up and indecently thrown, with others, into a hole made before the back door of the lodgings of the canons or prebendaries, in St. Margaret's Churchyard. Mrs. Cromwell appears to have been an excellent and amiable person ; and it is worthy of note that she is styled "a decent woman" by so strong a royalist as Lord Chancellor Clarendon.

The house occupied by Mrs. Cromwell, according to Mr. John Timbs, stood a little to the north of Blue Boar's Head Yard, on the west side of the street. If we may accept the testimony of Mr. G. H. Malone, its identity was ascertained by a search into the parish rate-books, and fixed to the north of the above-mentioned yard, and south of the wall of Ram's Mews. Among the Cole MSS. in the British Museum is a copy of a letter written by Cromwell at Dunbar, and addressed to his wife in this street.

One day a strange incident occurred to the Lord Protector as he was passing in his coach through this street, accompanied by Lord Broghill, afterwards better known by his superior title as Earl of Ossory, from whom the story has come down to us through his chaplain and biographer, Morrice :—"It happened that the crowd of people was so great that the coach could not go forward, and the place was so narrow that all the halberdiers were either before the coach or behind it, none of them having room to stand by the side. When they were in this posture, Lord Broghill observed the door of a cobbler's stall to open and shut a little, and at every opening of it his lordship saw something bright, like a drawn sword or a pistol. Upon which my lord drew out his sword with the scabbard on it, and struck upon the stall, asking who was there. This was no sooner done but a tall man burst out with a sword by his side, and Cromwell was so much frightened that he called his guard to seize him, but the man got away in the crowd. My lord thought him to be an officer in the army in Ireland, whom he remembered Cromwell had disgusted, and his lordship apprehended he lay there in wait to kill him. Upon this," adds Morrice, "Cromwell forbore to come any more that way, but a little after sickened and died."

And yet there was, at all events, one other occasion on which the Lord Protector passed along this narrow thoroughfare, and that was to his funeral in the Abbey. He died at Whitehall, in September, 1658 ; and as he died in the midst of his power and state, his obsequies were celebrated with the pomp and magnificence of a king. It would tax the pen of Macaulay to describe the scene : the road prepared for the passage of the hearse by gravel thrown into the ruts ; and the sides of the street lined with soldiery, all in mourning, as in solemn state the body was conducted to the great western entrance of the Abbey, where it was received by the clergy with the usual ceremonials.

Among the other residents in King Street were Sir Thomas Knevett, or Knyvett, who seized Guy Fawkes ; and Dr. Sydenham, on the site of Ram's Mews. Here, too, lived Erasmus Dryden, brother of "glorious" John Dryden, supporting himself by trade before his accession to the baronetcy as head of the family.

Dudley, the second Lord North, had a house in this street, about 1646, which was remarkable as being the first brick house in it. His son, Sir Dudley, as we learn in the "Lives of the Norths," was stolen by beggars, and retaken in an alley leading towards Cannon Row, while he was being stripped of his clothes. Bishop Goodman, during the Great Rebellion, lived here in great obscurity, and chiefly in the house of Mrs. Sybilla Aglionby, employing the greater part of his time in frequenting the Cottonian Library.

But there are other and more gloomy reminiscences which attach to King Street. Through it Charles I. was carried on his way to Westminster Hall on the first and last days of his trial. "On both these occasions," writes Mr. Jesse, "his conveyance was a sedan chair, by the side of which walked, bare-headed, his faithful follower, Herbert—the only person who was allowed to attend him. As he returned through King Street, after his condemnation, the inhabitants, we are told, not only shed tears, but, unawed by the soldiers who lined the streets, offered up audible prayers for his eternal welfare." Strange to say, among the residents in this street at the time was Oliver Cromwell himself; and it was from his abode here that, some months after the murder of his sovereign, he set forth in state, amid the blare of trumpets, to take upon himself the Lord Lieutenancy of Ireland. The house which was traditionally said to have been occupied by the Protector, was at the northern end, near Downing Street, and it was not demolished, says Mr. Jesse, until the present century.

Owing to its narrowness and want of light and air, and the crowded courts by which it was hemmed in on either side, King Street was among the first parts of Westminster to suffer from the plague in the year 1665. On its appearance so close to the gates of the royal palace, Charles II. and his train of courtiers, male and female, left Whitehall for Oxford. Accordingly, we find gossiping Samuel Pepys writing, under date June 20th : —" This day I informed myself that there died four or five at Westminster of the plague, in several houses, upon Sunday last, in Bell Alley, over against the Palace Gate." Again, on the 21st : " I find all the town going out of town, the coaches and carriages being all full of people going into the country." And, shortly after, on the 28th and 29th :—" In my way to Westminster Hall, I observed several plague-houses " (that is, houses smitten with the plague) " in King Street and the Palace. . . . To Whitehall, where the court was full of waggons and people ready to go out of town. This end of the town every day grows very bad of the plague." It appears from contemporary history that the example set by the King and Court was largely followed by

the nobility and the "quality ;" and that so great was the exodus that the neighbouring towns and villages rose up to oppose their retreat, as likely to sow the seeds of the disease still more widely, and to carry the infection further a-field. It is usually said by historians that the Great Plague in 1665 broke out at the top of Drury Lane, but Dr. Hodges, in his " Letter to a Person of Quality," states it as a fact that the pestilence first broke out in Westminster, and that it was carried eastwards by contagion.

King Street would seem to have been at one time noted for its coffee-houses, for in the fifth edition of Izaak Walton's additions to the "Complete Angler," (1676), " Piscator " says :—" When I dress an eel thus, I will he was as long and big as that which was caught in Peterboro' river in the year 1667, which was 3¾ feet long; if you will not believe me, then go and see it at one of the coffee-houses in King Street, Westminster."

Among these coffee-houses and hostelries was the " King's Head " Inn, where there was held an "ordinary," as far back as two centuries ago. Here a Mr. Moore told Pepys, in July, 1663, "the great news that my Lady Castlemaine is fallen from Court, and this morning retired ;" and the next day, at the same place, the same bit of scandal, he tells us, is confirmed by a " pretty gentleman," who, however, is in ignorance of the cause.

At another house in this street—the Bell Tavern —the "October Club" met early in the last century. The club, which consisted of about 150 members, derived its name from being composed of High Church Tory country gentlemen, who when at home drank October ale. The large room in which the club assembled was adorned with a portrait of Queen Anne, by Dâhl. After Her Majesty's death and the break-up of the club, the picture was purchased by the corporation of the loyal city of Salisbury, in whose council-chamber it may still be seen suspended.

In this street, also, the beautiful and talented actress, Mrs. Oldfield, earned her livelihood when a girl as a sempstress ; and through it she was carried, at the age of forty-seven, to her grave in the Abbey, her pall supported by noblemen and gentlemen, and her body being allowed to lie in state in the Jerusalem Chamber, as stated in a previous chapter. Such is the tide of destiny ; and well might it have been written on her hearse, " Voluit fortuna jocari."

Mr. John Timbs tells us, in his "Curiosities of London," that near the southern end of King Street, on the west side, was Thieven (Thieves) Lane, so called as being the regular passage along which thieves were led to the Gate House prison, so that they might not escape into the Sanctuary and set the law at defiance.

In Gardener's Lane, which leads from King Street to Duke Street, died in March, 1677, Hollar, the master of early etchers; he was buried on the 28th of that month in St. Margaret's Church-yard. He seems to have been as child-like and improvident as the rest of his fraternity. At all events, at the time of his last illness the bailiffs were in his rooms; and the dying artist, who had been the favourite of Lord Arundel, and the honoured inmate of his house, had to beg as a favour that the bed on which he lay might not be taken away till after his death. Hollar's widow survived him many years, and some time after his death sold to Sir Hans Sloane a large collection of the artist's works. This collection was subsequently acquired by the British Museum, and formed the nucleus of the magnificent collection of Hollar's works there existing. Hollar was of Bohemian extraction and of gentle blood; he was born at Prague in 1607. He came to England in the suite of Lord Arundel, whom we have already mentioned* as a lover and patron of art; and it was the death of his patron that plunged him into difficulties. It is probable that it was through Lord Arundel's influence that he became a member of the Roman Catholic faith, to which his father had formerly belonged.

Delahay Street, between King Street and St. James's Park, was so called from a family of that name formerly resident in the parish of St. Margaret's. At the southern end, at the corner of Great George Street, lived Lady Augusta Murray, the first wife of the Duke of Sussex.

At No. 19 in this street are the branch offices of the Society for the Propagation of the Gospel in Foreign Parts, Dr. Bray's Institution for Founding Libraries, the Colonial Bishoprics' Fund, the Ladies' Association for Promoting Female Education in India, and the Universities' Mission to Central Africa.

Duke Street, which ran in a line with Delahay Street and is now absorbed into it, was a poor and narrow thoroughfare at its best. Pope, in one of his Letters, tells an amusing anecdote relating to this street, but which serves to illustrate the cruel snares laid by the penal laws in force in his time against persons professing the Roman Catholic religion, who were not allowed to keep either carriages or horses of their own! He writes:—"By our latest account from Duke Street, Westminster, the con-

version of T. G. ——, Esq., is reported in a manner somewhat more particular. That, upon the seizure of his Flanders mares, he seemed more than ordinarily disturbed for some hours, sent for his ghostly father, and resolved to bear his loss like a Christian; till, about the hour of seven or eight, the coaches and horses of several of the nobility passing by his window towards Hyde Park, he could no longer endure the disappointment, but instantly went out, took the oath of abjuration, and recovered his dear horses, which carried him in triumph to the Ring. The poor distressed Roman Catholics, now unhorsed and uncharioted, cry out with the Psalmist, 'Some trust in chariots, and some in horses; but we will invocate the name of the Lord.'"

In this street died in 1826, aged eighty, Sir Archibald Macdonald, Bart., formerly M.P. for Hindon, &c., and Solicitor-General, and afterwards Chief Baron of the Exchequer. He was educated at Westminster School, to which he was so attached that he never omitted to be present at every college election and at every performance of the Westminster Play.

Here, too, lived Matthew Prior, in a house facing Charles Street. Bishop Stillingfleet, author of the "Origines Britannicæ," died here in 1699; Archbishop Hutton in 1758; and Dr. Arnold, the musical composer, in 1802.

The house once inhabited by the "infamous Judge" Jefferys, when Lord Chancellor, has been demolished during subsequent improvements in this locality. Down to the time of its removal, it was easily distinguished from its neighbours by a flight of stone steps, which James II. permitted the cruel favourite to make into the Park for his special accommodation; they terminated above in a small court, on three sides of which stood the once costly house. One portion of the mansion was used as the Admiralty House, until that office was removed by William III. to Wallingford House. The north wing of the house, in which Judge Jefferys heard cases, when he found it inconvenient to go to Lincoln's Inn or Westminster Hall, was afterwards converted into a chapel: Dr. John Pettingale, the antiquary, was for some time its incumbent.

The State Paper Office stood at the north end of Duke Street for many years. It was erected in 1833, to contain the documents of the Privy Council and Secretaries of State, formerly kept in Holbein's Gatehouse, and first arranged during the time when Lord Grenville was Premier.

In lodgings in Fludyer Street lived the eminent surgeon, Sir Charles Bell, in the early part of his career, before he joined the Middlesex Hospital.

* See Vol. III., p. 74.

This street was so named after Sir Samuel Fludyer, the ground-landlord, who, when Lord Mayor in 1761, entertained George III. and Queen Charlotte at Guildhall. It is said to occupy the site of the ancient Axe Yard, a haunt of Sir William of the "George and the Dragon." The houses in Great George Street were built shortly after the erection of Westminster Bridge, and the street covers ground which formed at that time an arm of the Thames. The tide flowed up from Bridge

THE BUXTON DRINKING FOUNTAIN. (*See page* 33.)

Davenant. The site is mentioned in a document of the time of Henry VIII., as "on the west side of Kynge Street, a great messuage or brew-house, commonly called the Axe." Pepys at one time had a house here.

Great George Street, the broad thoroughfare leading in a direct line from Bridge Street to Birdcage Walk and St. James's Park, derives its name from standing on the site of an old stable-yard which belonged to an inn close by, bearing the sign

Street, until it found its way into the canal of St. James's Park. From the frequency of inundations, Flood Street, which stood between the entrances of Dean's Yard and Tothill Street, derived its significant name.

In Great George Street lived, in 1763, John Wilkes, whilst carrying on his *North Briton* and fighting duels. It was in the front drawing-room of a house, No. 25 in this street, that in July, 1824, lay in state the body of Lord Byron, which had been brought over in the ship *Florida* from Missolonghi, in Greece, where he died fighting in the cause of Grecian independence. It was hoped that a grave would have been found for the author of "Childe Harold" in Poets' Corner in the Abbey hard by, but the Dean and Chapter refused to

Street, Westminster. At the house of Sir Edward it lay in state for two days, and was visited by hundreds of persons, who paid their last tributes to the genius of the mighty slumberer by gazing on his coffin-lid. After the lying in state had terminated, it was found necessary to remove the

HOUSE IN WESTMINSTER, SAID TO HAVE BEEN OCCUPIED BY OLIVER CROMWELL. (*See page* 27.)

allow his body to rest there; so, a day or two afterwards, the poet's remains were taken down into Nottinghamshire, and consigned to their last resting-place in Hucknall Church, near his home at Newstead Abbey. The scene itself is thus described by an American gentleman who was present:—"On being landed from the *Florida*, the body was removed to the house of Sir Edward Knatchbull, who then resided in Great George

body, for the purpose of placing it in a better constructed leaden coffin than that which had been prepared in Greece. A friend of mine kindly offered to procure me admission to the chamber where the removal of the body was to be effected—an offer which, I need not say, I gladly accepted. Accordingly, on the afternoon of the 11th of July, I proceeded to Sir Edward Knatchbull's, and found three or four gentlemen, attracted thither, like myself, to witness the solemn face of the poet for the last time, ere it should be shut up in the darkness of death. Mr. Samuel Rogers, the author of the 'Pleasures of Memory,' Mr. (now Sir) John Cam Hobhouse, and John Hanson, Esq. (the two last Lord Byron's executors), Dr. (afterwards Sir John) Bowring, Fletcher, his faithful valet, and one or two others, whose names I did not learn, were present.

"The body lay in the large drawing-room, on the first storey, which was hung with black cloth and lighted with wax candles. Soon after my arrival, the work of opening the coffin commenced. This was soon effected, and when the last covering was removed, we beheld the face of the illustrious dead, 'all cold and all serene.'

"Were I to live a thousand years, I should never, never forget that moment. For years I had been intimate with the mind of Byron. His wondrous works had thrown a charm around my daily paths, and with all the enthusiasm of youth I had almost adored his genius. With his features, through the medium of paintings, I had been familiar from my boyhood; and now far more beautiful, even in death, than my vivid fancy had ever pictured, there they lay in marble repose.

"The body was not attired in that most awful of habiliments—a shroud. It was wrapped in a blue cloth cloak, and the throat and head were uncovered. The former was beautifully moulded. The head of the poet was covered with short, crisp, curling locks, slightly streaked with grey hairs, especially over the temples, which were ample and free from hair, as we see in the portraits. The face had nothing of the appearance of death about it— it was neither sunken nor discoloured in the least, but of a dead, marble whiteness—the expression was that of stern repose. How classically beautiful was the curved upper lip and the chin! I fancied the nose appeared as if it was not in harmony with the other features; but it might possibly have been a little disfigured by the process of embalming. The forehead was high and broad—indeed, the whole head was extremely large—it must have been so to contain a brain of such capacity.

"But what struck me most was the exceeding beauty of the *profile*, as I observed it when the head was lifted in the operation of removing the corpse. It was perfect in its way, and seemed like a production of Phidias. Indeed, it far more resembled an exquisite piece of sculpture than the face of the dead—so still, so sharply defined, and so marble-like in its repose. I caught the view of it but for a moment; yet it was long enough to have stamped upon my memory as 'a thing of

beauty,' which poor Keats tells us is 'a joy for ever.' It is, indeed, a melancholy joy to me to have gazed upon the silent poet. As Washington Irving says of the old sexton who crept into the vault where Shakespeare was entombed, and beheld there the dust of ages, 'it was something even to have seen the dust of Byron.'"

This same house, which has a handsome architectural front, is now the home of the Institution of Civil Engineers. The institution was established in 1818, and was formally incorporated in June, 1828. It originated in a few gentlemen then beginning life, who, being impressed, "by what they themselves felt, with the difficulties young men had to contend with in gaining the knowledge requisite for the diversified practice of engineering, resolved to form themselves into a society for promoting a regular intercourse between persons engaged in its various branches, and thereby mutually benefiting by the interchange of individual observation and experience." The profession of the civil engineer is defined in the charter of incorporation as "the art of directing the great sources of power in nature for the use and convenience of man, as the means of production and of traffic in states, both for external and internal trade, as applied in the construction of roads, bridges, aqueducts, canals, river navigation, and docks, for internal intercourse and exchange; and in the construction of ports, harbours, moles, breakwaters, and lighthouses; and in the art of navigation by artificial power for the purposes of commerce; and in the construction and adaptation of machinery; and in the drainage of cities and towns."

The institution itself consists of four classes, viz., members, associates, graduates, and honorary members. Members are civil engineers by profession, or mechanical engineers of very high standing; associates are not necessarily civil engineers by profession, but their pursuits must in some way be connected with civil engineering; graduates are elected from the pupils of civil and mechanical engineers; honorary members are individuals who are eminent for scientific acquirements, and are enabled to assist in the prosecution of public works.

Here is a portrait of Thomas Telford, the engineer of the Menai Bridge, and for fifteen years president of the institution. Telford was the first president. His successors have been Mr. James Walker, Sir John Rennie, Sir M. I. Brunel, Sir William Cubitt, Mr. Thomas Hawksley, and Mr. J. F. Bateman.

At No. 29 in this street was established, at its first formation, in 1857, the National Portrait Gallery. This institution arose out of a suggestion of the late Earl of Derby; its object is the collection of a series of portraits of English men and women of note and celebrity, and forming them into a representative gallery belonging to the nation. The collection is largely recruited by gifts, as might naturally be expected, and a sum of £2,000 is voted annually in Parliament for its maintenance and support. In 1870, the portraits were removed to South Kensington, a portion of the building erected for the International Exhibition having been fitted up for their reception. In Great George Street were, till lately, the town mansions of several of the highest nobility. At No. 15, Edward Lord Thurlow resided, and from it in September, 1806, his remains were removed for interment in the Temple. Bishop Tomline, Pitt's tutor, lived for some time at No. 28. At his house here, on the 12th of December, 1849, died Sir Marc Isambart Brunel, the architect of the Thames Tunnel. At No. 31 died, in 1881, William Page Wood, Lord Hatherley, some time Lord Chancellor.

In July, 1816, the body of Richard Brinsley Sheridan was removed from Savile Row to the house of Peter Moore, Esq., in this street, whence it was carried to the grave in the Abbey, attended by several noblemen and gentlemen.

At the corner of Great George Street and St. Margaret's Churchyard is a conspicuous structure, with a spire and cross of imposing height, known as the Buxton Memorial Drinking Fountain. The base is octagonal, about twelve feet in diameter, having open arches on the eight sides, supported on clustered shafts of polished Devonshire marble around a large central shaft, with four massive granite basins. Surmounting the pinnacles at the angles of the octagon are eight figures of bronze, representing the different rulers of England; the Britons represented by Caractacus, the Romans by Constantine, the Danes by Canute, the Saxons by Alfred, the Normans by William the Conqueror, and so on, ending with Queen Victoria. The fountain bears an inscription to the effect that it is "intended as a memorial of those members of Parliament who, with Mr. Wilberforce, advocated the abolition of the British slave-trade, achieved in 1807; and of those members of Parliament who, with Sir T. Fowell Buxton, advocated the emancipation of the slaves throughout the British dominions, achieved in 1834. It was designed and built by Mr. Charles Buxton, M.P., in 1865, the year of the final extinction of the slave-trade and of the abolition of slavery in the United States." Mr. S. S. Teulon was the architect, and the fountain was erected at a cost of about £1,200.

Close by this fountain, and facing the Houses of Parliament, is a fine bronze statue of George Canning, standing upon a granite pedestal. It was executed by Sir Richard Westmacott, and erected in 1832. It formerly stood nearer to Westminster Hall, but was removed hither a few years ago, when sundry alterations were made in the laying out of the open space between King Street and the north door of the Abbey.

Soon after Canning's statue was put up in all its verdant freshness, the carbonate of copper not yet blackened by the smoke of London, Mr. Justice Gaselee was walking away from Westminster Hall with a friend, when the judge, looking at the statue (which is colossal), said, "I don't think this is very like Canning; he was not so large a man." "No, my lord," replied his companion, "nor so green."

On the western side of the Broad Sanctuary, and on the very foundations of the old belfry-tower of the Sanctuary, stands the Sessions House, which, as its name imports, is the place of meeting for the magistrates for the City and Liberties of Westminster. It is an octagonal building of no great architectural pretensions, with a heavy portico, supported by massive columns of the Doric order. It was erected in 1805 from the designs of Mr. S. P. Cockerell. The old Guildhall, apparently of great antiquity, stood on the west side of King Street; and an ancient painting, representing the foundation of this building, said to be a gift of the Duke of Northumberland, was transferred to the walls of the present Sessions House.

Fronting the Broad Sanctuary and the northern side of the nave of the Abbey, between the Sessions House and Victoria Street, stands the Westminster Hospital. It was established in 1719 for the relief of the sick and needy from all parts, and was the first subscription hospital erected in London. It was incorporated in 1836. Patients are admitted by order from a governor, except in cases of accident, which are received, without recommendation, at all hours of the day or night. The institution took its origin from the exertions of a few gentlemen, who set an infirmary on foot, inviting all kindly-disposed persons to aid them. Mr. Henry Hoare was the chief promoter of this charity; and at first the society was known as that "for relieving the sick and needy at the Public Infirmary in Westminster." In 1720, a house was taken for the purpose of an infirmary in Petty France; from which, in 1724, the institution was removed to Chapel Street, and some time after to James Street. The present spacious edifice was completed and opened in 1834. The building is an embattled structure of quasi-Gothic character, and was erected in 1834 by Messrs. Inwood. It has a frontage of about 200 feet, but has no pretensions to taste or beauty. The centre projects slightly, and is raised one storey higher than the wings. The entrance is by a flight of steps to a porch in three divisions, and is surmounted by an oriel. The hospital accommodates about 200 in-patients, and the total number of patients relieved annually is about 20,000.

The following document, which may be styled the first annual report of this institution, dated 1720, hangs framed and glazed on the wall of the secretary's room:—"Whereas a charitable proposal was published in December last (1719), for relieving the sick and needy, by providing them with lodging, with proper food and physick, and nurses to attend them during their sickness, and by procuring them the advice and assistance of physicians or surgeons, as their necessities should require; and by the blessing of God upon this undertaking, such sums of money have been advanced and subscribed by several of the nobility and gentry of both sexes and by some of the clergy, as have enabled the managers of this charity (who are as many of the subscribers as please to be present at their weekly meetings), to carry on in some measure what was then proposed:—for the satisfaction of the subscribers and benefactors, and for animating others to promote and encourage this pious and Christian work, this is to acquaint them, that in pursuance of the foresaid charitable proposal, there is an infirmary set up in Petty France, Westminster, where the poor sick who are admitted into it, are attended by physicians, surgeons, apothecaries, and nurses, supplied with food and physick, and daily visited by some one or other of the clergy; at which place the society meets every Wednesday evening for managing and carrying on this charity, admitting and discharging patients, &c."

Close to and in connection with the hospital, an institution has been opened, styled the Westminster Training School and Home for Nurses, having for its object the training of a superior class of nurses for the sick, for hospitals, and private families. An agreement has been entered into by its managers with the Westminster Hospital to undertake the whole of the nursing there. A limited number of probationers are received at the home, and to those who may be accepted is given the efficient training and practical instruction required.

The central schools of the National Society for Promoting the Education of the Poor in the Principles of the Church of England are situated contiguous to Westminster Hospital. These schools were instituted in 1811, and incorporated in 1817.

The institution, which has for its object the "Christianising of the children of millions in the densely-crowded streets of the metropolis, amid the ignorance of an agricultural population, and the restlessness of the manufacturing and mining districts," is supported by voluntary contributions. The number of schools in union with it amounts to upwards of 12,000. Here is the National Society's central depository for the sale, at a cheap rate, of books and apparatus for schools.

In May, 1789, Sir John Hawkins, the author of the "History of Music," and of a "Life of Dr. Johnson," whose executor he was, died at his house near the Broad Sanctuary—the same which had formerly been the residence of the famous Admiral Vernon—in a street leading towards Queen Square. The following anecdote about Sir John Hawkins's "History of Music" is taken from the *Harmonicon:*—"The fate of this work was decided, like that of many more important things, by a trifle, a word, a pun. A ballad, chanted by a fille-de-chambre, undermined the colossal power of Alberoni; a single line of Frederick the Second, reflecting not on politics but the poetry of a French minister, plunged France into the Seven Years' War; and a pun condemned Sir John Hawkins's sixteen years' labour to long obscurity and oblivion. Some wag wrote the following catch, which Dr. Callcott set to music:—

'Have you read Sir John Hawkins's History?
　Some folks think it quite a mystery;
　Both I have, and I aver
　That Burney's History I prefer.'

Burn his History was straightway in every one's mouth; and the bookseller, if he did not follow the advice *à pied de la lettre*, actually wasted, as the term is, or sold for waste paper, some hundred copies, and buried the rest of the impression in the profoundest depth of a damp cellar, as an article never likely to be called for, so that now hardly a copy can be procured undamaged by damp and mildew. It has been for some time, however, rising—is rising, and the more it is read and known the more it ought to rise—in public estimation and demand."

In Prince's Street, immediately behind the Westminster Hospital, and on the site of the Westminster Mews, stands a large building of no great architectural pretensions, which is entered by an archway, and surrounds a court. It is divided into two parts, the one of which, to the south, having formerly been a police-barrack, has been devoted, since 1854, to the purposes of Her Majesty's Stationery Office. This public office was first established as a separate department about the year 1790, the stationery used in the public service having been previously supplied by individuals who had lucrative patents. A yearly estimate is published of the amount required "to defray the expense of providing stationery, printing, binding, and printed books, for the several departments of Government in England, Scotland, and Ireland, and some dependencies; and of providing stationery, binding, printing, and paper for the two Houses of Parliament; and to pay the salaries and expenses of the establishment of the Stationery Office. The late Mr. J. R. M'Culloch, the eminent statistician, was for many years the Comptroller of this department.

Princes Street was formerly called "Long Ditch." At one time it contained an ancient conduit, the site of which has since been marked by a pump. At the bottom of the well, it is said, is a black marble image of St. Peter, and some marble steps. The southern extremity of this street was called "Broken Cross."

Parker Street, on the west side of Princes Street, was formerly called Bennet Street, so named after Bennet (now Corpus Christi) College, Cambridge, to which the land belongs. Its name was changed some years ago, when a number of disorderly occupants were ejected, and new tenants admitted. The new name refers to Archbishop Parker, who, having bequeathed his valuable library to Corpus Christi College, is regarded as one of its chief benefactors.

At the west end of Prince's Court—a narrow turning out of Prince's Street—resided, in 1788, the great civic notoriety, John Wilkes. It has been noticed that his name, and the offices which he successively filled, coupled with it, were composed of forty-five letters :—

John Wilkes, Esquire, Sheriff for London and Middlesex.
John Wilkes, Esquire, Knight of the Shire for Middlesex.
John Wilkes, Esquire, Alderman for Farringdon Without.
John Wilkes, Esquire, Chamberlain of the City of London.
The Right Honourable John Wilkes, Lord Mayor of London.

Opposite the Broad Sanctuary is a Gothic column, or cross, nearly seventy feet high, erected, in 1861, as a memorial to Lord Raglan, and other "old Westminster scholars," who fell in the Crimea, in 1854-5. It is of Aberdeen granite, and very picturesque, although somewhat incongruous, which is perhaps owing to its having been executed by various artists. Around the polished shaft, which rises from a decorated pedestal, are shields bearing the arms of those whom it commemorates. At the top of the sculptured capital are four sitting figures, under Gothic canopies, representing the successive founders and benefactors of the School and Abbey—Edward the Confessor, Henry III., Queen Elizabeth, and Queen Victoria. The whole is surmounted by a figure of St. George and the Dragon. The architect of this beautiful column was Sir G. Gilbert Scott; the figures of St. George and the Dragon, however, are by Mr. J. R. Clayton. In 1870, the memorial having become somewhat dilapidated, a sum of £30 towards its repair was voted by the Elizabethan Club, of which we have already spoken in our account of Westminster School.

CHAPTER IV.

MODERN WESTMINSTER.

"But times are altered."—Goldsmith.

HAVING in the preceding chapters dealt with the streets and thoroughfares forming the centre of the City of Westminster, we will now endeavour to point out some of the chief features of interest, and penetrate into some of the courts and alleys that lie scattered through its outlying regions.

Starting from the Broadway, skirting the southwestern corner of Dean's Yard, and running parallel to Abingdon Street, is Great Smith Street: this, with Little Smith Street, which joins it at right angles, and also Smith Square, derive their names, says Mr. Mackenzie Walcott, from a person who was clerk of the works at the time of the erection; but according to Hutton, from Sir James Smith, the ground-landlord, who resided here. At the commencement of the last century there was a turnpike in Smith Street. In Great Smith Street is St. Margaret's and St. John's Free Public Library, and also the Public Baths and Washhouses, two very useful institutions, the benefits of which are highly appreciated by a large number of that particular class of the inhabitants for whose service

days amused themselves at the game of bowls. The memory of the spot is still preserved in the name of Bowling Alley.

In Little Dean Street stood one of the chapels of the French Huguenot Refugees, removed hither about the year 1700, from Berwick Street, Soho.

JUDGE JEFFREYS' HOUSE IN DUKE STREET. *From an Original Drawing by Shepherd.* (*See page* 29.)

they were specially erected. In 1840, Dr. H. H. Milman, afterwards Dean of St. Paul's, laid in this street the first stone of the City of Westminster Literary, Scientific, and Mechanics' Institution. The building comprised a spacious lecture-room, reading-rooms, class-rooms for drawing and music, a museum, and a library.

To the south of College Street was the bowling-green, where the members of the convent in other

Tufton Street was built by Sir Richard Tufton, after whom it was named. He died in 1631, and was buried in the Abbey.

At No. 18 in this street is the Royal Architectural Museum. The building in itself has little or nothing architectural about it to merit special mention. It is simply a lofty plain brick edifice on the west side of the street, and is entered through an arched doorway and vestibule. The interior is lighted from the roof only, the walls being entirely covered with the various objects exhibited, such as castings of capitals and bases of columns, bosses, and other kinds of ornament. Two galleries run round the building, each of them likewise filled with specimens. The Museum was founded in 1851, in

practical object is to improve and perfect the art-workmanship of the present time, and to afford art-workmen the opportunity of studying casts or copies of those works, the originals of which neither their time nor their means will allow them to visit. Accordingly, a large collection of casts and actual

COLONEL BLOOD'S HOUSE. *From a Drawing in Mr. Crace's Collection.* (*See page* 38.)

Cannon Row, as the nucleus of a National Museum of Architectural Art, and subsequently for several years formed part of the collection exhibited at the South Kensington Museum. The intention of its founders was to supply to architects, artists, and art-workmen, the means of referring to and studying the architecture of past ages, and in com-bination with those arts which have their origin in or are dependent on architecture itself. Its direct

specimens has been formed from the finest mediæval examples, English and foreign, of complete archi-tectural works, arranged, as far as possible in the order of their dates; and of details, comprehending figures, animals, foliage, mouldings, encaustic tiles, mural paintings, roof ornaments, rubbings of sepul-chral brasses, stained glass, impressions from seals, and other objects. Schools of Classical Art are also represented, though not so fully or systematically. A special collection of marble reliefs from the ruins of one of the ancient capitals of India, situated in the great desert of Rajpootana, of the date of about 1100 A.D., is due to the generosity of Sir Bartle Frere. The museum is open to the public free; but a small fee is charged for the drawing and modelling classes.

In Tufton Street there was formerly a building devoted to the brutal and unmanly amusement of cock-fighting. It comprised a large circular area, with a slightly elevated platform in the centre, surrounded by benches, rising in gradation to nearly the top of the building. The cock-pit existed in this street long after that near St. James's Park was deserted.

Great Peter Street bears the name of the patron-saint of the Abbey. Upon the front of a house in it might be seen the following inscription, rudely cut: "This is Sant Peter Street, 1624. R. [a heart] W." In this street is the principal entrance to the gas-works, noticed in a preceding chapter. Here, too, stands the Church of St. Matthew, which was erected in 1849, to meet the wants of the over-crowded parish of St. John the Evangelist. The church is situated in a very close and poor neigh-bourhood, its site having been purchased piecemeal as the different miserable houses by which it was partly covered could be procured. It is of a very irregular and unfavourable form, something resem-bling the letter L, and presenting one narrow frontage to Peter Street, and one still narrower to St. Anne's Lane; the remainder is almost buried by houses. The architect has succeeded, however, in placing the church east and west, and in so arranging it as to present all the usual ecclesiastical features and proportions; and though the building externally is but little seen, the part exposed to view is bold and effective; while the interior, though simple, suffers but little from the cramped nature of the position, excepting that the north aisle is deprived of its side windows by the row of houses by which it is flanked. The chancel is lighted by a bold east window of five lights, and by three windows on the south, and one on the north side, the remainder of that side being occu-pied by a chancel-aisle and vestry. The nave, with its aisles, consists of five bays or arches in length, and is chiefly lighted from the clerestory and from a large west window which obtains light from above the surrounding houses. The nave and chancel occupying the whole available area of that part of the ground which lies east and west, but not affording the required accommodation, a third aisle is projected into the southern arm of the ground, so that the nave has one aisle on the

north and two on the south. The principal en-trance is through the tower, which projects again southward from the last-mentioned aisle and faces Peter Street. There are also a western entrance and one from St. Anne's Lane. The style is the later fashion of the geometrical variety of Middle-pointed, or, what is more frequently called, "Early Decorated." It is, however, very simple though bold in its details. The church is built to accom-modate 1,200 worshippers, and the cost of its con-struction was about £6,000.

At a house at the corner of Great Peter Street and Tufton Street, overlooking Bowling Alley, if tradition is correct, resided, during the latter part of his life, the notorious Colonel Blood, who, as told by us in a previous volume,* endeavoured to steal the Crown and Regalia from the Tower. While Edwards, the keeper, who so bravely saved the crown, was literally left to starve, Blood is stated to have retired hither—with a pension, too—after his daring exploit at the Tower, King Charles not only having pardoned, but actually conferred upon him an estate in Ireland, worth £500 a year. Truly, therefore, may we add, in the words of the poet of old—

"Ille crucem sceleris pretium tulit, hic diadema."

Colonel Blood was cast in a suit for libel against his former patron, the Duke of Buckingham, and sentenced to pay £10,000, by way of damages. This sentence he could not survive. He died here in August, 1680, and was buried in New Chapel Yard, near the Broadway. He had, how-ever, been such an eccentric scamp during his life, that the populace thought that his death was only a ruse and a sham; so his body was taken up and an inquest held upon it. It was identified beyond dispute by a malformation of the thumb, and ac-cordingly was put back into its grave, only to be again disturbed by the formation of Victoria Street.

In the Luttrell Collection of Broadsides in the British Museum is to be seen "An Elegy on Colonel Blood, notorious for stealing the crown," in which occur the two following lines:—

'Thanks, ye kind fates, for your last favour shown, For stealing Blood, who lately stole the crown."

The house is mentioned in 1820 as "no longer standing." It was distinguished by a shield and coat of arms, raised in relief on the brickwork on the front of the house.

St. Anne's Lane, a narrow turning out of Great Peter Street, was so named from the Chapel dedi-cated to the mother of the Virgin Mary. Henry Purcell, the musician, who was born in Westminster,

* See Vol. II., page 81.

lived for some time in this lane. One of the most important features of St. Anne's Lane at the present time is a range of spacious and convenient baths and wash-houses, which have been erected at a cost of about £10,000.

An amusing story with reference to St. Anne's Lane is related in the *Spectator*, No. 125:—"Sir Roger de Coverley was a schoolboy, at the time when the feuds ran high between the Roundheads and Cavaliers. This worthy knight, being then a stripling, had occasion to inquire which was the way to St. Anne's Lane, upon which the person to whom he spoke, instead of answering his question, called him 'a young Popish cur,' and asked him 'who had made Anne a saint?' The boy, in some confusion, inquired of the next he met which was the way to Anne's Lane; but was called 'a prick-eared cur,' and, instead of being shown the way, was told she had been 'a saint before he was born, and would be one after he was hanged." 'Upon this,' says Roger, 'I did not think fit to repeat the former question, but going into every lane in the neighbourhood, asked what they called the name of the lane.'"

There were two St. Anne's Lanes which might have cost Sir Roger some trouble to find: one "on the north side of St. Martin's-le-Grand, just within Aldersgate Street," according to Stow; and the other—which it requires sharp eyes to find in Strype's map—turning, as we have said, out of Great Peter Street. Mr. Peter Cunningham, in his "Handbook for London," prefers supposing that Sir Roger inquired his way in the latter neighbourhood.

There is an old saying among Londoners, quoted in Moryson's "Itinerarie," to the effect that "woe be to him who buys a horse in Smithfield, or who takes a servant from St. Paul's, or a wife out of Westminster." Judging from the appearance of the female part of the community inhabiting many of the narrow courts and alleys abounding in this neighbourhood, one would be almost inclined to feel that the latter part of the saying above quoted holds good even in the present day, notwithstanding the sweeping change that has been effected in this neighbourhood within the last few years under the auspices of the Westminster Improvements Commission.

Old and New Pye Streets, part of which has disappeared since the year 1845 in the formation of Victoria Street, derive their names from the well-known Sir Robert Pye, who resided in the New Way close by. He was by marriage a cousin of Oliver Cromwell.

In Old Pye Street is a large brick building devoted to the comfort and intellectual improvement of the poorest classes of the population of Westminster. It is known as the Westminster Working Men's Club and Lodging-house. About the year 1860 a very useful little institution was established in a small room in Duck Lane, near Strutton Ground, on the south side of Victoria Street. It was the first attempt made in London at a working men's club as distinguished from a mechanic's institute—a place of repose and recreation, opened every evening from six till half-past ten, on payment of a weekly subscription of one halfpenny. Several daily and weekly papers, with some monthly periodicals, were provided, besides draughts and chess; coffee and ginger-beer were supplied at cost price, no alcoholic beverages being admitted. Educational classes were held three times a week, and lectures, free to members and their families, were given every fortnight. A religious service (quite unsectarian) was also held for one hour on Sunday evenings. A penny bank was opened three nights a week, and in six months from the commencement, a labour loan society, enrolled by Mr. Tidd Pratt, was started. The institution soon proved so successful that it was necessary to enlarge the accommodation. Another room was built over the first one, and opened in December, 1861; the lower room was thus left free for general conversation, coffee, or smoking; the classes, lectures, and quiet reading being carried on upstairs. A temperance association was now formed by some of the members, with a sick benefit society attached, formed by paying a penny a week, the use of a room for the temperance meetings being accorded free of expense. A barrow club was also commenced in 1862, for furnishing the members who were costermongers with barrows. The cost of a barrow is 55s.; a weekly sum is paid, and when the price is liquidated the barrow becomes the property of the owner, instead of the latter always continuing to pay for the hire of one. In 1863, the accommodation having again become insufficient for its numerous members, an adjoining house was taken in, and the club entirely remodelled and improved, at a cost of more than £500, and re-opened in November of that year.

The demolition of Duck Lane, to make way for the progress of "the Westminster improvements," led to the erection, in Old Pye Street, of the pile of buildings above mentioned, which consists partly of a working men's club and partly of a dwelling-house, to accommodate between fifty and sixty of those families who are ineligible, from the lowness of their weekly wages or from their occupations, for any other lodging-houses, Mr. Peabody's included, where none but men earning 18s. or 20s. a week are admitted. The new Working Men's Club was opened in May, 1866. In the club building, which is quite distinct from the dwelling-house, there is, on the ground-floor, a spacious club-room, with a lavatory and other accommodation attached, as also a kitchen and library. A portion of the club at the corner of Old Pye Street and St. Ann's Lane has been fitted up as a double-fronted shop, where a co-operative store has been established by the members. Over the club-room are a lecture-room, a committee-room, and an office; the lecture-room can be at any time divided into two by a movable partition, so as to form a reading-room and a class-room.

In Pye Street lived for some time De Groot, the great-nephew of the learned Hugo Grotius, who was afterwards admitted as a poor brother into the Charter House, on the friendly intercession of Dr. Johnson.

Orchard Street was so called from being erected on the old orchard-garden of the monastery. Here, in 1757, the eccentric Thomas Amory, author of "Memoirs of John Buncle," lived the life of a recluse, venturing out only in the evening. He died in 1789, at a great age.

To the south-west of the Abbey is a district, between Great Smith Street and Victoria Street, which was and is known as "The Rookery." These "rookeries" or vagabond colonies, which meet us in various parts of "Modern Babylon," were originally the sites of sanctuaries and refuges for debtors and felons, or else of some "'spital" or "loke" for the reception of the poor, the maimed, and the lepers; the districts in which these asylums were located proving each the nucleus or nest of a dense pauper and criminal population. For just as the felon of our own days is too often found among the inmates of our "casual wards," so it is probable that of old the "sanctuary men" mixed with the diseased crowds and hordes of beggars that swarmed around a "'spital," associating of course with women of the lowest class, and so perpetuating the breed of outcasts and thieves, and turning the once "religious houses" into nests of poverty, misery, disease, and vice.

The region above alluded to formerly covered a much larger area than it does now, comprising as it did New Pye Street, Duck Lane, New Tothill Street, and portions of Orchard Street and Old Pye Street, together with a vast number of courts which diverged from them, all of which have been swept away since the year 1845, when the work of clearance was taken in hand by the Westminster Improvement Commission. It was in Orchard Street that Oliver Cromwell had one of his palaces; in those days Palmer's Village was close beside it, and was the seat of gentlemen's country residences. Lady Dacre, the foundress of Emmanuel Hospital, left to the City an estate of between two and three acres of ground—the garden ground—called "Palmer's Village" from the Rev. James Palmer, who here founded, in 1654, almshouses for twelve poor persons, and a school for twenty boys, known as the "Black-Coat School." This institution is now located in Rochester Row, where the almshouses were rebuilt in 1881. Palmer's Village at the early part of the present century, boasted of its village green, upon which the Maypole was annually set up; and there was an old wayside inn, bearing the sign of "The Prince of Orange." All this rurality, together with the nest and labyrinth of vile and dirty lanes and courts which surrounded it, has now disappeared, and in its place has been formed the broad and open thoroughfare, Victoria Street, which was commenced in 1845, and publicly opened in 1851.

"Nobody," writes the author of "A New Critical Review of the Public Buildings" in 1736, "will wonder, I presume, that I am for levelling the Gate House, demolishing a large part of Dean's Yard, and laying open a street at the west end of the Abbey, at least to an equal breadth with the building." Had the writer of these remarks lived to our own days he would have seen his wishes gratified.

Apropos of the improvements that have been of late years effected here, we may add that in 1766 was published Gwyn's "London and Westminster Improved," an important work, dedicated by permission to the King; the dedication and the preface, as we learn from Boswell, being from Dr. Johnson's pen. Mr. Croker thus remarks on it in his notes on Boswell:—"In this work Mr. Gwyn proposed the *principle*, and in many instances the *details*, of the most important improvements which have been made in the metropolis in our day. A bridge near Somerset House; a great street from the Haymarket to the New Road; the improvement of the interior of St. James's Park; quays along the Thames; new approaches to London Bridge; the removal of Smithfield Market; and several other suggestions on which we pride ourselves as original designs of our own times, are all to be found in Mr. Gwyn's able and curious work. It is singular that he denounced a row of houses *then* building in Pimlico, as intolerable nuisances to Buckingham Palace, and of these very houses the public voice now calls for the destruction.

Gwyn had what Lord Chatham calls 'the prophetic eye of taste.'"

Victoria Street is upwards of a thousand yards in length, extending from the Broad Sanctuary to Shaftesbury Place, Pimlico; it is eighty feet wide, and the houses on either side upwards of eighty feet high, mostly cut up into "flats." At the corner of this street, about three hundred yards west of the Abbey, stands the Westminster Palace Hotel, erected in 1861. Here the office of the Secretary of State for India was accommodated for a few years, until the new quarters for that department could be made ready for its reception. The hotel was built from the designs of Mr. A. Moseley. The hotel is traditionally said to stand on the site of the press set up in the Almonry, as already stated, by William Caxton, to whose memory the directors have subscribed a sum for the purpose of placing a statue of the first English printer in the entrance-hall.

A block of buildings of great magnitude, called Westminster Chambers, having a frontage of about 450 feet, stands immediately opposite the Hotel, and with it forms a striking entrance to this great street. The building contains about 530 rooms, disposed on the basement, ground, first, second, third, and fourth floors. It consists of two parallel ranges of building, each about 430 feet in length, separated by court-yards, access to the whole being obtained by seven stone staircases of easy gradients, and from seven arched entrances from Victoria Street. Each suite of rooms is approached from a separate entrance-door on the landings of these staircases, and consists of four or five rooms, as the case may be, with a few sets of two rooms each. There are 120 of these suites in the entire building. Party walls separate the building into fourteen compartments; making, as it were, fourteen separate self-contained houses; and thus, in case of fire, limiting the damage to the division or compartment in which it may occur.

In this street are the offices of the Metropolitan Drinking-fountain and Cattle-trough Association, of which the Duke of Westminster is the president. This is the only society which provides free supplies of water for animals in the streets of London, and the relief which it affords to horses, dogs, sheep, and oxen is well-nigh incalculable. The number of metropolitan fountains and troughs at the end of the year 1874 was as follows:—276 fountains, 72 large cattle-troughs, and 199 small troughs for sheep and dogs. In some cases the committee of the Association have to pay nearly £50 a year for the water consumed at a single trough. It is calculated that more than 1,200

horses, besides a large number of oxen, sheep, and dogs, frequently drink at a single trough in the course of one day. This invaluable association, we may add, as a hint to the charitable friends of dumb animals, is entirely "supported by voluntary contributions."

Duck Lane, which has quite disappeared in the formation of Victoria Street, probably took its name from the number of those birds which frequented the straight canals and runnels by which early maps represent the immediate vicinity to have been divided. There was a noted piece of water, called the Duck Pond, afterwards built over by the houses of this lane. In Duck Lane was first kept, in 1688, the Blue-Coat School, for boys only, and supported by voluntary contributions; and in 1709, a Mr. William Green built a school and masters' house in Little Chapel Street. A great part of the extensive grounds, including parts of Allington Street, Brewers' Green, St. Peter's Street, the Horseferry Road, and Orchard Street, was purchased by Mr. Green, who founded the Stag, or Elliot's Brewery.

In Horseferry Road, between the river and Victoria Street, about half a mile from the west end of the venerable Abbey, is a small and unpretending building, which for many years was the only chapel for the accommodation of the Roman Catholic poor who crowd the close courts abutting on the old Almonry. Down to 1792 they had no chapel at all, but were forced to practise their religion as best they could, in garrets and cellars, for fear of prosecutions under the penal laws. In that year a small chapel was opened in York Street, near Queen Square (now called Queen Anne's Gate), but it was closed for want of funds six years afterwards. In 1803 another attempt was made to maintain a chapel in Great Smith Street, under the auspices of the Chaplains of the Neapolitan Embassy, but this, too, came to an end after a three years' struggle. A temporary chapel in Dartmouth Street was next secured, and this lasted until 1813, when the present chapel was opened, mainly through the energy of the Rev. W. Hurst, the learned Professor of Theology at Valladolid, and translator of the writings of the Venerable Bede. It was enlarged and beautified in 1852, and is now served by Fathers of the Jesuit Order. The sculpture over the altar, representing the Annunciation of our Lady, by Phyffers, is much admired.

Between Victoria Street and St. James's Park is Queen Square, called by Strype "Queen Anne Square," and now altered by the authority of the Metropolitan Board of Works to "Queen Anne's

Gate." It tells its own tale so far as the date of its erection. It is a small oblong parallelogram, extending about fifty yards from east to west, but very narrow from north to south. Hatton, writing in 1708, speaks of it in terms of glowing, and, we fear must be added, undiscriminating praise, as "a beautiful square of very fine buildings." When Park Street was erected, the inhabitants of Queen Square, apprehending that carriages on their way also as a school and lecture-room, but formerly a chapel of ease to St. Peter's parish. It was originally a royal gift for the special use of the judges of Westminster, and was frequented by the members of the Royal Household. In it is a very handsomely carved pulpit, apparently of the seventeenth century, with an inscription, "Look upon me." In 1840 the chapel was much injured by fire; the altar-piece, then nearly destroyed, is

PALMER'S ALMSHOUSES, 1850. (*See page* 40.)

to Ranelagh would pass through the New Street, and make their hitherto quiet square a noisy thoroughfare, in order to avoid King Street, the Sanctuary, and Tothill Street, erected, by subscription, the wall and railing which separates Queen Square and Park Street. At the eastern entrance of the square, set up against one of the houses on the south side, is a statue of Queen Anne; it is, however, a poor specimen of art, and is so placed that it scarcely strikes the eye of the passer-by. The queen is dressed in her state robes, and has the sceptre and orb in her hands. At the beginning of this century, Mr. Henry J. Pye, poet laureate, resided in this square.

In the south-west corner of the square is a dull, heavy building, now used as a Mission Hall, and a fine specimen of wood-carving. The communion-table is said to be the same at which Queen Elizabeth made her first communion.

In Queen Square Place, where he had resided nearly half a century, died, in the year 1832, Jeremy Bentham, the eminent jurist, and writer on the philosophy of legislation. It was here that his brother, Sir Samuel Bentham, on his return from Russia, began to make machinery for all kinds of woodwork before unknown, and planned and constructed ships for the Admiralty, in which for the first time powder magazines were made safe. A singular anecdote is told concerning Jeremy Bentham, which we give for what it is worth:— "One day, returning to his home through Tothill Street, dressed in a suit of grey, of ancient cut, and

STOREY'S GATE, ST. JAMES'S PARK, IN 1820. (See page 47.)

with long grey hair falling over his shoulders, he sat down, tired, on a door-step. A lady passing, struck with his appearance, and taking him for a poor man, gave him a penny. He took it, enjoying the jest, and ever after kept it in his writing-desk." It is related of Jeremy Bentham, that he bequeathed his body to Dr. Southwood Smith, for the purposes of anatomical science.

In 1874 Queen Square and Park Street were re-numbered throughout, and together re-named Queen Anne's Gate, as stated above.

At No. 7, Park Street, on Sunday evenings, Mr. Towneley, the collector of the Towneley Marbles, &c., in the British Museum, one of the earliest revivers of the arts, was accustomed to entertain distinguished *literati* and artists, members of the Dilettanti Club; and Nollekens, Sir Joshua Reynolds, and Zoffany were generally found at his hospitable table. Here, in 1772, Mr. Towneley first assembled his collection of marbles, bronzes, and other works of art, which he had commenced in 1768 at Rome. We shall have more to say about this collection when we come to the British Museum.

In Little Park Street there was a curious alehouse called the "Three Johns," and the same sign, it is said, was also to be seen till lately near Queen Anne's Gate. It is thus described by Mr. Larwood:—"It represented an oblong table, with John Wilkes in the middle, John Horne Tooke at one end, and Sir John Glynn, serjeant-at-law, at the other. There is a mezzotint print of this picture, or the sign may have been taken from the print, and engraved by R. Houston in 1769. John Wilkes, on whom the popular gratitude for writing the Earl of Bute out of power has conferred many a sign-board, still survives in a few other spots also."

We have already seen that the Palace of Whitehall had its cock-pit,* and therefore our readers may be surprised to hear that there was a second cock-pit—called also the Royal—within three or four hundred yards off, in Birdcage Walk, facing the Park. It stood at the junction of Queen Square with Park Street, just at the top of Dartmouth Street, and was ornamented with a cupola. It was taken down in 1816; but in Ackermann's "Microcosm of London," published in 1808, there is a picture of its interior, as it was a few years previously, in a style worthy of Hogarth, who, by the way, has also immortalised it. It is drawn by Rowlandson and Pugin, and coloured, showing the style of dress worn by all grades, from the lord to

the Westminster "rough." Some of the figures introduced are evidently portraits of "peers and pick-pockets, grooms and gentlemen," mixed up in a strange medley. The rival cocks are being backed up by two boys, called feeders, dressed in red jackets and yellow trowsers—a sort of "royal" livery; the chief figure in the front row is an elderly gentleman, who seems to anticipate the loss of the battle, as also does his fat neighbour on the left, while a stupid look of despair in the countenance of a grim individual on the right proclaims that all is lost. The smiling gentleman on the left appears to be the winner, actual or expectant. The clenched fists and earnest looks of those in the two front rows show that a goodly sum of money is risked on the issue. Nearly in the centre of the back row of all are two figures apparently hurling defiance at the whole company; they are certainly offering odds which no one is disposed to take. At the back sits an officer in a cocked hat, and above him are the royal arms, the lion and the unicorn, to all appearance, looking down with composure on the fray, whilst some of the "roughs" are laying whips and thick sticks on the heads and shoulders of their neighbours. The whole picture is a study, and gives a far more perfect idea of such a scene than any words can convey. It seems strange that such scenes were tolerated and approved by royalty in the "good old days when George III. was king." In some families in the seventeenth century the patronage of cock-fighting would appear to have been as hereditary as is the keeping of hounds with certain nobles of a later date; for instance, the Herberts, concerning whom there is an old doggerel verse, often quoted :—

"The Herberts every cock-pit day,
    Do carry away, away, away !
    The gold and glory of the day."

It was at the Cock-pit in St. James's Park that Robert Harley, afterwards Earl of Oxford, was stabbed, though not fatally, with a penknife, by a French noble refugee, the Marquis de Guiscard, who was brought before him and the rest of the Cabinet Council by the Queen's Messenger, charged with treacherous correspondence with the rival Court at St. Germain, whilst drawing a pension from the English Court.

In the records of the Audit Office is an entry of a payment of "xxx*l.* per annum to the keeper of our Playhouse called the Cockpitt, in St. James's Parke."

Cock-fighting, and the still more barbarous sport of throwing at cocks, it may interest some of our readers to learn, was, in the days of our forefathers,

---

the chief amusement on Shrove Tuesday. Hence Sir Charles Sedley, in his epigram on a cock at Rochester, prays:—

"May'st thou be punished for St. Peter's crime,
And on Shrove Tuesday perish in thy prime!"

Such sports, it is fortunate to add, are now very nearly extinct among the educated classes, for public opinion has declared against them in an unmistakable manner. "Cock-fighting and bear-baiting," as Dr. Johnson said, "may raise the spirit of a company, just as drinking does, but they will never improve the conversation of those who take part in them."

Near the Cock-pit resided Sir John Germaine, who was tried for running off with the Duchess of Norfolk, whom her husband divorced in consequence. She was by birth a Mordaunt, a daughter of the Earl of Peterborough. It was sworn on the trial that Sir John and the duchess used to frequent Vauxhall almost daily in each other's company, a fact on which the divorce was based to a large extent, and which does not speak very much in praise of the morals of that place of amusement.

Much of the incongruous character of the Westminster of the era of Victoria may be traced back to the peculiarities of the ancient city. Du Chatelet, the celebrated French statistician, shows that the "Quartier de la Cité"—now the head-quarters of the thieves of Paris—was formerly the site of a well-known "sanctuary;" and just so it was also with the City of Westminster itself. "The church at Westminster," writes Stow, "hath had great privilege of sanctuary within the precinct thereof, from whence it hath not been lawful for any prince or any other to take any person that fled thither for any cause. The charter granted to it by Edward the Confessor conferred this privilege in the following terms:— 'I order and establish for ever that whatever person, of what condition or estate soever he be, from whence soever he come, or for what offence or cause it be, cometh for his refuge into the said Holy Church of the Blessed Apostle St. Peter, at Westminster, he be assured of his life, liberty, and limbs; . . . . and whosoever presumeth or doeth contrary to this my grant, I will that he lose his name, worship, dignity, and power, and that, with the great traitor, Judas, that betrayed our Saviour, he be in the everlasting fire of hell.'"

The neighbourhood of the Abbey two centuries, or even a century ago, it is to be feared, was low and disreputable. Pope tells us, for instance, how Curll's hack authors hung about this part: his historian at "the tallow-chandler's under the blind arch in Petty France; his two translators sharing a bed together; and his poet in the cockloft in Budge Row, where the ladder to get at it is in the hands of the landlady."

The author of "A New Critical Review of the Public Buildings, &c.," in the reign of George II., with the shallow and false taste of his time, dismisses the fair city in a very few words, as "though famous for its antiquity, yet producing very little worthy of attention and less of admiration." He would have written far otherwise, had he lived till the days of Queen Victoria.

Till within about a century most of the shops in the Strand and Westminster, as in the City, were open, as those of butchers are to the present day; and in this way not only articles of dress, but watches and jewellery were exposed for sale. In fact, they did not begin to be enclosed and glazed, as now, until about the year 1710. Thus, in the *Tatler* (No. 162), we find mentioned as novelties, "Private shops that stand upon Corinthian pillars, and whole rows of tin pots showing themselves through a sash window," the appearance of "pillars" and "sash-windows" being equally unwarrantable innovations. The appearance, too, of the master, under the first two Georges, if not to a later date, was equally unlike the dress of a modern trades-man. Then the old shopkeeper might be seen walking the quarter-deck of his own shop, with his hair full-powdered, his silver knee and shoe buckles, and his hands surrounded with the nicely-plaited ruffle hanging down to his knuckles, and his apprentices wearing the same livery, only with distinctions to mark their grade.

"By an Act of Parliament of the fourteenth and fifteenth of Henry VIII., c. 2, the jurisdiction of the City corporations was to extend two miles beyond the City; namely, the town of Westminster, the parishes of St. Martin-in-the-Fields and Our Lady in the Strand, St. Clement's Danes without Temple Bar, St. Giles's-in-the-Fields, St. Andrew's in Holborn, the town and borough of Southwark, the parishes of Shoreditch, Whitechapel, St. John's Street, Clerkenwell, and Clerkenwell, St. Botolph without Aldgate, St. Katharine's near the Tower, and Bermondsey.

"Such were the suburbs of our great metropolis in 1524. They were greatly detached, and the intervals were principally public fields. The Strand was then occupied by mansions and dwellings of the nobility, which were surrounded by large and splendid gardens; and a considerable portion of the parishes of St. Martin and St. Giles were literally, as they are still called, in the fields, as were also a great portion of the City of Westminster, and the villages of Clerkenwell, Shoreditch, and Whitechapel, and the borough of South-wark."

D'Israeli, in his " Curiosities of Literature," after noting the gradual union of Westminster and London, in spite of all edicts and Acts of Parliament, remarks that " since their happy marriage their fertile progenies have so blended together, that little Londons are no longer distinguishable from their ancient parents. We have succeeded in spreading the capital into a county, and have verified the prediction of James I., that ' England will shortly be London, and London England.' "

In Rymer's " Fœdera " (vol. xvi.) is given a proclamation of Elizabeth, issued for the purpose of restraining the increase of buildings about the metropolis. In it the high-handed Queen commands all persons, on the pain of her royal displeasure, and of sundry punishments besides, to desist from all new buildings of houses or tenements within three miles of any of the gates of London ; and in the same document it is ordered that unfinished buildings or new foundations are to be summarily pulled down. A strange contrast this to the policy of Queen Victoria, under whom the buildings and population of London and its suburbs have been more than doubled, without any let or hindrance on the part of the sovereign. The spirit of Elizabeth's proclamation was in due course repeated by James I. on his accession to his southern throne.

The fair city has numbered among its residents many distinguished and many eccentric personages, and has witnessed many freaks of fortune in the sudden rise or fall of individuals of less or more merit. Thus, we read in Erskine's " Dramatic Biography " the following bit of luck which befell a servant maid :—" Mrs. Jane Wiseman, who wrote a tragedy, entitled ' Antiochus the Great, or the Fatal Relapse ' (1702, 4to), was a servant in the family of Mr. Wright, Recorder of Oxford, where, having leisure time, she employed it in reading plays and novels. She began there that tragedy which she finished in London, and, soon after, marrying one Holt, a vintner, they were enabled, by the profits of her play, to set up a tavern in Westminster." It is devoutly to be hoped that this worthy pair made a fortune and " lived happily ever after."

Among the distinguished residents of Westminster in former times, as we learn from the " New View of London " (published in 1708), were Lord Scarsdale, who was living at a mansion in Duke Street ; Lord Stafford, at Tart Hall ; Lord

Rochester, " near Westminster Gate ; " Lord Essex, near Whitehall ; the Lord Portland, near the Banqueting House in Whitehall ; the Bishop of Norwich and the Archbishop of York in Petty France. Peter borough House, near the Horseferry, belonged to the Earl of Peterborough, but was let to a merchant, Mr. Bull. In Queen Square were living Lords North, and Grey, and Guernsey. Robert Harley, Principal Secretary of State under Queen Anne, lived in " York Buildings, near the water-side."

In the Market Place at Westminster was formerly an inn bearing the sign of " The Old Man." This probably refers to " Old Parr," of whom we have already spoken in our account of the Strand,[*] and who was celebrated in the ballads of the day as " The olde, olde, very olde manne." " The token of the inn," says Mr. Larwood, " represents a bearded bust in profile, with a bare head."

James I., with all his learning and pedantry, was, apparently, a patron of sports and pastimes ; at all events, we read that he granted to his groom-porter, one Clement Cottrell, the privilege of licensing, within the limits of London and Westminster, and within two miles therefrom, no less than forty taverns " for the honest and reasonable recreation of good and civil people, who for their quality and ability, may lawfully use the games of bowling, tennis, dice, cards, tables, nine-holes, or any other game hereafter to be invented."

We cannot turn our backs on Westminster without remarking that the two cities of London and Westminster for a number of years were totally distinct and separate—the one inhabited chiefly by the Scots, and the other by the English. It is believed that the union of the two crowns conduced not a little to unite these several cities ; " for," says an old writer, Howel, " the Scots greatly multiplying here, nestled themselves about the court, so that the Strand, from the mud walls and thatched cottages, acquired that perfection of building it now possesses ; " and thus went on the process which made London, according to the quaint fancy of the writer just named, like a Jesuit's hat, the brims of which were larger than the block ; and that induced the Spanish ambassador, Gondomar, to say to his royal mistress, after his return from London, and whilst describing the place to her, " Madam, I believe there will be no city left shortly, for all will run out of the gates to the suburbs."

---

* See Vol. III., p. 74.

CHAPTER V.

ST. JAMES'S PARK.

" A spark
That less admires the Palace than the Park."—*Pope.*

Storey's Gate—Origin of " Birdcage Walk "—The Wellington Barracks—Origin of the Guards—Mr. Harrington's House—Office of the Duchy of Lancaster—St. James's Park in the Reign of Henry VIII.—Rosamond's Pond—Charles II. and his Feathered Pets—Duck Island—Le Notre employed in Laying out and Improving the Park—The Decoy—The King and his Spaniels—William III.'s Summer-house—St. James's as a Deer-park—Le Serre's Description of the Park—Pepys' Account of the Works carried out here by Charles II.—The " Physicke Garden "—Waller's Poetic Description of the Park—The Canal—The Ornithological Society—The Waterfowl—Woodcocks and Snipes—Historical Associations of St. James's Park—Cromwell and Whitelock—Oliver Goldsmith—Peace Rejoicings after the Battle of Waterloo—Albert Smith's Description of St. James's Park and its Frequenters—The Mohawks—The Chinese Bridge—Skating on the " Ornamental Water "—Improvements in the Park by George IV.—The Horse Guards' Parade—Funeral of the Duke of Wellington—Robert Walpole and the Countryman—Dover House.

AT the western end of Great George Street, which we have already described, we find ourselves at Storey's Gate, the entrance of St. James's Park. This gate was so called from one Master Edward Storey, the "keeper of the king's birds," whose house stood on the spot. This fact has been doubted; but that Storey's Gate was so named after a real personage is proved by the entry in the registers of Knightsbridge Chapel, in the reign of Charles II., of the marriage of one Thomas Fenwick, "of St. Margaret's, servant to Storey, at ye Park Gate, and Mary Gregory, of ye same."

The birds, which were among the most innocent toys and amusements of the "merry monarch," were kept in aviaries ranged in order along the road which bounds the south side of the Park, and extends to Buckingham Palace, and which is still known by the significative name of "Birdcage Walk." To corroborate this derivation, we may mention here that the carriage-road between Storey's Gate and Buckingham Gate was, until 1828, open only to the Royal Family and to the Hereditary Grand Falconer, the Duke of St. Albans.

About one-half of the south side of Birdcage Walk, extending from Queen Anne's Gate to Buckingham Gate, is occupied by the Wellington Barracks, which consist of lofty and commodious ranges of buildings, for the use of the household troops. The barracks were first occupied by troops in the year before the battle of Waterloo. In the Military Chapel, which was opened in 1838, are preserved the tattered standards which were taken by Marlborough at Blenheim, and the colours of the Grenadier Guards which were used at Waterloo.

As there were no barracks during the reign of Charles II., and as by the Petition of Right it was declared unlawful to billet soldiers on private families, the alehouses and smaller inns of Westminster were always filled with privates of the regiments of Guards, which, from the first establishment of a standing army, have been generally stationed on duty near Whitehall and St. James's. Macaulay thus gives us the history of the origin of the Guards:—"The little army formed by Charles II. was the germ of that great and renowned army which has in the present century marched triumphant into Madrid and Paris, into Canton and Candahar. The Life Guards, who now form two regiments, were then distributed into three troops, each of which consisted of two hundred carabineers, exclusive of officers. This corps, to which the safety of the king and royal family was confided, had a very peculiar character. Even the privates were designated as 'Gentlemen of the Guard.' Many of them were of good families, and had held commissions in the Civil War. Their pay was far higher than that of the most favoured regiment of our time, and would in that age have been thought a respectable provision for the younger son of a country squire. Their fine horses, their rich houses, their cuirasses, and their buff coats, adorned with ribbons, velvet, and gold lace, made a splendid appearance in St. James's Park. A small body of grenadier dragoons, who came from a lower class, and received lower pay, was attached to each troop. Another body of household cavalry distinguished by blue coats and cloaks, and still called the Blues, was generally quartered in the neighbourhood of the capital. Near the capital lay also the corps which is now designated as the First Regiment of Dragoons, but which was then the only regiment of dragoons on the English establishment."

At the commencement of the present century a handsome building of one storey high, in the Chinese style, was, by order of Government, erected on the left angle of the recruiting-house, in the Birdcage Walk, for the purpose of serving as the armoury for the whole brigade of Guards. It consisted of four archways on the basement for the field-pieces, the room over it being for the small arms, and a range of rooms in the back, for cleaning. The two front angles had each a small house, one for a serjeant-major, and the other for a guard-room. This, we may infer, was the beginning of the barracks on this spot.

Near this part, as Aubrey tells us, a Mr. James Harrington had a "versatile timber house." He describes it as "built in Mr. Hart's garden, opposite to St. James's Park." "This eccentric individual," says Aubrey, "fancied that his perspiration turned to flies and bees, *ad cætera sobrius.* To try the

longing to the Hospital for Lepers, which in due course of time was converted, by the royal will and pleasure of "Bluff King Hal," into "our Palace of St. James's."

It was by the order of Henry that the meadow was drained and enclosed, formed into a "nursery for deer," and made also "an appendage to the Tilt-yard at Whitehall." At first this was but a small enclosure inside four brick walls; but in

WESTMINSTER ABBEY FROM ST. JAMES'S PARK, ABOUT 1740.

experiment, he would turn this house to the sun and sit towards it; then he had fox-tayles there, to chase away and massacre all the flies and bees." Mr. Harrington is said to have spent the last twenty years of his life in a house in the Little Almonry, near Dean's Yard, of which Aubrey gives us a curious description. "In the upper storey he had a pretty gallery, which looked into the yard, over a court, where he commonly dined and meditated, and smoked his tobacco."

At the western end of Birdcage Walk is the Duchy of Lancaster office, where all business relative to the revenues of the Prince of Wales, in right of that duchy, is transacted.

St. James's Park itself, which we now enter, was originally a low and swampy meadow, be-

course of time Henry VIII. added a "chase," which he threw out, like a wide open noose, from his palace at Westminster, forming, where the line of it fell, a large circle, which ran from St. Giles-in-the-Fields, up to Islington, round Highgate and Hornsey and Hampstead Heath, and so back again by Marylebone to St. Giles's and West-minster; and he forbade all his subjects of every degree either to hawk or hunt within those boun-daries. Though little more than three centuries and a half have passed away since this royal proclamation was issued, yet almost every mark of it has long since been blotted out. Edward VI. and Mary possessed no share of their "bluff" father's destructiveness, and the whole chase was gradually "disafforested."

Still, however, St. James's Park retains its verdant and rural character, and in it there are spots where the visitor may sit or walk with every trace of the great city around him shut out from his gaze, except the grey old Abbey, against the tall roof of which the trees seem to rest, half burying it in their foliage, just as they must have done three centuries ago.

In the south-west corner, near Birdcage Walk,

"This the blest lover shall for Venus take,
And send up vows from Rosamonda's lake."

The same is the drift of a dialogue in Southerne's comedy, *The Maid's Last Prayer*.

"Rosamond's Pond," writes the author of "A New Critical Review of the Public Buildings," &c., "is another scene where fancy and judgment might be employed to the greatest advantage; there is something wild and romantic round the sides of

"ROSAMOND'S POND" IN 1758.

and opposite to James Street and Buckingham Gate, was formerly a small sheet of water, known as "Rosamond's Pond," to which reference is constantly made in the comedies of the time as a place of assignation for married ladies with fashionable *roués*. The pond was made to receive the water of a small stream which trickled down from Hyde Park, and it is shown in one or two very scarce prints by Hogarth. It was filled up in 1770, soon after the purchase of Buckingham House by the Crown.

It is to its character as recorded above, and as being, in the words of Bishop Warburton to Hurd, "long consecrated to disastrous love and elegiac poetry," that Pope thus mentions it in the *Rape of the Lock* :—

it, of which a genius could make a fine use, if he had the liberty to improve it as he pleased." He adds, "The banks of it ought to be kept in better repair; and if a Venus in the act of rising from the sea with the Graces round her were raised in the midst of it, it would be neither an improper nor an useless decoration." From the same essay we gather that at this date the vineyard close by was in a most scandalously neglected state, and required much labour and art to make it a tasteful addition to the park. As to the Birdcage Walk, the writer calls it "exceeding pleasant, the swell of the ground in the middle having an admirable effect on the vista," and commanding a "simple and agreeable view down to the canal." He urges, however, that variety should be studied in its arrangement, and that the circle of trees should be made the " centre of a beautiful scene ;" in which case it would become " one of the most delightful arbours in the world." " Its romantic aspect, the irregularity of the ground, the trees which overshadowed it, and the view of the venerable Abbey, not only rendered it," writes Mr. Jesse, " a favourite resort of the contemplative, but its secluded situation is said to have tempted a greater number of persons, and especially of 'unfortunate' females, to commit suicide than any other place in London."

St. James's Park must have been a rural and pleasant enclosure in the reign of Charles II., when the avenues of trees were first planted along the northern side of the park, where now is the gravel walk known as "The Mall," under the direction of Le Notre, the French landscape gardener, who was also commissioned to lay out and improve the whole ; and when the south side was really, as its name still implies, a walk hung with the cages of the king's feathered pets. Its rural character, at that time, may be inferred from the title of Wycherley's successful comedy, *Love in a Wood, or St. James's Park*, which was first acted in 1672. Close by, at the east end of the water, which was in those days straight, and generally known as the " Canal," was a small decoy and an island, called " Duck Island," over which the celebrated St. Evremond was set as "governor" with a small salary. To this we find Horace Walpole alludes in a tone of pleasant banter when, recording in 1751 the appointment of Lord Pomfret as ranger of St. James's Park, he adds, " By consequence, my Lady [Pomfret] is queen of the Duck Island."

As to the island in the canal, the writer of the " New Critical Review" (1736) speaks of it—with some exaggeration, no doubt—as being on the one side a wilderness and a desert, and on the other " like a paradise in miniature ;" he complains that " the water is allowed to grow stagnant and putrid, and that the trees, shrubs, and banks all wanted attention "—remarks which show that whoever at that time was the " ranger" of the park must have had little eye for either beauty or taste. The canal itself appears to have been 100 feet in breadth and 2,800 feet long.

Duck Island was abolished and made into *terra firma* towards the close of the last century. In fact, " the island," says Pennant in 1790, " is lost in the new improvements."

Pope, who did not approve of Le Notre's stiff and formal style, censures him for the want of good sense—in company, it may be observed, with no less a master than Inigo Jones :—

" Something there is more needful than expense,
And something previous e'en to taste—'tis sense ;
Good sense, which only is the gift of Heaven,
And, though no science, fairly worth the seven ;
A light which in yourself you must perceive,
Jones and Le Notre have it not to give."

It is difficult to say to what omission Pope here makes special allusion. Le Notre was largely employed by Le Grand Monarque, Louis XIV., who also ennobled him. He died at Paris in the year 1700.

The " decoy" above mentioned consisted of five or six straight pieces of water all running parallel to each other and to the canal itself, with which they communicated by narrow openings.

King Charles appears to have been particularly fond of St. James's Park. We are told he would sit for hours on the benches in the walk, amusing himself with some tame ducks and his dogs, amidst a crowd of people, with whom he would talk and joke. It is fancied by some persons that no dogs are now left of the breed popularly called King Charles's breed, except a few very beautiful black-and-tan spaniels belonging to the late Duke of Norfolk, and which used to run riot over Arundel Castle much in the same way that their canine forefathers were formerly allowed to range about the palace at Whitehall. Charles was foolishly fond of these dogs ; he had always many of them in his bedroom and his other apartments ; as also so great a number of these pets lounging about the place, that Evelyn declares in his " Diary" that the whole court was made offensive and disagreeable by them.

Hard by, in a grove which rose round and between the miniature canals, a little later was a " tea-house" or rather summer-house, erected by order of William III. ; a place where that saturnine king would sometimes spend a summer evening with those of his friends whom he admitted into his confidence.

Although the park comprises less than ninety acres, Charles II. made a strict enclosure of the centre portion, which he surrounded with a ring fence for deer. " This day," writes Samuel Pepys, in his " Diary," under date August 11, 1664, " for a wager before the King, my Lord of Castlehaven, and Lord Arran, a son of my Lord Ormond's, they two alone did run down a stout buck in St. James's Park." During the reigns of Elizabeth and the first two Stuarts, the park was little more than a nursery for deer, and an appendage to the Tilt-yard of Whitehall. In the reign of Charles I. a sort of royal menagerie took the place of the deer with which the " inward park" was stocked in the days of Henry and Elizabeth. It was often called the

Inner or Inward Park, and apparently was not freely accessible to the public at large. At all events, Pepys tells us on one occasion in 1660 that when he went to walk there, he "could not get in," and saw "one man basted by the keeper for carrying some people over on his back through the water."

Le Serre, a French writer, in his account of the visit of the Queen-Mother, Mary de Medicis, to her daughter, Henrietta Maria, and Charles I., in the year 1633, mentions several particulars of St. James's Palace, as well as of the park, and the then state of the neighbourhood. The palace he calls the "Castle" of St. James's ; and describes it as embattled, or surmounted by crenelles on the outside, and containing several courts within, surrounded by buildings, the apartments of which (at least, those which he saw) were hung with superb tapestry, and royally furnished. "Near its avenue," says he, "is a large meadow, continually green, in which the ladies always walk in the summer. Its great gate has a long street in front, reaching almost out of sight, seemingly joining to the fields, although on one side it is bounded by houses, and on the other by the Royal Tennis Court;" then, after noticing the gardens, and the numerous fine statues in them, he adds, "These are bounded by a great park, with many walks, all covered by the shade of an infinite number of oaks, whose antiquity is extremely agreeable, as they are thereby rendered the more impervious to the rays of the sun. This park is filled with wild animals; but, as it is the ordinary walk of the ladies of the court, their [viz., the ladies'] gentleness has so tamed them, that they all yield to the force of their attractions rather than the pursuit of the hounds."

Pepys, in his gossiping manner, records from time to time the progress of the works carried out here by Charles II. Thus, in his "Diary," September 16, 1660, he writes :—"To the park, where I saw how far they had proceeded in the Pell Mell, and in making a river through the park, which I had never seen before since it was began." Again, a month later, October 11 : "To walk in St. James's Park, where we observed the several engines to draw up water, with which sight I was very much pleased. Above all the rest, I liked that which Mr. Greatorex brought, which do carry up the water with a great deal of ease." Further, under date July 27, 1662, we find this entry :—"I to walk in the park, which is now every day more and more pleasant, by the new water upon it."

Evelyn, in his "Diary," in April, 1664, tells us how that he went "to the Physicke Garden in St. James's Parke," and there "first saw orange-trees and other fine trees." The exact position of these gardens is not known now ; and as allusions to them are of rare occurrence, in all probability they were allowed to pass away and be forgotten, when a botanic garden on a larger scale was commenced under the highest auspices at Chelsea.

In 1661 we find the courtly Waller thus commemorating the improvements which had then been recently made in the park :—

> "For future shade, young trees upon the banks
> Of the new stream appear, in even ranks ;
> The voice of Orpheus, or Amphion's hand,
> In better order could not make them stand.
>
> *   *   *   *   *   *
>
> All that can, living, feed the greedy eye,
> Or dead the palate, here you may descry;
> The choicest things that furnish'd Noah's ark,
> Or Peter's sheet, inhabiting this park,
> All with a border of rich fruit-trees crown'd,
> Whose lofty branches hide the lofty mound.
> Such spacious ways the various valleys lead,
> My doubtful Muse knows not what path to tread.
> Yonder the harvest of cold months laid up,
> Gives a fresh coolness to the royal cup ;
> There ice, like crystal, firm and never lost,
> Tempers hot July with December's frost;
>
> *   *   *   *   *   *
>
> Here a well-polished Mall gives us the joy,
> To see our Prince his matchless force employ."

The most beautiful parts of St. James's Park are the walks beside the Ornamental Water, which is still called "the canal," in memory of its former unsightly shape. The water is alive with waterfowl, for whose comfort and protection a quiet and secluded island, with the Swiss cottage of the Ornithological Society, is reserved, at the southeastern extremity, nearly on the site of the old "decoy." The waterfowl here are natives of almost every climate in the world, and the Zoological Society itself has scarcely a finer or more varied collection. Those which are not foreign are mostly descendants of the ducks which Charles II. took such pleasure in feeding with his own royal hands. Around the "canal" stand many fine trees, which throw their green shadows into the water, "broken at times by a hundred tiny ripples which have been raised by the paddles of some strange-looking duck, or thrown up by the silver-breasted swans," as Mr. Thomas Miller quaintly remarks in his "Picturesque Sketches of London." It is almost needless to add that the banks of the "canal," and the bridge which spans it, are the haunt of children and their nurses, and the pieces of bread and biscuit which are given daily to the ducks, geese, and swans would well-nigh feed the inmates of a workhouse. At the western end of the lake there is a small island richly clothed with verdure, and also a fountain. The "Swiss cottage" above mentioned was erected in 1841, by means of a grant of £300 from the Lords of the Treasury. It contains a council-room, keeper's apartments, and steam-hatching apparatus; contiguous are feeding-places and decoys, and the aquatic fowl breed on the island, making their own nests among the shrubs and grasses. The water-fowl of the park can, at all events, boast that they have held undisturbed possession of the lake for more than two centuries. Pepys writes, under date of August, 1661 :—" To walk in St. James's Park, and saw a great variety of fowls which I never saw before."

In *Land and Water* of November 6th, 1869, Lord Lansdowne mentions having picked up a snipe, on the 26th of the previous month, under the wall of the Treasury Gardens, on the Horse Guards' Parade. It lay at the foot of a lamp, among some leaves, which had prevented the attention of passers-by being attracted. The spot was out of the line which any one carrying dead game could have taken, and the position in which the bird lay was that in which it might have fallen rather than been dropped. The lamp spoken of is opposite the end of the piece of water in St. James's Park. On examination at the office of *Land and Water* it was found to be a common jack-snipe. Its bill was fractured across, just at the point where it unites with the skull. It was probably flying at a great pace, and, attracted by the light of the lamp, flew against the iron post, when the force of the concussion killed it on the spot.

In the same publication, in March, 1873, a correspondent writes :—" As I was walking through St. James's Park, about ten a.m. on the 21st inst., a woodcock crossed me, flying rapidly and low, from the direction of the barracks towards Marl-borough House. It was well within gun-shot when I first saw it, and as my view of it as it crossed the water was quite unimpeded, I cannot for a moment question the accuracy of my observation, though in the case of such a *rara avis* I regret that I cannot produce a witness. In sending you this notice I am induced to add a list of the birds which I have noticed in St. James's Park during the past twelvemonth, as likely to interest those who think there are no birds but sparrows in London. They are :—1, sparrow-hawk, seen once flying from the east, in early morning; 2, great tit; 3, cole-tit; 4, blue tit, all occasionally seen; 5, fly-catcher, constant in summer; 6, rook; 7, jackdaw; 8, starling in small flocks when not breeding; 9, missel-thrush, once; 10, fieldfare, a small flock once in late autumn, one foggy morning; 11, song-thrush, constant; 12, blackbird, constant, the males seeming much more numerous than the females; 13, swallow; 14, martin; 15, swift, only once or twice; 16, pied wagtail, not unfrequent, but not apparently constant; 17, skylark, rare, generally flying high, and apparently moving on; 18, chaffinch, not common; 19, sparrow (*passer, passim*); 20, greenfinch, not common; 21, hedge-sparrow, constant; 22, robin-redbreast, constant; 23, white-throat, constant in summer on the eastern island, where its song is unmistakable; 24, wren, probably constant; 25, golden-crested wren, once only; 26, wood-pigeon, flying over in flocks in early morning, also once or twice birds probably strayed from Kensington Gardens, where they are common; 27, peewit, once, a flock flying north one foggy morning; 28, woodcock, once. Besides these I may mention the linnet, blackcap, willow-warbler, and wryneck, of which I cannot be quite positive, and last, not least, the Guards' raven, constant while his battalion is in town, on the trees near Buckingham Gate. Perhaps some other Cockney ornithologist will be able to verify and add to the above list."

A good story is told by Mr. W. C. Hazlitt respecting the waterfowl in this park and a young gentleman, a clerk in the Treasury, not over-gifted with brains, who used to feed the ducks with bread as he went daily from his home in Pimlico to the office. One day, having called the birds, as usual, he found that he had no bread in his pockets, and so threw a sixpence into the water, telling them to buy some. On reaching the office, he told the story with perfect simplicity to his fellow-clerks, with one of whom he was engaged to dine the next day. His friend accordingly ordered ducks for dinner, telling the cook to put a sixpence in the stuffing of one of them. The next day came, and with it the dinner, in the course of which the sixpence was found inside one of the birds, and the young man vowed that he would have the poulterer prosecuted for robbing the king, " for," said he, " I assure you, on my honour, that only yesterday I gave this very sixpence to one of the ducks in the park !"

St. James's Park is replete with historical associations, not the least interesting of which is the fact of Charles I. having passed through it on foot on the morning of his execution, from his bed-chamber in St. James's Palace to the scaffold at Whitehall. The king, as he passed along on that fatal morning, is said to have pointed to a tree which had been planted by his brother, Prince Henry, near Spring Gardens.

Strype, the historian, gives us a picture of the Princess Elizabeth's life during the reign of her brother, Edward VI., under date March 17th, 1551:—"The Lady Elizabeth, the King's sister, rode through London into St. James's, the King's Palace, with a great company of lords, knights, and gentlemen ; and after her a great company of ladies and gentlemen on horseback, about two hundred. On the 19th she came from St. James's through the Park unto the Court (at Whitehall), the way from the Park gate unto the Court being spread with fine sand. She was attended with a very honourable confluence of noble and worshipful persons of both sexes, and received with much ceremony at the Court gate." What would one not have given to have seen the young princess, thus gaily caparisoned, and in all her pride and beauty, before time had ploughed wrinkles on her brow, and ere the strong passions of middle life had stamped her countenance with their tell-tale marks !

Here Cromwell, as he walked with Whitelock, asked the latter, " What if a man should take upon him to be a king?" To which the memorialist replied, " I think that the remedy would be worse than the disease."

It is said that late in life Milton met James II., then Duke of York, whilst taking the air in the park. The duke, addressing him, asked whether the poet's blindness was not to be regarded as a judgment from Heaven upon him for daring to take up his pen against Charles I., his (the duke's) father, and his " own sovereign?" " Be it so, sir," replied Milton ; " but what then must we think of the execution of your Royal Highness's father upon a scaffold?" The story may be true or false : at all events it has been often told, and told as having happened here : we may say of it certainly, " Si non e vero, e ben trovato."

It may be added that the Princess Anne escaped twice from Whitehall through St. James's Park, once when she joined her husband and the Prince of Orange, and again when the palace was in flames.

This park was a favourite resort of Oliver Goldsmith. In his " Essays " we read that, " If a man be splenetic, he may every day meet companions on the seats in St. James's Park, with whose groans he may mix his own, and pathetically talk of the weather." The strolling player takes a walk in St. James's Park, " about the hour at which company leave it to go to dinner. There were but few in the walks, and those who stayed seemed by their looks rather more willing to forget that they had an appetite than to gain one."

Between the years 1770 and 1775 some extensive repairs and improvements were made in the park ; but notwithstanding this fact, the " rough, and intolerable" manner in which the walks were still kept caused much discontent and grumbling among its more fashionable habitués. Thus, for instance, in October, 1775, a letter appeared in the Middlesex Journal, addressed to Lord Orford, the ranger of the park, complaining bitterly of the disgraceful state of the walks. After some sarcastic remarks upon the delays of the workmen's wages, the writer plainly says that the public intend to petition his Majesty " on the subject of this unbearable grievance," and to " sign their real names ; which," he adds, " my lord, if all the complainants should do, I presume their number would far exceed that of any address ever presented." The writer finally proceeds to give vent to his feelings, and to entreat his Majesty for some instalment of reform, in the following lines, which he heads with the words—

AN ADDRESS TO THE KING.

" 'Tis yours, great George, to bless our safe retreats,
    And call the Muses to their native seats,
    To deck anew the flow'ry sylvan places,
    And crown the forest with immortal graces.
    Though barb'rous monarchs act a servile strain,
    Be thine the blessings of a peaceful reign ;
    Make James's Park in lofty numbers rise,
    And lift her palace nearer to the skies."

The park, in 1780, was occupied as a camp by several regiments of militia, during the alarm and panic caused by the Gordon riots. A print is extant which shows the long line of tents extending from east to west, from the " decoy" to " Rosamond's Pond," and to the south of the canal, and the king paying to the camp his daily visit."

On the occasion of the visit of the Allied Sovereigns, in 1814, Mr. Redding writes in his " Fifty Years' Recollections," " I stood without the iron palisades of Buckingham Old House. It was a childish affair there. But the illumination of the streets was really fine. Every window was lit up, and the blaze of light, from so great a mass of buildings, was thrown grandly upon the heavens. The park of St. James was prettily arranged with lamps in the trees, like another Vauxhall. A wooden bridge with a sort of tower, over the canal in St. James's Park, was illuminated too brightly. The edifice took fire, and the tower was consumed. One or two persons were killed."

The grand fête, which had long been in preparation, took place on the 1st of August, and an official programme was issued, in which the public were informed that a beautiful Chinese bridge had been thrown over the canal, upon the centre of which had been constructed an elegant and lofty pagoda, consisting of seven pyramidal storeys. "The pagoda to be illuminated with gas lights; and brilliant fireworks, both fixed and missile, to be displayed from every division of the lofty Chinese structure. Copious and splendid girandoles of rockets to be occasionally displayed from the summit, and from other parts of this towering edifice, so covered with squibs, Roman candles, and *pots de brin*, as to become in appearance one

remembered in connection with humorous frolics. In passing daily along the Mall he noticed a care-worn-looking man, with threadbare clothes, whom he discovered to be an officer on half-pay, with a wife and a large family, whom, for the sake of economy, he had been obliged to send down into Yorkshire. One day the duke sent a message asking him to dine with him next Sunday, and when his guest arrived he told him that he had

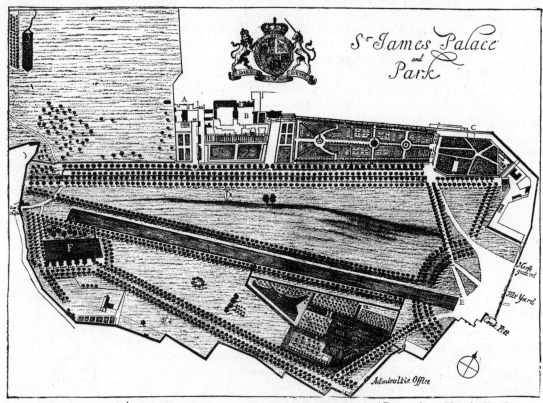

PLAN OF ST. JAMES'S PALACE AND PARK IN THE TIME OF CHARLES II. (*From a large Plate by Knyff.*)

A. Cleveland House.   B. St. James's Palace.   C. The Spring Garden.   D. The Mall.   E. The Canal.   F. Rosamond's Pond.
G. Birdcage Walk.   H. Duck Island and the Decoy.

column of brilliant fire. Various smaller temples and columns on the bridge to be vividly illuminated; and fixed fireworks of different devices on the balustrade of the bridge to contribute to heighten the general effect." The fireworks set light to the pagoda and burnt its three upper storeys. The canal was well provided with handsomely decorated boats at the disposal of those who wished to avail themselves of this amusement. The whole margin of the lawn was surrounded with booths for refreshment, open marquees with seats, &c. The Mall and the Birdcage Walk were illuminated with Chinese lanterns.

Among the residents in St. James's Park was the eccentric Duke of Montagu, whose name is still

asked a lady to meet him who had a most tender regard for him. On entering his grace's dining-room he found his wife and children, whom the duke had brought up to London from York-shire; and before he left the house the duke's solicitor brought out, and the duke signed, a deed settling on him an annuity of £200 a year. It is a pity that such practical jokes are not more often played by wealthy dukes and noble lords.

Here, at one time, used to take his daily walk the jovial and genial wit and poet, Matthew Prior, whom Gay calls, "Dear Prior, beloved by every muse." Swift and Prior were very intimate, and the latter is frequently mentioned in the "Journal to Stella." "Mr. Prior," writes Swift, "walks to

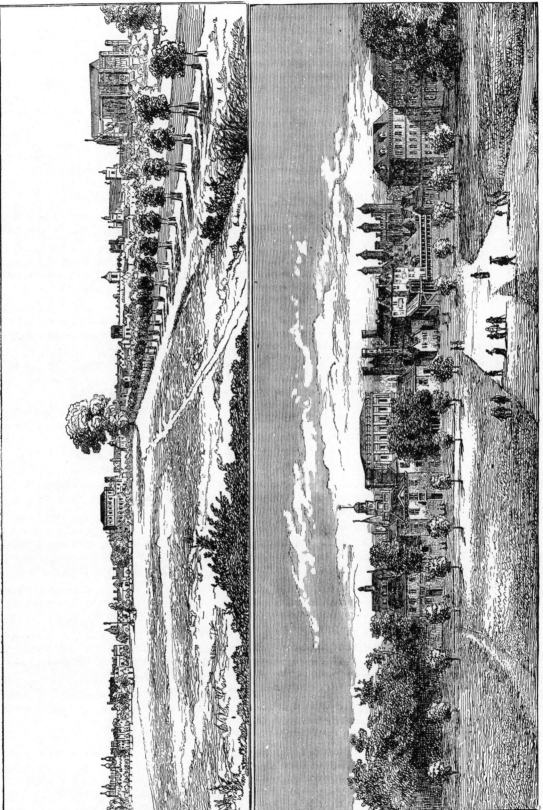

TWO OLD VIEWS IN ST. JAMES'S PARK. ABOUT 1680.   (*From Engravings by S. Rawle published in 1804 by F. T. Smith.*)

make himself fat, and I to keep myself down: we often walk round the park together."

Englishmen, as a rule, are not fond of out-door lounging, and, except in the extreme heat of the summer, they prefer taking the air on horseback or on a river steamer, or even on a railway, to sitting still on chairs and gazing leisurely on a green lawn and green trees, as they do in Paris by thousands. But in spite of this national tendency to in-door comforts, the Park of St. James's asserts its attractions so strongly, that at whatever time of the day we visit it, the seats have no lack of occupants; and in the hot days of July and August, when the West-End is emptied of all rank and ·fashion, thousands of "roughs" and idlers may be seen lying sound asleep on the grass under the shade.

Albert Smith has left us a graphic description of the scenes witnessed daily in the park, both in our own day and in days long gone by, which we here take the liberty of quoting:—"Although we do not find such crowds of idlers in the park at the present day, possibly the types encountered are more distinct. We say at the present day, because formerly the gayest of the gay thronged the walks, including royalty itself, with its attendant suite. Dear old Pepys has left us a mass of little mems thereanent. See where he says, on the 16th of March, 1662, that, while idling there in the park, 'which is now very pleasant,' he 'saw the King and Duke come to see their fowle play.' In 1661, in April, he says, 'To St. James's Park, where I saw the Duke of York playing at pall-mall, the first time that ever I saw the sport.' And later, which is quaintly interesting, he writes: 'Dec. 15. To the duke, and followed him into the park, where, though the ice was broken, he would go slide upon his skaits, which I did not like, but he slides very well.' We can imagine that Pepys was not strong upon skates. The first tumble—and nobody learns to skate without being sorely contused—would have been quite sufficient to have disgusted him with this then novel amusement. We find, however, that the love of feeding the ducks and skating in the park has not diminished. Afterwards, he tells us how he saw the King and Queen, with Lady Castlemaine and Mrs. Stuart *cum multis aliis*, walking about. He adds: 'All the ladies walked, talking and fiddling with their hats and feathers, and changing and trying one another's heads, and laughing. But it was the finest sight to see, considering their great beauties and dress, that ever I did see in all my life.'

"Evelyn is a little more scandalous. He says, on March 1, 1671:—'I once walked with the King through St. James's Park to the garden, where I both saw and heard a very familiar discourse between Mrs. Nellie, as they called an impudent comedian; she looking out of her garden on a terrace at the top of the wall, and ———— standing on the green walk under it. I was heartily sorry at this scene. Thence the King walked to the Duchess of Cleveland' (the Lady Castlemaine of Pepys), 'another lady of pleasure, and.curse of our nation.' Horace Walpole, eighty years afterwards, speaks of receiving a card from Lady Caroline Petersham to go with her to Vauxhall. 'And the party that sailed up the park, "with all our colours flying,"' he says, 'consisted of the Duke of Kingston, Lady Caroline, Lord March, Mr. Whitehead, 'a pretty Miss Beauclerc, and a very foolish Miss Sparre.' He adds, that 'Lady Caroline and little Ashe—or the Pollard Ashe, as they called her—had just finished their last layer of red, and looked as handsome as crimson could make them, and that they marched to their barge with a boat of French horns attending, and little Ashe singing.'

"Now-a-days the idlers in the park remind us but little of the personages in the above extracts. Poverty is far more frequently encountered there than wealth; and more, we fear, walk there to dine with 'Duke Humfrey' than to get an appetite for a meal elsewhere. At early morning, when the air is clearest, you encounter few persons; nor, somewhat later, do you find the crowds assembled to read the papers and discuss the politics after breakfast, as in Paris. You may, perhaps, encounter a student reading hard at some uninviting-looking book, and stumbling over the withies bent into the shuffled-out grass, as he moves along; or, perchance, an actor, as he threatens the lower boughs of the larger trees with his stick (most actors carry sticks), while he is rehearsing his part in some forthcoming play. And yet, lonely as the park is at this time, and half deserted, it is seldom chosen for the purpose of tender declarations, avowals, promises, oaths, quarrels, and all the other usual accompaniments of courtship. No: in this respect, perhaps, those chiefly concerned show their wit. The world—with its broad daylight, its tumultuous noise, and its distracted eyes—is far more adapted for secrecy than the shade and the retreat; and more than this, society will always lend itself as an accomplice of things which are not sought to be concealed.

"Towards noon, a movement of laughing mirth and noise commences by the arrival of the children and their nursery-maids; and in the children lies, in our opinion, the greatest attraction here offered —even beyond the ducks—the real zoological ducks. Not that we think slightingly of feeding them. We have heard, by the way, that it was one of the great O'Connell's favourite *délassemens*, and that he enjoyed it as much as the smallest fellow capable of tossing a bit of biscuit. It is great fun to see the rush made after a morsel : how the birds flash through the water to obtain it, and how, as in every community, the strongest always gets it. But if you want to enjoy the sport to perfection, throw in one of the small round rolls you get at evening-party supper-tables, and a fearful tumult is created. The prize is much too large for them to get hold of, as it is too valuable to be relinquished ; and so it is pushed and floated about, and vainly pecked at, surrounded by the whole tribe, squabbling, splashing, and fluttering— swayed, like large crowds, here and there—until it gets sufficiently soft to be accessible to their bills, when its consumption is speedily achieved.

"But to return to the children. We mean especially those who have not yet numbered eight years, and whose limbs have still all the smooth roundness of infancy. There is something very pleasing in their graceful movements, their fresh cheeks, and their beautiful hair, and a perfect charm in their gaiety ; in the innocent joy sparkling in their eyes, and the pure and living blood colouring their cheeks, which our brightest belles would give so much to imitate. This attraction, perhaps, belongs only to those who run about ; albeit it takes a great deal to beat the saucy beauty of an English baby. It is almost enough to make one a convert in favour of matrimony, even in these 'fast' times. The only pity is that these little people should ever be destined to become men."

The parks, though nominally they belong to royalty, are yet always regarded as somehow or other the property of the people. It was but an assertion of this principle that was uttered by Walpole, when, in reference to a design that was at one time entertained by one of the early Georges, of shutting up St. James's Park and converting it into a royal garden, and in answer to the question as its probable cost, he answered, " May it please your Majesty, only three crowns."

Since the time of Charles II., succeeding kings have given the people the privilege of walking in the park, and William III. granted to the public an entrance through the Spring Garden. The walks in the enclosure and the seats scattered about in such profusion beneath the shade of its trees have been a celebrated spot for love-making ever since the days of Charles II., and the park itself is often mentioned in this association in the works of the comic dramatists of the Stuart times. Horace

Walpole tells us that " pretty ladies " who walked in the park were sometimes "mobbed" by the crowd—a proof, if proof be needed, that other ages were not less marked by vulgarity than our own.

Like other parts of town, the park appears to have been frequented by those lawless rascals, the Mohocks, or Mohawks, of whom we have already made mention. Swift, for instance, writes under date of March, 1712, that he " walked in the park, and came home early to avoid the Mohocks ; " and apparently not without good reason, for, a day or two afterwards, a party of these armed ruffians assaulted a female servant of Lady Winchilsea's, at her mistress's garden-gate, " cutting her face and beating her without provocation."

It had been for many previous years the favourite amusement of dissolute young men to form themselves into clubs and associations for the cowardly pleasure of fighting and sometimes maiming harmless foot-passengers, and even defenceless women. They took various slang designations. At the Restoration they were Muns and Tityre-Tus ; then Hectors and Scourers ; later still, Nickers (whose delight it was to smash windows with showers of halfpence), Hawkabites, and lastly Mohocks. These last, as we learn from No. 324 of the *Spectator*, took their title from " a sort of cannibals in India, who subsist by plundering and devouring all the nations about them." Nor was the designation inapt ; for if there was one sort of brutality on which they prided themselves more than another, it was in tattooing, or slashing people's faces with, as Gay wrote, " new invented wounds." They began the evening at their clubs, by drinking to excess in order to inflame what little courage they possessed ; they then sallied forth, sword in hand. Some enacted the part of " dancing masters," by thrusting their rapiers between the legs of sober citizens in such a fashion as to make them cut the most grotesque capers. The hunt spoken of by Sir Roger de Coverley was commenced by a " view hallo ! " and as soon as the savage pack had run down their victim, they surrounded him, and formed a circle with the points of their swords. One gave him a puncture in the rear, which very naturally made him wheel about ; then came a prick from another ; and so they kept him spinning like a top till in their mercy they chose to let him go free. An adventure of this kind, in which the savages figure under the name of " Sweaters," is narrated in No. 332 of the *Spectator*.

Mr. John Timbs, in his " Curiosities of London," tells us that the park, as well as the palace, sheltered persons from arrest ; for, in 1632, one John Perkins, a constable, was imprisoned for serving the

Lord Chief Justice's warrant upon John Beard in St. James's Park. To draw a sword in the park was also a very serious offence. Congreve, in his *Old Bachelor*, makes Bluffe say, "My blood rises at that fellow. I can't stay where he is ; and *I must not draw in the park*." Traitorous expressions, when uttered in St. James's Park, were punished very severely. Thus, Francis Heat was whipped, in 1771, from Charing Cross to the upper end of the Haymarket, fined ten groats, and ordered a month's imprisonment, for here saying aloud, "God save King James III., and send him a long and prosperous reign!" and in the following year a soldier was whipped in the park for drinking a health to the Duke of Ormond and Dr. Sacheverel, and for saying he "hoped soon to wear his right master's cloth." The Duke of Wharton, too, was seized by the guard in St. James's Park for singing the Jacobite air, "The king shall have his own again."

Faithorne's plan of St. James's, taken shortly after the Restoration, shows the north half of the parade occupied by a square enclosure, surrounded by trees, with one tree in the centre ; and in the lower part of the parade broad running water, with a bridge of two arches in the middle. Later views show the park with long rows of young elm and lime trees, fenced with palings, and occasionally relieved by some fine old trees. A view of this park is worked in as a background to one of Hollar's charming and well-known etchings of the "Four Seasons."

Over the canal in this park during the Regency, when a taste for Eastern monstrosities of the kind was so prevalent, was built a little Chinese bridge, mainly of wood; but already, in 1823, it was beginning to fall to decay. Canova, when asked what struck him most forcibly during his visit to England in the year 1815, is said to have replied, "that the trumpery Chinese bridge in St. James's Park should be the production of the Government, whilst that of Waterloo was the work of a private company."

During the winter months, when the "ornamental water" is frozen over, this spot is much resorted to for the purposes of skating and sliding ; but the scene presented is doubtless very different now from what it was two centuries ago, when, as Pepys tells us in his "Diary" (December 1, 1662), he went "to my Lord Sandwich's, . . . and then over the parke, where I first in my life, it being a great frost, did see people sliding with their skates, which is a pretty art." Evelyn, too, has the following entry under the same date :—"Having seene the strange and wonderful dexterity of the sliders

in the new canal in St. James's Park, performed before their Majesties by divers gentlemen and others, with scheets, after the manner of the Hollanders, with what swiftness as they pass, how suddenly they stop in full career on the ice, I went home."

The park appears soon to have become a resort for all classes, for under date December 4, 1683 (when there was a very hard frost), the Duke of York records—"This morning the boys began to slide upon the canal in the park."

St. James's Park, much as we now see it, was laid out by George IV. between the years 1827 and 1829. In form, the enclosure takes somewhat the shape of a boy's kite, the head or broad part of which, towards Whitehall, is bordered by some of the principal Government offices—the Admiralty, the Horse Guards, the Treasury, and the India and Foreign Offices ; at the opposite end is Buckingham Palace. In 1857, a suspension bridge for foot-passengers was thrown across the water, so as to form a direct communication between Queen Anne's Gate and St. James's ; the bed of the lake was at the same time cleared out and raised, so that its greatest depth of water does not exceed four feet.

"Amongst the many improvements which have contributed to the convenience and ornament of the metropolis," writes Walker, in his "Original," in 1835, "none are more striking than those in the parks. The state in which they are kept does great credit to those who have the management of them. The right-lined formalities of St. James's Park seemed almost to defy the efforts of taste ; and I could not have conceived that without any advantages of ground the straight 'canal' and unpromising cow-pasture could have been metamorphosed into so graceful a piece of water, and so beautiful a shrubbery. In walking round the water, almost at every step there is a new and striking point of view of buildings and foliage. Buckingham Palace, Carlton Terrace, the Duke of York's Column, St. Martin's Church, the Horse Guards, Westminster Abbey, and other inferior objects, seen between and over the trees, form a combination and a variety I have never before seen equalled. . . . What a pity it is that the original design of making a gradual descent from Waterloo Place into St. James's Park was not allowed to be carried into execution! Besides the beauty of the plan, a horse-entrance there would have been an immense convenience to a numerous class. As that, however, is now out of the question, the nearest practical approach to it seems to be by the macadamisation of Pall Mall, with an entrance into the Park, if that could be permitted, between Marlborough House and the Palace. I know not how that would affect the Palace, but if it would be no inconvenience to royalty, it certainly would be a great boon to the equestrian public."

It is a pleasant task to record here the fact that in little more than a quarter of a century after the above-quoted words were written the entrance to St. James's Park between Marlborough House and St. James's Palace was thrown open, by permission of Her Majesty and the Ranger, not only to the "equestrian public," but to the commonalty who employ cabs and hired carriages, and that for such vehicles a right of way has been granted by the Queen to Pimlico and South Belgravia, across the once sacred precinct of the Royal Mall in St. James's Park, and under the very windows of Buckingham Palace.

It had always been the tradition of the Court to grant as little as possible to the public a right of way through St. James's Park. The following story, told of George I., shows that the privilege was not always allowed even to the children of a Stuart sovereign :—"Soon after his accession to the throne, the Duchess of Buckingham, a natural daughter of James II., asked for a passage for her carriage through the park, but was met with a polite refusal. She at once wrote off a letter to the king, abusing him in the grossest terms compatible with her character as a lady, affirming that he was an usurper, and that she had a better right to go through the park than a Hanoverian upstart. The king, instead of being offended, laughed, saying, 'The poor woman is mad, let her pass;' and thereupon gave an order that both her Grace and any other mad daughter of a Stuart king, who cared to obtain the privilege, might use it freely."

The park is still regularly patrolled at night by two of the horse guards whenever Her Majesty is in town—a standing proof of the old feeling of the insecurity of retired parts of London when entrusted to the old watchmen, or "Charlies." It was not till 1822 that St. James's Park was lighted with gas, although Pall Mall, adjoining, had been so lit fifteen years before.

The large open space laid down with gravel in front of the Horse Guards is popularly called the Parade, from the fact that the household troops are paraded here almost every day. Here, too, reviews of the troops occasionally take place ; as, also, such ceremonies as the presentation of medals to those of our "brave defenders" who may have taken part in foreign campaigns.

Here are two military trophies, curious pieces of foreign ordnance : the one is a large Turkish gun, captured by the English troops in Egypt, under Sir Ralph Abercromby ; the other is an immense mortar, cast at Seville by command of the great Napoleon ; it was used by the French under Marshal Soult at the siege of Cadiz, in 1812, but abandoned by them subsequently at Salamanca. Mr. Larwood, in his amusing book on the "London Parks," states that the carriage of the mortar was made at Woolwich under the direction of the Earl of Mulgrave : its ornamentation is said to bear reference to King Geryon, a monster with three bodies and three heads, whom Hercules slew at Cadiz, after "lifting" his anthropophagous cattle. Jekyll, the famous punster, however, explained it differently, and said that the dogs' heads were merely placed on it in order to justify the Latin inscription, which is certainly of a somewhat canine species.

As to the "Parade," a writer calls it (in the reign of George II.) a "grand and spacious area," and capable of being made one of the chief beauties "about the town," if surrounded by "noble and august buildings," and adorned with an equestrian statue to the memory of some departed hero. He suggests that it would be a fit place for the erection of one in particular to "the great and immortal Nassau"—meaning King William III.—and adds, "It is true that he has once been denied this piece of justice, but they were not soldiers who were guilty of so great an indignity." It is not, however, clear to what abortive attempt at doing justice to the "pious and immortal memory" of King William the writer means to allude.

Upon the Parade was marshalled the state funeral procession of the great Duke of Wellington, on the 18th of November, 1852. The body was removed from Chelsea Hospital on the previous midnight, and deposited in the audience-chamber at the Horse Guards. Beneath a tent erected on the parade-ground was stationed the funeral car, whereon the coffin being placed, and the command given, the *cortége*, in a slow and solemn manner, moved down the Mall, past Buckingham Palace, whence the procession was seen by Her Majesty and the Royal Family, before it made its way to St. Paul's.

We have already mentioned the fact that Sir Robert Walpole, when Prime Minister, lived constantly at the Treasury, at the corner of Downing Street. In the last century there was a carriage entrance to his house on the side of the park. A good story is told of a scene which occurred here. A countryman from Norfolk, having failed to obtain a post under Government, though recommended by one of Sir Robert Walpole's supporters in Parliament, resolved to trudge up to London, and to push his own request in person. Accordingly, he took up his quarters at the "Axe and Crown," an hostelry close by the Premier's house, and knocked at Sir Robert's door, but without success. The servants, however, told him that if he could speak to Sir Robert in person as he stepped into his

Between the Treasury and the Horse Guards is seen the back of Dover House (already mentioned in a former chapter), where the late Lord Dover made a very choice gallery of paintings. His early death, which took place in July, 1833, was much regretted by society at large. He was the author of a "Life of Frederick the Great;" "The True History of the State Prisoner, the Man in the Iron Mask;" and "Historical Enquiries respecting the

THE INDIA OFFICE, FROM ST. JAMES'S PARK. (*See page* 58.)

chariot, he would be sure to get what he wanted. Accordingly, for two or three days he watched the Premier go out, and at last waylaid him in the act of entering his chariot, and came out plump with his demand, adding that the post had been asked for him by his friend the M.P. for ——. "Well, my good man," said Sir Robert, "call on me another morning." "Yes, an please your honour, I'll be here and call on you every morning until I get the place." The man was as good as his word, and every day for at least a fortnight was at the same spot at the same hour, and made his bow to the Premier, who was either so amused or wearied with his blunt importunity, that he sent him back to Norfolk the richer and, it may be hoped, the happier, by the gift of a tide-waitership.

Character of Edward Hyde, Earl of Clarendon." He also edited "Horace Walpole's Correspondence" and "The Ellis Correspondence."

In the reign of the two first Georges, and perhaps even more recently, the situation of Dover House was quite rural; so much so indeed that the author of "A New Critical Review of the Public Buildings," in 1736, thus expresses himself about it :—"We will now step into the park, where we shall see a house in the finest situation, with the whole canal and park in prospect, yet so obscured with trees that, except in the garrets, it cannot have the advantage of either. Surely there can be no excuse for so egregious a mistake but that the house itself is in so wrong a taste that it was the owner's interest to hide it."

ARLINGTON HOUSE, 1700. *(See page 62.)*

CHAPTER VI.

BUCKINGHAM PALACE.

"The pillar'd dome magnific heaves
Its ample roof, and luxury within
Pours out its glittering stores."—*Thomson.*

The Palaces of England and France compared—The Mulberry Garden—John Dryden's Fondness for Mulberry Tarts—Arlington House—The House originally called Goring House—The First Pound of Tea imported into England—Demolition of Arlington House—Description of the First Buckingham House—John Sheffield, Duke of Buckingham—Singular Conduct of his Widow—The House purchased by George III., and called the "Queen's House"—Northouck's Description of Buckingham House in the Time of George III.—Dr. Johnson's Interview with George III.—Josiah Wedgwood and Mr. Bentley's Visits to the Palace—The Gordon Riots—Princess Charlotte—The Use of the Birch in the Royal Nursery—Queen Charlotte and her Christmas Trees—Building of the Present Palace—The Edifice described—The Gardens and Out-buildings—Queen Victoria takes up her Residence here—Royal Guests from Foreign Parts—"The Boy Jones"—Marriage of the Princess Augusta of Cambridge—The Queen and Charles Dickens—The Board of Green Cloth—Officers of the Queen's Household—Her Majesty's "Court" and "Drawing-rooms."

IT has often been said by foreigners that if they were to judge of the dignity and greatness of a country by the palace which its sovereign inhabits, they would not be able to ascribe to Her Majesty Queen Victoria that proud position among the "crowned heads" of Europe which undoubtedly belongs to her. But though Buckingham Palace is far from being so magnificent as Versailles is, or the Tuilleries once were, yet it has about it an air of solidity and modest grandeur, which renders it no unworthy residence for a sovereign who cares more for a comfortable home than for display. Indeed, it has often been said that, with the ex-

ception of St. James's, Buckingham Palace is the ugliest royal residence in Europe; and although vast sums of money have been spent at various times upon its improvement and embellishment, it is very far from being worthy of the purpose to which it is dedicated—lodging the sovereign of the most powerful monarchy in the world. It fronts the western end of St. James's Park, which here converges to a narrow point; the Mall, upon the north, and Birdcage Walk, upon the south, almost meeting before its gates.

The present palace occupies the site of what, in the reigns of Charles I. and Charles II., was known as the Mulberry Garden, then a place of fashionable resort. It was so called from the fact that the ground had been planted with mulberry-trees by order of James I., one of whose whims was the encouragement of the growth of silk in England as a source of revenue. With this object in view, he imported many ship-loads of young mulberry-trees, most of which were planted round the metropolis. Indeed, he gave by patent to Walter, Lord Aston, the superintendence of "the Mulberry Garden, near St. James's;" but all Lord Aston's efforts were unable to secure success; the speculation entered into by King James proved a failure, and the Mulberry Garden was afterwards devoted to a public recreation-ground.

Every reader of John Evelyn and Samuel Pepys will remember how they describe these gardens in their day—the former as "the best place about the towne for persons of the best quality to be exceedingly cheated at;" and the latter as "a silly place, with a wilderness somewhat pretty."

The Mulberry Garden is said by Mr. J. H. Jesse to have been a favourite resort of John Dryden, where he used to eat mulberry tarts. To this the author of "Pursuits of Literature" refers when he speaks of "the mulberry tarts which Dryden loved." It was in the years prior to his marriage, in 1665, as we learn from a note in his Life by Sir Walter Scott, that Dryden would repair hither, along with his favourite actress, Mrs. Reeve. "I remember," writes a correspondent of the *Gentleman's Magazine* for 1745, "plain John Dryden, before he paid his court with success to the great, in one uniform clothing of Norwich drugget. I have ate tarts with him and Madame Reeve at the Mulberry Garden, when our author advanced to a sword and a Chadreux wig." It would appear from the Epilogue of Otway's "Don Carlos," in 1676, that in all probability the connection of this fair lady with Dryden was brought to an end by her retreat into a cloister.

The public recreation-ground does not appear, however, to have lasted long, for in the course of a few years we find standing upon the southern portion of it a mansion known as Arlington House, the residence of Henry Bennet, Earl of Arlington, one of the "Cabal" Ministry, under Charles II. Dr. King thus alludes to these changes in his "Art of Cookery:"—

> "The fate of things lies always in the dark :
> What cavalier would know St. James's Park?
> For ' Locket's' stands where gardens once did spring,
> And wild ducks quack where grasshoppers did sing :
> A princely palace on that space does rise,
> Where Sedley's noble muse found mulberries."

The house was originally called Goring House; but its name was subsequently changed to that of Arlington House on its being occupied by the Earl of Arlington, whose name is, or ought to be, indissolubly linked with it, on one account at all events; for in the year of the great plague his lordship brought hither from Holland the first pound of tea which was imported into England, and which cost him sixty shillings; so that, as John Timbs remarks, "in all probability the first cup of tea made in England was drank where Buckingham House now stands."

On the demolition of Arlington House, in 1703, its site was purchased by John Sheffield, Duke of Buckingham, who built on it a mansion of red brick.

In the "New View of London," published in 1708, the original building is described as "a graceful palace, very commodiously situated at the westerly end of St. James's Park, having at one view a prospect of the Mall and other walks, and of the delightful and spacious canal; a seat not to be contemned by the greatest monarch. It was formerly," adds the writer, "called Arlington House, and being purchased by his Grace the present Duke of Bucks and Normanby, he rebuilt it, in the year 1703, upon the ground near the place where the old foundation stood. It consists of the mansion house, and at some distance from each end of that, conjoined by two arching galleries, are the lodging-rooms for servants on the south side of the court; and opposite, on the north side, are the kitchen and laundry, the fronts of which are elevated on pillars of the Tuscan, Dorick, and Ionick orders, thereby constituting piazzas. The walls are brick; those of the mansion very fine rubb'd and gagg'd (*sic*), adorned with two ranges of pilasters of the Corinthian and Tuscan orders. On the latter (which are uppermost) is an acroteria of figures, standing erect and fronting the court; they appear as big as life and look noble." They are thus described :—" 1. Mercury with his winged chapeau. 2. Secret, reposing its right arm on a pillar, and in the left hand a key. 3. Equity, holding a balance and a plummet. 4. Liberty, having in his right hand a sceptre, and a cap in the left. 5. Truth, holding the sun in his right hand, and treading on a globe. 6. Apollo, holding a lyre. Also, backward, are four figures beholding the west—Spring, Summer, Autumn, and Winter. Moreover, on the front of this mansion are these words, depensiled in capital gold characters : —' Sic siti lætantur Lares ;' ' Spectator fastidiosus sibi molestus ;' ' Rus in urbe;' and ' Lente suscipe, cito perfice.' The hall, partly paved with marble, is adorned with pilasters, the intercolumns are noble painture in great variety, and on a pedestal near the foot of the great staircase (whose steps are entire slabs) are the marble figures of Cain killing his brother Abel. In short, the whole structure is spacious, commodious, rich, and beautiful, but especially in the finishing and furniture. This house is now in the occupation of his Grace the Duke of Buckingham." Defoe in his "Journey" (1714) describes Buckingham House as "one of the great treasures of London, both by reason of its situation and its building," an opinion which will hardly be echoed now.

Sheffield's history furnishes another example of the instability of human greatness, and especially of titles. His only son, who held the title but a few short years, died, unmarried, in 1735, when the family honours became extinct. His father's great wealth was carried by his mother into her family by a previous marriage—the Phippses, now Marquises of Normanby. The duchess was grandmother of Mr. Phipps, afterwards Lord Mulgrave, who married the eldest daughter of Lepel, Lady Hervey, the friend of Pope and Horace Walpole. Lady Hervey was often a visitor at Buckingham House, the mansion being at the time an abode of mirth and cheerfulness, if we may judge from her letters.

In a letter to the Duke of Shrewsbury, printed in "London and its Environs," the Duke of Buckingham describes the house, and his style of living there, in the most minute detail. It is said that, at an annual dinner which he gave to his spendthrift friends, he used to propose as a toast, "May as many of us as remain unhanged till next spring meet here again!" He died in this house, and here his remains lay in state previous to their removal to Westminster Abbey, where they were consigned to their tomb in the stately chapel of Henry VII.

The duke's proud widow, Catherine Darnley, the natural daughter of James II. by Catherine Sedley, Countess of Dorchester, lived here after his death. "Here," writes Mr. J. H. Jesse, "on each successive anniversary of the execution of her grandfather, Charles I., she was accustomed to receive her company in the grand drawing-room, herself seated in a chair of state, clad in the deepest mourning, and surrounded by her women, all as black and as dismal looking as herself. Here, too, that eccentric lady breathed her last." "Princess Buckingham," writes Horace Walpole, "is either dead or dying. She sent for Mr. Anstes, and settled the ceremonial of her burial. On Saturday she was so ill that she feared dying before the pomp was come home. She said, 'Why don't they send the canopy for me to see? Let them send it, even though all the tassels are not finished.' But yesterday was the greatest stroke of all. She made her ladies vow to her that, if she should lie senseless, they would not sit down in the room before she was dead." By her own express directions, she was buried with great pomp beside her lord in the Abbey, where there was formerly a waxen figure of her, after the usual royal fashion, adorned with jewels, prepared in her life by her own hands. She was succeeded in her ownership of the house by the duke's natural son, Charles Herbert Sheffield, on whom his Grace had entailed it after the death of his son, the young duke.

George III., in his second year, bought the house for the sum of £21,000, and shortly afterwards removed hither from St. James's Palace. Here all his numerous family was born, with the exception of the Prince of Wales (afterwards George IV.), whose birth took place at St. James's. The King and Queen grew so fond of their new purchase that they took up their abode entirely here; and during their reign, St. James's Palace was kept up for use only on Court days and other occasions of ceremony.

In 1775 the property was legally settled, by Act of Parliament, on Queen Charlotte (in exchange for Somerset House, as we have stated in the previous volume); and henceforth Buckingham House was known in West-end society as the "Queen's House."

Northouck describes Buckingham House, in 1773, in terms which do not imply that the King and Queen had shown much taste in its approaches. "In the front it is enclosed with a semi-circular sweep of iron rails, which are altered very unhappily from the rails which enclosed it before it became a royal residence. Formerly an elegant pair of gates opened in the middle; but now, though a foot-opening leads up to where an opening naturally is expected in front, all entrance is forbidden, by the rails being oddly continued across without affording an avenue through. Whoever seeks to enter must walk round either to the right or left, and in the corners perhaps he may gain admittance. The edifice," he adds, "is a mixture of brick and stone, with a broad flight of steps leading up to the door, which is between four tall Corinthian pilasters, which are fluted and reach up to the top of the second storey." The illustration of the front which he gives shows a great resemblance to Kensington Palace. "Behind the house," he adds, "is a garden and terrace, from which there is a fine prospect of the adjacent country." The house is described, at the beginning of the present century, as having a mean appearance, being low and built of brick, though "it contains within," adds the writer, "apartments as spacious and commodious as any palace in Europe for state parade." On the marriage of the Prince of Wales (George IV.), "a suite of the principal rooms was fitted up in the most splendid manner; the walls of two of the levee rooms being hung with beautiful tapestry, then recently discovered with its colours unfaded in an old chest at St. James's. In the grand levee room," adds the writer, "is a bed of crimson velvet, manufactured in Spitalfields. The canopy of the throne likewise is of crimson velvet, trimmed with broad gold lace, and embroidered with crowns set with fine pearls of great value. This was first used on Queen Charlotte's birthday, after the union of the kingdoms of Great Britain and Ireland, and the shamrock, the badge of the Irish nation, is interwoven with the other decorations of the crown with peculiar taste and propriety."

At the south-east angle of the old house was an octagonal apartment, which contained for many years the cartoons of Raphael (now in the South Kensington Museum). They were transferred to Windsor Castle, and subsequently exhibited for a time at Hampton Court. The saloon was superbly fitted up as the throne-room, and here Queen Charlotte held her public drawing-rooms. Thus the mansion remained till the reign of George IV., externally "dull, dowdy, and decent; nothing more than a large, substantial, and respectable-looking red brick house," as it was styled by a writer of the time.

At the Queen's House, in February, 1767, when his Majesty had been seated little more than six years upon the throne, Dr. Johnson was honoured by George III. with a personal interview, as related by his biographers. Boswell tells us that the doctor had frequently visited those splendid rooms and noble collection of books, which he used to say was more numerous and curious than he supposed any person could have made in the time which the king had employed. "Mr. Barnard, the librarian, took care that he should have every accommodation that could contribute to his ease and convenience while indulging his literary taste in that place; so that he had here a very agreeable resource at leisure hours.

"His Majesty having been informed of his occasional visits, was pleased to signify a desire that he should be told when Dr. Johnson came next to the library. Accordingly, the next time that Johnson did come, as soon as he was fairly engaged with a book, on which, while he sat by the fire, he

seemed quite intent, Mr. Barnard stole round to the apartment where the king was, and, in obedience to his Majesty's commands, mentioned that Dr. Johnson was then in the library. His Majesty said he was at leisure, and would go to him; upon which Mr. Barnard took one of the candles that stood on the king's table, and lighted his Majesty through a suite of rooms, till they came to a private door into the library, of which his Majesty had the key. Being entered, Mr. Barnard stepped forward hastily to Dr. Johnson, who was still in a profound study, and whispered him, 'Sir, here is the king.' Johnson started up, and stood still. His Majesty approached him, and at once was courteously easy."

The king conversed with his learned subject freely and agreeably on the studies of Oxford, the two University libraries, the literary journals in England and abroad, the "Philosophical Transactions," Lord Lyttelton's "History," and other literary topics. Boswell continues: "During the whole of this interview Johnson talked to his Majesty with profound respect, but still in his firm, manly manner, with a sonorous voice, and never in that subdued tone which is commonly used at the levee and in the drawing-room. After the King withdrew, Johnson showed himself highly pleased with his Majesty's conversation and gracious behaviour."

Dr. Johnson, on this occasion, was pleased to pass a high compliment on the elegant manners of the sovereign. In speaking of this interview, the biographer writes: "He said to Mr. Barnard, the king's librarian, 'Sir, they may talk of the king as they will, but he is the finest gentleman I have ever seen.' And he afterwards observed to his friend Langton, 'Sir, his manners are those of as fine a gentleman as we may suppose Louis XIV. or Charles II.'" It was not often that Dr. Johnson condescended to express himself so approvingly of anybody, least of all of one whose position was one of direct antagonism to his beloved Stuart line; but we may well imagine that even the learned doctor's head was a little turned by the unexpected and flattering marks of condescension which he, so lately a poor and struggling man, had received from the King of England.

It is remarkable that Dr. Johnson should have seen four, if not five, of our sovereigns, and been in the actual presence of three, if not four, of them. Queen Anne "touched" him; George I. he probably never saw; but George II. he must frequently have seen, though only in public; George III. he conversed with on the occasion above mentioned; and he once told Sir John Hawkins that, in a visit to Mrs. Percy, who had the care of one of the young princes, at the Queen's House, the Prince of Wales (afterwards George IV.), being a child, came into the room, and began to play about; when Johnson, with his usual curiosity, took an opportunity of asking him what books he was reading, and, in particular, inquired as to his knowledge of the Scriptures. The Prince, in his answers, gave him great satisfaction. It is possible, also, that at that visit he might have seen Prince William Henry (William IV.), who, as well as the Duke of Kent, was afterwards under Mrs. Percy's care.

Among the occasional visitors to Queen Charlotte here were Josiah Wedgwood and his partner Bentley, who often had the opportunity of showing to their Majesties the "newest things" in the way of artistic pottery. "Last Monday," writes Bentley, in 1770, to a friend at Liverpool, "Mr. Wedgwood and I had a long audience of their Majesties, at the Queen's palace, to present some *bas-reliefs* which the Queen had ordered, and to show some new improvements, with which they were well pleased. They expressed in the most obliging and condescending manner their attention to our manufacture, and entered very freely into conversation on the further improvements of it, and on many other subjects. The King is well acquainted with business, and with the characters of the principal manufactures, merchants, and artists, and seems to have the success of all our manufactures much at heart, and to understand the importance of them. The Queen has more sensibility, true politeness, engaging affability, and sweetness of temper, than any great lady I ever had the honour of speaking to."

During the first two nights of the Gordon Riots, the King sat up with some of the general officers in the Queen's Riding House, whence messengers were constantly dispatched to observe the motions of the mob. "Between three and four thousand troops were in the Queen's Gardens, and surrounded Buckingham House. During the first night the alarm was so sudden, that no straw could be got for the troops to rest themselves on; which being told his Majesty, he, accompanied with one or two officers, went throughout the ranks, telling them, 'My lads, my crown cannot purchase you straw to-night; but depend on it, I have given orders that a sufficiency shall be here to-morrow forenoon; as a substitute for the straw, my servants will instantly serve you with a good allowance of wine and spirits, to make your situation as comfortable as possible; and I shall keep you company myself till morning.' The King did so, walking mostly in the garden, sometimes visiting the Queen and the children in the palace, and receiving all messages in the Riding House, it being in a manner head-quarters. When he was told that part of the mob was attempting to get into St. James's Palace, he forbade the soldiers to fire, but ordered them to keep off the rioters with their bayonets. The mob, in consequence of that, were so daring as to take hold of the bayonets and shake them, defying the soldiers to fire or hurt them; however, nothing further was attempted on the part of the rioters in that quarter."

In 1809 the King gave a reception to the Persian Ambassador, when an honour was conferred upon him that was hitherto confined to the Royal Family, namely, "the great iron gates fronting the park were thrown open for his entrance."

One of the ladies of the Court of the Princess of Wales thus mentions Buckingham House, in 1811:—"I was one of the happy few at H——'s ball, given in B——m House—a house I had been long anxious to see, as it is rendered classical by the pen of Pope and the pencil of Hogarth. It is in a woful condition, and, as I hear, is to be pulled down."

From its doors, in 1816, Princess Charlotte went forth to Carlton House, attired for her wedding with Leopold of Saxe-Coburg. The nation even now does not forget how, within a few short months, that brightest gem in the English crown was carried to the tomb.

George III. and Queen Charlotte, while living here, it appears, were strong believers in the literal application of the precept of Solomon, "Spare the rod and spoil the child." "The King," writes the Honourable Amelia Murray, in her "Recollections," "was most anxious 'to train up his children in the way they should go;' but severity was the fashion of the day; and although naturally a tender and affectionate father, he placed his sons under tutors who imagined that the 'rod' of Scripture could mean only bodily punishment. Princess Sophia," she adds, "once told me that she had seen her two eldest brothers, when they were boys of thirteen and fourteen, held by their arms at Buckingham Palace, to be flogged like dogs with a long whip!" Was it wonderful that the results proved anything but satisfactory?

Christmas-trees are now quite a common sight in almost every English household. But this was not the case half a century ago. Queen Charlotte, however, true to her German associations, as we learn in the work quoted above, regularly had one dressed up, either here or at Kew Palace, in the room of her German attendant. "It was hung," writes the authoress, "with presents for the children, who were invited to see it; and I well remember the pleasure that it was to hunt for one's own name, which was sure to be attached to one or more of the pretty gifts."

In 1825 the present edifice was commenced, from the design of John Nash, by command of George IV.; but as William IV. did not like the provements were effected, and new buildings added on the south side. The principal of these is the private chapel, which occupies the place of the old conservatory. It was consecrated in 1843. The pillars of this building formed a portion of the screen of Carlton House. Four years later other

THE KING'S LIBRARY, BUCKINGHAM HOUSE, 1775. (*See page* 64.)

situation or the building, Buckingham House was not occupied until the accession of Queen Victoria. It was at first intended only to repair and enlarge the old house; and therefore the old site, height, and dimensions were retained. This led to the erection of a clumsy building, as it was considered that Parliament would never have granted the funds for an entirely new palace. On the accession of her present Majesty, several alterations and im- and more extensive alterations were effected by the erection, at a cost of about £150,000, of the east front, under the superintendence of Mr. Blore. The palace, as constructed by Nash, consisted of three sides of a square, Roman-Corinthian, raised upon a Doric basement, with pediments at the ends; the fourth side being enclosed by iron palisades. In front of the central entrance stood, formerly, the Marble Arch, now at the north-east

BUCKINGHAM HOUSE IN 1775. (*See page* 63.)

corner of Hyde Park. It was removed to its present situation in 1851. On it was displayed the royal banner of England, denoting the presence of the sovereign. This flag is now displayed on the roof in the centre of the eastern front. The new east front of the palace is the same length as the garden front; the height to top of the balustrade is nearly eighty feet, and it has a central and two arched side entrances, leading direct into the quadrangle. The wings are surmounted by statues representing "Morning," "Noon," and "Night;" the "Hours and the Seasons;" and upon turrets, flanking the central shield (bearing "V. R. 1847"), are colossal figures of "Britannia" and "St. George;" besides groups of trophies, festoons of flowers, &c. Around the entire building is a scroll frieze of the rose, shamrock, and thistle.

It has been asserted that the mismanagement on the part of the Government nearly ruined the artist of the magnificent gates of the arch. Their cost was 3,000 guineas, and they are the largest and most superb in Europe, not excepting the stupendous gates of the Ducal Palace at Venice, and those made by order of Buonaparte for the Louvre at Paris. Yet the Government agents are reported to have conveyed these costly gates from the manufacturer's in a "common stage wagon," when the semi-circular head, the most beautiful portion of the design, was irretrievably mutilated; and, consequently, it has not been fixed in the archway to the present day.

The most important portions of the palace are the Marble Hall and Sculpture Gallery, the Library, the Grand Staircase, the Vestibule, the state apartments, consisting of the New Drawing-room, and the Throne-room, the Picture Gallery (where her present Majesty has placed a valuable collection of paintings), the Grand Saloon, and the State Ball-room.

The Entrance-hall is surrounded by a range of double columns, with gilded bases and capitals, standing on a continuous basement; each column consists of a single piece of Carrara marble. The Grand Staircase is of white marble, the decorations of which were executed by L. Gruner. The State Ball-room, on the south side, was finished in 1856, from Pennethorne's design, and decorated within by Gruner; and it has been more than once stated in print that it cost £300,000. It has ranges of scagliola porphyry Corinthian columns, carrying an entablature and coved ceiling, elaborately gilt. In this room are Winterhalter's portraits of the Queen and the late Prince Consort, also Vandyke's Charles I. and Henrietta Maria. This splendid room was the scene of two superb

costume balls in 1842 and 1845 : the first in the style of the reign of Edward III.; and the *fête* in 1845 was in the taste of George II.'s reign. The Library, which is also used as a waiting-room for deputations, is very large, and decorated in a manner combining comfort with elegance ; it opens upon a terrace, with a conservatory at one end and the chapel at the other, whilst over the balustrade are seen the undulating surface of the palace gardens. From this noble apartment, as soon as the Queen is ready to receive them, deputations pass across the Sculpture Gallery into the Hall, and thence ascend, by the Grand Staircase through an ante-room and the Green Drawing-room, to the Throne-room. The Sculpture Gallery contains busts of eminent statesmen and members of the Royal Family, and extends through the whole length of the central portion of the front of the edifice. The Green Drawing-room, which opens upon the upper storey of the portico of the old building, is a long and lofty apartment. Visitors on the occasions of state balls and other ceremonies are conducted through the Green Drawing-room to the Picture Gallery and the Grand Saloon. On these occasions refreshments are served in the Garter-room and Green Drawing-room, and supper laid in the principal Dining-room. The concerts, invitations to which seldom exceed 300, are given in the Grand Saloon. The Throne-room, which is in the eastern front, is upwards of sixty feet in length, and has the walls hung with crimson satin, the alcove with crimson velvet, and both are relieved by a profusion of golden hues; the ceiling is richly carved and gilt, emblazoned with armorial bearings, and the fringe adorned with bas-reliefs, illustrative of the Wars of the Roses.

The palace includes a Picture Gallery, containing a choice and extensive collection of specimens of ancient and modern masters; it can be viewed by orders from the Lord Chamberlain, which are granted only to persons who can give good references and guarantees of respectability. The Queen's Gallery contains a variety of the works of Dutch and Flemish artists, together with a few pictures of the Italian and English schools, collected by King George IV., who purchased the nucleus of the whole from Sir Thomas Baring, and was aided in his selection of others by Sir Charles Long, afterwards Lord Farnborough, whose taste in all that concerned fine arts was unquestioned. The gallery itself is an extensive corridor, upwards of 150 feet long, and lighted from the roof by skylights of ground glass, on which are exhibited all the stars of the various European orders. The "private apartments" of the Queen, which are very rarely shown, contain some fine portraits and miniatures of the late and present Royal Families, by Vandyck, Lely, Kneller, Gainsborough, Copley, Lawrence, &c.

The Yellow Drawing-room is generally considered the most magnificent apartment in the palace ; the whole of the furniture being elaborately carved, overlaid with burnished gold, and covered with broad-striped yellow satin. Several highly-polished syenite marble pillars are ranged against the walls. In each panel is painted a full-length portrait of some member of the Royal Family. This room, which is on the north side of the palace, communicates with the Queen's private apartments. The saloon, in the centre of the garden front, is superbly decorated ; the shafts of the Corinthian columns are composed of purple scagliola, in imitation of lapis lazuli ; the entablature, cornice, and ceiling are profusely enriched ; and the remaining decorations and furniture are of corresponding magnificence. The South Drawing-room contains three compositions in relief, by the late William Pitts—namely, the apotheosis of Spenser, of Shakespeare, and of Milton.

The last of the state rooms is the Dining-room, which is a very spacious and handsome apartment, lighted by windows on one side only, opening into the garden ; the spaces between these windows are filled with immense mirrors. At the southern end is a deep recess, the extremity of which is nearly filled by a large looking-glass, in front of which, during state balls or dinners, the buffet of gold plate is arranged, producing a most magnificent effect. The ceiling is highly enriched with foliage and floral ornamentation. On the eastern side are portraits of former members of the royal family, and Sir Thomas Lawrence's whole-length portrait of George IV. in his coronation robes, which was originally in the Presence Chamber at St. James's Palace.

The garden, or west front, of the palace, architecturally the principal one, has five Corinthian towers, and also a balustraded terrace, on the upper portion of which are statues, trophies, and bas-reliefs, by Flaxman and other distinguished sculptors.

The pleasure grounds cover a space of about forty acres, five of which are occupied by a lake. Upon the summit of a lofty artificial mound, rising from the margin of the lake, is a picturesque pavilion, or garden-house, with a minaret roof. In the centre is an octagonal room, with figures of "Midnight" and "Dawn," and eight lunettes, painted in fresco, from Milton's "Comus," by Eastlake, Maclise, Landseer, Dyce, Stanfield, Uwins,

Leslie, and Ross. Another room is decorated in the Pompeian style, and a third is embellished with romantic designs, suggested by the novels and poems of Sir Walter Scott.

The Royal Stables—or mews, as they are generally called—are situated on the west side of the garden, and are concealed from the palace by a lofty mound. They contain a spacious riding-school, a room expressly for keeping the state harness, stabling for the state horses, and houses for forty carriages. The magnificent state coach, which is kept here, was designed by Sir William Chambers, in 1762, and painted by Cipriani with a series of emblematical subjects ; its entire cost is said to have been little short of £8,000.

In 1837 it was a common joke of the day that Buckingham Palace could boast at all events of being the cheapest of all royal residences, having been " built for one sovereign and furnished for another." It was in July of the above year that Queen Victoria took up her residence here, since which period this palace has been the constant abode of Her Majesty, when in town. Here, in 1840 and 1841, were born the Princess Royal and the Prince of Wales ; and it has been the birth-place of most of the other children of Her Majesty. It is, too, occasionally set apart as the temporary residence of royal guests from foreign parts, when on visits to this country.

In March, 1841, a young lad, named Jones, caused some alarm to the inmates of the palace by making his way into the Queen's private apartments. Unlike the poor demented youth who in more recent times levelled an empty worn-out pistol to Her Majesty as she was leaving her carriage to enter the palace, the only object of "the boy Jones," as he was called, appears to have been notoriety, and this gratification certainly he obtained. Mr. Raikes, in commenting on this incident in his "Journal," says—"A little scamp of an apothecary's errand-boy, named Jones, has the unaccountable mania of sneaking privately into Buckingham Palace, where he is found secreted at night under a sofa, or some other hiding-place close to the Queen's bed-chamber. No one can divine his object, but twice he has been detected and conveyed to the police-office, and put into confinement for a time. The other day he was detected in a third attempt, with apparently as little object. Lady Sandwich wittily wrote that he must undoubtedly be a descendant of *In-I-go* Jones, the architect."

Here, in 1843, the Princess Augusta of Cambridge was married with great state to Frederick William, Grand Duke of Mecklenburg-Strelitz.

The King of Hanover came over for the occasion. Shortly afterwards, Mr. Raikes happening to be breakfasting with the Duke of Wellington, the latter told the following story :—" When we proceeded to the signatures of the bride and bridegroom, the King of Hanover was very anxious to sign before Prince Albert, and when the Queen approached the table, he placed himself by her side, watching his opportunity. She knew very well what he was about, and just as the Archbishop was giving her the pen, she suddenly dodged round the table, placed herself next to the Prince, then quickly took the pen from the Archbishop, signed, and gave it to Prince Albert, who also signed next, before it could be prevented. The Queen," added the duke, " was also very anxious to give the precedence at Court to King Leopold before the King of Hanover, and she consulted me about it, and how it should be arranged. I told Her Majesty that I supposed it should be settled as we did at the Congress of Vienna. ' How was that,' said she ; ' by first arrival ? ' ' No, Ma'am,' said I, ' but alphabetically ; and B. comes before H.' This pleased her very much ; and it was done."

It was by Buckingham Palace that the Duke of Wellington's funeral cortége passed, in November, 1852, on its way from St. James's Park to St. Paul's Cathedral ; and it was also in front of the Palace that the Scots Fusilier Guards paraded in the early dawn of a bleak March day in 1854, *en route* from the Wellington Barracks to Portsmouth, to embark for the Black Sea. The Queen, accompanied by the Prince Consort, the Prince of Wales, and three others of her elder children, looked down from the balcony to bid her soldiers farewell.

It was here, too, that Her Majesty favoured Mr. Charles Dickens with an interview, in the last few weeks of his life : the true account of this interview is given by Mr. John Forster, in his " Life " of the great novelist, in terms of which the following is the substance :—

" It had been hoped to obtain Her Majesty's name and patronage for some amateur theatrical performances on behalf of the family of Douglas Jerrold, in 1857 ; but, being a public effort on behalf of a private individual, it was feared that offence might be given if a like request should be refused in another case. The Queen, however, sent a request through Sir Charles Phipps, that Charles Dickens would select a room in the palace, and let her see the performance there. There were difficulties, however, in the way, and in return, Dickens proposed that Her Majesty should come on a private night to the Gallery of Illustration, having the room entirely at her own disposal and inviting her own company. This proposal the Queen accepted ; and she was so pleased with the performance, that she sent word round to the greenroom, requesting Mr. Dickens to come to the royal box, and accept her thanks. This, however, he could not do, being undressed and begrimed with dirt. Next year the Queen expressed a wish to hear Dickens read ' The Carol ;' but this, too, came to nothing. At last," writes Mr. Forster, " there came, in the year of his death, the interview with the author whose popularity dated from her accession, whose books had entertained a larger number of her subjects than those of any contemporary writer, and whose genius will be accounted one of the stories of her reign. Accident led to it. Dickens had brought with him from America some large and striking photographs of the battle-fields of the Civil War, and the Queen, having heard of this through Mr. Arthur Helps, expressed a wish to look at them. Dickens sent them alone, and went afterwards to Buckingham Palace with Mr. Helps, at Her Majesty's request, that she might see them and thank him in person. This was in the middle of March . . . . . The Queen's kindness left a strong impression on Dickens. Upon Her Majesty's expressing regret that she had not heard his readings, Dickens intimated that they had now been a thing of the past, while he acknowledged gratefully the compliment of Her Majesty in regard to them. She spoke to him of the impression made upon her by his acting in ' The Frozen Deep ; ' and on his stating, in reply to her inquiry, that the little play had not been very successful on the public stage, said that this did not surprise her, since it no longer had the advantage of his performance in it. . . . . . She asked him to give her his writings, and could she have them that afternoon ? but he begged to be allowed to send a bound copy. Her Majesty then took from the table her own book upon the ' Highlands,' with an autograph inscription ' to Charles Dickens,' and saying that ' the humblest of writers ' would be ashamed to offer it to ' one of the greatest,' but that Mr. Helps, being asked to give it, had remarked to her that it would be valued most from herself ; so she closed the interview by placing the book in his hands." Just two months from the day of the above interview with the Queen, Dickens was buried in Westminster Abbey.

The " Board of Green Cloth," the head-quarters of which are at Buckingham Palace, comprises five of the chief officers of Her Majesty's Household —namely, the Lord Steward, the Treasurer, the Comptroller, the Master of the Household, and the Secretary. They have the oversight and government of the Queen's Court bearing the above title, and also the supervision of the Household accounts, the purveyance of the provisions and their payment, and the good government of the servants of the Household. In Murray's "Official Handbook of Church and State," we learn that "the palace anciently formed an exempt jurisdiction, which was subject to the Court of the Lord Steward of the Household, held in his absence by the Treasurer, the Comptroller, or the Steward of the Marshalsea. This Court formerly possessed the power to try all treasons, murders, felonies, and other offences committed in the palace and within the verge; but this extensive jurisdiction, which was in part repealed by George IV., had long previously fallen into disuse, and the civil jurisdiction, which the Court continued to exercise till 1849, was abolished in that year by Act of Parliament. The Lord Steward of the Household fills an ancient office of great trust and dignity. He is the chief officer of the Queen's Household, all the officers and servants of which are under his control, except those belonging to the Chapel, the Chamber, and the Stable. His authority extends over the offices of Treasurer, Comptroller, and Master of the Household. The Lord Steward is at the head of the Court of the Queen's Household—the Board of Green Cloth. He is always sworn a member of the Privy Council. He has precedence before all peers of his own degree. He has no formal grant of his office, but receives his charge immediately from the Queen by the delivery of his white staff of office. He holds his appointment during pleasure, and his tenure depends upon the political party of which he is a member. His salary is £2,000 per annum. The Lord Steward has the selection and appointment of all the subordinate officers and servants of the Household, and also of the Queen's tradesmen, except those connected with the royal stables. The Treasurer of the Household acts for the Lord Steward in his absence. He is always a member of the Privy Council, and a political adherent of the Government in power. His salary is £904 per annum. The Comptroller is subordinate to the two preceding officers, for whom he acts in their absence. He is usually a member of the Privy Council. His particular duty consists in the examination and check of the Household expenses. His office is also dependent upon the Government of the day. His salary is £904 per annum. The Master of the Household stands next in rank to this department. He is an officer under the Treasurer, and examines a portion of the accounts; but his duties consist more especially in superintending the selection,

qualification, and conduct of the Household servants. His salary is £1,158 per annum. His appointment is during pleasure, and is not dependent upon party."

In this department an office was held by Mr. William Bray, F.S.A., some years Treasurer of the Society of Antiquaries, and the author (conjointly with Mr. Manning) of the "History of Surrey." He died in November, 1832, aged ninety-six.

It is at Buckingham Palace that Her Majesty usually holds her "Courts" and "Drawing-rooms." A court is held for the reception of the diplomatic and other official bodies, the general circle on the court list, and other persons having special invitations, the presentations being few in number. A writer in the *Graphic* gives us the following observations on these State receptions:—" A Court," he says, "is not so 'interesting' in some respects as a Drawing-room. The few presentations are principally of an official character, and the youthful *débutantes* who give such grace to Drawing-room days are but little represented. There is beauty you may be sure, as there must be in any assembly where English ladies compose a large proportion; and, apart from the splendour of the dresses, it forms the chief charm of the scene. And if the *débutante* element be wanting, there is no lack of youth as well as of beauty; charming faces indeed are everywhere, and fix the attention even more than the dazzling dresses of their owners. At Drawing-rooms, where people attend voluntarily, precautions are always taken to prevent an undue proportion of men being present, as most of us would prefer such an occasion to pay our respects to that of a Levee; so gentlemen have a polite invitation to stay away unless forming the escort of ladies. But here, where notifications are expressly sent by everybody, there is no necessity for the restriction; and the ladies are certainly in no danger of being overshadowed by members of the harder sex. As regards the latter, we notice one peculiarity: there are fewer military uniforms than on Levee and Drawing-room days, when the scarlet of Her Majesty's Forces is just a little in excess. But the dresses present not the less magnificent an appearance on that account. Apart from the foreign costumes, our own official uniforms are splendid enough; and the new general court dress is decidedly more pleasant to the eye than the old style, which, though still represented, is fast giving way to the new fashion sanctioned by authority. One obvious advantage which it possesses is in being something like the garments which gentlemen are accustomed to wear, instead of being a great deal like the garments which gentlemen are accustomed to put upon their foot-men. Indeed, the footmen have the best of it as far as splendour is concerned; for the old court dress has none of the bravery of Queen Anne's time, and that of the earlier Georges. It belongs to the period of the middle of the reign of George III., and is rather sombre than otherwise, except in respect to the variegated waistcoat, which is 'fine' in a certain sense of the term, but decidedly ugly

a dress of the kind when he wandered through the gallery at Whitehall, and scandalised himself—in the cause of his "Diary"—at the lax manners of Charles II.'s court. It would have been scarcely gay enough for Pepys. In our own day it ought to suit even the simple taste of Mr. Bright, who respectfully but firmly declined to costume himself in the old court style.

"Among the fair owners of the headdresses, of

THE THRONE-ROOM, BUCKINGHAM PALACE. (*See page* 68.)

to the eye of taste. The new dress is a little formal in cut; but this is a necessity where regulation is imperative; it would never do to have very marked peculiarities of style when the same costume is to be worn by persons of all sizes and variations of figure. There is room, too, for some exercise of the fancy. Private persons—that is to say, persons having no military or official uniform —may wear the coloured cloth suit, embroidered with gold, or they may disport themselves in black velvet from head to foot, with white lace at the collars and wrists. The cloth with its ornaments is more gay; but the velvet has the decided advantage in point of dignity, and the scholarlike appearance which it gives to the wearer. One can fancy Evelyn himself being appropriately clad in

feathers, blonde-lappets, and diamonds, the trains, and other elaborations, are, of course, a large number of men in military uniform, which is, after all, the most effective of any dress, if only for the reason that it seems to belong to the wearers. Not the least gorgeous of these are the Gentlemen-at-Arms, each of whom looks like a field-marshal in his own right, though he bears only the rank of a captain. They are on duty to-day, as may be supposed, and so are the Yeomen of the Guard, in their quaint uniform of the time of Henry VIII.; and a Guard of Honour of the Coldstream Guards is mounted in the court of the palace.

"All these important matters pass under our notice while the company is assembling preparatory to entering the royal presence. At the appointed

BUCKINGHAM PALACE: GARDEN FRONT. (*See page 69.*)

hour Her Majesty, who has arrived from Windsor, takes her place, having been joined by the Prince and Princess of Wales, and other members of the Royal Family, to say nothing of the Maharajah Duleep Singh, and the Nawab Nazim of Bengal—who goes everywhere just now—with their respective attendants. The scene on the staircase—the company being on their way to the Throne-room—is very splendid, and in the Throne-room itself it is gorgeous in the extreme.

"See the lady clad in black, with the coronet of diamonds and sapphires, and the white veil covered with large diamonds also; with the necklace, cross, and brooch of yet more diamonds; on her breast the blue riband and the Star of the Order of the Garter, the Orders of Victoria and Albert and Louise of Prussia, and the Coburg and Gotha Family Order. The dignity of her bearing, apart from all these insignia, would proclaim her to be the principal personage present. As she stands, surrounded by the members of her family, and the ladies and gentlemen of her household, she is evidently *reigning* actively, as a Queen is always supposed to do; and yet she is the same gentle lady who in her private life has made herself so pleasantly familiar to her subjects.

"Of the assembly who approach her a few are presented in form and kiss the Royal hand; the rest pass by Her Majesty in rotation, and file off by a sidelong retiring movement from the presence. The ceremony occupies a considerable time, as must be, owing to the large number present; and the scene during the continuance could scarcely be surpassed for splendour and costly state. The apartment in which it is enacted, too, is well worthy of the occasion, with its glass, and its gilding, and its crimson draperies.

"When the last lady and gentleman have passed the throne, Her Majesty retires with her suite; then there is a movement downstairs, a general call for carriages, and the first 'Court' of the season has fairly come to an end."

CHAPTER VII.

THE MALL AND SPRING GARDENS.

"The ladies gaily dress'd the Mall adorn
With various dyes and paint the sunny morn."— *Gay's* "*Trivia.*"

The Game of Mall—Discovery of Mailes and Balls used in playing the Game—Formation of the Mall, and Mr. Pepys' Visits thither—The Mall a Powerful Rival to the Ring in Hyde Park—Charles II. and Dryden—Courtly Insignia worn in Public—Congreve, the Poet—A Capuchin Monastery—French Huguenot Refugees—The Duke of York's Column—"Milk Fair"—Spring Gardens—A Bowling-green established there—Duels of frequent occurrence there—The Spring Garden closed, and a Rival Establishment opened—A Part of the Royal Menagerie kept in Spring Gardens—Courtier Life in the Reign of Charles I.—Mistaken Notions as to the Origin of the Name of Spring Gardens—King Charles on his Way to Execution—Thomson, the Poet—The "Wilderness"—Berkeley House—The Metropolitan Board of Works—The Celebrated Mrs. Centlivre—"Locket's Ordinary"—Drummond's Bank—The Old Duchess of Brunswick—Sir Astley Cooper and other Noted Residents—Spring Gardens Chapel—Its Destruction by Fire—St. Matthew's Chapel-of-Ease—The Medical Club—The Tilt-yard Coffee House—Warwick Street and Warwick House—Escape of Princess Charlotte in a Hackney Coach—Her Return to Warwick House—Exhibitions and Entertainments in the Neighbourhood—The "Rummer" Tavern—Prior, the Poet—Dr. Isaac Barrow and the Earl of Rochester—Pepys in the Hands of the Modeller—Miscellaneous Exhibitions in Cockspur Street—Origin of the Name of Cockspur Street—The "British Coffee House."

ON leaving Buckingham Palace, we walk through the Mall, on the north side of St. James's Park. This once fashionable lounge and promenade is described by Northouck as "a vista half a mile in length, at that time (Charles II.) formed with a hollow smooth walk skirted round with a wooden border, and with an iron hoop at the further end, for the purpose of playing a game with a ball called mall." The iron hoop was suspended from a bar of wood at the top of a pole, and the play consisted in striking a ball through this ring from a considerable distance.

In Timbs' "Curiosities of London" we read that in 1854 were found in the roof of the house of the late Mr. B. L. Vulliamy, No. 68, Pall Mall, a box containing four pairs of the mailes, or mallets, and one ball, such as were formerly used for playing the game of pall-mall upon the site of the above house, or in the Mall of St. James's Park. "Each maile was four feet in length, and made of lance-wood; the head was slightly curved, measuring outwardly $5\frac{1}{2}$ inches, the inner curve being $4\frac{1}{2}$ inches; the diameter of the maile-ends was $2\frac{1}{2}$ inches, each shod with a thin iron hoop; the handle, which was very elastic, was bound with white leather to the breadth of two hands, and terminated by a collar of jagged leather. The ball was of box-wood, $2\frac{1}{2}$ inches in diameter." These relics of a bygone, almost forgotten game were presented to the British Museum by Mr. George Vulliamy.

The "Mall" is the name now conventionally

given to the wide gravel walk running under the windows of Carlton Terrace, from the Green Park as far as Spring Gardens. This was not the original "Mall" of the days of Charles II., which seems to have lain to the north, and to have been as nearly as possible identical with "the present street of Pall Mall." No doubt, when a new and broad thoroughfare like the old one, and so close to it, was opened in its place to the public, the name was transformed the more easily and obviously, as the former, like the present, was the northern boundary of the park, and indeed formed part of it.

Under date of April 2, 1661, there is an entry in Pepys' "Diary" which implies that the "Pell Mell" was then newly finished :—"To St. James's Park, where I saw the Duke of York playing at Pellmell,

opportunity for displaying a carriage, horses, and smart livery. Equipages at that time became more and more the fashion, and to be seen afoot in the Mall was by many considered the height of vulgarity. There appeared in 1709 a satire, entitled "The Circus, or the British Olympus," in the preface of which occurs the following remark :—"If gentlemen are never such dear companions now, they must have no conversation together but upon equal terms, lest some should say to the man of figure, 'Bless me, sir! what strange, filthy fellow was that you bow'd to parading in the Mall, as you were driving to the Ring?'"

The following story of the Mall, though told in "Spence's Anecdotes," will amuse many of our readers to whom it may be news :—"It was Charles II. who gave to Dryden the hint for writing his

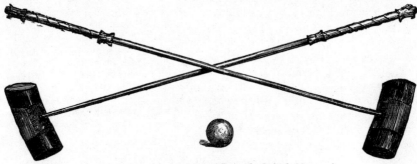

PALL MALL IMPLEMENTS. (*From the British Museum.*)

the first time that ever I saw the sport." And on the 15th of May, 1663, he tells us how that he "walked in the parke, discoursing with the keeper of the Pell Mell, who was sweeping it." It appears to have been covered with fine gravel, mixed with cockle-shells finely powdered and spread to keep it fast; which, "however," complains Mr. Samuel Pepys, "in dry weather turns to dust and deads the ball." In the following January the diarist is here again, and in his record of this visit, says it pleased him "mightily" to "hear a gallant, lately come from France, swear at one of his companions for suffering his man (a spruce blade) to be so saucy as to strike a ball while his master was playing on the Mall."

Since the reign of Charles II. the Mall had become a powerful rival to the Ring in Hyde Park. In Etheredge's "Man of Mode" (1676), a young lady observes that the Ring has a better reputation than the Mall; "but," says she, "I abominate the dull diversions there, the formal bows, the affected smiles, the silly bywords and amorous tweers in passing; here [in the Mall] one meets with a little conversation now and then." On the other hand, the Ring had this advantage, that it gave the

poem called 'The Medal.' One day, as the king was walking in the Mall and talking with Dryden, he said, 'If I were a poet . . . . . I would write a poem on such a subject in the following manner, and then gave him the plan for it. Dryden took the hint, carried the poem as soon as it was written to the king, and had a present of a hundred broad pieces for it."

The Mall was a fashionable lounge, and is constantly alluded to in the anecdote literature and gossip of the Stuart and Hanoverian times. Thus Swift tells "Stella" that "when he passes the Mall in the evening, it is prodigious to see the number of ladies walking there;" and, speaking of St. John says, "His father is a man of pleasure that walks the Mall, and frequents St. James's Coffee House, and the Chocolate House."

In the time of the first and second Georges it was usual for noblemen of the highest rank to wear the insignia of their orders in public places. The writer of the "Town Spy" for instance, tells us, in 1725, how he was walking in the Mall with a gentleman whom he had met "at a coffee-house within the verge," when there passed before them "a nobleman vested with a blue Garter." His servants, he adds, "were worried about by the people to know what duke it was. It turned out, however, to be only an earl after all."

Congreve, the poet, was one of the gallants who were fond of displaying their fine dress in the haunts of fashion. Hence Thackeray's remark, that "Louis Quatorze in all his glory is hardly more splendid than our Phœbus Apollo of the Mall and the Spring Garden."

Close to St. James's Palace, nearly on the site where now stands the German chapel, was built, in the reign of Charles II., a monastery for the use of the Capuchin monks who attended Catherine of Braganza. It is thus described by Pepys in his "Diary," under date January 23, 1666–7 :—"My Lord Brounkir and I walking into the park, I did observe the new buildings ; and my lord seeing I had a desire to see them, they being the place for the priests and friers, he took me back to my Lord Almoner ; and he took us quite through the whole house and chapel, and the new monastery, shewing me most excellent pieces in wax-worke ; a crucifix given by a Pope to Mary Queene of Scotts, wherein is a piece of the Cross ; two bits set in the manner of a cross in the foot of the crucifix ; several fine pictures, but especially very good prints of holy pictures. I saw the dortoire and the cells of the priests, and we went into one ; a very pretty little room, very clean, hung with pictures, set with books. The priest was in his cell, with his hair-clothes to his skin, bare-legged with a sandall only on, and his little bed without sheets, and no feather bed ; but yet, I thought, soft enough. His cord about his middle ; but in so good company, living with ease, I thought it a very good life. A pretty library they have, and I was in the refectoire, where every man has his napkin, knife, cup of earth, and basin of the same ; and a place for one to sit and read while the rest are at meals. And into the kitchen I went, where a good neck of mutton at the fire, and other victuals boiling. I do not think they fared very hard. Their windows all looking into a fine garden and the park ; and mighty pretty rooms all. I wished myself one of the Capuchins."

In the reign of William III. we find a congregation of the French Huguenot refugees established in the "French Chapel Royal," St. James's.

On the site of what is now the basement or sub-structure of Carlton House Terrace, which nearly the whole distance eastward bounds the north side of the Mall, was once a row of fine old trees, which overhung the road by the park-wall. Half way along the Terrace is an opening from Waterloo Place, formed by command of William IV., as had

been the Spring Garden Gate, more than a century earlier, by William III.

The column which crowns the steps leading up from the park into Waterloo Place was erected by public subscription in 1830–33, to the memory of the late Duke of York, many years Commander-in-Chief. The cost of it was £26,000. It consists of a plain circular shaft of Aberdeen granite about 120 feet high, from the designs of Mr. B. Wyatt. The statue of the duke which surmounts it is the work of the late Sir Richard Westmacott, R.A.

The column and statue, as might be expected, was the subject of many witticisms. Take, for instance, the following lines in the *New Monthly Magazine* :—

"Thou pillar, longitudinally great,
　And also perpendicularly straight.

　　　*　　　　　*　　　　　*　　　　　*

Thou art, I fear, but flattery's handiwork,
Being a tribute unto royal York.
Thy royal highness (ah ! too like to *His*)
Prompts us somewhat to stare, somewhat to quiz,
Railing surrounds above thy lofty brow,
And passers-by do likewise rail below.
That mortal Prince whom thou to Cherubim
Wouldst raise, what record canst thou give of him ?
Of his great deeds few words the Muse can dish up ;
But, for his virtues, was he not a bishop ?"

The allusion in the last line is to the fact that the duke enjoyed by courtesy the lay title of Prince-Bishop of Osnaburg.

At the end of the Mall, in the shade of the tall trees, near the Spring Gardens entrance, is an "institution "—if we may so call it—of considerable date, and a proof of the former rural character of the spot, which has flourished here perhaps almost since the formation of the Mall. It is known as "Milk Fair," and is held by a privilege granted from royalty to the gatekeepers. In Tom Brown's time (1700) the noisy milk-fools in the park cried, "A can of milk, ladies ! A can of red cow's milk, sir !" If we may judge from a fashionable conceit in Gay's "Trivia," we may conclude that not only cows' but asses' milk was at one time sold here as a restorative for bodily ailments—

"Before proud gates attending asses bray,
　Or arrogate with solemn pace the way ;
　These grave physicians with their milky cheer,
　The love-sick maid and dwindling beau repair."

It may be added, that the vendors of milk of the present day in Spring Gardens are almost, without exception, descendants from those who have had their stalls here for the last century or more.

Spring Gardens—more properly "The Spring Garden"—as late as the reign of Elizabeth, and possibly down to a still more recent date, was a rural garden. This spot bears its name from a fountain or "spring" of water, which in the days of Queen Bess was set in motion by the spectator treading on some secret machinery, which proved a novel puzzle for the good people of Westminster.

Hentzner, in his "Travels" (1598), thus describes the scene :—" In a garden belonging to this palace there is a *jet d'eau*, with a sun-dial, at which, while strangers are looking, a quantity of water forced by a wheel which the gardener turns at a distance, through a number of little pipes, plentifully sprinkles those that are standing around." Mr. P. Cunningham assures us that such watersprings as this were common in gardens in the days of Queen Bess, and that one of the same kind was to be seen at Chatsworth as late as 1847. Be this, however, as it may, Nares, in his "Glossary," tells us that the Spring Garden described by Plot was in existence at Enstone, in Oxfordshire, in 1822.

This place appears to have been a sort of adjunct to the Royal Palace of Whitehall, though " across the road," and to have been covered occasionally with scaffolds, in order to enable "the quality" to see the tilting in the Tilt-yard. It contained a pleasant yard, a pond for bathing, and some butts to practise shooting.

Charles I., by royal patent in 1630, made it a " bowling-green," but the patent was revoked, and the " bowling-green " brought to an untimely end four years later. The reason of the withdrawal of its licence may be gathered from the following extract from a letter addressed by a Mr. Gerrard to Lord Strafford :—" There was kept in it an ordinary of six shillings a meal, when the king's proclamation allows but two elsewhere ; continual bibbing and drinking wine all day under the trees ; two or three quarrels every week. It was grown scandalous and insufferable ; besides, my Lord Digby being reprehended for striking in the king's garden, he said he took it for a common bowling place, where all paid money for their coming in." It is clear from this that Lord Digby thought that if he only paid for admission, he had a right to " strike " where and whom he pleased ; and if this was the general idea entertained by " persons of quality," it is not difficult to see how "two or three quarrels "—or, in other words, duels—would arise there every week.

One result of the shutting up of the " Spring Garden " was the opening of a rival, the " New Spring Garden," by one of the Lord Chamberlain's household, too. It appears, however, that the old place was re-opened ere long ; for in June, 1649, John Evelyn paid it a visit, " treating divers ladies of his relations," as he tells us in his " Diary."

Under date May 10, 1654, however, he writes :—" My Lady Gerrard treated us at Mulberry Garden, now the only place of refreshment about the towne for persons of the best quality to be exceedingly cheated at ; Cromwell and his partisans having shut up and seized on the Spring Garden, which till now had been the usual rendezvous for the ladys and gallants at this season." In spite of the sour-visaged Puritans, however, its gates were again thrown open ; for the writer of " A Character of England," published five years later, thus speaks of it, and in the present tense :—" The inclosure is not disagreeable, for the solemnness of the grove, and the warbling of the birds, and as it opens into the spacious walks at St. James's." He adds :—" It is not unusual to find some of the young company here till midnight ; and the thickets of the garden seem to be contrived to all advantages of gallantry, after they have refreshed with collation, which is here seldom omitted, at a certain cabaret in the middle of this paradise, where the forbidden fruits are certain trifling tarts, neats' tongues, salacious meats, and bad Rhenish."

Soon after the Restoration, a part at least of the ground occupied by these rival places of amusement seems to have been built over, and distinguished as the " inner " and the " outer " Spring Garden respectively ; a trace of which doubtless still remains in the present name of Spring Garden*s*. Prince Rupert occupied a house in Spring Gardens from 1674 until his death.

We have already in a previous chapter spoken of the " menagerie " which James I. established in St. James's Park ; some of the animals, however, appear to have been located in Spring Gardens. " At all events," says Larwood, in his " Story of the London Parks," " they were there in the second year of the reign of Charles II. This appears from a document preserved among the State papers, being an order dated January 31, 1626, for £75 5s. 10d. a year to be paid for life to Philip, Earl of Montgomery, 'for keeping the Spring Garden, and the *beasts and fowls* there.' "

The Parliament passed a decree in March, 1647, in the true spirit of Puritan intolerance, ordering " That the keeper of the Spring Garden be hereby required and enjoined to admit no person to come into or walk in the Spring Garden on the Lord's Day or any of the public fast days, and that no wine, beer, ale, cakes, or other things be sold there either upon the Lord's Day or public fast days."

Isaac D'Israeli, in his " Curiosities of Literature," tells us an amusing story illustrative of courtier life in Spring Gardens in the early days of Charles I.

"The king and the Duke of Buckingham," he writes, " were in the Spring Garden looking at the bowlers ; the duke put on his hat. One Wilson, a Scotchman, first seizing the duke's hand, snatched it off, saying, ' Off with your hat before the king ! ' Buckingham, not able to restrain his quick feelings, kicked the Scotchman ; but the king interfering, said, ' Let him alone, George ; he is either mad or a fool.' ' No, sir,' replied Wilson ; ' I am a sober

apparently another writer, R. Brome, who asks his friend, "Shall we make a fling to London, and see how the spring appears there in the Spring Gardens ? "

Mr. J. H. Jesse tells us that down to the present day every house in Spring Garden Terrace has its separate well. He also gives currency to a tradition to the effect that as he walked through the park from St. James's Palace to the scaffold at

PLAYING AT PALL MALL. (*From a Contemporary Print.* (*See page* 75.)

man ; and if your Majesty would give me leave, I would tell you that of this man, which many know, and none dare speak.' "

Evelyn tells us in May, 1658, how he went to see the coach race in Hyde Park, and afterwards "collationed" in Spring Gardens ; and it would seem from other sources that the latter formed an agreeable house of call on the way to and from the park.

Margaret, the learned Duchess of Newcastle, tells us that when young she and her sisters used to ride in their coaches about the streets to see the concourse and recourse of people, and in the spring time to visit the Spring Gardens, Hyde Park, and the like places. From this it is probable that her Grace mistook the origin of the name, as does

Whitehall, King Charles stopped, weary and faint, to drink a glass of water at one of the springs, at the same time, as we have before remarked, pointing out to Bishop Juxon and Herbert a tree close by as having been planted by the hands of his elder brother, Prince Henry.

Among the inhabitants of this place enumerated by Mr. Peter Cunningham are Sir Philip Warwick (after whom Warwick Street is named), Philip Earl of Chesterfield (1670), Prince Rupert, the "mad" Lord Crofts, Sir Edward Hungerford, Colley Cibber, and, last but not least, George Canning. An advertisement in the *Daily Courant* of January, 1703, gives us Cibber's *locale* as "near the ' Bull Head' Tavern, in Old Spring Garden." John Milton, too, during the Commonwealth, occupied lodgings at the house of a tradesman named Thomson, "next door to the 'Bull Head Tavern.'"

In a room over the shop of one Egerton, a bookseller, near this spot, where he resided on first coming to London, a raw Scottish lad, James Thomson wrote part of his "Seasons." We are told that at this time he was "gaping about the town listlessly, getting his pockets picked, and forced to wait on great persons with his poem of

denominated the 'Wilderness' so lately as 1772, in which year Frederick Augustus, Earl of Berkeley, obtained leave to build messuages and gardens in a place called 'the Wilderness,' on the north-west side of the passage from Spring Gardens to St. James's Park. This grant, no doubt, occasioned the disappearance of the last vestige of the once famous place of amusement."

At the northern end of Spring Gardens, at the

THE MALL IN 1450.

'Winter,' in order to find a patron." Most luckily, fond as he was of freedom, he did not carry his love of freedom so far as to close against himself the doors of powerful patrons. "He obtained," writes Leigh Hunt, "an easy place, which required no compromise of his principles, and passed the latter part of his life in his own house at Richmond," where he died and is buried.

As late as the reign of George I., the Spring Gardens are laid down in maps as forming an enclosure limited by rows of houses in Warwick Lane and Charing Cross, and containing a house with a large flower-garden in front, situated in the midst of an orchard or a grove of trees. "It is this plantation, perhaps," says Mr. Jacob Larwood, in his "Story of the London Parks," "which was

corner of the footway leading into the Mall of St. James's Park, stood the above-named dull and unattractive mansion, known as Berkeley House, from having been the town residence of the Earls of Berkeley for the best part of a century. Here George Prince of Wales, and many of his boon companions, were frequent visitors. It was purchased by the Government in 1862, and pulled down. On its site are built the offices of the Metropolitan Board of Works. This edifice is spacious and lofty, and well adapted to the purposes for which it was erected. It is in the Italian style of architecture, and has at once a bold and striking appearance. The Metropolitan Board of Works was established in 1855. Under the Metropolitan Building Act, passed in the same year, it exercises a supervision over all buildings erected within the limits of its jurisdiction. The powers of the Board were extended in 1858, to enable it to effect the purification of the Thames by constructing a new system of Main Drainage on both sides of the river. The construction of the Thames Embankments was also carried on under its supervision. It is empowered by the Act under which it is constituted to raise loans for carrying out public works of this nature, the repayment and interest of which are guaranteed by Government, and secured by a tax of 3d. in the pound on property in the metropolis. The principal general duties of the Board comprise the control over the formation of streets, and the maintenance of the Fire Brigade, the Main Drainage system, and of the parks and commons.

In Buckingham Court, at the southern end of Spring Gardens, died, December 1, 1723, the celebrated Mrs. Centlivre, the witty and pretty dramatist, author of *The Busybody*, and *The Bold Stroke for a Wife*, and the wife of three husbands in succession. She is said to have been a great beauty, an accomplished linguist, and a good-natured, friendly woman. Pope immortalised her in his "Dunciad," it is said, for having written a ballad against his translation of Homer, when she was a child. "But," as Leigh Hunt suggests, "the probability is that she was too intimate with Steele, and other friends of Addison, while the irritable poet was at variance with them. It is not impossible, also, that some raillery of hers might have been applied to him—not very pleasant from a beautiful woman against a man of his personal infirmities, and who was actually jealous of not standing well with the fair sex." Mrs. Centlivre is said to have accompanied her first lover, Anthony Howard (the father of the author of "Love Elegies"), to Cambridge, in boy's clothes. This, however, did not hinder her from marrying a nephew of Sir Stephen Fox, who died a year afterwards, nor from having two other husbands in succession. Her second husband was an officer of the name of Carroll, who was killed in a duel. Her third husband, Mr. Centlivre, who had the formidable title of "Yeoman of the Mouth," being chief cook to Queen Anne, fell desperately in love with her when she was playing the part of Alexander the Great, at Windsor; for she seems to have acted on the stage in the provinces, though she did not appear on London boards. Leigh Hunt says of her plays that "they are not after the taste of Mrs. Hannah More, but the public seem very fond of them. They are still," he adds, in 1835, "acted as often as if they had just come out. The reason is that, careless as they are in dialogue,

and not very scrupulous in manners and morals, they are full of action and good humour."

Her house must have stood near the spot where now is Messrs. Drummond's bank; close by was a house known as "Locket's," or "Locket's Ordinary," a house of entertainment much frequented by the gentry and "persons of quality" in the reign of Queen Anne, and partaking very much of the old character of the gardens on which it rose. Dr. King thus commemorates it, in his "Art of Cookery," with a quaint and not very first-rate pun :—

"For Locket's stands where Gardens once did spring."

The exact site of "Locket's Ordinary" is not known, though Leigh Hunt is inclined to identify it with the "Northumberland" Coffee House of a later date. "It is often mentioned," observes the writer of a MS. in Birch's "Collection," quoted in the Notes to the *Tatler*, "in the plays of Colley Cibber, Vanbrugh, &c., where the scene is sometimes laid. It was much frequented by Sir George Etheredge, as appears from the following anecdotes, picked up in the British Museum :—Sir George and his company, provoked by something amiss in the entertainment or the attendance, got into a violent passion, and abused the waiters. This brought in Mrs. Locket. 'We are so provoked,' said Sir George, 'that I could find it in my heart to pull that nosegay out of your bosom, and throw all the flowers into your face.' This turned all the anger of the guests into a loud fit of laughter. Sir George Etheredge, it appears, discontinued Mrs. Locket's ordinary, having run up a score which he could not conveniently discharge. Mrs. Locket sent a man to dun him, and to threaten him with a prosecution. He bade the messenger tell her that he would kiss her if she stirred a step further in the matter. When this answer was brought back to her, she called for her hood and scarf, and told her husband, who interposed, that 'she'd see if there was any fellow alive who had the impudence to do so.' 'Pry'thee, my dear,' replied her husband, 'don't be so rash; you don't know what folly a man may do in his passion.'"

The banking-house of Messrs. Drummond stands at the corner of Spring Gardens and Charing Cross. It was founded early in the eighteenth century, and is consequently one of the oldest West-end banks. At a day when it was customary for the younger sons of Scottish noblemen to seek their fortunes by commerce, Andrew Drummond, fifth son of Sir John Drummond, the third Laird of Machany, younger brother of the fourth Viscount Strathallan, came to London as an agent for some of the chief Jacobite houses, about the year 1713, and founded this business on the opposite side of Charing Cross as a banker and a goldsmith. The business was removed to its present site a year or two afterwards. Mr. A. Drummond is represented by Malcolm, in his "Genealogical Memoirs of the House of Drummond," as a man of great integrity and ability. He married a Miss Strahan, daughter of a London banker, and bequeathed the business to his three sons. Messrs. Drummond have had, and still have, a large Scottish connection.

Mr. Peter Cunningham tells us that the founder of Drummond's bank obtained his great position by advancing money to the Pretender, and by the king's consequent withdrawal of his account. This step on the part of the king led to a rush of the Scottish nobility and gentry with their accounts to Charing Cross, and to the ultimate advancement of the bank to its present position.

There is a tradition in the house that Sir Robert Walpole, in his zeal for the House of Hanover, wished to inspect the books of Messrs. Drummond's bank, in order to keep his eye on the adherents of the Pretender. It is needless to add that his wish was not gratified, and Mr. Drummond, on meeting Sir Robert soon afterwards at Court, turned his back on the Minister, in order to mark his sense of the affront; and the King, so far from being offended with him, showed Mr. Drummond a special mark of his royal favour, either then or at a later date.

On one occasion, it is said, Messrs. Drummond refused to advance the sum of £500 to the Princess of Wales, when she was in pecuniary difficulties. Hence that lady writes to a friend:—"Messrs. Drummond certainly shall not be the banker to George IV.'s Queen; for any historian, who would write the biography of the ex-Princess of Wales, would not a little astonish the world, in relating that she could not procure the sum of £500, at the rate of paying £500 a *year* per annum for it!!" It is only fair to add that this statement, coming from an angry lady's pen, may very possibly be mere gossip and scandal after all.

There is a portrait of the founder of the bank, painted by Zoffany; an engraved copy of it hangs in the inner room of the bank. Pope had an account at this bank, though few poets of modern times are so fortunate as to enjoy the luxury of a banker. The bank was rebuilt in 1881.

In 1810, the old Duke and Duchess of Brunswick, the parents of Princess (afterwards Queen) Caroline, were living in a dingy and old-fashioned house in New Street. Neither the road nor the royal carriages would appear to have been of the best, for we find one of the ladies of the princess's suite at Kensington writing thus to a friend. "We rumbled in her (the princess's) old tub all the way to New Street, Spring Gardens, much to the discomfiture of my bones . . . We were ushered into the dirtiest room I ever beheld, nearly empty and devoid of comfort. A few filthy lamps stood on a sideboard, common chairs were placed around very dingy walls, and in the middle of this empty space sat the old duchess, a melancholy spectacle of decayed royalty."

In New Street lived Sir Astley Cooper, in the height of his fame as a surgeon. Excellent as was his surgical skill, he liked to display it, and was often accused of a sort of anatomical sleight of hand. "No one," writes the author of the "Family Joe Miller," "will deny that the first requisite for an operating surgeon is nerve, and that to a degree which appears to spectators to amount to want of feeling. Sir Astley Cooper possessed this quality thoroughly. He always retained perfect self-possession in the operating theatre; and his unrivalled manual dexterity was not more obvious than his love of display during his most critical and dangerous *performances* on the patient, whose courage he tried to keep up by lively and facetious remarks. When Sir Astley was in the zenith of his fame, a satirical Sawbones sang thus:—

> ' Nor Drury Lane, nor Common Garden,
> 　　Are, to my fancy, worth a farden;
> 　　　I hold them both small beer.
> 　　Give me the wonderful exploits,
> 　　And jolly jokes between the sleights,
> 　　　Of *Astley's Amphitheatre.*' "

In 1815 Sir Astley Cooper settled in Spring Gardens, and a few years afterwards he was employed professionally by George IV. He long enjoyed a very large share of public patronage, and his reputation both at home and abroad was such as rarely falls to the lot of a professional man.

Lord Campbell—then " plain John Campbell "—was living in New Street, Spring Gardens, in his early Parliamentary days, 1830–35. In the same street, at the same time, lived Sir James Scarlett (afterwards Lord Abinger), whose daughter Campbell married, and whom he helped to raise to the peerage. Joseph Jekyll, the witty contemporary of Selwyn and friend of the Prince Regent, was also an inhabitant of New Street.

In the reign of William III. we find some of the French Huguenot refugees established in Spring Gardens Chapel. The chapel itself was set on fire in the year 1726, when King George I. was in Hanover; and his son, the Prince of Wales (afterwards George II.), happening to take an active part in the work of extinguishing it, the following epigram was written off-hand by Nicholas Rowe, with a covert comparison or rather contrast of the Prince of Wales with Nero, who "fiddled while Rome burnt:"—

> "Thy guardian, blest Britannia, scorns to sleep,
> When the sad subjects of his father weep.
> Weak princes by their fears increase distress :
> He faces danger, and so makes it less.
> Tyrants on blazing towns may smile with joy,
> George knows to save is greater than destroy."

Great alarm was caused in the neighbourhood, as the chapel adjoined some depôts of gunpowder; but these were saved. The chapel, however, and an inn called the "Thatched House Tavern" adjoining, were destroyed.

In 1731, a new chapel was built by the Hon. Edward Southwell. A chapel subsequently erected by one of the De Clifford family still stands at the corner of New Street; it is dedicated to St. Matthew, and is a monument of the low architectural taste of the time ; it was styled a chapel-of-ease to St. Martin's parish, but it is to be feared that it proved in the event a frequent bone of clerical contention between Lord De Clifford and the Vicar of St. Martin's.

Nearly the whole of Spring Gardens is about to be removed, to make room for new public offices, and to form a thoroughfare from Whitehall to St. James's Park.

We have already spoken of the Tilt-yard, which formerly occupied part of the space now known as Spring Gardens. Close by it, in Stow's time, "were divers handsome houses lately built before the park." One of these "handsome houses" afterwards became Jenny Man's "Tilt-yard Coffee House," upon the site afterwards occupied by the Paymaster-General's office. It was the resort of military officers, until supplanted by "Slaughter's" in St. Martin's Lane, which more recently was, in its turn, ruined by the military clubs. The *Spectator* states that the mock military also frequented the Tilt-yard Coffee House—"fellows who figured in laced hats, black cockades, and scarlet suits ; and who manfully pulled the noses of such quiet citizens as wore not swords." As Theodore Hook wrote in "Sayings and Doings," no doubt with a retrospect of his own youthful days : "When he fell really in love, Bond Street lounges and loungers became a bore to him; he sickened at the notion of a jollification under the piazza; and even the charms of the pretty pastry-cooks at Spring Gardens had lost their piquancy."

Warwick Street, built in 1681, was named after Sir Philip Warwick. Strype says that in his day it led to the back gate of the king's garden, "for

the conveniency of her late Majesty's principal gardener."

At the western end of this street, which formed a *cul de sac*, stood Warwick House, adjoining Carlton House Gardens, for some time the residence of the Princess Charlotte, in her girlish years, when heiress to the throne. Here she was brought up by Lady De Clifford, as her governess; and hence in 1814 she "bolted off" in a hackney coach to her mother's house at Connaught Place, from which it required the united pressure of the Lord Chancellor Eldon and the Archbishop of Canterbury (Dr. Manners Sutton) to induce her to return; and even this was not accomplished without much difficulty and remonstrance from her friends, until an early hour next morning, when she was brought back in one of the royal carriages.

"On the 7th of July, 1814," to use Lady Brownlow's words in her "Reminiscences of a Septuagenarian," "all the London world was startled by hearing that the Princess Charlotte on the previous evening had left Warwick House unobserved, and gone off in a hackney coach to the Princess of Wales in Connaught Place. The cause of this sudden and unaccountable proceeding has never transpired to the world at large. That it was perfectly unexpected and unwished-for by the Princess of Wales there seems no doubt. The Duke of York, the Duke of Sussex, Lord Eldon, and Mr. Brougham all repaired to Connaught Place, and after several hours of discussion the Princess Charlotte returned to Warwick House."

We learn accidentally that the Lord Chancellor (Clarendon) was living at Warwick House in 1660, for in that year Pepys records the fact of having carried a letter thither to him from Whitehall.

In this street, close to where stood old "Warwick House," is to be seen a small public-house, with the sign of "The Two Chairmen"—referring, of course, to the time when "sedan chairs," or as they were commonly called "chairs," were in vogue.

At a time when Regent Street was not built, and when Bond Street was too near to Marylebone to be central, Spring Gardens were the head-quarters of those exhibitions which abound in town in "the season," and disappear at its close. Here, towards the end of the last century, the Incorporated Society of Arts held its exhibitions ; and "here in 1806," as Mr. Timbs reminds us, "at Wigley's Rooms, were shown Serre's Panorama of Boulogne, and other foreign cities, and sea pieces; also Maillardet's automatic figures, including a harpsichord-player, a rope-dancer, and a singing bird. Here also was exhibited Marshall's 'Peristrophic' Panorama of the Battle of Waterloo "—so called because the spectators themselves were turned round by machinery whilst they viewed it. A similar contrivance more recently was adopted at the Coliseum, when the Panorama of London was exhibited here.

In the reign of Queen Anne there was to be seen "over against the Mews' Gate, at Charing Cross, close to the 'Spring Gardens,' by Royal permission, a collection of strange and wonderful creatures from most parts of the world, all alive." It certainly was most miscellaneous, including a black man, a dwarf, a pony only two feet odd inches high, several panthers, leopards, and jackalls, and last not least, "a strange monstrous creature brought from the coast of Brazil, having a head like a child, legs and arms very wonderful, and a long tail like a serpent, wherewith he feeds himself as an elephant does with his trunk." Mr. Frost, in his "Old Show-men," conjectures that this last-named "monstrous creature" may have been, after all, only a spider-monkey, one variety of which is said by Humboldt to use its prehensile tail for the purpose of picking insects out of crevices.

Among the other objects of curiosity exhibited here from time to time, not the least attractive was the "Mechanical and Picturesque Theatre," which was, as the advertisements of the day tell us, "illustrative of the effect of art in imitation of nature, in views of the island of St. Helena, the city of Paris, the passage of Mount St. Bernard, Chinese artificial fireworks, and a storm at sea."

"Punch," if not a native of this locality, at all events first here made his appearance in England. Mr. Frost, in his "Old Showmen of London," says: "The earliest notices of the representation in London of 'Punch's moral drama,' as an old comic song calls it, occur in the overseers' books of St. Martin's-in-the-Fields, for 1666 and 1667, in which there are four entries of sums ranging from twenty-two shillings and sixpence to fifty-two shillings and sixpence, as 'Received of Punchinello, yᵉ Italian popet player, for his booth at Charing Cross.'"

Somewhere on this side of Charing Cross, though its actual site is unknown, stood the tavern called the "Rummer," where Prior was found reading "Horace" when a boy. In 1685 it appears to have been kept by one Samuel Prior; and this would tally with what Dr. Johnson tells us in his "Lives of the Poets." Prior is supposed to have fallen, by his father's death, into the hands of his uncle, a vintner near Charing Cross, who sent him for some time to Dr. Busby, at Westminster School; but not intending to give him any education beyond that of the school, took him, when he was well edu-cated in literature, to his own house, where the Earl of Dorset, celebrated for his patronage of genius,

found him by chance (as Burnet relates) reading Horace, and was so well pleased with his profi-ciency that he undertook the care and cost of his academical education. It is well known that all through his life the poet showed a strong propensity for tavern life and pleasures; and Johnson probably is not far from the truth when he adds: "A survey of the life and writings of Prior may exemplify a sentence which he doubtless well understood when he read Horace at his uncle's house. 'The vessel long retains the scent which it first receives;' for in his private relaxation he revived the tavern."

In mean lodgings over a shop close by the en-trance to Spring Gardens, which down to our own times was a saddler's, died the celebrated divine and preacher, Dr. Isaac Barrow, one of the most illus-trious scholars and writers; and his wit has been spoken of by no less an authority than Dr. Johnson, as the "finest thing in the language." We quote an instance of the doctor's ready wit. In meeting the Earl of Rochester one day, the worthy peer exclaimed, "Doctor, I am yours to the shoe-tie;" to which the clergyman replied, "My lord, I am yours to the ground." The peer rejoined, "Doctor, I am yours to the centre." "My lord," retorted the doctor, "I am yours to the antipodes." Deter-mined not to be outdone, his lordship blasphe-mously added, "Doctor, I am yours to the lowest pit of hell;" on which Barrow turned on his heel and said, "And *there*, my lord, I leave you."

There is a tradition mentioned by Pyne, that with the intention of painting the proclamation of George III., Hogarth stood at a window near Charing Cross, making sketches of the yeomen of the guard, the heralds, and the sergeant and trumpeter's band, who had their rendezvous hard by. So, at least, says Mr. Timbs, who accepts the statement as probably true.

This would appear to have been the neighbour-hood in which ingenious devices of new arts and trades abounded even in the Stuart era. Pepys writes, under date February 10, 1668-9:—"To the plaisterer's at Charing Cross, that casts heads and bodies in plaister: and there I had my whole face done; but I was vexed first to be forced to daub all my face over with pomatum. Thus was the mould made; but when it came off there was little pleasure in it as it looks in the mould, nor any resemblance, whatever there will be in the figure when I come to see it cast off."

In 1748 a female dwarf, the "Corsican Fairy," was shown in Cockspur Street, at half-a-crown a head, drawing almost as large levees as "General Tom Thumb" in our own days. In the same year was exhibited, "in a commodious room facing

Cragg's Court," a strange monstrosity, a "double cow." From the work of Mr. Frost, on "Old Showmen," we learn of yet another and still stranger sight exhibited in the same year at the "Heath Cock, at Charing Cross," namely, "a surprising young mermaid, taken on the coast of Aquapulca, which" (says the prospectus), "though the generality of mankind think there is no such thing, has been seen by the curious, who express their

with the "Mews" which adjoined it. It probably derived its name from some association with the Cock-pit at Whitehall, which we have already mentioned. As it now stands it is quite a modern street, having been built towards the close of the last or beginning of the present century.

As the tide of fashion gradually set westwards from Covent Garden, this street became more and more frequented by the wits and critics of *bon ton*;

MILK FAIR, ST. JAMES'S PARK. (*See page* 76.)

utmost satisfaction at so uncommon a creature, being half like a woman and half like a fish, and is allowed to be the greatest curiosity ever exposed to the public view." Here, too, was exhibited O'Brien, the Irish giant, whom we have already mentioned (vol. iii., p. 46); and here he died.

In 1772, and again in 1775 and in 1779, in a large room in Cockspur Street, appeared the conjuror Breslau, whose tricks of legerdemain were interspersed with a vocal and instrumental concert, and imitations by an Italian, named Gaietano, of the notes of the "blackbird, thrush, canary, linnet, bullfinch, skylark, and nightingale."

The origin of the name of Cockspur Street is uncertain; and Mr. Peter Cunningham can suggest no better derivation of it than a fancied connection

and among its most pleasant memories is the name of the "British Coffee House," which was largely frequented by gentlemen from "the north of the Tweed." Its northern connection, kept together by hosts and hostesses from Scotland, is incidentally to be gathered from a letter of Horace Walpole to his friend Sir H. Mann, in which, speaking of some Scottish question pending in the House of Lords, he writes :—"The Duke of Bedford . . . had writ to the sixteen [Scotch representative] peers to solicit their votes; but with so little difference, that he enclosed all their letters under one cover, directed to the 'British Coffee House.'"

Concerning a dinner at this coffee-house, Mr. Cyrus Redding tells a sad story in his "Fifty Years' Reminiscences:"—"While on this short visit to town, the proprietors of the 'Pilot' gave a dinner to some of the officers of the Horse Guards at the 'British Coffee House.' After a sumptuous repast, in the fashion of the time, we sat down to wine. There was present a bustling little man, a Scotch colonel, named Macleod, with his son, a fine young

Mall East stands an equestrian statue of King George III. It is of bronze, between ten and eleven feet high, and stands upon a granite pedestal about twelve feet high. It was executed by Mr. Matthew C. Wyatt, and the cost of its erection amounted to £4,000, the sum being

WARWICK HOUSE, ABOUT 1810. (*See page 82.*)

man, about twenty years old, who sat by me. He was an only son, with a number of sisters. The bottle was pushed hard. The youth partook too freely for one of his years. He was seized with fever and died. The estate entailed went by his death to distant relatives; and his mother and sisters, who would have had to depend on him, were left penniless on the father's demise."

At the junction of Cockspur Street with Pall

defrayed by public subscription. It was set up about the year 1836. Although the likeness of the king is good, the statue is not generally admired, on account of its costume; and the pig-tail at the back of the royal head has often been made the subject of waggish and uncomplimentary remarks. Altogether, it can hardly be said that this statue is calculated to raise the credit of English sculpture in the eyes of foreign visitors.

CHAPTER VIII.

CARLTON HOUSE.

"At domus interior regali splendida luxu
Instruitur."   *Virgil: Æneid.*

Carlton House in the Reign of George II.—A Facetious Remark—The Screen, or Colonnade—The Building described—The Gardens—The Riding House—"Big Sam," the Royal Porter—Carlton House from a Foreigner's Point of View—A Secret Conclave—The Miniature Court of Frederick Prince of Wales—Carlton House occupied by the Princess of Wales—Lord Bute—Carlton House a Focus of Political Faction—How the Marriage of the Prince of Wales and the Princess Caroline was brought about—The Regency of George IV.—Mrs. Fitzherbert—The Reckless Way in which the Princess of Wales would speak of her Unhappy Life—The *Début* of Princess Charlotte—The Prince of Orange and Prince Leopold of Belgium—Death of Princess Charlotte—Life at Carlton House under the Regency—"Romeo" Coates—George Colman, the Younger—"Beau Brummell"—General Arabin—Mike Kelly, the Actor—Death of George III. and Proclamation of the New King—Demolition of Carlton House—Carlton Terrace and its Principal Residents.

As stated in the previous chapter, the north side of the Mall, in St. James's Park, is nearly all occupied by the lofty mansions of Carlton House Terrace. They cover the site of Carlton House, the palace of Frederick, Prince of Wales, father of George III., and subsequently for many years the residence of George IV., when Prince of Wales. The building is mentioned by the author of the "New Critical Review of the Public Buildings" in the reign of George II., as "now belonging to his Royal Highness," meaning Prince Frederick. He describes it as "most delightfully situated for a palace of elegant and costly pleasure," adding, however, that "the building itself is tame and poor," and that "hardly any place is capable of greater improvements, and hardly any place stands in more need of them."

The house was distinguished by a row of pillars in front; whilst York (now Dover) House, Whitehall, the residence of the Prince's brother, the Duke of York, was marked by a circular court, serving as a sort of entry hall, which still remains. These two buildings being described to Lord North, who was blind during the latter period of his life, he facetiously remarked, "Then the Duke of York has been sent, as it would seem, to the *Round-House*, and the Prince of Wales to the *Pillory*." John Timbs attributes this *bon mot* to Sheridan.

The house itself stood opposite what is now Waterloo Place, looking northward, and the forecourt was divided from Pall Mall by a long range of columns, handsome in themselves, but supporting nothing. Hence the once famous lines—

"Care Colonne, qui state qua?
    Non sapiamo in verità:"

thus Anglicised by Prince Hoare—

"Dear little columns, all in a row,
    What *do* you do there?
Indeed we don't know."

Lord North's allusion to these columns, quoted above, was scarcely much more complimentary.

This screen, or colonnade, of single pillars, with the long line of cornice or entablature which rested upon them, formed a disagreeable impediment to the view of the front of the palace. "When I first saw England," writes Thackeray in "The Four Georges," "she was in mourning for the young Princess Charlotte, the hope of the empire. With my childish attendant I remember peeping through the colonnade at Carlton House, and seeing the abode of the Prince Regent. I can yet see the guards pacing before the gates of the palace. What palace? The palace exists no more than the palace of Nebuchadnezzar. It is but a name now."

The façade of the palace consisted of a centre and two wings, rusticated, without pilasters, and an entablature and balustrade which concealed the roof. The portico, by Holland, was of the Corinthian order, consisting of six columns, with details taken from the Temple of Jupiter Stator, in the Forum at Rome. Above this was an enriched frieze, and a tympanum, adorned with the Prince's arms. All the windows were plain and without pediments, except two in the wings.

There were in the building several magnificent apartments, which were fitted up and furnished in the most luxurious manner; and there was also an armoury, said to be the finest in the world. The collection was so extensive as to occupy five rooms, and consisted of specimens of whatever was curious and rare in the arms of every nation, with many choice specimens of ancient armour.

The building was modernised at a vast expense in the year 1788, and in 1815 further alterations were made in the interior. The edifice at this period is thus described in the "Beauties of England and Wales:"—"From the hall, which is exceedingly magnificent, you pass through an octagonal room, richly and tastefully ornamented, conducting to the grand suite of apartments on the one side, and to the great staircase on the other. The latter cannot be seen till you advance close to it, when the most brilliant effect is produced by the magical management of the light.   Opposite the entrance is a flight of twelve steps, thirteen feet long, and on either side of the landing-place at the top of these is another flight of steps of the same length, which takes a circular sweep up to the chamber floor. Underneath is another staircase descending to the lower apartments.   On a level with the first floor are eight divisions, arched over; two of these are occupied by Time pointing to the hours on a dial; and Æolus supporting a map of a circular form, with the points of the compass marked round it. The central division forms the entrance to an ante-room; and the others are adorned with female figures of bronze, in the form of termini, supporting lamps.   The railing is particularly rich, glittering with ornaments of gold, intermixed with bronze heads.   The skylight is embellished with rich painted glass, in panes of circles, lozenges, Prince's plumes, roses, &c."

One of the most splendid apartments in the palace was the crimson drawing-room, in which the Princess Charlotte was married, in 1816, to Prince Leopold of Saxe-Coburg.   This apartment was embellished with the most valuable pictures of the ancient and modern schools, bronzes, ormolu furniture, &c.   The other state apartments on the upper floor were the circular cupola room, of the Ionic order; the throne-room, of the Corinthian order; the splendid ante-chamber; the rose-satin drawing-room, &c., all of which were furnished and embellished with the richest satins, carvings, cutglass, carpetings, &c.   On the lower level, towards the gardens and St. James's Park, were other equally splendid suites of apartments, used by the Court for domestic purposes, and for more familiar parties. These rooms, which were designed by Mr. Nash, consisted of a grand vestibule, of the Corinthian order; the Golden Drawing-room, the Gothic Dining-room, a splendid Gothic Conservatory, and the Library.

The mansion was first erected for Lord Carlton, in 1709, and was bequeathed to his nephew, the Earl of Burlington, from whom it was purchased by Frederick, Prince of Wales, in 1732.   The house in its original state was of red brick, and differed but little from any of the houses of noblemen and gentlemen which surrounded it.   The necessary alterations for the reception of the Prince were at once begun, and the palace was new-fronted with stone.   Flitcroft is said to have drawn for the Prince, in 1734, a plan intended as an improvement on the existing house; and Kent designed a cascade in the same year for the garden, where a saloon was afterwards erected, and paved

with Italian marble brought to England by Lord Bingley and Mr. George Dodington.   The walls were adorned with statuary and paintings, and the chair of state was of crimson velvet embroidered with gold, said to have cost five hundred pounds. Rysbrack sculptured statues of Alfred and Edward the Black Prince, which were placed on marble pedestals in the garden.   The grounds, which extended westward as far as Marlborough House, were in summer a perfect mass of umbrageous foliage; and in them men of the last generation remember to have heard nightingales singing. Indeed, the grove of trees was so tall and so thick, that it contained a rookery so lately as the year 1827.   This fact is commemorated by some amusing verses entitled "The Emigration of the Rooks from Carlton Gardens," published in "Hone's Table Book," in that year.

Adjoining the palace was a Riding House, which, when the palace was demolished, was allowed to stand for some years, and was converted into a storehouse for some of the public records.   It was long known as Carlton Ride.   Its antiquarian contents were subsequently transferred to the great central building in Fetter Lane.

In one of the lodges dwelt " Big Sam," the royal porter to George III. and IV. ; he is said to have stood nearly eight feet high.

The whole of Carlton House was pulled down in 1828, in order to make room for the central opening of Waterloo Place.   Some of the Corinthian columns, which formed the colonnade in front of the house, were used in the portico of the National Gallery, and others were made use of in the chapel at Buckingham Palace.

The author of an amusing " Tour of a Foreigner in England," published in 1825, thus expresses himself (or herself) with respect to Carlton House :— "Though the royal or government palaces are among the most remarkable in London, they serve to show how little the dignity of the sovereign is respected in England in comparison with other countries of Europe.   To say nothing of St. James's Palace (which the present sovereign has not thought fit for his residence) there are in Paris many hotels preferable to Carlton House.   This pretended palace is adorned with a Corinthian portico, the elegance of which, at first glance, pleases the eye, but its columns support nothing except the entablature which unites them.   On one of these pillars an Italian artist chalked the following lines in the name of Pasquin and Marfori :—

> ' Belle colonne che fate la ?
> Io no lo so en verità.' "

The shadowy and extravagant court kept up

here by Frederick, as described by one who knew several of its members, Sir N. W. Wraxall, was not such as to convey a very favourable impression of the good sense of the father of George III. "His court," writes that author, "seems to have been the centre of Cabal, torn by contending candidates for the guidance of his future imaginary reign. The Earl of Egmont and Dodington were avowedly at the head of two great hostile parties. In November, 1749, we find his royal highness, in a secret conclave held at Carlton House, making all the financial dispositions proper to be adopted on the demise of the king his father, and even framing a new Civil List. At the close of these deliberations he binds his three assistants to abide by and support his plans, giving them his hand, and making them take each other's hands as well. The transaction, as related by Dodington, who was himself one of the party, reminds the reader of a similar convocation commemorated by Sallust, and is not unlike one of the scenes in 'Venice Preserved.' It was performed after dinner, however, which may perhaps form its best apology. The diversions of the prince's court appear equally puerile. Three times within thirteen months preceding his decease, Dodington accompanied him and the Princess of Wales to fortune-tellers; the last of which frolics took place scarcely nine weeks before his death. After one of these magical consultations, apparently dictated by anxiety to penetrate his future destiny, the party supped with Mrs. Connor, the Princess's midwife. From Carlton House, too, Frederick used to go disguised to Hockley-in-the-Hole to witness bull-baiting; and either Lord Middlesex or Lord John Sackville was commonly his companion on such expeditions. As far as we are authorised from these premises to form a conclusion, his premature death before he ascended the throne ought not to excite any great national regret."

It was partly at Carlton House that Frederick, Prince of Wales, in the lifetime of his father George II., held his miniature court, and amused himself with sketching out future administrations, in which his friends the Duke of Queensberry, the Earl of Middlesex, "Jack" Spencer, Lord John Sackville, and Francis, Earl of Guildford, were to have their parts. Sir N. W. Wraxall tells us in his "Memoirs" that Lady Archibald Hamilton, the Prince's *chere amie*, resided close to Carlton House, the Prince having allowed her to construct some apartments, the windows of which commanded a view over the gardens of that house, and which, indeed, communicated with the house itself.

Among the guests here in the time of Frederick, Prince of Wales, was Pope, who paid his royal highness very many compliments. "I wonder," said the Prince, "that you, who are so severe on kings, should be so complimentary to me." "Oh, sir," replied the crafty poet, "that is because I like the lion before his claws are full grown."

After the accession of George III. Carlton House was occupied by the Princess of Wales; and hither the young king was accustomed to repair of an evening, and pass the hours with his mother and her special favourite, Lord Bute, the world supposing that the trio formed a sort of interior cabinet, which controlled and directed the ostensible administration. Here, too, the lucky Scotchman whom good fortune, almost in a jest, raised to the premiership, used to pay his mysterious visits to the Princess of Wales—the mother of George III.—in Miss Vansittart's sedan chair, to the great scandal of the entire court.

The extraordinary degree of favour accorded to Lord Bute, and the predilection with which he was known to be regarded by the Princess of Wales, afforded fuel to popular discontent; and the public mind was inflamed by a series of satirical prints, in which her royal highness was held up to odium and reproach, the most odious comparisons being drawn between the Premier and herself and Mortimer and the Queen-Dowager Isabella, of the time of Edward III. The *North Briton* employed the pen of most powerful satire in the same direction.

One of the maids of honour in the establishment of the Princess of Wales at this house was Miss Elizabeth Chudleigh, better known a few years later as the Duchess of Kingston. When reproached for some irregularities by her royal mistress, whose *penchant* for the society of Lord Bute was notorious, she replied, with her usual wit and insolence, "Ah! madame, votre altesse royale sait bien que chacune ici a son *But*."

It is well known that throughout his boyhood and youth, and even in his early manhood, George III. lived a very quiet and secluded life: how quiet and how secluded, may be gathered from Sir N. W. Wraxall's "Memoirs of his Own Time." He writes: "During near ten years which elapsed between the death of his father, early in 1751, and the decease of his grandfather, a period when the human mind is susceptible of such deep impressions, he remained in a state of almost absolute seclusion from his future people, and from the world. Constantly resident at Leicester House or at Carlton House when he was in London; immured at Kew whenever he went to the country; perpetually under the eye of his mother and of Lord Bute, who acted in the choicest unity of design; he saw comparatively few other persons, and those only chosen individuals of both sexes. They naturally obtained, and long preserved, a very firm ascendancy over him. When he ascended the throne, though already arrived at manhood, his very person was hardly known, and his character was still less understood, beyond a narrow circle. Precautions, it is well ascertained, were even adopted by the Princess-dowager to preclude as much as possible access to him, precautions which, to the extent of her ability, were redoubled after he became king. It will scarcely be believed, but it is nevertheless true, that in order to prevent him from conversing with any persons, or receiving written intimations, anonymous or otherwise, between the drawing-room and the door of Carlton House, when he was returning from thence to St. James's or Buckingham House after his evening visits to his mother, she never failed to accompany him till he got into his sedan-chair."

Carlton House, from time to time, proved a focus of political faction. Sir N. W. Wraxall describes with great minuteness the entertainment given here by the Prince of Wales in May, 1784, in honour of the return of Fox for Westminster, after a prolonged and exciting contest in which both parties put forth all their strength. In order to give piquancy to the event, the Prince chose the day after the election, when all the rank, beauty, and talent of the opposition (Whig) party were assembled by invitation on the lawn of his palace for the *fête*, precisely at the time when the King, his father, was proceeding in state down St. James's Park to open the new Parliament. The wall of Carlton Gardens, and that barrier only, formed the separation between them. Then, while the younger part of the company were more actively engaged, there might be contemplated under the shade of the trees an exhibition such as fancy places in the Elysian Fields. . . Lord North, dressed, like every other individual invited, in his new livery of buff and blue, beheld himself surrounded by those very persons who, scarcely fifteen months earlier, affected to regard him as an object of national execration, deserving of capital punishment. Lord Derby and Lord Beauchamp, two noblemen long opposed to each other, Colonel North and George Byng, lately the most inveterate enemies, Fitzpatrick and Adam, depositing their animosities at the Prince's feet, or either at the altar of ambition or interest—were here seen to join in perfect harmony."

A few days afterwards, a second banquet even more magnificent was given by the Prince in the same interest—antagonistic, of course, to his father and his father's ministers—"a banquet," if we may believe the same writer, "prolonged, in defiance of usage and almost of human nature, from the noon of one day to the following morning. Every production," adds the gossiping writer, "that taste and luxury could assemble, was exhausted, the foreign ministers resident in London assisting at the celebration. A splendid banquet was served up to the ladies, on whom, in the spirit of chivalry, his royal highness and the gentlemen present waited while they were seated at table. It must be owned that on these occasions, for which he seemed peculiarly formed, the Prince appeared to great advantage. Louis XIV. himself could scarcely have eclipsed the son of George III. in a ball-room, or when doing the honours of his palace, surrounded by the pomp and attributes of luxury and royal state."

Here, also, in 1789, the Prince used to give dinners on Saturdays and Sundays to the hangers-on of the Whig party, in the hope of confirming them in their allegiance to Fox. The guests were often thirty or forty in number. Sir N. W. Wraxall says, "Wine, promises, and personal attentions were not spared. Governments, regiments, offices, preferments, titles, here held out in prospect, retained the wavering and allured the credulous and discontented; private negotiations were likewise set on foot to gain over supporters to the Government." Here the Prince of Wales, in 1789, received the deputation from the House of Commons, with Pitt at its head, which first offered the Regency to his acceptance.

It is well known that George II. and his eldest son, Frederick, Prince of Wales, during several years previous to the early death of the latter, lived "at daggers drawn" with each other, and without even the veil of decency being drawn before their expressions of mutual dislike. To a certain extent, though not to the same degree, the court of Carlton House under George IV., as Prince of Wales, was maintained in constant hostility to that of the King his father at St. James's and at Kew.

In Mr. T. Raikes's "Journal," we get some insight of the manner in which the unfortunate marriage of the Prince of Wales was brought about. The author, as he tells us, was often in the company of the Duke of Wellington, who talked much about the Royal Family in his time, and on one occasion more especially with reference to the above marriage. "'The marriage,' he said, 'was brought about by Lady ——, who exercised great influence over him: the Prince, who was easily led, imparted his wishes to the King, which were immediately and readily complied with; and as soon as his marriage was accomplished with the Princess Caroline of Brunswick, Lady —— promoted their separation.' I said that this was amply corroborated by what I had lately read in Lord Malmesbury's Papers, who was selected by King George III. to go over to Brunswick, to make the formal proposals and bring the bride over to England. They had a wretched journey home, accompanied by the old Duchess, attempting to go through Holland, and embark at Rotterdam, where the squadron was waiting for them, Queen Caroline on reaching England could not speak a word of English. So Samuel Rogers tells us in his " Diary."

It is impossible at this interval of time to conceive the bitterness with which Queen Caroline was assailed by the Tory press, at the head of which,

GRAND STAIRCASE IN CARLTON HOUSE, 1820. (*See page* 87.)

them, but they were stopped by the French armies, and confined for a long time at a miserable Dutch inn, where they met with so many hardships, that the old Duchess was taken ill, and obliged to return home. Lord M———— and his charge were also forced to beat a retreat, countermand the orders given to the men-of-war, and, after six or seven weeks' miserable adventures, they at last embarked at Embden and arrived in England."

for wit and influence, stood the *John Bull*, with Theodore Hook as its editor. It is with a dash of dry humour that Hook's biographer, in an article in the *Quarterly*, makes these observations :— "There is little to be said in defence of the early virulences of *John Bull* except that they were, we believe without exception, directed against the Queen and her prominent partisans ; and that the Whig leaders, both in Parliament and in society,

FRONT OF CARLTON HOUSE, 1820. (See page 86.)

had, from the commencement of the Regency, countenanced attacks equally malignant on the private life and circle of George IV.—nay, encouraged, in times then freshly remembered, the long series of libels by which the virtues and the afflictions of King George III. were turned into matter of contemptuous sport. The truth is, the Liberals—as they about this period began to style themselves— had shown a fervid desire to domineer in a haughty monopoly of wicked wit : their favourites among the literati almost resented any interference with it as an intolerable invasion of 'vested rights.' The ultimate result of the struggle was, we think, highly beneficial to both parties. In the words of Thomas Moore—

> ' As work like this was unbefitting,
> And flesh and blood no longer bore it,
> The Court of Common Sense then sitting
> Summoned the culprits both before it.'

On either side, when there came coolness enough for measuring the mutual offences and annoyances, all persons of influence seem to have concurred in the determination that such things should no longer be tolerated."

On the meeting of both Houses of Parliament on the 30th of November, 1810, a report of the physicians on the state of the King's health was brought in and laid before the members. The final issue of all the debates which followed was, that the Prince of Wales should be Regent, under certain restrictions ; and that the Queen should have the care of the King's person, her Majesty being assisted by a council. The ceremony of conferring the regency on the Prince was performed at Carlton House with great pomp, on the 5th of February, 1811 ; and in the following June, the Prince Regent gave here a grand supper to 2,000 guests, a stream with gold and silver fish flowing through a marble canal down the central table.

One of the first acts of the Regent, after his being sworn in in due form before the Privy Council, was to receive here the address of the Lord Mayor and Common Council of the City of London on the occasion ; and as he on the same day held a council, all the Ministers of State were present, when it was read in a very solemn manner. The address of the City was partly condoling and partly congratulatory. Among the grievances was specified "the present representation in the Commons House of Parliament, a reform in which was necessary for the safety of the Crown, the happiness of the people, and the independence of the country." To this the Prince Regent returned a kind and dignified answer, assuring the City that he should esteem it as the happiest moment of his life, when he could resign the powers delegated to him into the hands of his sovereign, and that he should always listen to the complaints of those who thought themselves aggrieved.

The household of the Prince Regent here was full of bickerings and quarrels. As a proof of the absurd stress laid by his Royal Highness upon the merest trifles, it may be mentioned that on one occasion the sub-governess of the Princess Charlotte was obliged to resign her situation at Court because her youthful ward, in a freak, had made a childish will in rhyme, leaving her poll parrot to ———, and all her *non*-valuables to Miss Campbell, as residuary legatee. Indeed, it is said by Miss Amelia Murray, in her "Recollections," that the sub-governess was even accused before the Privy Council of treason, for allowing the heiress presumptive to the throne to make a will, even in jest ! It is to be hoped that the authoress is guilty here of a little feminine exaggeration.

The Princess of Wales herself, as is too well known, had anything but happiness in her married life. On one occasion, as we learn from the "Diary of the Times of George IV.," when all her Royal Highness' ladies had been invited by the Prince Regent to a *fête*, from which she herself was excluded, she presented each of them with a very handsome dress ; and to one her Royal Highness wrote : " Dear ———, pray do me de favour to accept and wear de accompanying gown ; and when you are in de ball at Carlton House, tink of me, and wish me well. For ever your affectionate, C. R."

If the Prince ever really cared for any woman, it was for Mrs. Fitzherbert. After his accession to the throne, and the trial of Queen Caroline, he shut himself up almost wholly from the public gaze, and lived chiefly within the walls of Carlton House, his table being presided over by the beautiful Marchioness of Conyngham, whose brilliant wit, according to his Majesty's estimate, surpassed that of all his friends, male or female.

The Princess of Wales always spoke highly of Mrs. Fitzherbert ; she would say :—" That is the Prince's true wife ; she is an excellent woman ; it is a great pity for him he ever broke vid her. Do you know, I know de man who was present at his marriage, the late Lord Bradford. He declared to a friend of mine, that when he went to inform Mrs. Fitzherbert that the Prince had married me, she would not believe it, for she knew she was herself married to him."

The author of " Memories of the Times of George IV." mentions several instances of the unguarded and reckless way in which the Princess would speak of the situation in which she was then placed, and also of her previous life. She would dwell, in conversation with her friends, on the drunken habits of her husband, which were then notorious to the world. How he spent the first night of his marriage in a state of intoxication is known by all the readers of the "Memories" above mentioned, the author of which says that after the birth of the Princess Charlotte, the unhappy lady received through Lord Cholmondeley a message to the effect that in future the Prince and she would occupy separate establishments. "Poor Princess!" continues the writer, "she was an ill-treated woman, but a very wrong-headed one. Had she remained quietly at Carlton House, and conducted herself with silent dignity, how different might have been her lot. It is true, as her Privy Purse, Miss Hamilton, once told a person of my acquaintance, she was so insulted whilst there, that every bit of furniture was taken out of the room she dined in, except two shabby chairs; and the pearl bracelets, which had been given her by the Prince, were taken from her to decorate the arms of Lady Jersey. Still, had the Princess had the courage which arises from principle, and not that which is merely the offspring of a daring spirit, she would have sat out the storm, and weathered it."

For the following description of the *début* of the Princess Charlotte at Carlton House in the year 1813, we are indebted to Captain Gronow, who was present as a guest. He writes: "At the period to which I refer, Carlton House was the centre of all the great politicians and wits who were friends of the Prince Regent. The principal entrance of the palace in Pall Mall, with its screen of columns, will be remembered by many. In the rear of the mansion was an extensive garden that reached from Warwick Street to Marlborough House; green sward, stately trees (probably two hundred years old), and beds of the choicest flowers, gave to the grounds a picturesque attraction perhaps unequalled. It was here that the heir to the throne of England gave, in 1813, an open-air *fête*, in honour of the battle of Vittoria. About three o'clock p.m. the *élite* of London society, who had been honoured with invitations, began to arrive— all in full dress; the ladies particularly displaying their diamonds and pearls, as if they were going to a drawing-room. The men were, of course, in full dress, wearing knee-buckles. The regal circle was composed of the Queen, the Regent, the Princesses Sophia and Mary, the Princess Charlotte, the Dukes of York, Clarence, Cumberland, and Cambridge.

"This was the first day that her Royal Highness the Princess Charlotte appeared in public. She was a young lady of more than ordinary personal attractions; her features were regular, and her complexion fair, with the rich bloom of youthful beauty; her eyes were blue and very expressive, and her hair was abundant, and of that peculiar light brown which merges into the golden; in fact, such hair as the middle-age Italian painters associate with their conceptions of the Madonna. In figure her royal highness was somewhat over the ordinary height of women, but finely proportioned and well developed. Her manners were remarkable for a simplicity and good-nature which would have won admiration and invited affection in the most humble walks of life. She created universal admiration, and I may say a feeling of national pride, amongst all who attended the ball. The Prince Regent entered the gardens giving his arm to the Queen, the rest of the royal family following. Tents had been erected in various parts of the grounds, where the bands of the Guards were stationed. The weather was magnificent, a circumstance which contributed to show off the admirable arrangements of Sir Benjamin Bloomfield, to whom had been deputed the organisation of the *fête*, which commenced by dancing on the lawn.

"The Princess Charlotte honoured with her presence two dances. In the first she accepted the hand of the late Duke of Devonshire, and in the second that of the Earl of Aboyne, who had danced with Marie Antoinette, and who, as Lord Huntly, lived long enough to dance with Queen Victoria. The Princess entered so much into the spirit of the *fête* as to ask for the new fashionable Scotch dances. The Prince was dressed in the Windsor uniform, and wore the garter and star. He made himself very amiable, and conversed much with the Ladies Hertford, Cholmondeley, and Montfort. Altogether, the *fête* was a very memorable event."

Lady Clementina Davies writes in her "Recollections of Society:"—"The Princess Charlotte was treated by all parties as the brightest hope of England. When she made her *début* at Carlton House a brilliant circle attended. The Queen, the Regent, the Princesses, and the four Royal Dukes, were there, but all eyes were engrossed by the royal girl."

The Princess could not well help resenting the affronts offered to her mother. Indeed, as a child, and throughout her girlhood, she had a most difficult part to play, for, as she often used to say, "if she showed affection or respect for one of her parents, she tacitly blamed the other, and, of course, was blamed in return."

It has often been asked what induced the Princess Charlotte so suddenly to give his *congé* to the Prince of Orange, and suddenly to accept Prince Leopold of Saxe-Coburg in his stead. The Hon. Amelia Murray in her "Recollections," writing of the visit of the Allied Sovereigns in 1814, thus solves the mystery :—"The Prince of Orange was not particularly attractive ; Prince Leopold, on the contrary, was a handsome young man, though not then specially noticed ; but very soon it was discovered that the Princess Charlotte preferred him to her former lover. Small blame to the young Princess ! but I have strong reason to believe that it was through a Russian intrigue that she had been thrown in the way of the handsomest prince in Germany, and that the Grand Duchess of Russia came here for the purpose of disgusting the Princess of England with her intended husband. It did not suit Russian views that England and Holland should be so closely connected. The Grand Duchess of Oldenburg came to this country, I verily believe, for the purpose of ' putting a spoke into that wheel.' She took an hotel in Piccadilly ; she earnestly sought the acquaintance of Miss Elphinstone, who was known to be on intimate terms with the Princess. She gave grand dinners, and took care to invite the Prince of Orange on the night when he was to waltz in public with the Princess as her *fiancé*. The Grand Duchess plied him well with champagne, and a young man could hardly refuse the invitations of his hostess. In fact, he was made tipsy, and the Princess was disgusted. Then, in Miss Elphinstone's apartments, the charming Prince Leopold was presented. Was it to be wondered at that a girl of seventeen should prefer him to the former lover? The Prince of Orange accordingly was speedily dismissed, and in due time he married the Duchess of Oldenburg's sister. This intrigue accounts for all that happened subsequently."

The story of the engagement of the Princess Charlotte to Prince Leopold of Saxe-Coburg is told, however, somewhat differently in the gossiping pages of Captain Gronow's "Anecdotes and Reminiscences." He writes : "The Duke of York said one day to his royal niece, ' Tell me, my dear, have you seen any one among the foreign princes whom you would like to have for a husband ?' The Princess replied, with much *naïveté*, that she was most agreeably struck with Prince Leopold of Coburg. She had heard of his bravery in the field, and especially of his famous charge in the battle of Leipsic, for which he was rewarded by the Order of Maria Theresa. In a few months afterwards she became the wife of the man whom she so

much admired, and from whom she was so soon afterwards torn away by the hand of death." It will be remembered that she died in childbirth having given birth to a dead infant. Her death was felt as a blow by the whole nation. Miss Amelia Murray, who held a post at Court, and may be supposed to have been well informed on such subjects, does not hesitate to express her opinion that "the Princess Charlotte was starved to death," her medical attendant, Sir Richard Croft, having forbidden her to eat meat so as to keep up her strength. Sir Richard was so much affected by the calamity that he committed suicide shortly afterwards.

It was wittily said of those who were admitted in former days to the circle of Carlton House, that they learnt there the value of being good listeners, or else afterwards came to lament the want of that qualification. Hear what you like, but say as little as possible, was the rule with that gay and heartless coterie who gathered round the Prince Regent in those gilded *salons*.

Cyrus Redding wrote in the *Times* a witty " Dialogue between Carlton House and Brandenburg House," which caused a sensation in town.

The following is an extract from a letter dated February 23rd, 1812 :—" The Prince Regent went yesterday in grand state to the Chapel Royal—the first time of his appearance as virtual sovereign. As he proceeded from Carlton House to St. James's surrounded by all his pomp, &c., not a single huzza from the crowd assembled to behold him ! Not a hat off ! Of this I was assured by a gentleman present, on whom I can depend."

Of the Prince Regent himself, who so long held his court here, Captain Gronow, who was much behind the scenes, has but little that is favourable to say. According to the Captain's anecdotes, the Prince, so far from being "the first gentleman in Europe," was " singularly imbued with a petty and vulgar pride. He would rather be amiable and familiar with his tailor than agreeable and friendly with the most illustrious of the aristocracy of the kingdom ; and would rather joke with ' Beau ' Brummell than admit to his confidence a Howard or a Somerset. And yet he took good care always to show good manners in public. His misfortune was his marriage with a most unattractive and almost repulsive woman, Caroline of Brunswick ; and his debts were at the bottom of his ill-starred union. He sold himself, in fact, for a million sterling."

Sir N. W. Wraxall tells a good anecdote about Lord Carhampton, who, as Colonel Luttrell, had contested the representation of Middlesex against

John Wilkes:—"In 1812, soon after the restrictions imposed by Parliament on the Prince Regent were withdrawn, Lord Carhampton was lying in an apparently hopeless state at his house near Berkeley Square, whence premature intelligence of his death was carried by some officious person to Carlton House. The Prince, who was at dinner at the time, immediately gave away his regiment, the Carabineers, to a general officer present, who actually 'kissed hands' on his appointment. No sooner did the report reach Lord Carhampton next day, than he dispatched a friend to Pall Mall with a message for the Prince, informing his Royal Highness that he was still happily in the land of the living, and humbly entreating him to dispose of any other regiment in the service except the Carabineers. Lord Carhampton, with much humour, added, that the Prince might rest assured that, in case of his own death, he would give special directions to his servants to lose not a moment, when he was really no more, in notifying the fact at Carlton House. The Prince very much enjoyed the joke, and Lord Carhampton got well enough to laugh at it in his company."

Another story is told of one of Theodore Hook's hoaxes, the scene of which was Carlton House under the Regency. On the 17th of June, the Prince gave here a *fête* of "surpassing magnificence." "Romeo" Coates was at this time in all his glory—murdering Shakespeare at the Haymarket, and driving his bright-pink cockle-shell, with the life-like chanticleers in gilt traps, about the parks and the streets of the West-end. Hook, who could imitate almost any and every handwriting, contrived to get into his possession one of the Chamberlain's tickets for this *fête*, and produced a fac-simile commanding the presence of Signor Romeo at Carlton House. He next equipped himself in a gorgeous uniform of scarlet, and delivered in person the flattering missive at Mr. Coates's door. The delight of Romeo must be imagined. "Hook," says one of his biographers, "was in attendance when the time for his sallying forth arrived, and had the satisfaction of seeing him swing into his chariot, bedizened in all his finery, with a diamond-hilted sword and the air of Louis le Grand. Theodore was also at the front entrance of Carlton House when the amateur's vehicle reached its point. He saw him mount up the broad steps and enter the vestibule. The stranger passed in without remark or question; but when he had to show his ticket to the Private Secretary, that eye caught the imposture. Mr. Coates was politely informed that a mistake had occurred, and had to retrace his course to the portico. The

blazoned chariot had driven off; in wrath and confusion he must pick his steps as he might to the first stand of hackney-coaches. Hook was at his elbow well muffled up. No such discomfiture since the Knight of the Woeful Countenance was unhorsed by the Bachelor Sampson Carrasco. We must not omit that the Prince, when aware of what had occurred, signified his extreme regret that any one of his household should have detected the trick, or acted on its detection. Mr. Coates was, as he said, an inoffensive gentleman, and his presence might have amused many of the guests, and could have done harm to no one. His Royal Highness sent his secretary next morning to apologise in person, and to signify that as the arrangements and ornaments were still entire, he hoped Mr. Coates would come and look at them. And Romeo went. In this performance Hook had no confidant. To do him justice, we believe he never told the story without some signs of compunction."

One day, at a party at Carlton House, the Prince Regent gaily observed that there were present two "Georges the Younger," alluding to himself and George Colman, Junior, but that he should like to know which was "George the Youngest." "Oh!" replied Colman, with a happy sally of wit, "I could never, sir, have had the rudeness to come into the world before your Royal Highness." The Prince was highly amused, and never forgot the joke or its author.

In April, 1814, as we learn from Allen's "History of London," "when Marshal Blucher arrived at Carlton House, all attempts to keep the populace out of the court-yard were in vain: the two sentinels at the gate, with their muskets, were laid on the ground; and the porter was overpowered. To indulge the public, the doors of the great hall were thrown open on the occasion; and here the first interview of the General with the Prince Regent took place."

One of the most constant frequenters of Carlton House in the days of George Prince of Wales was George Brummell, or "Beau Brummell," as he was known to his friends, and is still known to history. He was born in 1777, and sent to Eton, where he enjoyed the credit of being the best scholar, the best oarsman, and the best cricketer of his day. His father was under-secretary to Lord North, and is said to have left to each of his children some £30,000. Whilst at Eton, he made plenty of aristocratical friends; and being regarded as a sort of "Admirable Crichton," obtained the *entrée* to the circle of Devonshire House, where the Duchess of Devonshire introduced him to the Prince Regent, who gave him a commission in the 10th Hussars.

When he left the army he lived in Chesterfield Street, where he often had the Prince to sup with him in private. Notwithstanding the great disparity of rank, the intimacy continued for several years. He spent his days mainly at Brighton and at Carlton House, keeping a well-appointed resi-

bidden to approach the royal presence. Even this, however, blew over, and having been lucky enough to win a large sum at cards, he was once more invited to Carlton House. Here, in joy at meeting once more with his old friend, the Prince, he took too much wine. The Prince said quietly

OLD CARLTON HOUSE, 1709. (*See page* 87.)

dence in town, and belonging to "White's" and other clubs, where high play prevailed. His canes, his snuff-boxes, his dogs, his horses and carriage, each and all were of the first class, and distinguished for taste ; and the cut of his dress set the fashion to West-end tailors, who vied with each other in their efforts to secure his patronage. After a few years, however, a coolness sprang up between him and the Prince, as he espoused the cause of Mrs. Fitzherbert, and finally, the mirror of fashion was for-

to his brother, the Duke of York, "I think we had better order Mr. Brummell's carriage before he gets quite drunk," so he left the palace never to return. It is said by Captain Gronow, that in treating his guest thus, the Regent merely retaliated on him for an insult which he had received from him a year or two before at Lady Cholmondeley's ball, when the "Beau," turning to her ladyship, and pointing to the Prince, inquired, "And pray who is your fat friend?" Another version of the rupture between the Prince and "Beau" Brummell is, that one day he risked some freedom of speech to his royal patron, to whom he is reported to have said, "George, ring the bell!" This he always denied; but it is certain that whatever his words were, they never were forgotten or forgiven by the Prince. Every one knows Brummell's subsequent career and fate. For a few

Late in life he "cut" the Prince, like George Brummell, and revenged himself by writing a volume of scurrilous memoirs of Carlton House and its inmates. The book is mentioned by Cyrus Redding as in MS., and we do not think it has ever yet seen the light.

Then there was a man named Lade, who, from having had the management of the royal stables,

BEAU BRUMMELL. *From a Miniature by John Cooke in Jesse's "Life of Brummell."* (*See page* 95.)

years he was a hanger-on at Oatlands, the seat of the Duke and Duchess of York; then, having lost large sums at play, was obliged to fly the country, and, having lived in obscurity for some years at Calais, obtained the post of British Consul at Caen, where he died, in anything but affluent circumstances, in 1840—another proof, if any proof be needed, of the precarious existence of those who live by basking in the sunshine of royalty.

Another of the friends and companions of the Prince Regent was General Arabin, the writer of witty prologues and epilogues for lords and ladies.

and having married a very pretty wife, formerly a cook in the royal establishment, received the honour of knighthood from the Prince Regent. Sir John Lade's ambition, however, even after he became a "Knight Batchelor," was to imitate the groom in dress and in language. "I once heard him," writes Mr. Raikes in his "Journal," "asking a friend on Egham racecourse to come home and dine. 'I can give you a trout spotted all over like a coach-dog, a fillet of veal as white as *alablaster* (*sic*), a pantaloon cutlet, and plenty of pancakes.' It was then the fashion to drive a phaeton and four-in-hand. The Prince of Wales used to drive a phaeton and six as more magnificent. . . . As a boy, I have often seen the Prince driving round and round the park in this equipage, followed by a dozen others of the same description, including Lord Sefton, Lord Barrymore, and other notorious 'whips.'"

Tommy Moore was a constant guest here, under George IV., who, as Regent and as King, "played the cheap and easy part of Polycrates to the Irish Anacreon." Some of our readers will not have forgotten Moore's whimsical description of the Prince Regent's breakfast-room at Carlton House during the London season :—

> "Methought the Prince in whisker'd state
> Before me at his breakfast sate ;
> On one side lay unread petitions,
> On t'other hints from five physicians ;
> Here tradesmen's bills, official papers,
> Notes from ' my lady,' drams for vapours ;
> There plans for saddles, tea and toast,
> Death-warrants, and—the *Morning Post*."

Mike Kelly, the Irish comedian, was another frequent visitor here, and of him Cyrus Redding, in his " Recollections," tells us many anecdotes :— " Kelly was a good after-dinner man. He told many stories of the characters of his time, and of the ' Prince, God bless him ! ' to use his own words in relation to George IV. All the boon companions of the Prince were friends of Kelly's. After the ' true prince,' Sheridan was Kelly's hero. The veteran composer spoke of one tainted in appearance from such a connection during his life's prime. He looked flaccid from past indulgences. The best of those, high or low, who had come within the influence of the same circle, exhibited similar resemblances to half-worn rakes."

When Dr. Parr dined at Carlton House by royal command, the Prince Regent most good-naturedly allowed him to sit after dinner and quietly smoke his pipe.

The likeness so often drawn between the Regent in his youth to the Hal of Shakespeare, and the similar change of conduct with that Prince when he came to the throne, and which is made an excuse for every caprice of humour and every change of system, has told the tale long ago of an heir-apparent and a crowned monarch. There was, however, nothing new in the conduct of the Prince Regent: all princes who scorn their father's ministers and measures during their minority, generally adopt both when they come to reign.

It was whilst residing here, in 1780—soon after attaining the dignity of a separate royal household —that the Prince of Wales became passionately attached to Mrs. Mary Robinson, the popular actress, better known by her name of " Perdita." In vain did George III. remonstrate with his son upon his infatuation. The Prince appeared in public with the lovely " Perdita" by his side ; and the assumed name of " Florizel," under which royalty sought her plebeian hand, became known to, and was commented on, by the fashionable world without any reserve. It was only a more honourable love for Mrs. Fitzherbert, which dated from the following year, that induced the then heir-apparent to the British throne to give up the most foolish of semi-romantic unions by which a royal personage was ever entangled. " Florizel," in due course, became king ; but " poor Perdita" died in debt and broken-hearted less than twenty years afterwards, and lies at rest in the parish churchyard of Old Windsor, where she had spent the last few years of her life.

At Carlton House the Prince was privately married, on the 21st of December, 1785, by a clergyman of the Established Church, to Mrs. Fitzherbert, a Roman Catholic lady of high family and connections —just a week after writing a letter to Charles James Fox, denying the truth of a rumour to the effect that he had contracted a morganatic marriage.

On the 29th of January, 1820, the venerable King, George III., died at Windsor Castle; and on the following morning, in pursuance of established usage, the cabinet ministers assembled at Carlton House, and here George IV. held his first court. This was numerously and brilliantly attended by all ranks and parties, who eagerly offered their homage to the new king ; the re-appointment of the Lord Chancellor, and several ministers, was the first exercise of sovereign power, the oaths of allegiance being administered to those present. A council was, in compliance with the royal ordinance, immediately holden ; and all the late king's privy councillors then in attendance were sworn as members of the new council, and took their seats at the board accordingly.

The proclamation of the new king took place publicly in the metropolis, on Monday, January 31st. The first proclamation was made on the steps of Carlton House, in the presence of his Majesty, his royal brothers, and the principal officers of state. The procession then formed in the following order, and proceeded to Charing Cross :—Farriers of the Life Guards with their axes erect ; French horns of the troop ; troop of Life Guards ; the beadles of the different parishes in their long cloaks ; constables ; two knights marshals' officers ; knight marshal and his men ; household drums ; kettle drums ; trumpets ; the pursuivants ; Blue Mantle ;

Rouge Croix; Rouge Dragon and Portcullis; the Kings of Arms in their tabards and collars; Garter, Sir I. Heard, knt., supported by two sergeants at arms, with their maces; Clarencieux and Norroy; heralds in their full dress; the procession being concluded by a troop of Life Guards.

On arriving at Charing Cross, the proclamation was again read, and the procession proceeded to Temple Bar, where the usual formalities of closing the gates, and admitting one of the heralds to shew his authority, having been gone through, the cavalcade entered the City, and were joined by the Lord Mayor, sheriffs, and several of the aldermen; the proclamation was read at the end of Chancery Lane, at the end of Wood Street, Cheapside, and at the Royal Exchange, when the heralds and the military returned.

In the year 1828, as above stated, Carlton House was demolished; much of the ornamental interior details—such as marble mantelpieces, friezes, and columns—being transferred to Buckingham Palace. Upon the site of the gardens have been erected the York Column and Carlton House Terrace; the balustrades of the latter originally extended between the two ranges of houses, but were removed to form the present entrance to St. James's Park, by command of William IV., soon after his accession to the throne. Upon the site of the court-yard and part of Carlton House are the United Service and the Athenæum Club-houses, and on the east side of the intervening area facing Waterloo Place, have been set up, on granite pedestals, bronze statues of Field-Marshal Lord Clyde, the hero of the Punjab and Lucknow, who died in 1863, and of Lord Lawrence, some time Viceroy of India. The latter statue was erected in 1882. On the west side of the area is a statue, also of bronze, of Sir John Franklin, the Arctic navigator; the pedestal is ornamented with bas-reliefs of scenes in the Arctic regions.

The house in Carlton House Terrace next but one eastward from the Duke of York's Column was the residence of Mr. Gladstone for some years before and during his premiership, in 1868-74. Curiously enough, it was occupied for a time, some thirty years earlier, by another Prime Minister, the late Earl of Derby, then Lord Stanley. A curious and interesting anecdote is told concerning this house by Mr. Forster in his "Life of Charles Dickens." He writes :—"The story is, that Lord Derby, when Mr. Stanley, had on some important occasion made a speech which all the reporters found it necessary greatly to abridge; that its

essential points had, nevertheless, been so well given in the *Chronicle* that Mr. Stanley, having need of it for himself in greater detail, had sent a request to the reporter to meet him in Carlton House Terrace and take down the entire speech; that Dickens attended and did the work accordingly, much to Mr. Stanley's satisfaction; and that, on his dining with Mr. Gladstone in recent years, and finding the aspect of the dining-room strangely familiar, he discovered afterwards, on inquiry, that it was there he had taken the speech. The story, as it actually occurred, is connected with the brief life of the 'Mirror of Parliament.' It was not at any special desire of Mr. Stanley's, but for that new record of debates, which had been started by one of the uncles of Dickens, and professed to excel 'Hansard' in giving verbatim reports, that the famous speech against O'Connell was taken as described. The young reporter went to the room in Carlton Terrace because the work of his uncle Barrow's publication required to be done there; and if, in later years," adds Mr. Forster, "the great author was in the same room as the guest of the Prime Minister, it must have been but a month or two before he died, when, for the first time, he visited and breakfasted with Mr. Gladstone."

The house No. 9 has been for some years the official residence of the German Ambassador, and here, in 1873, died Count Bernstorff. At No. 14, Lord Lonsdale's, is a very fine collection of old furniture of various styles and dates, with a profusion of Sèvres china, among which is the splendid service given by Louis XV. to the Empress Catharine. At No. 1, Mr. George Tomline has a fine gallery of paintings, including some Murillos. No. 18, the last on the southern side, was the Duke of Hamilton's; but its contents were sold off under the auctioneer's hammer in 1870, and the house afterwards occupied by Earl Granville.

In 1840 the Prince Louis Napoleon (afterwards Emperor of the French) was living here, in the house of Lord Ripon, No. 1, in Carlton Gardens. This mansion accordingly became the centre of preparations for his famous descent upon Boulogne in the August of that year—an abortive attempt to revive the "Napoleonic Idea" in France, which led to the Prince's imprisonment in the fortress of Ham. It is said, indeed, by Mr. B. Jerrold, in his "Life of the Emperor," that in this house the Prince and his friends amused themselves with coining military buttons for a "regiment of the future."

CHAPTER IX.

ST. JAMES'S PALACE.

"The home and haunt of kings."—Spenser.

A Hospital for Leprous Women—The Structure demolished by Henry VIII., and the Palace built—The Gate-house, and Vicissitudes of the Clock—The Colour Court, and Proclamation of Queen Victoria—The Chapel Royal—Perseverance of George III. in his attendance at Chapel—Doing the "Civil Thing"—Royal Marriages—The Gentlemen and Children of the Chapel Royal—"Spur-money"—The "Establishment" of the Chapel Royal—The Chair Court and the State Apartments—The Yeomen of the Guard—The Chapel of Queen Catharine of Braganza, and Pepys' Visit there—The Lutheran Chapel—The Ambassadors' Court—The Royal Library—Office of the Lord Chamberlain's Department—Clarence House—Charles Dartineuf and his Partiality for Ham-pie—Historical Reminiscences of St. James's Palace—Marie de Medicis and her Miniature Court—Charles I. and his last parting from his Children—King Charles II. and Dr. South—La Belle Stewart, afterwards Duchess of Richmond—Dissolute Hangers-on about the Court—Court Balls of the Time of Charles II.—Marriage of William Prince of Orange—Mary Beatrice of Modena and her Court—Morality of the Court under the Georges—Death-bed Scene of Queen Caroline—Strange Conduct of an Irish Nobleman—The Palace partially destroyed by Fire—The Duke of Cumberland and his Italian Valet.

SOME quarter of a mile to the westward of Charing Cross, there stood, in very early times, a hospital for leprous women : it was a religious foundation, and was dedicated to St. James the Less, Bishop of Jerusalem.

St. James's Palace now occupies the site of the above-mentioned hospital, showing what changes a place may undergo by the operation of the whirligig of time. The endowment of the hospital was for women only, "maidens that were leprous" being the sole objects of the charity. Eight "brethren," however, were attached to the house, in order to solemnise the religious services, and to discharge the "cure of souls."

According to Stow, the house had appended to it "two hides of land," with the usual "appurtenances," in the parish of St. Margaret, Westminster; "it was founded," he goes on to say, "by the citizens of London, before the time of man's memory, for fourteen sisters, maidens, that were lepers, living chastely and honestly in divine service. Afterwards," Stow continues, "divers citizens of London gave six-and-fifty pounds rents thereto. . . . . After this, sundry devout men of London gave to the hospital four hides of land in the fields of Westminster, and in Hendon, Chalcote, and Hampstead, eight acres of land and wood."

King Edward I. confirmed these gifts to the hospital, granting to its inmates also the privilege and profits of a fair "to be kept on the eve of St. James, the day and the morrow, and four days following;" "and this," says Mr. Newton, "was the origin of the once famous 'May Fair,' held in the fields near Piccadilly."

Henry VIII., however, set his covetous eyes on the place ; and seeing that it was fair to view, while the sisters were defenceless, he resolved to possess himself of it, much as Ahab resolved to become master of Naboth's vineyard. He pulled down the old structure, "and there," as Holinshed tells us, "made a faire parke for his greater comoditie and

pleasure;" and also erected a stately mansion, or, as Stow denominates it, "a goodly manor." This was in the year of his marriage with Anne Boleyn, when he had every motive for wishing to break off with the ancient faith.

St. James's was at that time more of a country seat than would now be supposed ; indeed, more than had been any of the other residences of our sovereigns near London, except Kennington. The latter was now abandoned ; the sovereign came to dwell on the Middlesex instead of on the Surrey side of the Thames ; and St. James's, no doubt, was intended by the fickle-minded monarch to take its place. It stood in the middle of fields, well shaded with trees ; and these fields, now the park, were enclosed as the private demesne of the palace. Incredible as it may now seem, they were then well stocked with game. The king lost no time in surrounding himself here with all the appliances for amusement, and there were both a cock-pit and a tilt-yard in front of Whitehall, nearly on the site of the present Horse Guards, as we have stated in a previous chapter.

From the gates of St. James's Palace, Miss Benger tells us, in her "Life of Anne Boleyn," Henry VIII. delighted, on May morning, to ride forth at daybreak, having risen with the lark, and with a train of courtiers all gaily attired in white and silver, to make his way into the woods about Kensington and Hampstead, whence he brought back the fragrant May boughs in triumph.

"The gateway, a part of which now forms the Royal Chapel, and the chimney-piece of the old presence chamber," says Mr. A. Wood, "are all that remain of the palace erected by Henry. The last bears on its walls the initials of Henry and Anne," twined, as he might have added, in that love-knot of which he was then so fond, but which he severed by the axe in four short years afterwards.

Henry, even whilst residing here, held his court still at the old palace, first at Westminster, and then at Whitehall, after he had taken the latter from Wolsey, thus curiously anticipating the present day, when St. James's Palace is "our Court of St. James's," and contains the Throne Room and other state apartments, though it is no longer the residence of the sovereign.

Henry's gatehouse and turrets, built of red brick, face St. James's Street, and with the Chapel Royal, which adjoins them on the west side, cover the site of the ancient hospital, which, to judge from the many remains of stone mullions, labels, and other masonry found in 1838, on taking down some parts of the Chapel Royal, was of the Norman period. The lofty brick gatehouse bears upon its roof the bell of the great clock, dated A.D. 1731, and inscribed with the name of Clay, clockmaker to George II. The clock originally had but one hand. When the gatehouse was repaired, in 1831, the clock was removed, and was not put up again on account of the roof being reported unsafe to carry the weight. The inhabitants of the neighbourhood then memorialised the king (William IV. for the replacement of the time-keeper, when his Majesty, having ascertained its weight, "shrewdly inquired how, if the palace roof was not strong enough to carry the clock, it was safe for the number of persons occasionally seen upon it to witness processions, &c." The clock was forthwith replaced, and a minute-hand was added, with new dials; the original dial was of wainscot, "in a great number of very small pieces, curiously dovetailed together."

The archway of the gatehouse leads into the quadrangle, or "Colour Court," as it is usually called, from the colours of the military guard of honour being placed there. Here, according to ancient practice, a regiment of the sovereign's "foot-guards" parade daily at eleven a.m., accompanied by their band, for the purpose of exchanging the regimental standard, and handing over the keys of the palace to the incoming commandant. Here each new sovereign is formally proclaimed on his (or her) accession to the throne. It was on the 21st of June, 1837, that Her Majesty Queen Victoria was proclaimed "Queen of the United Kingdoms of Great Britain and Ireland, Defender of the Faith." Soon after nine in the morning a troop of the 1st Life Guards drew up in line across the quadrangle, and at ten the youthful sovereign made her appearance at the opened window of the Tapestry Room, where she was so overcome by the affecting scene—the exclamations of joy and clapping of hands, the waving of hats and handkerchiefs—in conjunction with the eventful occurrences of the preceding day, that she instantly

burst into tears; and, says an eye-witness, "notwithstanding her earnest endeavours to restrain them, they continued to flow in torrents down her now pallid cheeks until she retired from the window; Her Majesty, nevertheless, curtsied many times in acknowledgment of her grateful sense of the devotion of her people." Meanwhile the heralds and pursuivants, dismounted and uncovered, had taken up their accustomed position immediately beneath the window at which the Queen was standing; and silence being obtained, Clarencieux King of Arms, Sir William Woods, in the absence of Garter King at Arms, read the Proclamation, which had been issued at Kensington Palace on the preceding day. At its conclusion, Sir William gave the signal by waving his sceptre, and loud and enthusiastic cheering followed, which Her Majesty graciously and frequently acknowledged. A flourish of trumpets was then blown, and the Park and Tower guns fired a salute in token that the ceremony of proclamation had been accomplished.

On the west side of the great gateway is the Chapel Royal. It is oblong in plan, and plain, and has nothing about it to call for particular mention, excepting, perhaps, the ceiling, which is divided into small painted squares, the design of which was executed by Hans Holbein. The Royal Gallery is at the west end, opposite the communion-table. In this chapel there is a choral service on Sundays, at twelve o'clock, which is largely attended by the aristocracy when in town for the London season. The Duke of Wellington, during the last twenty or thirty years of his life, was a constant attendant. Entrance is to be obtained, we fear it must be added, most effectively by aid of a silver key.

George III., when in town, used to attend the services in this chapel, a nobleman carrying the sword of state before him, and heralds, pursuivants-at-arms, and other officers walking in the procession. So persevering was his Majesty's attendance at prayers, that Madame d'Arblay, one of the robing-women, tells us "the Queen and family, dropping off one by one, used to leave the King, the parson, and his Majesty's equerry to freeze it out together."

It is to be feared that not all the frequenters of the Chapel Royal come to attend its services with very devout hearts, if the following story, amusingly told by Mr. Raikes, may be taken as a specimen of the body at large :—"One Sunday morning the Dowager Duchess of Richmond went with her daughter to the Chapel Royal at St. James's, but being late they could find no places.

After looking about some time, and seeing the case was hopeless, she said to her daughter, 'Come away, Louisa; at any rate, we have done the *civil* thing.'" This was completely realising the idea of the *card-leaving* dowager of her day.

Here were married Prince George of Denmark

the 10th of February, 1840, when was celebrated the marriage of Her Majesty Queen Victoria and Prince Albert. The ceremony was performed by the Archbishop of Canterbury, assisted by the Archbishop of York and the Bishop of London, the latter officiating as Dean of the Chapel Royal.

CHAPEL ROYAL, ST. JAMES'S. (*See page* 101.)

and the Princess Anne; Frederick Prince of Wales and the daughter of the Duke of Saxe-Coburg; George IV. and Queen Caroline; Queen Victoria and Prince Albert; and the Princess Royal and the Crown Prince of Germany. Before the building of the chapel at Buckingham Palace, Her Majesty and the Court used to attend the service here.

Upon no occasion, perhaps, did the chapel present a gayer appearance than on the morning of

The Duke of Sussex "gave away" his royal niece, and at that part of the service where the archbishop read the words, "I pronounce that they be man and wife together," the Park and Tower guns were fired. When the wedding ring was put by Prince Albert on the Queen's finger, we are told, Lord Uxbridge, as Lord Chamberlain, gave a signal, and the bells of Westminster rung a merry peal. The fittings of the chapel and palace on this occasion are stated to have cost upwards of £9,000.

VIEW OF ST. JAMES'S PALACE, TIME OF QUEEN ANNE. (From an Old Engraving.)

The "Gentlemen and Children of the Chapel Royal," as the members of the choir are styled, were the principal performers in the religious drama, or "mysteries," when such performances were in fashion; and a "Master of the Children" and "singing children" occur in the chapel establishment of Cardinal Wolsey. In 1583 the "Children of the Chapel Royal," afterwards called the "Children of the Revels," were formed into a company of players, and thus were among the earliest performers of the regular drama. In 1731 they performed Handel's *Esther*, the first oratorio heard in England; "and they continued to assist at oratorios in Lent," says Mr. John Timbs, "as long as those performances maintained their ecclesiastical character entire."

In *Notes and Queries*, No. 30, we read that the "spur-money"—a fine upon all who entered the chapel with spurs on—"was formerly levied by the choristers, at the door, upon condition that the youngest of them could repeat his gamut; if he failed, the spur-bearer was exempt." In a tract dated 1598, the choristers are reproved for "hunting after spur-money;" and the ancient cheque-book of the Chapel Royal, dated 1622, contains an order of the Dean, "decreeing" the observance of the custom. "Within my recollection," writes Dr. Rimbault, in 1850, "the Duke of Wellington (who, by the way, is an excellent musician) entered the Royal Chapel 'booted and spurred,' and was, of course, called upon for the fine. But his Grace calling upon the youngest chorister to repeat his gamut, and the 'little urchin' failing, the impost was not demanded." As stated above, the Duke used to attend the service here regularly; and Mr. A. C. Coxe, an American clergyman, devotes half a chapter of his "Impressions of England" to a description of an early service here, at which he knelt side by side with the hero of Waterloo.

The establishment of the Chapel Royal consists of a Dean (usually the Bishop of London), a Sub-Dean, Lord High Almoner, Sub-Almoner, Clerk of the Queen's Closet, deputy-clerks, chaplains, priests, organists, and composer; besides "violist" and "lutanist" (now sinecures), and other officers; and, until 1833, there was also a "Confessor to the Royal Household." The forty-eight "Chaplains in Ordinary" to Her Majesty are appointed by the Lord Chamberlain. They receive no payment for their services, and their duties are confined to the work of preaching one sermon each in turn yearly; but the appointment is generally regarded as a stepping-stone to something better. The Dean of the Chapel Royal is nominated by the sovereign; he has a salary of £200 a year.

In spite of modern alterations this is substantially the same chapel as that in which Evelyn so often anxiously marked the conduct of King Charles, and of his brother the Duke of York, at the celebration of the sacrament. The gold plate and offertory basin are the same as those used in the days of our last Stuart sovereign.

Eastward of the Colour Court are the gates leading to the quadrangle formerly known as "the Chair Court." The State Apartments, in the south front of the Palace, face the garden and St. James's Park. The sovereign enters by the gate on this side; it was here, on the 2nd of August, 1786, that Margaret Nicholson made an attempt to assassinate George III. as he was alighting from his carriage.

The State Apartments are said by the guide-books to be commodious and handsome, but they certainly are not very imposing, and indeed may, with truth, be pronounced mean, with reference to the dignity of English royalty. They are entered by a passage and staircase of great elegance. At the top of the latter is a gallery or guard-room converted into an armoury. The walls are tastefully decorated with daggers, muskets, and swords, arranged in various devices, such as stars, circles, diamonds, and Vandyke borders. This apartment is occupied by the Yeomen of the Guard on the occasion of a Royal levee. The Yeomen of the Guard are 140 in number; it is part of their duty to carry up the dishes to the royal table. They also take care of the baggage when the sovereign removes from one place to another. Their principal duty, however, consists in keeping the passages about the palace clear on state days. In former days the yeomen dined together, and kept a good table too. "Cannot one fancy," writes Thackeray, "Joseph Addison's calm smile and cold grey eyes following Dick Steele, as he struts down the Mall to dine with the Guard at St. James's, before he himself turns back, with his sober pace and threadbare suit, to walk back to his lodgings up the two pair of stairs in the Haymarket?"

The old Presence Chamber—or, as it is now called, the Tapestry Chamber—is the next room entered. The walls are covered with tapestry, which was made for Charles II., but was never actually hung until the marriage, in 1795, of the Prince of Wales, it having lain, by accident, in a chest undiscovered until within a short time of the event. In this room, over the fire-place, are some relics of the period of Henry VIII.; among which may be mentioned the initials "H. A." (Henry and Anne Boleyn) united, as stated above, by a true-lover's knot; the fleur-de-lis of France, formerly emblazoned with the arms of England; the portcullis of Westminster; and the rose of Lancaster.

When a drawing-room is held, a person attends here to receive the cards containing the names of the parties to be presented, a duplicate being handed to the lord in waiting, to prevent the presentation of persons not entitled to that privilege. From this room is obtained entrance to the state apartments, the first of which is very splendidly furnished; the sofas, ottomans, &c., being covered with crimson velvet, and trimmed with gold lace. The walls are covered with crimson damask, and the window curtains are of the same material; here is a portrait of George II., in his robes; paintings of Lisle and Tournay; and an immense mirror, reaching from the ceiling to the floor. The apartment is lighted by a chandelier, hanging from the centre of the ceiling, and by candelabra at each end.

The Great Council Chamber was the place where the accession and birthday odes of the Poet Laureate were performed and sung in the last century. During the present century, as far back, at least, as the memory of man runneth, these productions have been "taken as read."

The second room is called Queen Anne's Room; it is fitted up in the same splendid style, and contains a full-length portrait of George III., in his robes of the Order of the Garter; on each side of him hang paintings of the great naval victories of the First of June and Trafalgar. Here the remains of Frederick Duke of York lay in state, in January, 1827. From the centre of the ceiling hangs a richly-chased Grecian lustre, and on the walls are three magnificent pier-glasses, reaching the full height of the apartment.

The third room is called the Presence Chamber; in it Her Majesty or her representative holds levees; although similar in style of decoration, it is far more gorgeous than the two described above. The throne, which is on a raised daïs, is of crimson velvet, covered with gold lace, surmounted by a canopy of the same material. The state chair is of exquisite workmanship. The window-curtains are of crimson satin trimmed with gold lace. Here are placed paintings of the battles of Vittoria and Waterloo, by Colonel Jones. The "Royal Closet" is the name conventionally given to the room in which the Queen gives audiences to ambassadors, and also receives an address annually on her birthday from the clergy of the Established Church.

On the east side of the Palace, close to where now stands Marlborough House, as already stated in our chapter on the Mall (see page 76 of the present volume), was in former times a friary, occupied by some Capuchin priests, who came into England with Catharine of Braganza, on her marriage with Charles II. The buildings included a refectory, dormitory, chapel, and library, with cells for the religious. Pepys, in his "Diary," gives us an account of a visit which he paid to the place, where he was shown a crucifix that had belonged to Mary Queen of Scots—which we may suppose he believed—and contained a portion of the true cross, which he probably did *not* believe.

The chapel, as prepared for the use of Queen Catharine of Braganza, is thus described by Pepys, in his "Diary," September 21st, 1662:—"To the parke; the Lord's Day. The Queen coming by in her coach going to her chapel at St. James's (the first time that it hath been ready for her), I crowded after her, and I got up to the room where her closet is, and there stood and saw the fine altar, ornaments, and the fryers in their habits, and the priests come in with their fine crosses, and many other fine things. I heard their musique, too, which may be good, but it did not appear so to me, neither as to their manner of singing, nor was it good concord to my ears, whatever the matter was. The Queen very devout; but what pleased me best was to see my dear Lady Castlemaine, who, tho' a Protestant, did wait upon the Queen to chapel. By and by, after masse was done, a fryer with his cowl did rise up and preach a sermon in Portuguese, which I not understanding, did go away, and to the King's Chapel, but that was done; and so up to the Queen's presence-chamber, where she and the King were expected to dine; but she staying at St. James's, they were forced to remove the things to the King's presence, and there he dined alone."

Pepys alludes to the Roman Catholic services in the Royal Chapel at Whitehall in terms which would seem to imply that he had a strong dislike for them. Thus he writes, 10th May, 1663: "Put on a black cloth suit, with white lynings under all, as the fashion is to wear, to appear under the breeches. I walked to St. James's, and was there at masse, and was forced in the crowd to kneel down"—no bad thing, by the way, for such a worldly and sceptical Christian.

When Charles I. married Henrietta Maria it had been stipulated that the Queen should be allowed the free practice of her religion in London, in spite of the severe laws in force against Roman Catholics in England; but the King found it convenient in this, as in other matters, to forget his promise, and ordered "the French," as he contemptuously called them, to be driven out of St. James's Palace. From thence they went in a body to Somerset House, where for some time they performed mass and heard confessions, until "Steenie," Duke of Buckingham, was ordered to dislodge them thence also, and to pack them off without ceremony to their own country.* On leaving St. James's, we are told, "the women howled and lamented as if they had been going to execution, but all in vain, for the Yeomen of the Guard, by Lord Conway's appointment, thrust them and all their country folk out of the Queen's lodging, and locked the doors after them." A contemporary account adds: "The Queen, when she understood the design, grew very impatient, and brake the glass windows with her fist; but since, I hear, her rage is appeased, and the King and she, since they went together to Nonsuch, have been very jocund together."

A community of the Benedictine order was established at St. James's in the reign of James II., but it was suppressed after the Revolution.

On the site of the chapel above mentioned now stands the Lutheran or German Chapel, which seems almost to intrude upon the grounds of Marlborough House. It was here that the late Queen Dowager Adelaide used to attend on Sundays, preferring the simplicity of its service to the Chapel Royal. In 1851, its use was granted, by permission of the Bishop of London, to the foreign Protestants who had flocked to see the Great Exhibition in Hyde Park.

Westward of the Colour Court is the Ambassadors' Court, where are the apartments of the ex-King of Hanover, and of certain other branches of the Royal Family, and beyond it the Stable Yard, so named from covering the site of the ancient stable-yard of the Palace. Here are now Stafford House, the mansion of the Duke of Sutherland, and Clarence House, the residence of the Duke of Edinburgh; besides a few other mansions inhabited by the nobility.

Mr. Cunningham says that, in 1814, during the visit of the Allied Sovereigns, Marshal Blucher was lodged in the dingy brick house on the west side of the Ambassadors' Court, or West Quadrangle, where he would frequently sit at the drawing-room windows and smoke, and bow to the people, pleased with the notice that was taken of him. At this time the state apartments were fitted up for the Emperor of Russia and the King of Prussia.

In the reign of George II. the Royal Library stood nearly on the site of the present Stafford House, detached from the rest of the buildings of the Palace; there is no print of it in existence,

and it is said to have possessed few architectural pretensions. In fact, literature was not one of the "hobbies" of the first two monarchs of our Hanoverian line.

Here, in the Ambassadors' Court, is the office of the Lord Chamberlain's Department. It is poor and mean enough, and gives but little idea of the importance of the work transacted within its walls. Persons to be "presented at Court," either at levees or drawing-rooms,† are required to send their cards to the Lord Chamberlain; and it is his duty to see that such persons are entitled, by station and character, to be presented to the sovereign. Levees only, however, now take place at St. James's Palace. "The Lord Chamberlain," as we learn from Murray's "Official Handbook," "is an officer of the Household of great antiquity, honour, and trust. He has the supreme control over all the officers and servants of the royal chambers (except those of the bedchamber); also over the establishment of the Chapel Royal, and the physicians, surgeons, and apothecaries of the Household. He has the oversight of the Queen's band, and over all comedians, trumpeters, and messengers. All artificers retained in Her Majesty's service are under his directions. The ancient office of Keeper of the Great Wardrobe was abolished in 1782, and the duties, which consisted in providing the state robes of the royal family, the household, and the officers of state, were transferred to the Lord Chamberlain. The public performance of stage plays in the metropolis and at Windsor, and wherever there is a royal palace, is not legal unless in a house or place licensed by the Lord Chamberlain, who may suspend or revoke his licence. Nor is the performance of any new play, or part of a play, anywhere in Great Britain, legal until his licence has been obtained."

Clarence House was for many years the residence of the Duchess of Kent. In 1874 it was assigned as a residence for the Duke and Duchess of Edinburgh, and greatly enlarged, a storey being added to it in height, and its entrance being made to face the Park on the south instead of being in the narrow passage on the west. The entrance portico was formerly on the west side, facing Stafford House; but this has now been pulled down, and in its place, and also in the balcony above, have been substituted three large windows. Fronting St. James's Park, a new portico entrance, with a conservatory, supported on four columns, has been erected, and two gateways for ingress and egress, flanked by lodges and a stone sentry-box,

---

* See Vol. III., p. 91.

† A levee is confined to gentlemen only; a drawing-room is attended by gentlemen and ladies, the latter forming the larger proportion.

have been constructed on the south-west side. The old court-yard, and a number of ancient buildings extending to St. James's Palace, have been demolished, and the area thus obtained has been thrown into the basement, which is set apart for the general domestic offices and servants' apartments; and on the old court-yard site a one-storey building has been erected as a dormitory for the servants. On the west side of the building is the *bijou* "Greek Church," fitted up for the private devotions of the Duchess of Edinburgh; the altar, flooring, walls, &c., are inlaid with rich mosaic work. A portion of St. James's Palace has been thrown into the new premises, thus affording increased accommodation, while the gardens of the two establishments have been thrown into one, and laid out in uniform terraces and slopes.

In 1806, just before his death, Charles James Fox was residing at Godolphin House (the site of which is now covered by Stafford House), in the Stable Yard.

Among the now forgotten dwellers in the out-quarters of the Palace was Charles Dartineuf, or Dartinave, said by some to have been a son of Charles II., by others a member of a refugee family. He was Paymaster of the Board of Works, and Surveyor of the Royal Gardens and Roads in 1736. He was, as Swift describes him, a "true epicure," and a man "that knows everything and everybody; where a knot of rabble are going on a holiday, and where they were last." His partiality for ham-pie has been confirmed by Warburton and Dodsley. Pope, he said, had done justice to his taste; if he had given him *sweet pie*, he never could have pardoned him. Lord Lyttelton, in his "Dialogues of the Dead," has introduced Dartineuf discoursing with Apicius on the subject of good eating, ancient and modern. His favourite dish, ham-pie, is there commemorated; but Dartineuf is made to lament his ill fortune in having lived before turtle-feasts were known in England.

In the "New View of London," published in 1708, St. James's Palace is said to be "pleasantly situated by the Park;" the writer adds, "Though little can be said of its regular design in appearance, yet it contains many noble, magnificent, and beautiful rooms and apartments."

This edifice was the London residence of our sovereigns from 1697, when Whitehall Palace was consumed by fire, until about the middle of the last century, when George III. made Buckingham Palace his home in London. Since 1809, when part of the south-eastern wing was destroyed by fire, a part only of the palace has been rebuilt, but it was put into ornamental repair on the accession of George IV., during the years 1821–23. In this palace died Queen Mary I.; Henry, Prince of Wales, eldest son of James I.; and Caroline, Queen of George II. Here also were born Charles II., James, "the Old Pretender," son of James II., and George IV.

In 1638 this palace was given up by Charles I. as a residence for Marie de Medici, the mother of his consort, Henrietta Maria; but in this, as in nearly all his other acts of imprudent generosity, the King came in for a large share of unpopularity. She was welcomed to London with a public reception and a procession through the streets, and a copy of most courtly verses by the court poet, Edmund Waller; as witness these lines :—

"Great Queen of Europe! where thy offspring wears
    All the chief crowns; where princes are thy heirs;
    As welcome thou to sea-girt Briton's shore,
    As erst Latone, who fair Cynthia bore
    To Delos, was."

The miniature court, however, which she maintained here for three years, was never acceptable to the nation, who regarded her as the symbol of arbitrary power. In the end, the Parliament voted to her a sum of £10,000 if she would only leave the country; and she quitted England for the free city of Cologne in August, 1641. Lilly thus notices her departure :—"I saw the old Queen-mother of France departing from London. A sad spectacle it was, and produced tears in my eyes and those of many other beholders, to see an aged, lean, decrepit, poor queen, ready for her grave, necessitated to depart hence, having no other place of residence left her but where the courtesy of her hard fate assigned. She had been the only stately and magnificent woman of Europe, wife to the greatest king that ever lived in France, mother unto one king and two queens." She died at Cologne in 1642, in a garret, and with scarcely more than the bare necessaries of life!

It was at St. James's that Charles I., so soon about to earn the title of "the Martyr," took his farewell of his young children, who were brought from Sion House for that purpose—an affecting scene, which has been a favourite subject for pictorial representation; and here the King's last night on earth was spent. "He slept," as the historians tell us, "more than four hours; his attendant, Herbert, resting on a pallet by the royal bed. The room was dimly lighted by a great cake of wax, set in a silver basin. Before daybreak the king had aroused his attendant, saying, 'He had a great work to do that day.' Prayer, communion, and the announcement of the executioners waiting for their victim—the glass of claret and the morsel of bread, lest faintness on the scaffold might be felt, and be misinterpreted—the long procession to Whitehall—the silent and dejected faces of the soldiers—the mutual prayers, and the last inquiry, 'Does my hair trouble you?'—the outstretched hands for the signal—all these, and many more

It must have been trying to the proud spirit of Queen Henrietta Maria in her widowhood, when she had seen the bodies of Cromwell, Ireton, and Bradshaw dragged on hurdles to Tyburn, and their heads set, as we have said, on the front of Westminster Hall, to have been compelled, in deference

COUNCIL CHAMBER, ST. JAMES'S PALACE, 1840. (*See page* 105.)

such gloomy sights, go to make up a mournful picture. As the cloak of the king falls from his shoulders, the faithful Juxon receives from the hand of his beloved master, with the single and mysterious word, 'Remember!' the 'George' which he had removed from his neck. So ended the domestic history of poor King Charles; and with him, in one sense, for a long time, the domestic happiness of his country."

to the will of her son, the King, to salute here publicly at court as Duchess of York, and consort of the presumptive heir to the throne, the offspring of Lord Chancellor Hyde and his low-born wife.

We learn from Whitelock that St. James's was temporarily occupied by Monk, Duke of Albemarle, before he had made up his mind that it was time to effect the Restoration.

In former times a dinner was laid regularly every

day in the out-quarters of the Palace for the royal chaplains. A good story is told about this dinner and the witty Dr. South, who obtained a reprieve for it when there was a talk of its being discontinued. King Charles II. one day came in to dine with the reverend gentlemen; and it was Dr. South's turn to say grace. Instead of using the regular form, "God *save* the King, and *bless* our dinner," he transposed the verbs, saying, "God *bless* the

queen to marry her, and was half distracted when, by her clandestine marriage with the Duke of Richmond, she eluded his grasp. The personal charms of La Belle Stewart have been commemorated by Grammont, Pepys, and others. The secretary, indeed, was enraptured with her appearance—her "cocked hat and a red plume," her "sweet eye," and "little Roman nose." Miss Stewart had been so annoyed by the attentions of

COURT-YARD OF ST. JAMES'S PALACE, 1875. (*See page* 101.)

King, and *save* our dinner." "How say you, Dr. South?" said the King; "and it *shall* be saved, I promise, on the word of a king." It is to be hoped that on this occasion his Majesty did not break his word.

One of the chief ornaments of the Court of St. James's in the reign of Charles II. was La Belle Stewart, afterwards Duchess of Richmond, to whom Pope has alluded as the "Duchess of R.," in the well-known line—

"Die and endow a college or a cat."

She was Frances Stewart, grand-daughter of Lord Blantyre, and as such she inspired Charles II. with the purest and strongest passion he seemed capable of entertaining. He would have divorced his

Charles and the manners of his profligate court, that she had already resolved to marry any gentleman of £1,500 a year, when, fortunately, the Duke of Richmond solicited her hand. Her consent was, according to Pepys, "as great an act of honour as ever was done by woman!" In a few years the duchess became a widow, and continued so for thirty years, dying October 15, 1702. The endowment satirised by Pope has been favourably explained by Warton. She left annuities to certain female friends, with the burden of maintaining some of her cats: a delicate way of providing for poor, and probably proud, gentlewomen, without making them feel that they owed their livelihood to her mere liberality. It would have been easy, however, to have effected the same object in a way less liable to ridicule. The "effigy" of the duchess still exists, along with some others, in Westminster Abbey. She left money by her will, desiring that her image, as well done in wax as could be, and dressed in coronation robes and coronet, should be placed in a case, with clear crown glass before it, and should be set up in Westminster Abbey. A more lasting and popular "effigy" is the figure of Britannia on our copper coins, which was originally modelled from a medal struck by Charles II. in honour of the fair Stewart.

In addition to the "sweet little Barbara," Countess of Castlemaine *in esse*, and Duchess of Cleveland *in posse*, there hung about the Court, here and at Whitehall, the Duke of Buckingham and the Earl of Rochester, the handsome Sidney, the pompous Earl of St. Albans, and his vain and giddy nephew, Harry Jermyn; the Earls of Arran and Ossory, and the dissolute Killigrew, who together governed the privacy of their master as readily and easily as Clarendon and Ormond controlled his public measures. King Charles II. being here, on one occasion, in company with Lord Rochester and others of the nobility, Killigrew, the jester, came in. "Now," said the king, "we shall hear of our faults." "No, faith," said Killigrew, "I don't care to trouble my head with that which all the town talks of."

Here, in the bedroom of the Princess, took place, on the 4th of November, 1677, the marriage of Mary, daughter of James Duke of York and of his first wife, Anne Hyde, with William Prince of Orange—a marriage so fatal afterwards to her father and her step-mother, Mary of Modena, who at the time was hourly expecting her confinement. Three days afterwards the boy was born, but he did not live to the end of the year, being carried off by the smallpox. Waller, the Court poet, in a graceful little poem on the death of this infant, alludes to the extreme youth of the royal mother, to which he ascribes the early deaths of her other offspring, and from the same circumstance insinuates consoling hopes for the future :—

> "The failing blossoms which a young plant bears
> Engage our hopes for the succeeding years.
>
> *   *   *   *   *
>
> Heaven, as a first-fruit, claimed that lovely boy ;
> The next shall live to be the nation's joy."

When, in 1688, the Prince of Orange, with the forces at his command, was advancing towards London, King James sent him an invitation to take up his quarters here. The Prince accepted it, but at the same time hinted to the King, his father-in-law, that he must leave Whitehall. With

respect to this event, Dalrymple, in his "Memoirs," tells the following story :—"It was customary to mount guard at both palaces. The old hero, Lord Craven, was on duty at the time when the Dutch guards came marching through the Park to relieve, by order of their master. From a point of honour he had determined not to quit his station, and was preparing to maintain his post ; but, receiving the command of his sovereign, he reluctantly withdrew his party, and marched away in sullen dignity."

Here Mary Beatrice of Modena spent the first years of her wedded life with James Duke of York ; and even after she became Queen Consort she always preferred its homely apartments to the gilded and gorgeous rooms of the great Palace at Whitehall. Here, too, when she found that she was once more about to become a mother, in the summer of 1688, she resolved that the child should be born, who, if a son, was destined thereafter to become the heir to the English throne. "Mary Beatrice," writes Miss Strickland, "never liked Whitehall, but always said of it that it was one of the largest and most uncomfortable houses in the world. But her heart always clung to her first English home, which had been endeared to her by those tender recollections that regal pomp had never been able to efface."

Here, too, the son of James II. and Mary Beatrice, afterwards so well known to history as "the Elder Pretender," was born on Sunday, the 10th of June, 1688, being Trinity Sunday, between nine and ten in the morning. This chamber is memorable as the scene of the alleged fraud by which the king and queen were said to have tried to foist upon the nation as its future sovereign a child brought into the palace in a warming-pan. Mr. Peter Cunningham tells us that there is extant "a contemporary plan of the palace, dotted with lines to show the way by which the child was said to have been conveyed to her Majesty's bed in the great bedchamber." Those who would wish to read in detail the narratives of this event cannot do better than study them in the "Life" of that queen by Miss Strickland, who states that nearly every member of the court was present on the occasion, to the number of sixty-seven persons, and all saw that a son was born to the queen.

"The Court of Mary Beatrice at St. James's Palace," writes Miss Strickland, "was always magnificent, and far more orderly than that at Whitehall." Like Whitehall, St. James's Palace, under the Stuart sovereigns, was constantly the scene of the ceremony of "touching for the King's evil." Many instances of its performance are on record. Thus we are told that on the 30th of

March, 1712, some 200 persons were brought before Queen Anne at St. James's Palace to be healed by the "royal touch." Among this number was one whose name was destined to become great—Samuel Johnson, then a child about two years and a half old. His mother had brought him from Lichfield to London to be touched by the Queen on the advice of Sir John Floyer, a physician of fame in Lichfield; a proof of the high estimation in which the royal "healing" was generally held early in the last century. When asked, late in life, if he could remember Queen Anne, the doctor used to state that he had "a confused but somehow a sort of solemn recollection of a lady in diamonds and a long black hood."

The morals of the Court of Charles II. are matters of history; and even the court balls at St. James's, in his reign, in spite of the influence of his excellent queen, were not marked with any great propriety, if contemporary diaries may be trusted. But, if the Palace was the scene of much that was discreditable and immoral under the Stuarts, it did not gain much in morality under the first two Georges, who kept here their dull English and German mistresses, just as Charles and James had maintained their more attractive French ladies. In the court chronicles and scandalous memoirs of the time we may read plenty of anecdotes of such court ladies as the Duchess of Kendal and Miss Brett, the rival favourites of George I.; and of Mrs. Howard, afterwards Countess of Suffolk, who, in the reign of George II., had "apartments" within its walls, under the very nose and eyes of Queen Caroline, who apparently cared little about her existence. Those who are interested in such scandals may read in Mr. Peter Cunningham's "Handbook of London" an interesting account of a passage at arms between the above-mentioned Miss Brett and her "protector's" granddaughter, the Princess Anne, who ordered to be bricked up again a door which that lady had made to connect her apartments with the Palace garden. The strife was at its height when the sudden death of the King put an end to the reign of Miss Brett, and the Princess triumphed. And Horace Walpole tells us how the accident of Lord Chesterfield having won a heavy sum of money, and having deposited it late at night with Mrs. Howard, led the Queen to suspect him of too great intimacy in that quarter, and so almost forced him into opposition to the Ministry.

Cunningham adds further, as a separate bit of scandal, that Mrs. Howard's husband presented himself one night in the quadrangle of the Palace to claim his wife; but, after many noisy protesta-tions, was induced to desist, "selling to the King," as Walpole had heard, "his noisy honour and the possession of his wife for a pension of twelve hundred a year!" While such scenes were transacted in the eighteenth century, it certainly cannot be allowed that either of the first two Georges had a right to throw the first stone at Charles II. or James II.

Lord Orford, in his "Reminiscences," tells an amusing story of one of the German ladies who came over with King George I. On being abused by the mob, she put her head out of the coach, and cried in bad English, "Good people, why you abuse us? We come for all your goods." "Yes," answered a fellow in the crowd, "and for our *chattels* too."

The death-bed scene of Queen Caroline has been told by Lord Hervey and other writers of the time. It was on the 9th of November, 1737, that the Queen was taken ill, and continued getting worse. On the 11th, the Prince of Wales—who, as our readers will have already seen, was then living at enmity with his parents—sent to request that he might see her; but the King said it was like one of the *scoundrel's* tricks, and he forbade the Prince to send messages, or even to approach St. James's. The Queen herself was no less decided. She was then dying from the effects of a rupture, which she had courageously concealed for fourteen years, and she would have died without declaring it, had not the King communicated the fact to her attendants. This delicacy was not, as Lord Hervey says, merely an ill-timed coquetry at fifty-four, that would hardly have been excusable at twenty-five. She feared to lose her power over the King, which she had held firmly in spite of all his mistresses, and was in constant apprehension of making herself distasteful to her husband. The Prince of Wales continued to send messages to the dying Queen, and the messengers got into the Palace; but the Queen wished to have the *ravens* (who, she said, were only there to watch her death, and would gladly tear her to pieces whilst she was alive) turned out of the house, and the old King was inexorable. About the seventh day of the Queen's illness, the Archbishop of Canterbury (Dr. Potter) was sent for. He continued to attend every morning and evening, but her Majesty did not receive the sacrament.

Some of Lord Hervey's revelations are curious enough. Her Majesty, it appears, advised the King, in case she died, to marry again. George sobbed and shed tears. "Whilst in the midst of this passion, wiping his eyes and sobbing between every word, with much ado he got out this answer:

'Non, j'aurai des maîtresses;' to which the Queen made no other reply than 'Ah! mon Dieu! cela n'empêche pas.'

"When she had finished all she had to say on these subjects, she said she fancied she could sleep. The King said many kind things to her, and kissed her face and her hands a hundred times; but even at this time, on her asking for her watch, which hung by the chimney, in order to give it to him to take care of her seal, the natural *brusquerie* of his temper, even in these moments, broke out, which showed how addicted he was to snapping without being angry, and that he was often capable of using those worst whom he loved best; for, on this proposal of giving him the watch to take care of the seal with the Queen's arms, in the midst of sobs and tears, he raised and quickened his voice, and said, 'Ah, my God! let it alone: the Queen has always such strange fancies. Who should meddle with your seal? Is it not as safe there as in my pocket?'"

During their night watches, the King and Lord Hervey had many conversations, all which the Court Boswell reports fully. George wished to impress upon the Privy Seal that the Queen's affectionate behaviour was the natural effect of an amorous attachment to his person, and an adoration of his great genius! He narrated instances of his own intrepidity, during a severe illness and in a great storm; and one night while he was discoursing in this strain, the Princess Emily, who lay upon a couch in the room, pretended to fall asleep. Soon after, his Majesty went into the Queen's room. When his back was turned, Princess Emily started up, and said, 'Is he gone? How tiresome he is!' Lord Hervey replied only, "I thought your Royal Highness had been asleep. 'No,' said the Princess Emily, 'I only shut my eyes that I might not join in the *ennuyant* conversation, and wish I could have shut my ears too. In the first place, I am sick to death of hearing of his great courage every day of my life; in the next place, one thinks now of mamma, and not of him. Who cares for his old storm? I believe too, it is a great lie, and that he was as much afraid as I should have been, for all what he says now.'"

Other glimpses of the interior of this strange Court at this time are furnished by Lord Hervey. At length the last scene came. There had been about eleven days of suffering:—"On Sunday, the 20th of November, in the evening, she asked Dr. Tesier—with no seeming impatience under any article of her present circumstances but their duration—how long he thought it was possible for all this to last? to which he answered, 'Je crois que votre Majesté sera bientôt soulagée.' And she calmly replied, 'Tant mieux.' About ten o'clock on Sunday night, the King being in bed and asleep, on the floor, at the foot of the Queen's bed, and the Princess Emily in a couch bed in a corner of the room, the Queen began to rattle in the throat; and Mrs. Purcel giving the alarm that she was expiring, all in the room started up. Princess Caroline was sent for, and Lord Hervey, but before the last arrived the Queen was just dead. All she said before she died was, 'I have now got an asthma; open the window.' Then she said, 'Pray:' upon this the Princess Emily began to read some prayers, of which she scarce repeated ten words before the Queen expired. The Princess Caroline held a looking-glass to her lips, and finding there was not the least damp upon it, cried, "'Tis over.'"

George did not marry again, but contented himself with "des maîtresses." He survived nearly twenty-three years, dying suddenly on the 25th of October, 1760. He directed that his remains and those of the Queen should be *mingled together;* and accordingly, one side of each of the wooden coffins was withdrawn, and the two bodies placed together in a stone sarcophagus.

George III., at his accession, was not much more popular than his grandfather had been before him; and on several occasions the populace showed that he held the throne by a very precarious tenure. Sir N. W. Wraxall tells us, in his gossiping "Memoirs of his Own Time," that in one popular outbreak, in 1769, a hearse, followed by an excited mob, decorated with insignia of most unmistakable meaning, was driven into the court-yard of St. James's Palace, an Irish nobleman, Lord Mountnorris, personating an executioner, holding an axe in his hands, whilst his face was covered over by a veil of crape. "The king's firmness, however," adds Wraxall, "did not forsake him in the midst of this trying ebullition of democratic rage. He remained calm and unmoved in the drawing-room, whilst the streets surrounding his palace echoed with the shouts of an enraged multitude, who seemed disposed to proceed to those extremities to which, eleven years later, they actually went, in the 'Gordon' riots."

On the 22nd of January, 1809, as stated above, about half-past two in the morning, a fire was discovered in St. James's Palace, near the King's back stairs. The whole of the private apartments of the Queen, those of the Duke of Cambridge, the King's court, and the apartments of several persons belonging to the royal household, were destroyed; the most valuable part of the property was preserved. The Hon. Miss Amelia Murray tells us this fire was believed at the time to be the work of an incendiary.

About the year 1810 the Palace was the scene of a horrid tragedy, which, for a time at least, drew down great popular indignation on one member of the royal family. The Duke of Cumberland had an Italian servant named Sellis, who made his way into his master's bedroom and tried to assassinate him in the night. The duke awoke, and was able not only to defend himself, but to drive away the would-be assassin, who, when he found himself foiled in his dastardly attempt, crept back to his own room and cut his throat. A coroner's inquest being held on the body, a verdict of "felo-de-se" was returned. The affair, nevertheless, caused great excitement at the time, and many suspicions were entertained, and many cruel insinuations made against the duke, who was, from youth, the most unpopular member of the royal house; and even to the present day there is a sort of floating tradition to the effect that the duke—who, in 1837, left England on becoming King of Hanover, and scarcely ever afterwards came to this country—was the murderer of his valet.

A good story is told by Miss Murray, in her "Recollections," concerning the wife of the Duke of Cumberland, who in early life was more than suspected of levity of conduct. Old Queen Charlotte was resolved to keep her court pure, in the persons of its female part, at least; and when her eldest son, the Prince Regent, endeavoured to smooth over the Duchess's faults, and procure for her a public reception at Court, her Majesty replied, that "she would receive the Duchess of Cumberland as a daughter-in-law when she received the Princess of Wales also. But this arrangement did not suit the Prince Regent's book."

With regard to the kitchen of St. James's Palace in the time of George III., it need only be said that it was very similar in its appearance to the kitchens of other large establishments. Our illustration (page 120) shows the principal features of the place at the above period. It may be added here that the grass-plot which lies beneath the southern windows of the Palace, now enclosed with high walls, is substantially the same as it was in the reign of Charles II., who, on a summer evening, was often to be seen here, playing at bowls with the fair ladies of his court.

CHAPTER X.

ST. JAMES'S PALACE (continued).

"They say there is a Royal Court,
Maintained in noble state,
Where every able man and good
Is certain to be great."—Tom Hood.

A Drawing-room in the Reign of Queen Anne, and one of the Present Day—Court Wits—Sedan Chairs at St. James's—Influence of Monarchical Institutions on Social Etiquette—Sociality of Great Kings—Courtly Leaders of Fashion—Court Dresses—Costume in the Reign of George III.—Queen Elizabeth's Partiality for Black Silk Stockings—Killigrew and King Charles's Tailor—Hair-powder and Full-bottomed Wigs—Farthingales and Crinoline—The Poet-Laureate and his Butt of Sherry—Royal Patronage of Poetry and Literature—Stafford (formerly Cleveland) House—Appearance of St. James's at the Beginning of the Seventeenth Century.

FOR upwards of two hundred years—indeed, even before the burning of Whitehall—the name of St. James's has been identified in English literature with the English Court, and all that is refined and courtly. Mr. Harrison Ainsworth, therefore, has only given expression to a popular idea of long standing, when he names one of his works "St. James's and St. Giles's," as the very antipodes of each other; and it is almost superfluous to add, that in his historical romance of St. James's he has given us an insight into the inner life of the Court of Queen Anne, scarcely inferior in minuteness to the picturesque peeps of the same court which we find in the "Diaries" of Samuel Pepys and John Evelyn. Here, for instance, is a picture of St. James's Street en fête in February, 1707,

on the occasion of a "drawing-room" held in celebration of the birthday of Queen Anne. It is worth giving entire, as a sketch taken from life:—
"The weather was in unison with the general festivity, being unusually fine for the season. The sky was bright and sunny, and the air had all the delicious balminess and freshness of spring. Martial music resounded within the courts of the Palace, and the trampling of the guard was heard, accompanied by the clank of their accoutrements, as they took their station in St. James's Street, where a vast crowd was already collected.

"About an hour before noon the patience of those who had taken up their positions betimes promised to be rewarded, and the company began to appear, at first somewhat scantily, but speedily in great numbers. The science of the whip was not so well understood in those days as in our own times, or perhaps the gorgeous and convenient though somewhat cumbersome vehicles then in vogue were not so manageable ; but from whichever cause, it is certain that many quarrels took place among the drivers, and frequent and loud oaths and ejaculations were poured forth. The footpath was invaded by the chairmen, who forcibly pushed the crowd aside, and seemed utterly regard-

respective habiliments, military and naval commanders in their full accoutrements, foreign ambassadors, and every variety of character that a court can exhibit. The equipages were most of them new, and exceedingly sumptuous, as were the liveries of the servants clustering behind them.

"The dresses of the occupants of the coaches were varied in colour, as well as rich in material, and added to the gaiety and glitter of the scene. Silks and velvets of as many hues as the rainbow

AMBASSADORS' COURT, ST. JAMES'S PALACE, 1875. (*See page* 106.)
(*Showing the Room in which the Duke of Cumberland's Valet died.*)

less of the ribs and toes of those who did not make way for them. Some confusion necessarily ensued ; but though the crowd were put to considerable inconvenience, jostled here, squeezed there, the utmost mirth and good-humour prevailed.

"Before long the tide of visitors had greatly increased, and coaches, chariots, and sedans were descending in four unbroken lines towards the Palace. The curtains of the chairs being for the most part drawn down, the attention of the spectators was chiefly directed to the coaches, in which sat resplendent beauties bedecked with jewels and lace, beaux in their costliest and most splendid attire, grave judges and reverend divines in their

might be discovered, while there was every kind of peruke, from the courtly and modish Ramillies just introduced, to the somewhat antiquated but graceful and flowing French Campane. Neither was there any lack of feathered hats, point-lace cravats and ruffles, diamond snuff-boxes and buckles, clouded canes, and all the *et cetera* of beauish decoration."

Another writer in describing the scene witnessed at St. James's on the occasion of a Drawing-room in more recent times, remarks that, "after all, magnificence is a tawdry thing, when viewed under the searching blaze of sunshine. Jewels lack lustre— gold appears mere tinsel—the circumstantialities of dress are too much seen to admit of any general

OLD VIEW OF ST. JAMES'S PALACE, BEFORE THE GREAT FIRE OF LONDON.

effect ; and even beauty's self becomes less beautiful. The complexion becomes moistened by the stifling atmosphere of the crowded rooms. As to ladies of a certain age," continues the writer, "let them, above all things, avoid the drawing-room : such a revelation of wrinkles, moles, beards, rouge, pearl-powder, pencilled eyebrows, false hair and false teeth, as were brought to light, I could scarcely have imagined. Many faces, which I had thought lovely at 'Almack's,' grew hideous when exposed to the tell-tale brightness of the meridian sun ; the consciousness of which degeneration rendered them anxious, fretful, and doubly frightful. Two or three dowagers, with mouths full of gold wire, chinstays of blond to conceal their withered deficiencies, and *tulle illusion* tippets, were really horrific ; painted sepulchres—ghastly satires upon the hollowness of human splendour.

"I have often heard it asserted that an English girl, with the early bloom of girlishness on her cheek, is the prettiest creature in the world ; and have thence concluded that a drawing-room, where so many of these rosebuds are brought forward to exhibit their first expansion, must present a most interesting spectacle. This morning I particularly noticed the *demoiselles* to be presented ; and the ghastliness of the ladies of a certain age was scarcely less repulsive than a *niaiserie* of several of these budding beauties. Nothing but a young calf is so awkward as a girl fresh from the schoolroom, with the exhortations of the governess against forwardness and conceit still echoing in her ears ; knowing no one—understanding nothing—afraid to sit, to stand, to speak, to look—always in a nervous ague of self-misgiving. The blushing, terrified, clumsy girls I noticed yesterday will soon refine into elegant women ; but what will then become of the delicacy of their complexion and the simplicity of their demeanour ? "

A " Drawing-room," therefore, is an institution organised to fulfil the object of every fair young *débutante's* ambition, by enabling her to be " presented at court," the event which marks her entry into " fashionable life," and gives her an *entrée* and passport in every European capital.

A Levee or a Drawing-room has always formed the head-quarters of witty retort and polite badinage. Of all Court wits perhaps George Selwyn was the readiest and the happiest. Among other witticisms uttered by him within the precincts of the Court, was one related by Mr. W. C. Hazlitt in his "New London Jest Book." "Lord Galloway was an avowed enemy to the Bute administration. At the change of the Ministry consequent on Lord Bute's fall, he came to St. James's for the

first time in George III.'s reign. He was dressed in plain black, and in a very uncourtly style. When he appeared at the Levee, the eyes of the company were turned on him, and inquiries were murmured as to who he could be. George Selwyn being asked, replied that he was not sure, but thought he was 'a Scotch undertaker, come up to London to bury the late administration.'"

There are extant many sketches of the front of the Palace Gate on the day of a Levee or a Drawing-room under the later Stuarts and the Hanoverian sovereigns. The illustration on page 103 shows the king arriving in his coach with the company in carriages and sedan-chairs. As they look at it, some of our readers may possibly remember the lines ascribed to Pope :—

" Roxana, from the Court returning late,
  Sighed her soft sorrow at St. James's Gate ;
  Such heavy thoughts lay brooding in her breast,
  Not her own chairmen with more weight oppressed."

In 1626 sedan chairs were novelties confined to the upper classes and persons "of quality." They were introduced at the West-end by Sir Sanders Duncombe, who represented to the King that "in many parts beyond the seas people are much carried in chairs that are covered, whereby few coaches are used among them," and prayed for the privilege of bringing them into London. Duncombe was patronised by the royal favourite, Buckingham, through whose influence he obtained a concession of the privilege for fourteen years, and made, no doubt, a good round sum of money by the monopoly.

Sedan chairs, which once were as common at the West-end as hansom cabs, and as much used by men as well as ladies of "the quality," figure frequently in Hogarth's pictures of London life. In his day the sedan chair was the courtly vehicle, and in one of the plates of the " Modern Rake's Progress" we see the man of fashion using it in attending court. The chair continued to be in use all through the Georgian era, and even to a later date ; and in some large houses, in the early part of Her Majesty's reign, a specimen of it was to be seen in the hall or lobby of large houses in the West-end, laid up like a ship in ordinary. It was used even to a later date occasionally at Bath, Cheltenham, and Edinburgh, where the chairmen were a very quaint and humorous body, mostly natives of the Highlands.

It is far from uninteresting to mark the introduction of such modes of conveyance, as they become curious in the retrospect, and give us a very fair insight into the habits and manners of past years.

The Sedan chair, though so called from the place where it was originally made, did not come to England from France, but from Spain, being introduced from Madrid by Charles I., when, as Prince of Wales, he went to that city to look for a wife. On his departure from Spain, as we learn from Mendoza's " Relation of what passed in the Royal Court of the Catholic King, our Lord, on the departure of the Prince of Wales," the Prime Minister of Spain, and favourite of Philip IV., Olivarez, gave the Prince " a few Italian pictures, some valuable pieces of furniture, and three sedan chairs of curious workmanship." Another contemporary writer tells us that on his return to England, Charles gave two of these chairs to his favourite, the Duke of Buckingham, who raised a great clamour against himself by using them in the streets of London. Bassompierre, the French Ambassador, in his " Memoirs of the English Court," states that " the popular outcry arose to the effect that the Duke was reducing freeborn Englishmen and Christians to the condition of beasts of burden." When, however, the populace found out that money was to be made out of them, and that to start a " sedan " was a good speculation, they swallowed their scruples, and, like shrewd and sensible persons, invested their savings in building and buying them, so that in a short time they came into common use, not only in London, but in the chief provincial towns. In the country they were never popular.

Amongst those who came to St. James's in " a chair" was John Duke of Marlborough, after his crowning victory of Ramillies, then at the summit of his popularity, and almost worshipped by the people, who measure everything by success. He tried to smuggle himself into the levee in a chair, but in spite of his attempt at privacy he was discovered, and in a few minutes was surrounded by thousands who rent the air with their acclamations.

A courtly and polished condition of society among the wealthier circles is a natural consequence of our monarchical institutions. Mr. N. P. Willis, the American writer, confesses as much when he writes, " The absence of a queen, a court, and orders of nobility, gives us in the States a freedom from trammel in such matters which would warrant quite a different school of polite usages and observances of ceremony. Yet up to the present time," he adds, " we have followed the English punctilios of etiquette with almost as close a fidelity as if we were a suburb of London." So deeply engrained in human nature is the observance of an orderly and regulated ceremonial, even in the minutiæ of daily life.

Johnson remarked that it had been suggested that kings must be unhappy, because they are deprived of the greatest of all satisfactions, easy and unreserved society. " That is an ill-founded notion. Being a king does not exclude a man from such society. Great kings have always been social. The King of Prussia, the only great king at present, is very social. Charles II., the last king of England who was a man of parts, was social; and our Henrys and Edwards were all social."

It is one of the least observed but perhaps not among the least equivocal proofs of a great advancement in the ideas of freedom entertained by the British people, that their king and queen for the time being may be said to be the only sovereigns in Europe who have ceased to have the power of dictating the fashions to their people.

In days of old—nay, so late as the reign of George II.—it was with the English, as it is still with the other nations : the first personages in the kingdom (from being supposed to be the best informed) led the fashions. As the king and queen, so their whole court, and all the higher ranks of the public, were habited, from the celebrated ruff of the good Queen Bess to the elegant head-dress of the amiable Queen Caroline. But the reign of George III. introduced a new era. " Queen Charlotte, on her arrival in this country, evinced a desire to fall in with its national modes, and a chasteness in her own ideas of improvement in dress, which well entitled her to take the lead of her adopted countrywomen in this respect ; but English ladies, it seemed, were not now to be led, even by their queen. Her Majesty's first endeavour was to reduce their toupee to a size more suited to the length and breadth of the face, than it had been usual to wear them ; and next to introduce a cap neither so diminutive as to be nearly invisible, nor of such a magnitude as to bury the features of the wearer. But in vain were her efforts. Broad and towering head-dresses continued still the rage ; and so continued till a love of novelty induced the ladies, of their own accord, to change to something less absurd. As for the gentlemen of those days, they seemed more inclined to follow the manners and dresses of the King's Guards than of the King himself. His Majesty's wig and large hat found as few imitators among his subjects as his domestic virtues. Nor at any time during the many years which George III. and his virtuous consort presided over society in this country, could their influence over the fashions be said to have much increased. The annual fashions among the ladies continued as usual to take date from the day on which her Majesty's birthday was celebrated; but the fashions themselves had little or no regard to what her Majesty wore on such occasions, but rather to what was the most admired among the very splendid varieties presented for general imitation."

This may not be literally true, for the dress of her present Majesty and her mode of arranging her hair on first ascending the throne, were most servilely followed by nearly all the young ladies of England.

The court dress of ladies has varied to a very great extent with the fashions of the age, and the sovereign from time to time has laid down very precise regulations as to what is, and what is not, allowable in the female costume on court occasions. The court dress of gentlemen, however, has undergone but very slight modification during the past century: though wigs and hair-powder are no longer worn, yet the plum-coloured suit of livery with light silk facings, worn till our own time at levees by men, would remind us of so many lacqueys, were it not for the sword which accompanies them. Some slight modifications in this dress were made a few years ago by the authority of the Lord Chamberlain, the most important being the admission of velvet as an optional substitute for the plum-coloured cloth above-mentioned, and the recognition of trousers instead of knee-breeches; but the court costume of the male sex is still somewhat of an anachronism.

At the commencement, and indeed to almost the middle of the reign of George III., a nobleman or a gentleman of "quality" was known by his dress, which he wore not only on "court" days and special occasions, but in the streets, and at evening parties or other gatherings, at home, or at the coffee-houses and clubs. "That costume," writes Sir N. W. Wraxall in 1814, "which is now confined to the levee or drawing-room, was forty years ago worn by persons of condition, with few exceptions, everywhere and every day. Mr. Fox and his friends, who might be said to dictate [social laws] to the town, affecting a style of neglect about their own persons, and manifesting a contempt of all the usages hitherto established, first threw a discredit on the court dress. From the House of Commons and the Clubs in St. James's Street, it spread through the private assemblies of London. But though gradually undermined, and insensibly perishing of an atrophy, dress never totally fell till the era of Jacobinism and equality, in 1793 and the following year. It was then that pantaloons, cropped hair, and shoe-strings, as well as the total abolition of buckles and ruffles, together with the disuse of

hair-powder, characterised the dress of Englishmen." To the same influence he traces the decline of a distinctive dress among the ladies also; and expresses a hope, and indeed a prophecy, that "it will be necessary at no very distant period to revive the empire of dress."

The huge hoops worn by the ladies of a century or more ago have occasionally been of service. Sir Robert Strange, for instance, the eminent engraver, being "out in '45," as the phrase then went, being hard driven for shelter from the searchers of the victorious army, hid himself under the ample folds of the petticoats of a Miss Lumsden, whom he requited for the service by marrying her soon afterwards.

The first pair of silk stockings brought into England from Spain was presented to Henry VIII., who greatly prized them. In the third year of Elizabeth's reign, her "tiring" woman, Mrs. Montagu, presented her Majesty with a pair of black silk stockings as a new-year's present; whereupon her Majesty asked if she could have any more, in which case she would wear no more cloth stockings. Silk stockings were equally rare things in the Royal Court of Scotland, for it appears that before James VI. received the ambassadors sent to congratulate him on his accession to the English throne, he requested one of the lords of his court to lend him his pair of silk hose, that he "might not appear as a scrub before strangers."

Apropos of court dresses, we may be pardoned for extracting the following from "Joe Miller's Jest-book:"—"King Charles II. having ordered a new suit of clothes to be made, just at a time when addresses were coming up to him from all parts of the kingdom, Tom Killigrew went to the tailor, and ordered him to make a very large pocket on one side of the coat, and one so small on the other, that the king could hardly get his hand into it; which seeming very odd, when they were brought home, he asked the meaning of it. The tailor said, "Mr. Killigrew ordered it so." Killigrew being sent for and interrogated, said, "One pocket was for the addresses of his Majesty's subjects, and the other for the money they would give him."

Hair-powder was introduced into Europe in the year 1614. It is said that at the accession of George I., only two ladies wore powder. At the coronation of George II. there were but two hairdressers in London: in 1795, there were 50,000 in England.

The full-bottomed wigs which envelope and cloud some of the most distinguished portraits of the Stuart era were still in fashion during the reign of William and Mary. Lord Bolingbroke was one of the first to reduce them by tying them up. At this Queen Anne was much offended, and said to a bystander, that "he would soon come to court in a night-cap." Soon after this, tie-wigs, instead of being regarded as undress, became part and parcel of the high court dress at St. James's and Kensington.

Archbishop Tillotson, who was the first English prelate represented in a wig, says :—"I can well remember since the wearing the hair below the ears was looked upon as a sin of the first magnitude ; and when ministers generally, whatever their text was, did either find or make occasion to reprove the great sin of long hair ; and if they saw any one in the congregation guilty in that kind, they would point him out particularly, and let fly at him with great zeal." It is stated that as far as the women were concerned, there was nothing to blame in this innocent fashion of long locks let free from unnatural constraint ; and the glossy ringlets of the young gentlewomen of 1640, confined only by a simple rose, jewel, or bandeau of pearls, was one of the most elegant head-dresses ever invented to please the eye of man : this, as is well known, is the style that has been transmitted to us in the bewitching portraits of the beauties of the court of Charles II. The decorations of the men's heads were not anything half so simple, for, after the frizzing up the hair from the forehead, and then suffering it to fall in the wild luxuriance that called forth the censures of the clergy, they next proceeded to ornament themselves with borrowed hair, and the odious invention of the peruke, or periwig, made in imitation of the long, waving curls of the "Grand Monarque," came next into fashion. Charles II., it is well known, adopted this fantastic fashion ; and very soon not a gentleman's head or shoulders were considered to be complete without a French wig.

The farthingale of the sixteenth and beginning of the seventeenth centuries was—as our readers, no doubt, well know—the originator of the hooped petticoat of the eighteenth and of the crinoline of the nineteenth century ; but in many respects the men offered a still broader mark for the satirist, the cavalier being adorned in silk, satin, or velvet of the richest colours, with loose, full sleeves, slashed in front ; the collar, too, of this superb doublet was of the costliest point lace ; his sword-belt, of the most magnificent kind, was crossed over one shoulder, whilst a rich scarf, encircling the waist, was tied in a large bow at the side.

Charles II. curtailed the doublet of its fair proportions, made it excessively short, and opened it in front to display a rich shirt, bulging out without any waistcoat, wearing at the same time Holland sleeves of extravagant size and fantastic contrivance. The ladies' dresses, however, and their drapery were not much affected by the example of royalty.

That the dress of the court fops in the Georgian era was a somewhat expensive commodity, we may infer from " Beau" Brummell's answer to a question once put to him. Being asked by a lady how much she ought to allow her son for dress, he replied, that it might be done for £800 a year, *with strict economy!*

Among the curious customs and ceremonies of the Court, which have been handed down to us from the Stuart times, is that of presenting the poet-laureate—who, by the way, is an "officer of the household of the sovereign"—with a butt of sherry from the royal cellars. Although .the earliest mention of a poet-laureate in England occurs in the reign of Edward IV., it was not till 1630 that the first patent of the office seems to have been granted. Since 1670 the following poets have held the office of laureate :—Dryden, Tate, Rowe, Colley Cibber, William Whitehead, Warton, Pye, Southey, Wordsworth, and Alfred Tennyson.

Mention of the office of poet-laureate leads us naturally to speak of the success attending the poetical and literary efforts of such as have owed their rise in life to royal and courtly patronage. Most of the persons mentioned in the following extract from a modern periodical must have frequently crossed the threshold of St. James's Palace to worship the rising or risen sun of royalty :— " In the reigns of William III., of Anne, and of George I., even such men as Congreve and Addison would scarcely have been able to live like gentlemen by the mere sale of their writings. But the deficiency of the natural demand for literature was at the close of the seventeenth, and at the beginning of the eighteenth century, more than made up by artificial encouragement—by a vast system of bounties and premiums. There was, perhaps, never a time at which the rewards of literary merit were so splendid—at which men who could write well, found such easy admittance into the most distinguished society, and to the highest honours of the state. The chiefs of both the great parties into which the kingdom was divided, patronised literature with emulous munificence. Congreve, when he had scarcely attained his majority, was rewarded for his first comedy with places which made him independent for life. Smith, though his ' Hippolytus and Phædra ' failed, would have been consoled with £300 a year but for his own folly. Rowe was not only poet-laureate, but land surveyor of the Customs in the port of London,

Clerk of the Council to the Prince of Wales, and Secretary of the Presentations to the Lord Chancellor. Hughes was Secretary to the Commissions of the Peace. Ambrose Philips was Judge of the Prerogative Court in Ireland. Locke was Com-

unconquerable prejudice of the Queen, would have been a bishop. Oxford, with his white staff in his hand, passed through the crowd of suitors to welcome Parnell, when that ingenious writer deserted the Whigs. Steele was a Commissioner of Stamps

KITCHEN OF ST. JAMES'S PALACE IN THE TIME OF GEORGE III.

missioner of Appeals, and of the Board of Trade. Newton was Master of the Mint. Stepney and Prior were employed in embassies of high dignity and importance. Gay, who commenced life as apprentice to a silk-mercer, became a Secretary of Legation at five-and-twenty. It was to a poem on the death of Charles II., and to the 'City and Country Mouse,' that Montague owed his introduction into public life, his Earldom, his Garter, and his Auditorship of the Exchequer. Swift, but for the

and a Member of Parliament. Arthur Mainwaring was a Commissioner of the Customs, and Auditor of the Imprest. Tickell was Secretary to the Lords Justices of Ireland. Addison was Secretary of State."

On the western side, and within what we may style the precincts of St. James's Palace, commanding a view both of St. James's Park and the Green Park, stands Stafford House, or as it was called till recently, Cleveland House. The old house derived its name from Barbara, Duchess of Cleveland, one of the mistresses of Charles II. By birth she was a Villiers, the daughter and heiress of the Irish Viscount Grandison; and she was created Baroness of Nonsuch, Countess of Northampton, and Duchess of Cleveland, by her royal admirer, to whom she had borne two sons—Charles Fitz Roy, Earl of Southampton, and George Fitz Roy, Duke of Northumberland. This lady died

his state of health, and catch at every hope of his amendment. As he grew worse he ceased to go out in his carriage, and was drawn in a garden chair, at times, round the walks. . . . His manner was as easy and his mind as penetrating and vigorous as ever; and he transacted business in this way, though heavily oppressed by his disorder, with perfect facility." After his death at the Duke of Devonshire's villa at Chiswick, his body rested

CLEVELAND HOUSE. (*From a Print published in* 1799.)

at Chiswick in 1709. Seven years before that, apparently she had resigned her interest in this house, as in 1702 we find it granted by the Crown to Henry, Duke of Grafton: it was then called Berkshire House, from its former owner. The present house covers also very nearly the site of a smaller mansion, Godolphin House, which at the beginning of the present century was occupied by the Duke of Bedford. It is deserving of a passing note as having been the residence of Charles James Fox during his last illness. We learn from his biographer, Trotter, that during this anxious period " the garden of the house in the Stable Yard was daily filled with anxious inquirers; the foreign ambassadors and ministers, and private friends of Mr. Fox, walked there, eager to know

here for a night or two previous to his public funeral in Westminster Abbey. In the last century Godolphin House became the residence of the Duke of Bridgewater, who new-fronted the mansion with stone.

Stafford House was built about the year 1825 by the Duke of York. It is said by Mr. Chambers, in his " Handy Guide to London," that it was built with money lent to him by the Marquis of Stafford, whose grandson is the present owner. Be this as it may, the Stafford family became possessed of it, and have spent at least a quarter of a million upon it and its decorations. The mansion was built by the Duke of York on the site of a former residence, where he and the duchess gave pleasant dinners and receptions, devoting the evenings to whist, at which the duke was a first-rate player. Among his most constant guests were Lords Alvanley, Lauderdale, De Ros, and Hertford, "Beau" Brummell, and the Duke of Dorset. It is said that he planned and built the house from his own designs. The duke was very fond of collecting here curiosities of every description—jewels, bronzes, coins, and articles of *vertu;* he also spent large sums in purchasing old chased plate, with which his sideboards groaned; and on his walls he had a fine collection of portraits of officers in curious old uniforms. When he left the Stable Yard the duke took up his abode at Cambridge House, in South Audley Street. He died at Rutland House, at the north-western corner of Arlington Street, but his body was afterwards brought to St. James's Palace, where it lay in state, in January, 1827.

It may be mentioned here that Stafford House marks the extreme south-western limit of the parish of St. James's, Piccadilly.

The money received for the sale of Stafford House by the Crown was devoted in 1842 to the purchase of Victoria Park in the East-end of London as a recreation-ground for the people. The form of the mansion is quadrangular, and it has four perfect fronts, all of which are cased with stone. The north or principal front, which is the entrance, exhibits a portico of eight Corinthian columns. The south and west fronts are alike; they project slightly at each end, and in the centre are six Corinthian columns supporting a pediment. The east front differs a little from the preceding, as it has no projecting columns. The vestibule, which is of noble dimensions, leads to the grand staircase. The library is situated on the ground floor; and on the first, or principal floor, are the state apartments, consisting of dining-rooms, drawing-rooms, and a noble picture gallery, 130 feet in length, in which is placed the Stafford Gallery, one of the finest private collections of paintings in London; it is particularly rich in the works of Titian, Murillo, Rubens, and Vandyck. The private rooms contain many valuable art treasures.

The noble suite of drawing-rooms have been often lent by the late and the present Duchesses of Sutherland for the purposes of meetings of gentlemen and ladies who are interested in social reforms, so that the interior of the house is known to very many persons. One of the most novel exhibitions, perhaps, which have taken place here, or anywhere, was in the summer of 1875, when there was held in the garden a show of wicker coffins of all sorts, sizes, and patterns—*apropos*, of course, of the much-vexed question of " earth

to earth," which at the time had been so frequently agitated in the newspapers.

Even so lately as 1660, St. James's Palace stood in somewhat open country, as shown by a drawing of that date in the Towneley Collection, which corresponds very closely to the description of the place given by Le Serre in his "Entrée Royale," &c., fol. 1639. "Near the avenues of the palace," says the latter, "is a large meadow, always green, in which the ladies walk in summer; its great gate has a long street in front, reaching nearly to the fields." A long low wall runs eastwards, along what is now the south side of Pall Mall, and a thick grove of trees covers what is now the site of Marlborough House. As nearly as possible, where now stands the Junior Carlton Club, on the north side of Pall Mall, is a small barn or shed and a haystack; and in the front of the print, not far from the centre of what is now St. James's Square, stands a handsome conduit, with ornamental brickwork and a lofty crenellated roof; and the meadow in which it stands, apparently, was not at that time surrounded even by a hedge.

We fear it must be owned to be as true in 1875 as it was half a century before, that the sovereign of England is still without a London residence becoming the head of so great an empire. Though Windsor Castle is unequalled as a mediæval stronghold, we have in London nothing that answers to what the Tuileries was; and Hampton Court is at best but a poor substitute for the Château of Versailles.

With reference to the mean appearance of St. James's Palace, the author of the "Beauties of England and Wales" writes, in 1815:—"Few ideas of superior grandeur or magnificence are excited by a partial view of the exterior of this royal palace. And when it is considered that, in fact, this is the only habitation which the monarch of a mighty empire like ours possesses in his capital, strangers are at a loss whether to attribute the circumstance to a penuriousness or meanness of our national character. It arises, in fact, from neither. It has been justly remarked that the disparity between the appearance of this palace, and the object to which it is—or rather has been—appropriated, has afforded a theme of wonder and pleasantry, especially to foreigners, who, forming their notions of royal splendour from piles erected by despotic sovereigns, with treasures wrung from a whole oppressed nation, cannot at once reduce their ideas to the more simple and economical standard which the head of a limited monarchy is compelled to adopt in its expenditure."

CHAPTER XI.

PALL MALL.

" Oh, bear me to the paths of fair Pall Mall !
Safe are thy pavements, grateful is thy smell ;
At distance rolls along the gilded coach,
Nor sturdy carmen on thy walks encroach ;
No lets would bar thy ways were chairs denied—
The soft supports of laziness and pride :
Shops breathe perfumes, through sashes ribbons glow,
The mutual arms of ladies and the beaux."—*Gay's "Trivia,"* Book ii.

Appearance of Pall Mall in the Time of Charles II.—Charles Lamb prefers Pall Mall to the Lakes of Westmoreland—Bubb Dodington—Cumberland House—Schomberg House—Bowyer's Historic Gallery—The "Celestial Bed"—The *Beggar's Opera* concocted—The Society for the Propagation of the Gospel in Foreign Parts—Nell Gwynne's House—A Relic of Nell Gwynne—The First Duke of St. Albans—Messrs. Christie and Manson's Sale-rooms in Pall Mall—Buckingham House—Lord Temple and Lord Bristol—The Duchess of Gordon as the Tory "Queen of Society"—The War Department—Statue of Lord Herbert of Lea—Marlborough House—The Great Duke of Marlborough—Sarah, Duchess of Marlborough—The Mansion bought by the Crown—Its Settlement upon the Prince of Wales—The Vernon Gallery—Literary Associations of Pall Mall—The "Tully's Head"—The "Feathers"—The Shakespeare Gallery—Notable Sights and Amusements—The British Institution—*Habitués* of Pall Mall during the Regency—The "Star and Garter" Hotel—Duel between Lord Byron and Mr. Chaworth—Introduction of Gas.

PALL MALL is described by Strype, in his edition of Stow, as "a fine long street," adorned with gardens on the south side, many with raised mounds and fine views of the royal gardens and St. James's Park beyond ; nevertheless, three centuries ago, the whole of the space between St. James's Palace and Charing Cross was only a tract of fields. In the time of Charles II. it was sometimes styled Catharine Street, out of compliment to the king's unhappy and neglected consort, Catharine of Braganza. We know that at a far later period it was the favourite haunt of the beaux and dandies of the Regency in a summer afternoon ; and few will have forgotten the popularity of the song of the jovial and genial Captain Morris—

"Oh ! give me the sweet shady side of Pall Mall ! "

In the days of Pepys, Pall Mall had really a "sweet shady side," as there grew along it a row of elm-trees, a hundred and fifty in number, "in a very decent and regular manner on both sides of the walk ; " and the few houses which stood on the south side of it were " fair mansions enclosed with gardens." The north side was entirely open, and one or two hay-stacks might be seen on the spot now occupied, as has already been mentioned, by the Junior Carlton Club. At that time the Mall was the fashionable walk of the "upper ten thousand," who afterwards transferred their affections, when the trees were cut down, to the Long Walk in Kensington Gardens.

Some celebrated characters have been remarkable for their fondness for London, and especially for the West-end. The reader may possibly remember that when Charles Lamb was invited by Wordsworth to come down and stay with him by the side of the Westmoreland Lakes, he sighed for the silversmiths' shops about Charing Cross, and the "sweet shady side of Pall Mall."

On the south side, in a house which overlooked the Park and its gardens, resided George Bubb Dodington, afterwards Lord Melcombe, whom Pope immortalised as "Bubo." Lord Hervey tells us in his "Memoirs," that his house "stood close to the garden which the Prince (Frederick, Prince of Wales) had bought of Lord Chesterfield," and that "during Dodington's favour, the Prince had suffered him to make a door out of his house into his garden, which, upon the first decay of his interest, the Prince shut up—building and planting before Dodington's house, and changing every lock to his own house, to which he had formerly given Dodington keys." Dodington was a witty, generous, ostentatious, and, in a political sense, unprincipled man ; but he was the kind patron of James Thomson (who dedicated to him his "Summer"), and also the early friend of Richard Cumberland. To him Dr. Young inscribed his third Satire, and Lord Lyttelton his second Eclogue. The unwarrantable publication of his "Diary" by a person to whom he had left his papers on condition of his printing such only as would do credit to his memory, reveals him to the light as politically the type of profligacy, though probably he was not worse than many of his cotemporaries, who were wise enough not to commit their thoughts to paper. Dodington is thus portrayed by Walpole :—"A man of more wit and more unsteadiness than Pulteney ; as ambitious, but less acrimonious ; no formidable enemy, no sure political, but an agreeable private friend. Lord Melcombe's speeches were as daring and pointed as Lord Bath's were copious and wandering from the subject. Ostentatious in his person, houses, and furniture, he wanted in his expense the taste which he never wanted in his conversation. Pope and Churchill treated him more severely than he deserved—a fate that may attend a man of the greatest wit, when his parts are more suited to society than to composition. The verse remains; the *bon mots* and sallies are forgotten."

"Soon after the arrival of Frederick, Prince of Wales, in England," says his biographer, "Dodington became a favourite, and submitted to the Prince's childish horse-play, being once rolled up in a blanket, and tumbled down stairs; nor was he negligent in paying more solid court, by lending his Royal Highness money. 'This is a strange country, this England,' said his Royal Highness once; 'I am told Dodington is reckoned a clever man; yet I got £5,000 out of him this morning, and he has no chance of ever seeing it again." In 1761 he was advanced to the peerage, under the title of Lord Melcombe Regis; and in the following year he died, at the age of seventy-one." "Poor Lord Melcombe," writes Lady Hervey, "an old friend, and a most entertaining and agreeable companion, has lately been subtracted from the friends I had left. He is really a great loss to me; I saw him often; and he kept his liveliness and his wit to the last."

A good anecdote is told of Lord Melcombe; when his name was Bubb, he was appointed ambassador to Spain. Lord Chesterfield told him it would not do, as the Spaniards could not suppose a man to possess any dignity whose name was a monosyllable. "You must make an addition to it." "But how?" answered Lord Melcombe. "Oh," replied Lord Chesterfield, "I can help you to one: suppose you make it *Silly* Bubb."

As nearly as possible on the site of what is now Carlton Gardens, stood as lately as 1786, if not much later, Cumberland House. It was a large brick mansion, retiring from the street. According to Thornton's "Survey of London," it was built for Edward, Duke of York, but afterwards became the residence of his brother, whose name it bore. Thornton describes it as "a lofty and regular building, with a back-front commanding a beautiful prospect of the Park." The house fell into a neglected state after the duke's death, in 1790. When the union of England and Ireland was in agitation, it was resolved to establish a club in honour of the event; a number of gentlemen then purchased the house and fitted it up for an hotel. It bore the name of the "Albion."

The houses Nos. 81 and 82 formed originally one mansion, known as Schomberg House, which was built during the Commonwealth. Like the adjoining house of Nell Gwynne, it had in its rear a garden with a handsome raised terrace commanding a view of the royal gardens and of the Park beyond. At the Restoration it was tenanted by Edward Griffin, one of the high officers of the court of Charles II. Here afterwards lived the Duke of Schomberg, one of the Dutch generals brought over in his train by William, Prince of Orange, and who fell at the battle of the Boyne: the house was named after him. It was beautified for Frederick, the third and last duke, for whom Peter Berchett painted the grand staircase with landscapes in lunettes. The rest of the history of the mansion shall be told in the words of the author of " Curiosities of London : "—" In 1699 the house was near being demolished by a body of disbanded soldiers; and in the Gordon Riots of 1780 attempts were made to sack and burn it. William, Duke of Cumberland, the hero of Culloden, became tenant of the house in 1760. John Astley, the painter and the 'beau,' who lived here many years, divided the mansion into three, and placed the bas-relief of 'Painting' above the middle doorway. Astley built also on the roof a large painting-room—his country-house, as he called it—overlooking the Park, to which and to some other apartments he had a private staircase. After Astley's death, Cosway the portrait-painter became the tenant of the central portion. Gainsborough occupied the west wing from 1777 to 1788, when he died in a second-floor room. He sent for Sir Joshua Reynolds and was reconciled to him; and then exclaiming, 'We are all going to heaven, and Van Dyke is of our number,' he immediately expired. Part of the house was subsequently occupied by Robert Bowyer for his 'Historic Gallery,' and by Dr. Graham, the empiric, for his 'Celestial Bed,' and other impostures, advertised by two gigantic porters stationed at the entrance, with gold-lace cocked hats and liveries. The house was a good specimen of the red-brick mansion of the seventeenth century. It was partly occupied by Messrs. Payne and Foss, with their valuable stock of old books, until 1850, soon after which the eastern wing was taken down and rebuilt in the Italian style, though incongruously, for the War Department." The house is still remarkable for its foreign design, with wings, pediment, and caryatide porticos.

Many years after the duke's death it was bought from the Earl of Holdernesse, who then owned it, by a portrait painter named John Astley, who, as stated above, divided it into three houses. Gainsborough and his works of art have made one of these houses known far and wide. Astley himself occupied the central house, and raised it by a storey. During the latter part of the eighteenth century it was hired by various speculators in succession as a gallery for the exhibition of pictures, &c., and it is said that more shillings were taken at its doors than at any other house in the time of George III. Early in the present century it was converted to more strictly literary uses, becoming the bookshop of Mr. Thomas Payne, whose father, "honest Tom Payne of immortal memory," had been for forty years a bookseller at the Mews Gate. It was here that was first concocted the dramatic scheme of the *Beggars' Opera*. It was originally proposed to Swift to be named the *Newgate Opera*, as the first thought of writing such a gross and immoral drama originated with him. Swift also, who was an ardent admirer of the poetic talents of Gay, delighted to quote his Devonshire pastorals, they being very characteristic of low, rustic life, and congenial to his taste; for the pen of the Dean revelled in vulgarity. Under the influence of such notions, he proposed to Gay to bestow his thoughts upon the subject, which he felt assured he would turn to good account, namely, that of writing a work to be entitled "A Newgate Pastoral;" adding, "and I will, *sub rosâ*, afford you my best assistance." This scheme was talked over at Queensberry House, and Gay commenced it, but soon dropped it, with something of disgust. It was ultimately determined that he should commence upon the *Beggar's Opera*. This proposal was approved, and the opera written forthwith, under the auspices of the Duchess of Queensberry, and performed at the theatre in Lincoln's Inn Fields, under the immediate influence of her Grace, who, to induce the manager, Rich, to bring it upon his stage, agreed to indemnify him all the expenses he might incur, providing that the *daring* speculation should fail.

No. 79, adjoining Schomberg House, was for very many years the head-quarters of the venerable Society for the Propagation of the Gospel in Foreign Parts, prior to its removal, about the year 1870, to Park Place, St. James's Street. The house has been identified as that occupied by Nell Gwynne during the heyday of her career as the favourite of King Charles II. To the south side of it was attached a garden, adjoining that of the King; and we have already told our readers how Evelyn was a witness on this spot to "a familiar discourse between the King and Mrs. Nelly, as they call an impudent comedian; she looking out of her garden on a terrace on the top of the wall, the King standing on a green walk under it." According to Mr. John Timbs, part of this "terrace," or raised mound of earth, is still to be seen "under the Park wall of Marlborough House," and the same authority tells us that a bill for erecting this very mound was found among Nell Gwynne's papers. It is interesting to learn that whilst basking in the sunshine of the royal favour Nelly did not forget her poor mother, and that the same doctor's bill which mentions the medicine sent for her own use and that of her little son, includes also "a cordial for old Mrs. Gwynne." Maintained in decent comfort after the King's death, whose last words were "Do not let poor Nelly starve," she died in Pall Mall in November, 1687, and was buried in the church of St. Martin's-in-the-Fields, the vicar, Dr. Tenison, preaching her funeral sermon.

With respect to this residence of Nell Gwynne, Mr. Peter Cunningham writes:—"Nelly at first had only a lease of her house, which as soon as she discovered, she returned the conveyance to the King, with a remark characteristic alike of her wit and of the monarch to whom it was addressed. The King enjoyed the joke, and perhaps admitted its truth; so the house in Pall Mall was conveyed *free* to Nell and her representatives for ever. The truth of the story," he adds, "is confirmed by the fact that the house which occupies the site of the one inhabited by her, No. 79, is the only freehold on the southern or Park side of Pall Mall. No entry, however, of the grant is to be found in the Land Revenue Record Office." The house rebuilt upon the site of that given by Charles II. to Nell Gwynne was some years since occupied by Dr. Heberden.

Previously to living on this side of Pall Mall, Nell Gwynne had occupied a house on the north side, whither she had removed in 1670, soon after the birth of her eldest son by Charles II. That house is described by Pennant as the first good one on the left hand of St. James's Square, as we enter from Pall Mall. Its site is now covered by the Army and Navy Club. When Pennant wrote, it belonged to Mr. Thomas Brand, afterwards Lord Dacre; it subsequently was the town residence of Lord De Mauley. Pennant says, "The back room on the ground floor was, within memory, entirely of looking-glass, as also was said to have been the ceiling. Over the chimney was her picture, and that of her sister was in a third room." Mr. John Timbs adds the fact that in Lord De Mauley's house was a relic of Nell Gwynne—namely, her looking-glass; "this," he tells us, "was bought with the house, and is now in the Visitors' Room of the Club."

Bishop Burnet calls Nell Gwynne the indiscreetest and wildest creature that was ever in a king's court, and says she was maintained at a great expense. The Duke of Buckingham, he says, told him that at first she asked only £500 a year;

but at the end of the fourth year she had received from the King £60,000. Throughout her whole life she continued negligent in her dress, but that might have arisen from the acknowledged fact that whatever she wore became her. Her eldest son,

the name of Beauclerk, and created him Earl of Burford; and shortly before his death made him Duke of St. Albans. In the next house west to Schomberg House lived Mrs. Fitzherbert, of whom we have already spoken.

MESSRS. CHRISTIE AND MANSON'S ORIGINAL AUCTION ROOMS.
From an original Drawing in the possession of Mr. Crace. (See p. 128.)

by Charles II., was born in May, 1670, and the tradition of his first elevation to the peerage is as follows:—Charles one day going to see Nell Gwynne, and the little boy being in the room, the King wanted to speak to him. "Come hither, you little bastard, and speak to your father." "Nay, Nelly," said the King, "do not give the child such a name." "Your Majesty," replied Nelly, "has given me no other name by which I may call him!" Upon this the King conferred upon him

Pall Mall is styled by Malcolm, in 1807, a "handsome street, but subject to the endless rattle of coaches, and the lounging place of strings—or rather links, or chains—of men of fashion, and their humble imitators, during the months in which London is tolerable, that is, from December to June." It could not at this time have been well kept or watered, for he complains that "it becomes a desert when the pavements are dry and the carriage way is fit for crossing." He enumerates

MRS FITZHERBERT'S HOUSE, 1820.

NELL GWYNNE'S HOUSE, 1820.

SCHOMBERG HOUSE, 1820.

(From original Drawings in the possession of Mr. Crace.)

as its chief attractions, Carlton House, Kelly's Opera Saloon, or rather music shop—"made fashionable by an odd set of lattices, distributed over the west front,"—and lastly by Christie's Auction Room, which then stood on the south side, next to Schomberg House.

"The late Mr. Christie," observes Malcolm, "was perhaps the most eminent auctioneer in the world"—George Robins, it may be observed by us in passing, was not then known to fame—"and the value of property which waited the tap of his hammer would almost baffle the powers of calculation. The manors, estates, jewels, plate, and collections of pictures which he sold, were situated in or collected from all parts of the kingdom; and he had the singular fortune to dispose of the rich articles and paintings of but too many noble fugitives from France, Italy, and Holland during the French Revolution. This house was and is," he adds, "the exhibition of everything curious in the arts, under his son and successor, who to his father's abilities adds a rich stock of classical attainments." It may be added that the first auction in London is said to have been held in 1700.

Among the other various relics which here passed under the hammer of Messrs. Christie, was the famous Shakspeare Cup, which is thus described by Mr. J. T. Smith:—"The much-famed cup, carved from Shakespeare's mulberry-tree, lined with and standing on a base of silver, with a cover surmounted by a branch of mulberry leaves and fruit, also of silver-gilt, which was presented to Mr. Garrick on the occasion of the Jubilee at Stratford-upon-Avon." It was sold early in the present century by Mr. Christie, who addressed the assembly, adjuring them "by the united names of Shakespeare and Garrick" to offer biddings worthy of the occasion. The first bid was 100 guineas; and it was knocked down ultimately for 121 guineas, the purchaser being Mr. J. Johnson, of Southampton Street, Covent Garden.

How thoroughly these rooms held their position not merely as a mart and market, but also as a criterion of the arts, may be inferred from the first stanza of a poem by Mr. Richard Fenton, published just a century ago :—

" As Painting and Sculpture now bending with years
    Proclaimed an assembly at Christie's great room,
  For adopting an heir, and reflected with tears
    On the days when they boasted their vigour and bloom;
  The doors were scarce opened, when thronging the space
    With different pretensions the candidates pressed."

And so on. What happened does not much matter; but the lines certainly imply that there was

at that time no other "repository" in London where the special works of two at least of the Muses would be likely to find competent critics. Messrs. Christie's sale room was removed in the year 1823 to King Street, St. James's Square.

It is mentioned incidentally by Miss Meteyard, in her "Life of Wedgwood," that in 1768 the great master of pottery was in treaty for some premises in Pall Mall, which had been formerly used as auction rooms, but were then occupied as an "Artists' Exhibition Gallery;" and she gives a print of the house as it then stood. The negotiation, however, passed off.

On the south side also, nearly opposite to the entrance leading to the west side of St. James's Square, is a mansion of the last century, built by Sir John Soane, formerly belonging to Lord Temple, and afterwards to his son, the Marquis of Buckingham, and sometimes therefore called Buckingham House. One night, if we may believe Sir N. W. Wraxall, Mr. (afterwards Lord) Nugent was at a party at Lord Temple's, when, in a foolish frolic, he laid a bet with his host that he would spit in Lord Bristol's hat. He coolly did so, then pretended to apologise for the indecorum, and asked to be allowed to wipe off the affront with his pocket-handkerchief. With a coolness and high breeding which marks the perfect gentleman, Lord Bristol took out his own handkerchief, and performed that office for himself, and then sat down to a rubber of whist. Next morning, however, Lord Bristol addressed him a note demanding an apology or instant satisfaction. Mr. Nugent, judging the matter serious, and not wishing to be made the laughing-stock of the town by fighting a duel for so silly a freak, found himself obliged to tender an apology, to which Lord Temple also was forced to subscribe, both asking his pardon at White's Club. Lord Bristol declared himself satisfied, and there the matter happily ended without blood being shed. This Lord Bristol was George, the eldest son of the famous Lord Hervey, whom Pope has most unjustly handed down to posterity as "Sporus" and "Lord Fanny," and like his father, he had an effeminate manner, which led Mr. Nugent to take the liberty of insulting him—with what result we have seen.

Mr. Nugent is the same individual of whom the same writer tells us another capital story. When he was a member of the House of Commons, in the early part of the reign of George III., a bill was introduced for the better watching of the streets of London and Westminster. One of the clauses proposed that watchmen should be made to go to sleep in the day-time, so as to make them the more active at night. Mr. Nugent, with admirable humour, got up, and in his usual Irish accent, begged the Ministers to include him personally in the provisions of the bill, as he was frequently so tormented with the gout that he could sleep neither by day nor by night. Glover, in speaking of this Mr. Nugent, describes him in very just terms, as " a jovial and voluptuous Irishman, who had left Popery for the Protestant religion, widows, and money." Singularly enough, a great part of his wealth in the end came to the son of this same Lord Temple, afterwards Marquis of Buckingham, by his marriage with Lord Nugent's daughter and heiress.

Buckingham House was the head-quarters of the Tory party in the eventful days of the struggles between Pitt and Fox. Accordingly it suffered some indignities from the mob who marched from Covent Garden to Devonshire House, carrying Mr. Fox in triumph on their shoulders as member for Westminster, in 1784. Five years later, the mansion of Lord Buckingham was tenanted by the Duchess of Gordon, whom Pitt and Dundas put forward as the Tory " Queen of Society," in opposition to the Duchess of Devonshire. With her five unmarried daughters she brought together here the leaders of the " constitutional" party, both Lords and Commons, summoning doubtful members to her receptions, questioning and remonstrating with them, and using all other feminine arts for confirming their allegiance to Pitt.

Buckingham House now forms part of the Government Offices, having been purchased by the War Department. The department of the Secretary for War, the duties of which were formerly performed at the Horse Guards, was established in the year 1856. Up to that time, as we learn from " Murray's Official Handbook," the business had formed part of the duty of the Secretary of State ; but the consolidation of the finance of the army in his department had become so inconvenient, that this separate office was then created. Since the remodelling of the administration of our military department after the Crimean war, the Secretary of State for War has been really the supreme controller of the army, assuming and exercising a power which essentially minimises that of the Commander-in-Chief. " Not a soldier can be moved," writes the author of the " Personal History of the Horse Guards," " not an alteration effected, or a comfort administered which involves the expenditure of a shilling, unless it pleases the Secretary for War ; he is the prime originator, the Commander-in-Chief the instrument ; the one pulls the strings, the other is the puppet."

Before the War Office is a statue of Lord Herbert of Lea, its pedestal inscribed with the name by which he is better known, " Sidney Herbert." " It stands," observes the writer above quoted, " in front of the office which he had dignified by his labours and accomplishments."

At the western end of Pall Mall, and on the south side, almost completely shut out from view by the walls and out-buildings which partially enclose it, and also by the buildings forming the southern side of the street, stands Marlborough House, the town residence of the Prince of Wales. Built in 1709-10, by Sir Christopher Wren for John, Duke of Marlborough, on ground leased on easy terms to his Duchess by Queen Anne ; it occupies the site of the old pheasantry of St. James's Palace, and of the garden of Mr. Secretary Boyle, the latter of which was taken out of St. James's Park. The supplement to the *Gazette* of April 18th, 1709, says :—" Her Majesty having been pleased to grant to his Grace the Duke of Marlborough the Friary next St. James's Palace, in which lately dwelt the Countess du Roy, the same is pulling down in order to rebuild the house for his Grace ; and about a third of the garden lately in the occupation of the Right Hon. Henry Boyle, her Majesty's Principal Secretary of State, is marked out in order to be annexed to the house of his Grace the Duke of Marlborough." The lease of the site was for fifty years, at a low rental ; and this was nearly the only boon which the haughty and grasping Duchess of Marlborough obtained from her royal mistress, as she boasts in a letter of Vindication which was published in her name. How true this statement is will be seen presently.

Marlborough House is thus described by Defoe in his " Journey through England " in 1722 :— " The palace of the Duke of Marlborough is in every way answerable to the grandeur of its master. Its situation is more confined than that of the Duke of Buckinghamshire, but the body of the house is much nobler, more compact, and the apartments better composed. It is situated at the west end of the King's Garden on the Park side, and fronts the Park, but with no other prospect but that view. Its court is very spacious and finely paved ; the offices are large, and on each side as you enter ; the stairs, mounting to the gate, are very noble."

The building is a stately red-brick edifice, ornamented with stone. The front is very extensive ; and the wings on each side are decorated at the corners with stone rustic-work. A small colonnade extends on the side of the area next the wings; the opposite side of the area is occupied by sundry offices. The top of the house was originally finished with a balustrade, but that was subsequently altered, and the first storey crowned by an attic raised above the cornice. The front towards the Park resembles the other; only instead of there being two wings, there are niches for statues; and instead of the area as in front, there is a descent by a flight of steps into the gardens. The vestibule was painted with a representation of the battle of Hochstet, in which the most remarkable incident was the taking of Marshal Tallart, the French general, and several other officers of distinction, prisoners; the long series of battles in which the illustrious duke was engaged, including of course those of Malplaquet and Blenheim, were painted by La Guerre as ornaments for the house.

If Marlborough House, even now, is quiet and retired, what must it have been when it was first built, when it was shut in upon two sides by a grove of chestnut-trees, its west front open to the gardens of the Palace, its south to the Park, then private? " Here, and at Blenheim," observes Malcolm, " it might have been supposed that the conqueror of so many battles would have enjoyed the honours lavished on him; but party, ambition, and peculation stepped in, and prevented him from enjoying repose. Had he fallen in battle on the day of his last victory, his memory would have been more gratefully remembered by his countrymen."

It is well known to readers of history that the Duke of Marlborough outlived not only his fame but his reason, and during his latter years was reduced to a state of imbecility, of which he was so conscious that he never liked to be seen by strangers, becoming, as it has been said, a "driveller and a show;" though Archdeacon Coxe, in his "Life" of the duke—the substance of which was inspired by the family—appears to represent him as having retained his powers to the last. One day the witty Dr. Monsey being at Marlborough House, and wishing to get slily a view of the duke, hid himself behind a door in the hall, but did not manage to escape detection. Taylor tells us in his "Recollections" that "the duke, all the while that he was getting into his (sedan) chair, and when he was seated, kept his eye fixed on the doctor, and at the moment when the chairmen were carrying him away, the doctor saw the duke's features gather into a whimper like those of a child, and the tears start into his eyes."

Lord Sackville used to say that one of his earliest memories was that of being carried, when a child

of five years old, to the gate of St. James's Palace, in order to see the great Duke of Marlborough, as he came away from court. "He was then (1721) in a state of caducity, but he still retained the vestiges of a most graceful figure, though he was obliged to be supported by a servant on either side, whilst the tears ran down his cheeks, just as he is drawn by Dr. Johnson. The populace cheered him as he passed through the crowd to enter his carriage. I have, however, heard my father say," adds Lord Sackville, "that the duke by no means fell into settled or irrecoverable dotage, as is commonly supposed, but manifested at times a sound understanding till within a very short period of his decease, occasionally attending the Privy Council, and sometimes speaking in his official capacity on matters of business with his former ability."

For the Duke of Marlborough's first step on the ladder of advancement, as Macaulay hints in his "History of England," he was perhaps indebted to the fact of his sister Arabella Churchill being the mistress of James II., as this led to his introduction to the gay scenes of court life. Of the duke in his early days, Macaulay tells a story to the effect that he was one day nearly surprised by the King in the chamber of the Duchess of Cleveland, but effected his escape by leaping out of the window in time to shield his paramour. The duchess rewarded her youthful lover with a present of £5,000, which the prudent young officer laid out in the purchase of a well-secured annuity. Pope adds, it is to be hoped untruly, though we know that the duke grew very avaricious in his old age :—

> " The gallant, too, to whom she paid it down,
> Lived to refuse his mistress half-a-crown."

So intense was the avarice of the old duke, who at his death in 1722 left a million and a half behind him, that he would walk home from the Palace or from his neighbour's house, however cold the night, in order to save sixpence in the hire of a sedan chair.

Pope often satirised the Duke of Marlborough. In the early editions of the " Moral Essays " the following lines were inserted, though subsequently suppressed :—

> " Triumphant leaders at an army's head,
> Hemm'd round with glories, pilfer cloth, or bread;
> As meanly plunder as they bravely fought,
> Now save a people, and now save a groat."

The satire here is general as respects the army —and nothing could be more lax or extravagant than the system of military accounts and supplies—

but the poet evidently points to Marlborough, whose avarice he frequently condemns. The general did not *pilfer*, but he had taken presents from army contractors. One of the most striking illustrations of his penurious habits, and the best comment on Pope's verses, is an anecdote related by Warton, on the authority of Colonel Selwyn. The night before the battle of Blenheim, after a council of war had been held in Marlborough's tent, at which Prince Louis of Baden and Prince Eugene assisted, the latter, after the council had broken up, stepped back to the tent to communicate something he had forgotten, when he found the duke giving orders to his aide-de-camp at the table, on which there was now only a single light burning, all the others having been extinguished the moment the council was over. "What a man is this," said Prince Eugene, "who at such a time can think of saving the ends of candles!"

After her husband's death his widow, Sarah, continued to live here, and, as we know from the diaries of the time, delighted to speak of "neighbour George," as she styled the Hanoverian King who lived in St. James's.

The readers of English history, and of Mr. Harrison Ainsworth's historical romance of "St. James's," will not need to be reminded of the character of this imperious and ambitious woman, who kept Queen Anne, as well as her court, in awe of her power. It may be well, however, to say that, from the day of that Queen's accession, she lost no opportunity of aggrandising her husband's family and her own at the cost of the patient and long-enduring public. She quickly obtained from the personage whom she styled "her royal mistress," besides large pensions, the posts of Groom of the Stole, Keeper of the Great and Home Parks, and of the Privy Purse, and Mistress of the Robes, whilst she extended her female influence by uniting her eldest daughter, Lady Henrietta Churchill, to the eldest son of the Earl of Godolphin, the Lord High Treasurer; her second daughter, Lady Anne, to the Earl of Sunderland; her third, Lady Elizabeth, to the Earl of Bridgewater; and her youngest, Lady Mary, to the Marquis of Monthermer, afterwards by her interest created Duke of Montagu. Hence the Marlborough and Godolphin party, having almost a monopoly of court influence and favour, were called by their opponents "The Family."

The duchess was accustomed to give here an annual feast, to which she invited all her relations, many of whom were expectant legatees in case of her demise. At one of these family gatherings, she exclaimed, "What a glorious sight it is to see such a number of branches flourishing from the same root!" "Alas!" sighed Jack Spencer to a first cousin next him, "the branches would flourish far better if the root were under ground."

Here, too, in October, 1744, having survived all her children but one, and her husband by more than twenty years, the duke's haughty and imperious widow died at the age of eighty-four. The youngest of the three daughters of a plain country gentleman, Mr. Richard Jennings, of Holywell, on the outskirts of the town of St. Albans, she was sent to London at twelve years old, to become the playmate of the Princess Anne at the court of James II., in each of whose wives she found a patroness in succession. At nineteen she married Colonel John Churchill, "the handsome Englishman," whose merits Turenne had even then acknowledged. Though fond of her husband almost to a fault, she became so intimate a friend of the Princess that they agreed to call each other "Mrs. Freeman" and "Mrs. Morley" respectively. She had apartments in the "Cock-pit" at Whitehall before the abdication of James, and so played her cards as to become a necessary adjunct to the courts of Mary and of Anne, in both of which successively she reigned as "Queen Sarah," at once a beauty and a wit. For the first ten years of Anne's reign she governed the Queen herself without a rival, her husband's successes in war serving to consolidate her power. The accession of Harley and the Tory and High Church party to place and power to some extent shook her influence at Court, which was still further imperilled by her opposition to Queen Anne's wish to exclude the Hanoverian succession. She now became head of the opposition, and exerted in this capacity a really formidable power. She was attacked by Swift, and waged war to the knife with Sir John Vanbrugh, all the years during which he was building Blenheim, and also with Sir Robert Walpole, in spite of his Whig principles. To attempt to give an outline of her career, however, would be to write the history of three reigns, which would be foreign to our purpose here.

Many anecdotes of the Duchess of Marlborough are to be gleaned from books of cotemporary memoirs; none, however, show her character more forcibly than the following:—After the death of her husband, the great Duke of Marlborough, her hand was solicited—partly, no doubt, on account of her wealth—by Charles Seymour, the "Proud" Duke of Somerset, whose first wife had been the heiress of the Percies, and who thought that he honoured her by making the offer of his hand. "The widow of Marlborough shall never become the wife of any other man," was her haughty reply. Whilst she filled the *salons* of Marlborough House with the leaders of the Whig party, the "queen" of the Jacobite Tory circles was the Duchess of Buckingham, a natural daughter of James II. For

retorted her Grace of Buckingham; "since I made the request, I have seen the undertaker, who tells me that he can make as good a one for twenty pounds."

Many other stories, as may easily be imagined,

MARLBOROUGH HOUSE, 1710. *From a contemporary Engraving.* (*See p.* 129.)

her rival she felt both contempt and aversion. Her Grace of Buckingham, on being left a widow, made for him a funeral just as splendid as that with which "Queen" Sarah had honoured her lord; and when her son died, she even sent to Marlborough House to borrow the funeral car on which the hero of Blenheim had been conveyed to his tomb. "It carried my Lord of Marlborough," cried the duchess fiercely, "and it never sha carry any other." "It is of no consequence,"

are current respecting the Duchess of Marlborough. It is said she once pressed the duke to take a medicine, adding, with her usual warmth, "I'll be hanged if it do not prove serviceable." Dr. Garth, who was present, exclaimed, "Do take it, then, my lord duke, for it must be of service one way or the other." Among the duchess's constant guests was Bishop Burnet, whose absence of mind was notorious. Dining with her Grace after her husband's fall, he compared that great general to

Belisarius. " But," said the duchess, eagerly, " how came it that such a man was so miserable, and universally deserted?" "Oh, madam," exclaimed the *distrait* prelate, " he had such a brimstone of a wife !"

Horace Walpole tells an amusing anecdote about

never been removed. The reason is given by Thornton in his "Survey of London and Westminster:"—" When this noble structure was first finished, the late Duchess of Marlborough intended to have opened a way to it from Pall Mall, directly in the front, as appears from the manner in which

SARAH, DUCHESS OF MARLBOROUGH.　(*From the Portrait by Lely.*)

the haughty duchess in her last days. He writes :— " Old Marlborough is dying ; but who can tell? Last year she had lain a great while ill, without speaking. Her physician said, ' that she must be blistered, or she will die.' She called out, ' I won't be blistered, and I won't die !' And she kept her word ; at all events, she recovered for a time."

Many Londoners, no doubt, have often wondered why the houses between Marlborough House and Pall Mall, which so obstruct the view, have

the court-yard is formed. But she reckoned without her host : Sir Robert Walpole having purchased the house before it, and not being on good terms with the duchess, she was prevented from executing her design."

The mansion was bought by the Crown, in the year 1817, for the Princess Charlotte and Prince Leopold, but the Princess died before the purchase was actually completed. Her widower, however (afterwards King of the Belgians), lived in it for several years.

In 1828 there was a talk, but only a talk, as we learn from the Correspondence of the Duke of Wellington, about pulling down Marlborough House and building a street upon its site. The question appears to have been discussed among the Lords of the Treasury on financial grounds, and then to have died away; probably their decision, if any was arrived at, was based on the experience gained at Carlton House.

In 1837 the mansion was thoroughly repaired, decorated, and furnished, and settled by Act of Parliament on Queen Adelaide as a Dowager house. She occupied it till her death in 1849.

Considering that Marlborough House has been the residence of the Prince and Princess of Wales ever since their marriage in 1863, having been settled in 1850 on the Prince on his coming of age, it seems strange to find the following paragraph in the *Weekly Post* of 1714:—"The Duke of Marlborough has presented his house to the Prince and Princess of Wales; and it is said a terrace walk will be erected, to join the same to St. James's House (*sic*)." The mansion then lent to the one Prince of Wales is now the property of the other.

Shortly after the settlement of Marlborough House upon the Prince of Wales, the lower part of the building was appropriated to the accommodation of the Vernon collection of pictures, and others of the English school, until they could be fitly hung in the National Gallery. The upper rooms were set apart for the use of the Department of Practical Art, for a library, museum of manufactures, the ornamental casts of the School of Design, a lecture-room, &c. Here, in 1852, was designed the Duke of Wellington's funeral car, which was subsequently exhibited to the public in a temporary building in the court-yard.

A few of the literary associations of Pall Mall in the last century are thus briefly recorded by Mr. John Timbs in his "Curiosities of London:"—"In gay bachelor's chambers in this street lived 'Beau Fielding'—Steele's 'Orlando the Fair;' here he was married to a supposed lady of fortune, brought to him in a mourning coach and dressed in widow's weeds, which led to his trial for bigamy. Fielding's namesake places Nightingale and Tom Jones in Pall Mall, when they leave the lodgings of Mrs. Miller in Bond Street. Letitia Pilkington for a short time kept here a pamphlet and print shop. At the sign of 'Tully's Head,' Robert Dodsley, formerly a footman, opened a shop in 1735, with the profits of a volume of his poems and of a comedy, published through the kindness of Pope; and this soon afterwards was followed by the 'Economy of Human Life,' and Sterne's

'Tristram Shandy.' Robert Dodsley retired in 1759, but his brother James, his partner, continued the business until his death in 1797; he is buried at St. James's, Piccadilly." The "Tully's Head" was the resort of Pope, Chesterfield, Lyttelton, Shenstone, Johnson, and Glover, as also of Horace Walpole, the Wartons, and Edmund Burke.

The sign of Dodsley's house—which, by the way, was in an age before shops were designated by numbers—was set up out of his regard for Cicero. It is thus mentioned in a newspaper of the time:—

> " Where Tully's bust and honour'd name
> 　Point out the venal page,
> There Dodsley consecrates to fame
> 　The classics of the age.
> Persist to grace this humble post
> 　Be Tully's head the sign,
> Till future booksellers shall boast,
> 　To sell their tomes as thine."

At Dodsley's, in the winter of 1748-49, was held a meeting at which Warton, Moore, Garrick, Goldsmith, Dr. Johnson, and other literary men were present: on this occasion the title of the then newly intended periodical, the *Rambler*, was discussed. "Garrick," says Boswell, "proposed that it should be called the 'Salad,' on account of the variety of its ingredients"—a name which, by a curious coincidence, was afterwards applied to himself by Goldsmith :—

> " Our Garrick's a salad, for in him we see
> 　Oil, vinegar, sugar, and saltness agree !"

Dodsley proposed that it should be called the *World*, and at last the company parted without any suggestion of which they all approved being offered. Johnson, it is well known, the same night sat down by his bedside, and resolved that he would not go to sleep till he had fixed a title. "The *Rambler* seemed to me the best," he says, "and so I took it."

At Dodsley's shop was published in 1759 the first volume of the *Annual Register*, planned and prepared by Edmund Burke, whose name had recently become known to the world by his "Essay on the Sublime and Beautiful." To it Burke contributed for many years the department entitled "The Historical Chronicle," as well as some philosophical and other essays. The result was to establish the reputation of the *Annual Register* as a standard work of reference and general information, and for a century and more a fit companion for our library shelves to the *Gentleman's Magazine*.

Dodsley's shop, as already remarked, was the

recognised rendezvous and centre of all who were learned or who cultivated a literary taste. Hence when Burke anonymously published his " Vindication of Natural Society" as a satire on and imitation of Lord Bolingbroke, we read that the poet David Mallet rushed into Mr. Dodsley's when it was most crowded, and made an open disclaimer of its authorship on behalf of both Bolingbroke and himself.

In 1780, Mr. H. Payne, whose shop, as we learn from his title-pages, stood " opposite Marlborough House in Pall Mall," published for an unknown and unbefriended writer named George Crabbe, " The Candidate ; a Poetical Epistle to the Authors of the *Monthly Review*." Crabbe was poor; within a few weeks his publisher failed ; and the young poet was plunged into great perplexity, which led him to seek aid—but in vain—in high circles, where afterwards, when he no longer needed it, he found ready assistance and support. So selfish and blind is human nature.

Apropos of the literary character or reputation of this locality in former times, it may be stated that Pall Mall has given a name to more than one newspaper, all of which perhaps have almost passed clean out of memory. In 1865 was commenced the evening paper bearing the title of the *Pall Mall Gazette;* this, however, has little or nothing to do with Pall Mall, except that it is supposed to retail much of Club talk and gossip. There was published in the reign of George II. a collection of loose tales and biographical sketches, mainly taken from West-end life, and named the " Pall Mall Miscellany." It went through several editions.

As a proof of the rural character of this part of the town, it may be mentioned that in the reign of Charles II. there was in Pall Mall—as at a later time in Piccadilly—an inn rejoicing in the name of the " Hercules' Pillars," denoting, of course, the very westernmost extremity of what then was the metropolis.

" The Feathers " is, of course, the symbol of the Prince of Wales ; and there can be no doubt that, considering the fact of the Prince and Princess of Wales being resident at Marlborough House, the sign of " The Feathers" would be by far the most popular now-a-days, if it were still the fashion to denote the houses in Pall Mall and elsewhere by signs instead of numbers.

There was a sign of " The Feathers" in Pall Mall during the time of the Great Plague, as is clear from the following advertisement in one of the newspapers published at that time :—" The late Countess of Kent's powder has been lately experimented upon divers infected persons with admirable success. The virtues of it against the plague and all malignant distempers are sufficiently known to all the physicians of Christendom, and the powder itself, prepared by the only person living that has the true receipt, is to be had at the third part of the ordinary price at Mr. Calvert's, at ' The Feathers,' in the old Pall Mall, near St. James's," &c.

On the north side of Pall Mall, a little to the east of St. James's Street, stood formerly the Shakespeare Gallery, the creation of that real and true patron of art, and especially of historical painting and engraving, Alderman Boydell, whose name is far less well known than it deserves to be among artists and men of taste. Beginning life as an engraver, he spent a larger sum than any nobleman had done up to that time in encouraging a British school of engraving; for, as he tells us in one of his appeals, " when he commenced business nearly all the fine engravings sold in England were imported from abroad, and more especially from France." The outbreak of the French Revolution seriously embarrassed his venture in this artistic business, and in 1789 he was obliged to make arrangements for disposing of his Gallery. He brought out, happily, a costly edition of the works of Shakespeare, the profits of which, together with a Shaksperian lottery, saved him from bankruptcy. After his death, however, the Gallery was for some years vacant, and Malcolm in 1807 speaks of it as " a melancholy memento of the irretrievable ruin of the arts in England."

When Alderman Boydell first proposed, in the interest of the fine arts, to issue his superb edition of Shakespeare, an envious cotemporary imputed his patriotism to sheer vanity, and the following lines appeared in one at least of the journals :—

" Old Father Time, as Ovid sings,
Is a great eater up of things,
And without salt or mustard
Will gulp down e'en a castle wall
As easily as at Guildhall
An alderman eats custard.

But Boydell, careful of his fame,
By grafting it on Shakespeare's name,
Shall beat his neighbours hollow :
For to the Bard of Avon's stream
Old Time has said, with Polypheme,
' You'll be the last I'll swallow.'

In the last century, the pillory was occasionally set up here, as well as at Charing Cross ; one of the last sufferers from this punishment in Pall Mall was a notorious lady of the stamp of Mrs. Cornelys, who was pelted with rotten eggs by the gentry as well as by the rabble, and, if tradition may be believed, by the soldiery as well. She had probably been plying her trade in the neighbourhood of St. James's.

John Timbs reminds us that Pall Mall had at an early date its notable sights and amusements. "In 1701 were shown here models of William III.'s palaces at Loo and Hunstaerdike, 'brought over by outlandish men,' with curiosities disposed of 'on public raffling days.' In 1733 'a holland smock, a cap, checked stockings, and laced shoes,' were run for by four women in the afternoon, in Pall Mall; and one of its residents, the High Constable of Westminster, gave a prize laced hat to be run for by five men, which created so much riot and mischief that the magistrates issued precepts to prevent future runs to the very man most active in promoting them!" In the old "Star and Garter" house, westward of Carlton House, was exhibited, in 1815, the Waterloo Museum of portraits and battle scenes, cuirasses, helmets, sabres, firearms, and trophies of Waterloo; besides a large picture of the battle painted by a Flemish artist. At No. 121 Campanani exhibited his Etruscan and Greek Antiquities, in rooms fitted up as the "Chambers of Tombs."

At No. 52, on the north side, now the Marlborough Club, the British Institution was founded as far back as 1805 for the encouragement of native art, by affording to English artists facilities for the exhibition and sale of their productions. The Institution had two exhibitions every year; the former from February to May for the works of living artists, and the latter from June to the end of the summer for the works of old masters, lent by their owners for the occasion. Here was exhibited West's large picture of "Christ healing the Sick in the Temple," bought by the British Institution for 3,000 guineas, and presented to the National Gallery. Pall Mall has always been a place for exhibitions, especially of pictures. In the present year (1882) here are three or four galleries devoted to the fine arts:—No. 53 is the Institute of Painters in Water Colours; the British Gallery of Art is at No. 57; and No. 120, further eastward, is the Exhibition of Paintings by Continental Artists.

On the site of the British Institution, in the early part of the reign of George III. (1764-5), was "Almack's Club." It was celebrated as the home of Macaronis and high play. It was afterwards known as "Goose-tree's" Club, and William Pitt was one of its frequenters. It was here that he made the acquaintance of Wilberforce. Of the association so long known as "Almack's" we shall have more to say when we come to King Street. Mr. Timbs mentions here a club called the "*Je ne sais quoi*" Club, of which he says that the Prince of Wales, the Dukes of York, Clarence, Orleans, Norfolk, and Bedford, were members; but no details of its history are known to exist.

Among the *habitués* of Pall Mall, in the days of the Regency, was George Hanger, the eccentric "Lord Coleraine." Mr. C. Redding says in his "Recollections:"—"He might be seen in Pall Mall riding his grey pony without a servant; then dismounting at a bookseller's shop, he would get a boy to hold his horse, and sit upon the counter for an hour, talking to Burdett, Bosville, or Major James, who used to haunt that shop, Budd and Calkin's then or afterwards. He was a very rough subject, but honest to the backbone, and plain speaking. He carried a short, thick shillelagh, and now and then took his quid. A favourite of the Prince of Wales, he administered a well-merited reproof to the Prince and the Duke of York one day at Carlton House for the grossness of their language. His name in consequence became no longer on the list of guests there. Upon this, as often related by others, he advertised himself as a coal merchant. Meeting the Prince one day on horseback afterwards, the former addressed him, 'Well, George, how go coals now?' 'Black as ever, please your Royal Highness,' was the quick reply."

In this street was living Lord George Germain, when Secretary of State for the American department in 1781; and here Sir N. W. Wraxall, Lord Walsingham, and a large party were dining in the November of that year, when a messenger arrived announcing the defeat and surrender of the forces in America under Lord Cornwallis. The tidings sent on to the King at Kew, Wraxall tells us, never disturbed the King's dignity nor affected his self-command, deeply as it grieved his heart.

At her residence in Pall Mall, in 1815, at the age of eighty-three, died the celebrated Mrs. Abington, the first actress who played the part of *Lady Teazle* in the "School for Scandal." "Of all the theatrical ungovernable ladies under Mr. Garrick's management," says Mr. Raikes, in his "Book for a Rainy Day," "Mrs. Abington, with her capriciousness, inconsistency, injustice, and unkindness, perplexed him the most. She was not unlike the miller's mare, for ever looking for a white stone to shy at. And though no one has charged her with malignant mischief, she was never more delighted than when in a state of hostility, often arising from most trivial circumstances, discovered in mazes of her own ingenious construction. Mrs. Abington, in order to keep up her card-parties, of which she was very fond, and which were attended by many ladies of the highest rank, absented herself from her abode to live *incog*. For this purpose she generally took a small lodging in one of the passages leading from Stafford Row, Pimlico, where plants are so placed at the windows as nearly to shut out the light, at all events, to render the apartments impervious to the inquisitive eye of such characters as Liston represented in 'Paul Pry.' Now and then, she would take a small house at the end of Mount Street, and there live with her servant in the kitchen, till it was time to reappear; and then some of her friends would compliment her on the effects of her summer's excursion."

In the year 1756 a gentleman named William Backwell, one of the partners in the banking-house of Messrs. Child, of Temple Bar, started on his own account a bank in Pall Mall, and named it "The Grasshopper." It dragged on its existence, in anything but prosperity, down to 1810, when it closed its accounts, and its business was absorbed into other establishments. The Army and Navy Club occupies the site of the bank.

As one of the leading thoroughfares in the neighbourhood of the Court and the aristocracy, Pall Mall is very naturally associated in our minds with the coaches and sedan chairs of our grandfathers' days. Nor will the English reader probably have forgotten how Gay alludes to the latter in his "Trivia:"—

> " For who the footman's arrogance can quell,
> Whose flambeau gilds the sashes of Pall Mall,
> When in long ranks a train of torches flame,
> To light the midnight visits of the dame?"

But of these we have already spoken in our chapter on St. James's Palace.

In this street was an old and fashionable hotel, now long forgotten, named the "Star and Garter." Here, as we learn from the title-page of a small publication on the rules of that English game, were "The Laws of Cricket revised on February 25, 1774, by a committee of noblemen and gentlemen." The " Rules " are prefaced by a woodcut of the bat then in use, which appears to have been curved, and with a face perfectly flat, whereas the modern bat is quite straight, and has a face slightly convex. Perhaps the best information about the early history of the game is to be found in " The Young Cricketer's Tutor, by John Nyren," who was for many years a celebrated member of the Hambledon Club.

In one of the public rooms of the " Star and Garter," in 1762, was fought the fatal duel between William, fifth Lord Byron, and his neighbour in Nottinghamshire, old Mr. Chaworth. The ground of the quarrel was a trivial one, arising out of a heated argument over a dinner-table; but in little more than an hour from its commencement, Mr. Chaworth received a mortal wound from his opponent. Lord Byron — who was the great-uncle and immediate predecessor of the poet—was tried for the capital offence; but the House of Lords found him guilty of manslaughter only, and, as he pleaded his privilege of peerage, he was let off, and discharged from custody on payment of the fees! The "Star and Garter" was famous for its choice dinners and its exorbitant prices, as we learn from the *Connoisseur* of 1754.

It may sound strange when we tell our readers that, as late as the year 1786, a highway robbery was committed on one of his Majesty's mails in Pall Mall. At all events, Horace Walpole writes in January of that year: "On the 7th, half an hour after eight, the mail from France was robbed in Pall Mall—yes, in the great thoroughfare of London, and within call of the Guard at the palace. The chaise had stopped, the harness was cut, and the portmanteau was taken out of the chaise itself. What think you of banditti in the heart of such a capital?"

The Hon. Amelia Murray writes, in her " Recollections," under the year 1811: " It was about this time that gas was first introduced into England; a German of the name of Winsor gave lectures about it in Pall Mall. He had made his first public experiments at the Lyceum, in the Strand, in 1803. He afterwards lighted with gas the walls of Carlton Palace Gardens, on the king's birthday, in 1807, and during 1809 and the following year he lighted a portion of Pall Mall. He died in 1830. My eldest brother," she adds, "and my uncle were so convinced of the importance of the discovery, that they exerted themselves to get a bill through Parliament which gave permission for an experiment to be made ; and my uncle established the first gas-works. Like all the pioneers in great works, he was ruined, and his country place, Farnborough Hill, came to the hammer. Since then the old house has been taken down, and a modern mansion has been built by the present possessor of the property ; and it is a curious circumstance that the new house is lit throughout by gas made upon the spot. The greatest chemists and philosophers may be mistaken. In 1809, Sir Humphry Davy gave it as his opinion that it would be as easy to bring down a bit of the moon to light London, as to succeed in doing so with gas!" Walker says, in his " Original:" " The first exhibition of gas was made by Winsor, in a row of lamps in front of the colonnade before Carlton House, then standing on the lower part of Waterloo Place; and I remember hearing Winsor's plan of lighting the metropolis laughed to scorn by a company of very scientific men." To our disgrace, Grosvenor Square was the last public place in the West-end of London where gas was adopted.

Macaulay thus records the state of the metropolis, in respect to lighting, two centuries ago :— "It ought to be noticed that, in the last year of the reign of Charles the Second, began a great of one night in three. But such was not the feeling of his contemporaries. His scheme was enthusiastically applauded, and furiously attacked. The friends of improvement extolled him as the greatest of all the benefactors of his city. What, they asked, were the boasted inventions of Archimedes, when compared with the achievement of the man who had turned the nocturnal shades into noon-day? In spite of these eloquent eulogies

THE SHAKESPEARE GALLERY, PALL MALL. *From a Drawing in Mr. Crace's Collection.* (*See p.* 135.)

change in the police of London, a change which has perhaps added as much to the happiness of the body of the people as revolutions of much greater fame. An ingenious projector, named Edward Heming, obtained letters patent conveying to him, for a term of years, the exclusive right of lighting up London. He undertook, for a moderate consideration, to place a light before every tenth door, on moonless nights, from Michaelmas to Lady Day, and from six to twelve of the clock. Those who now see the capital all the year round, from dusk to dawn, blazing with a splendour beside which the illuminations for La Hogue and Blenheim would have looked pale, may perhaps smile to think of Heming's lanterns, which glimmered feebly before one house in ten during a small part the cause of darkness was not left undefended. There were fools in that age who opposed the introduction of what was called the new light, as strenuously as fools in our age have opposed the introduction of vaccination and railroads. Many years after the date of Heming's patent there were extensive districts in London in which no lamp was seen."

Those who may wish for further information on the subject of gas will find it in a work called "Angliæ Metropolis," 1690, sect. 17, entitled, "Of the New Lights," and in two works on gas-lighting by the late Mr. Samuel Clegg, jun. (son of the inventor of the gas-meter), and by Mr. Samuel Hughes, both published some years ago in Weale's "Educational Series."

OLD HOUSES IN PALL MALL, ABOUT 1830. (*From an Original Drawing in Mr. Crace's Collection.*)

CHAPTER XII.

PALL-MALL.—CLUB-LAND.

"Man is a social animal."—Aristotle, "Politics."

Advantages of the Club System—Dr. Johnson on Club-Life—Earliest Mention of Clubbing—Club-Life in Queen Anne's Time—The "Albion" Hotel—The "King's Head" and the "World" Club—Usual Arrangements of a Club House—The "Guards'" Club—"Junior Naval and Military"—The "Army and Navy"—The "United Service"—The "Junior United Service"—The "Travellers'"—The "Oxford and Cambridge"—The "Union"—The "Athenæum"—Sam Rogers and Theodore Hook—An Anecdote of Thomas Campbell, the Poet—The "Carlton"—The "Reform"—M. Soyer as *Chef de Cuisine*—The Kitchen of the "Reform" Club—Thackeray —at the "Reform" Club The "Pall Mall" "Marlborough," and "Century" Clubs—Sociality of Club-Life.

As Pall Mall and the immediate neighbourhood of St. James's have been for a century the head-quarters of those London clubs which have succeeded to the fashionable coffee-houses, and are frequented by the upper ranks of society, a few remarks on Club-land and Club-life will not be out of place here.

As Walker observes in his "Original," the system of clubs is one of the greatest and most important changes in the society of the present age from that of our grandfathers, when coffee-houses were in fashion. "The facilities of life have been wonderfully increased by them, whilst the expense has been greatly diminished. For a few pounds a year, advantages are to be enjoyed which no fortunes, except the most ample, can procure. . . . For six guineas a year, every member has the command of an excellent library, with maps; of the daily papers, London and foreign, the principal periodicals, and every material for writing, with attendance for whatever is wanted. The building is a sort of palace, and is kept with the same exactness and comfort as a private dwelling. Every member is a master without the troubles of a master. He can come when he pleases, and stay away as long as he pleases, without anything going wrong. He has the command of regular servants, without having to pay or to manage them. He can have whatever meal or refreshment he wants at all hours, and served up with the cleanliness and comfort of his own home. He orders just what he pleases, having no interest to think of but his own. In short, it is impossible to suppose a greater degree of liberty in living. To men who reside in the country and come occasionally to town, a club is particularly advantageous. They have only to take a bed-room, and they have everything else they want, in a more convenient way than by any other plan. Married men whose families are absent find in the arrangements of a club the nearest resemblance to the facilities of home; and bachelors of moderate incomes and simple habits are gainers by such institutions in a degree beyond calculation. They live much cheaper, with more ease and freedom, in far better style, and with much greater advantages as to society, than formerly. Before the establishment of clubs, no money could procure many of the enjoyments which are now within the reach of an income of three hundred a year. . . . Neither could the same facilities of living, nor the same opportunities of cultivating society, have been commanded twenty years since" [he wrote this in 1835] "on any terms. . . . In my opinion, a well-constituted club is an institution affording advantages unmixed with alloy."

In these remarks Mr. Walker draws for his experience on the club to which he belonged, the "Senior Athenæum;" and he enters into some interesting calculations as to the cost of living, if a man makes such a club his head-quarters. From the accounts of his club in 1832, it appeared that the daily average of dinners was forty-seven and a fraction, and that the dinners for the year, a little over 17,000 in number, cost on an average two shillings and ninepence three farthings, and that the average quantity of wine drunk by each diner was a small fraction over half a pint! It is to be feared that all the clubs in the West-end could not show an equally abstemious set of diners; but still, it may fearlessly be said that the majority of them exhibit a simplicity which contrasts very favourably with the old taverns and coffee-houses of fifty or sixty years ago, and the excesses to which they too often ministered occasion. And although the ladies, as a body, do not like "those clubs," because they are more or less antagonistic to early marriages, yet Mr. Walker defends them on even what may be called the matrimonial ground, asserting that "their ultimate tendency is to encourage marriage, by creating habits in accordance with those of the married state;" and he adds emphatically: "In opposition to the ladies' objections to clubs, I would suggest . . . . that they are a preparation, and not a substitute, for domestic life. Compared with the previous system of living, clubs induce habits of economy, temperance, refinement, regularity, and good order; and as men are in general not content with their condition as long as it can be improved, it is a natural step from the comforts of a club to those of matrimony, and . . . there cannot be better security for the good behaviour of a husband than that he should have been trained in one of these institutions. When ladies suppose that the luxuries and comforts of a club are likely to make men discontented with the enjoyments of domestic life, I think they wrong themselves. One of the chief attractions of a club is, that it offers an imitation of the comforts of home, but only an imitation, and one which will never supersede the reality."

The London system of clubs, grouping, as it does, around Pall Mall and St. James's, finds its outward expression in buildings that give dignity and beauty to the thoroughfare in which they stand by their architectural splendour. They afford advantages and facilities of living which no fortunes, except the most ample, could procure, to thousands of persons most eminent in the land, in every path of life, civil and military, ecclesiastical, peers spiritual and temporal, commoners, men of the learned professions, those connected with literature, science, the arts, and commerce, in all its principal branches, as well as to those who do not belong to any particular class. These are represented by the " Carlton," the " Reform," the " University," the " Athenæum," the " Union," the " United Service," the " Army and Navy," the " Travellers'," and a host of others.

The opinion of Dr. Johnson on the subject of clubs and club-life is well known to every reader of Boswell. A gentleman venturing one day to say to the learned doctor that he sometimes wondered at his condescending to attend a club, the latter replied, " Sir, the great chair of a full and pleasant town club is, perhaps, the throne of human felicity." Again, the learned doctor touches on this phase of life in the great metropolis, in the following conversation, also related by Boswell :— " Talking of a London life," he said, " the happiness of London is not to be conceived but by those who have been in it. I will venture to say, there is more learning and science within the circumference of ten miles from where we now sit, than in all the rest of the kingdom." Boswell : " The only disadvantage is the great distance at which people live from one another." Johnson : " Yes, sir ; but that is occasioned by the largeness of it, which is the cause of all the other advantages." Boswell : " Sometimes I have been in the humour of wishing to retire to a desert." Johnson : " Sir, you have desert enough in Scotland."

Addison, who knew something about the coffee-house, and what we may call the " club-life" of his day, has given us, in his own graphic style, a sketch of St. James's Coffee-house, which stood near the western end of Pall Mall. We have already spoken of him as a frequenter of " Button's "* in Covent Garden, and as a member of the celebrated Kit-cat Club,† in Shire Lane ; indeed, he modestly surmised that his detractors had some colour for calling him the King of Clubs, and oracularly said that " all celebrated clubs were founded on eating and drinking, which are points where most men agree, and in which the learned and the illiterate, the dull and the airy, the philosopher and the buffoon, can all of them bear a part." But it is not every club that has avowed itself by its name or title as formed on this basis. " The Kit-Kat itself," says Addison, in illustration of the proposition quoted from him above, " is said to have taken its original from a Mutton-Pye. The Beef-Steak and October Clubs are neither of them averse to eating and drinking, if we may form a judgment of them from their respective titles."

The truth is, that two centuries ago clubs were the natural resorts of men who, though socially inclined, did not enjoy the social position, and could not, therefore, command the introductions into high circles which were accorded to Pepys or Evelyn in the seventeenth, and to Horace Walpole in the eighteenth century.

Pall Mall, if we may trust John Timbs, was noted for its tavern clubs more than two centuries since. " The first time that Pepys mentions it," writes Peter Cunningham, " is under date 26th July, 1660, where he says, ' We went to Wood's, our old house for clubbing, and there we spent till ten at night.' " The passage is curious, not only as showing how, even at that time, Pall Mall was famous for houses of entertainment, but also as the earliest instance of the use of the verb " to club " in the sense in which we now commonly use it.

Thackeray describes the club-life at the West-end, in Queen Anne's day, with his usual felicity : " It was too hard, too coarse a life, for the sensitive and sickly Pope. He was the only wit of the day . . . . who was not fat. Swift was fat ; Addison was fat ; Steele was fat ; Gay and Thomson were preposterously fat. All that fuddling and punch-drinking, that club and coffee-house boozing, shortened the lives and enlarged the waistcoats of the men of that age." " The chief of the wits of his time, with the exception of Congreve," he writes again, " were what we should now call ' men's men.' They spent many hours of the four-

and-twenty, nearly a fourth part of each day, in clubs and coffee-houses, where they dined, drank, and smoked. Wit and news went by word of mouth : a journal of 1710 contained the very smallest portion of either the one or the other. The chiefs spoke ; the faithful *habitués* sat around ; strangers came to wonder and to listen. . . . The male society passed over their punch-bowls and tobacco-pipes almost as much time as ladies of that age spent over spadille and manille."

We see few traces of club-life in the gossiping writings of Horace Walpole, though so many of his personal friends—George Selwyn, for example —were devoted to its pleasures. For himself, it is scarcely uncharitable to add that he was scarcely robust enough to live in such an element.

The clubs in London in the days of the Regency belonged exclusively to the aristocratic world. In the words of Captain Gronow : " My tradesmen," as King Allen used to call the bankers and the merchants, had not then invaded White's, Boodle's, Brookes's, or Wattier's, in Bolton Street, Piccadilly ; which, with the Guards', Arthur's, and Graham's, were the only clubs at the West-end of the town. " White's" was decidedly the most diffi-cult of entry ; its list of members comprised nearly all the noble names of Great Britain. Its politics were decidedly Tory. Here play was carried on to an extent which made many ravages in large fortunes, the traces of which have not disappeared at the present day. General Scott, the father-in-law of George Canning and the Duke of Portland, was known to have won at " White's " a large fortune ; thanks to his notorious sobriety and knowledge of the game of whist. The general possessed a great advantage over his companions by avoiding those indulgences at the table which used to muddle other men's brains. He confined himself to dining off something like a boiled chicken, with toast and water ; by such a regimen he came to the whist-table with a clear head, and possessing as he did a remarkable memory, with great coolness and judg-ment, he was able to boast that he had won honestly no less than £200,000.

It is traditionally said that the first modern mansion in Pall Mall which was used as a club in the present sense of the word was No. 86, now part of the War Office, and originally built for Edward Duke of York, brother of George III. It was opened as a " subscription house," and called the " Albion Hotel." This must have been towards the end of the last century.

Cyrus Redding tells us that in 1806, when he first came up from Cornwall to London, single men, of all classes, including the best, still passed

a good part of their time in coffee-houses ; the great objection to which plan, he seems to think, was the bad ventilation of these places, and fatal to young men fresh from their country hills. They used to be crowded, especially in the evening, and the conversation in them was general. " The sullen club-house, united with the *rus in urbe* dwelling, and the out-of-town life, not further off than the suburbs, have diminished sociality, and changed the aspect of town intercourse." He means to add, no doubt, " for the worse ;" and possibly the accusation may be true.

Spence tells us in his " Anecdotes " that there was a club held at the " King's Head " in Pall Mall, which arrogantly styled itself " The World." Among its members was Lord Stanhope, after-wards Earl of Chesterfield. " Epigrams were pro-posed to be written on the glasses by each member after dinner : once, when Dr. Young was invited thither, the Doctor would have declined writing because he had no diamond. Lord Stanhope lent him his own diamond, and the Doctor at once improvised the following :—

" Accept a miracle instead of wit :
See two dull lines with Stanhope's pencil writ."

Dr. Johnson, as we have already seen, con-sidered that " the full tide of human life could be seen nowhere save in the Strand ;" but in fifty years after his death the centre of social London had moved somewhat further west, and Theodore Hook, in the reign of William IV., maintained that " the real London is the space between Pall Mall on the south, and Piccadilly on the north, St. James's Street on the west, and the Opera House to the east." At this period, it is to be observed that he himself lived just outside that world which he defined with such geographical precision, being then tenant of a house in Cleveland Row.

Many of the old clubs have passed away, for though some of them, or similar societies, may still exist, they live behind the scenes, instead of figur-ing conspicuously upon the stage of London life. Quite a new order of things has come up : from small social meetings held periodically, the clubs have become permanent establishments, luxurious in all their appointments—some of them indeed occupy buildings which are quite palatial. No longer limited to a few acquaintances familiarly known to each other, they count their numbers by hundreds, and, sleeping accommodation ex-cepted, provide for them abundantly all the com-forts and luxuries of an aristocratic home and admirably-regulated *ménage*, without any of the trouble inseparable from a private household, unless it be one whose management is, as in a club-house, confided to responsible superintendents. Each member of a club is expected to leave his private address with the secretary; but this, of course, remains unknown to the outside world, and considerable advantage frequently results from the arrangement, inasmuch as it was some years ago determined by a County Court judge, who before his elevation to the bench had been sadly annoyed by such visitants, that the interior of a club was inviolable by the bearers of writs, summonses, orders, executions, and the like. Besides those staple features, news-room and coffee-room, the usual accommodation of a club-house comprises library and writing-room, evening or drawing-room, and card-room, billiard and smoking rooms, and even baths and dressing-rooms; also a "house dining-room," committee-room, and other apartments, all appropriately fitted up according to their respective purposes, and supplied with almost every imaginable convenience. In addition to the provision thus amply made for both intellectual and other recreation, there is another important and tasteful department of the establishment—namely, the *cuisine.*

As to the management of a club household, nothing can be more complete or more economical, because all its details are conducted systematically, and therefore without the slightest confusion or bustle. Every one has his proper post and definite duties, and what contributes to his discharging them as he ought is that he has no time to be idle. The following is the scheme of government adopted:—At the head of affairs is the committee of management, who are generally appointed from among the members, and hold office for a certain time, during which they constitute a board of control, from whom all orders emanate, and to whom all complaints are made and irregularities reported. They superintend all matters of expenditure and the accounts, which latter are duly audited every year by others, who officiate as auditors. The committee further appoint the several officers and servants, also the several tradespeople. The full complement of a club-house establishment consists of secretary and librarian, steward, and housekeeper; to these principal officials succeed hall-porter, groom of the chambers, butler, under butler; then, in the kitchen department, clerk of the kitchen, *chef,* cooks, kitchenmaids, &c.; lastly, attendants, or footmen, and female servants, of both which classes the number is greater or less, according to the scale of the household. It may be added that most of the clubs distribute their broken viands to the poor of the surrounding parishes.

So far as the general arrangement of the club-houses is concerned, one description may serve for the whole, as there is little difference between the majority of them. The kitchen, cellars, store-rooms, servants' hall, &c., are situated in the basement of the building. On the ground floor the principal hall is usually entered immediately from the street; in other instances it is preceded by an outer vestibule of smaller dimensions and far more simple architectural character. At a desk near the entrance is stationed the hall-porter, whose office it is to receive and keep an account of all messages, cards, letters, &c., and to take charge of the box into which the members put letters to be delivered to the postman. The two chief apartments on this floor usually are the morning-room and coffee-room, the first of which is the place of general rendezvous in the early part of the day, and for reading the newspapers. In some club-houses there is also what is called the "strangers' coffee-room," into which members can introduce their friends as occasional visitors. The "house dining-room" is generally on this floor. Here, although the *habitués* of the club take their meals in the coffee-room, some of the members occasionally—perhaps about once a month—make up a set dinner-party, for which they previously put down their names, the day and number of guests being fixed: these, in club parlance, are styled "house dinners." Ascending to the upper or principal floor, we find there the evening or drawing room, and card-room; the library, the writing-room. So far as embellishment or architectural effect is concerned, the first mentioned of these rooms is generally the principal apartment in the building. The writing-room is a very great accommodation to members, for many gentlemen write their letters at, and date them from, their club. Upon this floor is generally the committee-room, and likewise the secretary's office. The next, or uppermost floor—which, however, in most cases does not show itself externally, it being concealed in the roof—is appropriated partly to the billiard and smoking rooms, and partly to servants' dormitories, the divisions being kept distinct from each other. Being quite apart from the other public rooms, those for billiards, &c., make no pretensions to outward appearance.

With these preliminary remarks as to our present club system and the usual arrangements of a club-house, we will proceed to speak more individually of the clubs which abound in Pall Mall.

The Guards' Club, which is restricted to the officers of Her Majesty's Household Troops, is the oldest club now extant, having been established in 1813. It was formerly housed in St. James's Street, next to "Crockford's." The present club-house, however, was erected only as far back as 1848; it was built from the designs of Mr. Henry Harrison, and is said to be "remarkable for its compactness and convenience, although its size and external appearance indicate no more than a private house. As Captain Gronow tells us in his "Anecdotes and Reminiscences," it was established

child betwixt its jaws. On the right side of the entrance hall, which is paved with encaustic tiles, is the smoking-room, and in the rear is a noble dining-room. The entire frontage of the first floor is occupied by the morning-room; in the rear is the billiard-room. The second floor consists of billiard and card rooms, and five bed-rooms for members, others being also on the third and fourth floors. In the rear of the fourth floor a large roof

WAR OFFICE, PALL MALL, 1850. (*See page* 129.)

for the three regiments of Foot Guards, and was conducted on a military system. Billiards and low whist were the only games indulged in. The dinner was, perhaps, better than at most clubs, and considerably cheaper.

Close by the Guards' Club, and adjoining the grounds of Marlborough House, is the Beacons-field Club. The edifice, which was erected in 1875, originally belonged to the Junior Naval and Military Club. It is six storeys high, and is built of Portland stone; the base and columns of the entrance are of polished Aberdeen granite, and over the doorway at each side are two life-sized recumbent female figures supporting shields bearing medallions of Nelson and Wellington; whilst over the centre of the doorway is a huge lion's head with the head of a

or flat has been carried out, overlooking the grounds of Marlborough House; this is paved with encaustic tiles, and during the summer it can be converted into a covered lounge for smokers.

The Army and Navy Club—or rather a part of it—covers the site of what was once Nell Gwynne's house. Pennant thus describes it: "As to Nell Gwynne, not having the honour to be on the Queen's establishment, she was obliged to keep her distance (from the Court) at her house in Pall Mall. It is the first good one on the left hand of St. James's Square, as we enter from Pall Mall. The back room on the ground floor was within memory (he wrote in 1790), entirely of looking-glass, as was said to have been the ceiling also. Over the chimney was her picture, and that of her sister was in a third room. At the period I mention this house was the property of Thomas Brand, Esq., of the Hoo, in Hertfordshire"—an ancestor, we may add, of the Lords Dacre.

This club—which bears the colloquial nickname as far back as the end of the war in 1815, stands at the corner of Pall Mall and the opening into St. James's Park. This club took its rise, says the author of "London Clubs," when so many of the officers of the army and navy were thrown out

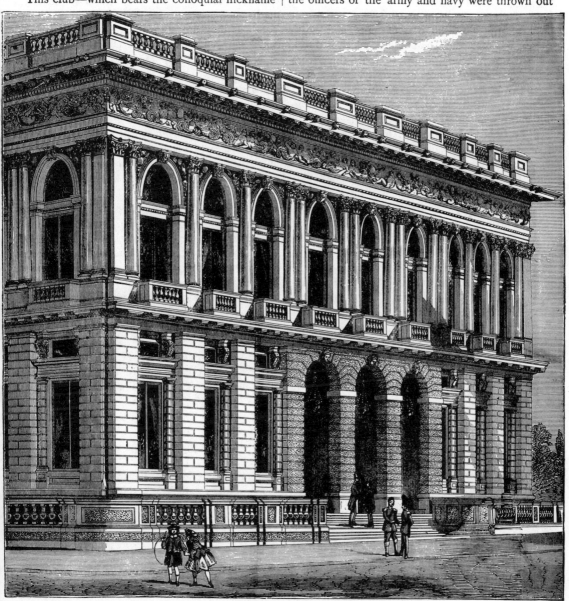

FRONT OF THE ARMY AND NAVY CLUB.

of the "Rag and Famish," arising out of a joke in *Punch*—was originally held at a private mansion in St. James's Square, and the present club-house was finished in 1850, at the cost of nearly £100,000. The house is luxuriously furnished, and the smoking-room has the reputation of being one of the best in London.

The "United Service," which was established

of commission. Their habits, from old mess-room associations, being gregarious, and their reduced incomes no longer affording the luxuries of the camp or barrack-room on full pay, the late Lord Lynedoch, on their position being represented to him, was led to propose some such institution as a mess-room, in peace, for the benefit of his old companions in arms. A few other officers of influence in both branches of the service concurred, and the United Service Club was the result. It was first established at the corner of Charles Street, Waterloo Place, where the junior establishment of the same name now stands; but the funds soon becoming large, and the number of candidates for admission rapidly increasing, the present large and classic edifice was erected. The building, which is devoid of much architectural embellishment—the decorations being simple almost to severity—was erected from the designs of Mr. John Nash.

This is considered to be one of the most commodious, economical, and best managed of all the London club-houses. Among the pictures that adorn the walls of the principal rooms are Clarkson Stanfield's "Battle of Trafalgar," and the "Battle of Waterloo," by George Jones, R.A. There are also several portraits of the sovereigns of England, of the Stuart and Brunswick lines. Among them are James I., James II., Charles II., William III., and Queen Mary, original picture, by Sir Godfrey Kneller; Queen Anne, the four Georges, William IV., and Queen Victoria, by Sir Francis Grant; and an original portrait of the late Prince Consort, by J. Lucas. The members of this club consist of princes of the blood royal, and officers of the army, navy, marines, regular, militia, and Her Majesty's Indian Forces, of the rank of commander in the navy, or major in the army, in active service or retired; the lords lieutenants of counties in Great Britain and Ireland, &c., are also eligible.

The "Junior United Service," although perhaps not quite within the limits of "Club-land," standing as it does at the corner of Charles Street and Waterloo Place—may be introduced here. It was established in 1827, to provide for officers not of field rank, and also for those general officers whom the Senior Club was unable to receive. The house was rebuilt and enlarged in 1857, from the designs of Messrs. Nelson and Innes. The club accommodates fully as many members as the old club, as well as four or five hundred additional, or "supernumeraries." Many of the senior members of each club now belong to both, it having been considered a high honour, when the Junior was established, for the more distinguished individuals in the ranks of the Senior Club to be elected as honorary members, although those belonging to the new institution could not, of course, attain a similar distinction, unless of the requisite grade.

The Travellers' Club dates its existence from the year 1819. Sir Charles Barry was the architect of the club-house, which was built in the year 1831. In 1850 it had a narrow escape from destruction by fire; the damage, however, was principally confined to the billiard-room, in which it originated. This club is exceedingly select, numbering among its members the highest branches of the peerage, and the most distinguished of the lower House of Parliament. It consists of only about 700 members, but they are amongst the *élite* of the land; and Talleyrand, with some of the most eminent representatives of foreign powers, have been enrolled in the list of its honorary members. When ambassador to this country from the French Court, the veteran diplomatist was wont to pass his leisure hours at this favourite retreat in Pall Mall, and, we are told, "steered his way as triumphantly through all the mazes of whist and *écarté*, as he had done amid the intricacies of the thirteen different forms of government, each of which he had sworn to observe."

The "Oxford and Cambridge," in Pall Mall, midway on the "sweet shady side," and the "United University," at the corner of Suffolk Street, in Pall Mall East, may both be mentioned together as being restricted to University men, and, indeed, to such only as are members of Oxford or Cambridge. The former is a handsome structure, and was built from the. joint designs of Mr. Sidney Smirke and his brother, Sir Robert. In panels over the upper windows, seven in number, are a series of bas-reliefs, executed by Mr. Nicholl, who was also employed on those of the Fitzwilliam Museum at Cambridge. The subject of that at the east end of the building is Homer; then follow Bacon and Shakespeare. The centre panel contains a group of Apollo and the Muses, with Minerva on his right hand, and a female, personifying the fountain Hippocrene, on his left. The three remaining panels represent Milton, Newton, and Virgil. The "Oxford and Cambridge," which is the more recent of the two in its origin—having been established in 1830, whereas the "University" dates from 1822 —consists chiefly of the younger spirits of the universities, and is less "donnish." The other is, for the most part, composed of the old and graver members. The serious members of Parliament who have received university education are almost invariably to be found in the latter. It also contains a considerable number of the judges, and no small portion of the beneficed and dignified clergy.

The "Union," at the corner of Trafalgar Square and Cockspur Street, is one of the oldest of the clubs, and for many years enjoyed the reputation of being one of the most *recherché* of all. It was founded in 1822, and consists of politicians, and the higher order of professional and commercial men, without reference to party opinions. The club-house itself was built in 1824, from the designs of the late Sir Robert Smirke, R.A.

The "Athenæum" was established in 1824, and the club-house, built by Mr. Decimus Burton, was opened about two years later. The building showed considerable progress with regard to ornateness and finish, for it presented the then somewhat extravagant novelty of a sculptured frieze. It is surmounted by an imposing statue of Minerva, by Baily, R.A. In the interior the chief feature is the staircase. The library, as perhaps may be expected, is very extensive, consisting of several thousand volumes. A sum of £500 a year from the funds of the club was, several years ago, voted to be set apart for the purchase of new works of merit in literature and art. Above the mantelpiece is a portrait of George IV., painted by Lawrence, upon which he was engaged but a few hours previous to his decease, the last bit of colour this celebrated artist ever put upon canvas being that of the hilt and sword-knot of the girdle; thus it remains, unfinished.

The expense of building the club-house, we are told, was £35,000, and £5,000 for furnishing; the plate, linen, and glass cost £2,500; library, £4,000; and the stock of wine in the cellar is usually worth £4,000. The yearly revenue is about £9,000. It does not admit strangers to its dining-room under any circumstances. The economical management of the club has not, however, been effected without a few sallies of humour from various quarters. In 1834 we read, " The mixture of Whigs and Radicals, *savants*, foreigners, dandies, authors, soldiers, sailors, lawyers, artists, doctors, and members of both Houses of Parliament, together with an exceedingly good average supply of bishops, render the *mélange* very agreeable, despite some two or three bores, who 'continually do dine,' and who, not satisfied with getting a 6s. dinner for 3s. 6d., 'continually do complain.'"

The "Athenæum" was founded by a number of gentlemen connected with the learned professions and higher order of the fine arts and literature; and, with the exception, perhaps, of the "United Service," it is the most select establishment of the kind in London. Previous to the year 1824, if we except the occasional festive gatherings of the Royal Society, there was no place in London where those gentlemen who were more interested in art and literature than in politics could meet together for social intercourse. To remedy this acknowledged want, a preliminary meeting was held in the February of that year, at the rooms of the Royal Society, at Somerset House, at which it

was resolved to institute a literary club. Among those present were Sir Walter Scott, Sir Francis Chantrey, Richard Heber, Thomas Moore, Davis Gilbert, Mr. J. W. Croker, Sir Humphry Davy, Lord Dover, Sir Henry Halford, Sir Thomas Lawrence, Joseph Jekyll, and other well-known celebrities. It was at first called " The Society," but the name was subsequently changed to its present. Its members made their rendezvous at the Clarence Club until 1830.

For many years after its establishment, smoking was not permitted within the walls of this club. At last, however, about 1860, a concession was made, and a smoking-room added—apart, however, from the rest of the house, a part of the garden on the south front being sacrificed.

The number of ordinary members is fixed at twelve hundred. Samuel Rogers and Thomas Campbell, the poets, were among the first to join it, and Theodore Hook, too, was also one of its most popular members. Almost all the judges, bishops, and members of the Cabinet belong to it; and the committee have the privilege of electing annually, without ballot, nine persons, eminent in art, science, or literature. It is said that at the "Athenæum" the dinners fell off in number by upwards of 300 yearly after Theodore Hook disappeared from his favourite corner near the door of its coffee-room. " That is to say," observes one of his biographers, " there must have been some dozens of gentlemen who chose to dine there once or twice every week of the season, merely for the chance of his being there, and allowing them to draw their chairs to his little table in the course of the evening. . . . The corner alluded to will, we suppose, long retain the name which it derived from him, " Temperance Corner.'" It may be added, by way of explanation, that when Hook wanted brandy or whisky, he asked for it under the name of tea or lemonade, in order not to shock the grave and dignified persons who were members of the "Athenæum" in his day.

A falling-off in the number of its members being at one time anticipated, says the writer of an able article in the *New Quarterly Review*, a report was foolishly set abroad that " the finest thing in the world was to belong to the 'Athenæum,' and that an opportunity offered for hobnobbing with archbishops, and hearing Theodore Hook's jokes. Consequently, all the little crawlers and parasites, and gentility-hunters, from all corners of London, set out upon the creep; and they crept in at the windows, and they crept down the area steps, and they crept in, unseen, at the doors, and they crept in under bishops' sleeves, and they crept in in peers' pockets, and they were blown in by the winds of chance. The consequence has been that ninety-nine hundredths of this club are people who rather seek to obtain a sort of standing by belonging to the 'Athenæum,' than to give it lustre by the talents of its members. Nine-tenths of the intellectual writers of the age would be certainly black-balled by the dunces. Notwithstanding all this, and partly on account of this, the 'Athenæum' is a capital club. The library is certainly the best club library in London, and is a great advantage to a man who writes."

As may well be supposed from its literary constituency, no modern club in London, except the Garrick, is richer than the Athenæum in anecdotes and *bons mots*. In the library of this club lounging-chairs, writing-tables, and like conveniences are abundantly provided; and it was in some such apartment as this, probably in this identical room, where creditors pressed him, that, as we are told, " the unhappy, the defiant, the scorning, but eventually scorned and neglected Theodore Hook wrote the greater part of his novels, undisturbed by all the buzz and hum of the more fortunate butter-flies around."

Mr. E. Jesse used to tell a story to the effect that Thomas Campbell, the poet, was led home one evening from the Athenæum Club by a friend. There had been a heavy storm of rain, and the kennels were full of water. Campbell fell into one of them at the steps of the club, and pulled his friend after him, who exclaimed, in allusion to a well-known line of the poet's, " It is not *I*ser rolling rapidly, but *We*ser."

The " Athenæum " has reckoned among its members at least half of the illustrious names of the last half century; among others, Mr. D'Israeli, Lord Granville, Lord Coleridge, Thackeray, Sir John Bowring, Sir Roderick Murchison, Sir Benjamin Brodie, Sir Charles Wheatstone, Dr. Hooker, Sir Henry Holland, George Grote; Professors Sedgwick, Darwin, Tyndal, Huxley, Willis, Owen, Phillips, Maurice, and Conington; Lord Lytton, Macaulay, Bishop Thirlwall, Charles Dickens, Dean Stanley, Lord Shaftesbury, Bishop Wilber-force, Lord Romilly, Ruskin, Maclise, Thackeray, Serjeant Kinglake, Dean Milman, Lord Mayo, and Sir Edwin Landseer. The first secretary was no less eminent a person than Professor Faraday, but he retained the post only for a year.

In 1832—during the exciting era which culminated in the passing of the First Reform Bill—the friends of the Constitution, somewhat alarmed perhaps at the " sweeping measures " which were supposed to be about to follow, founded the

" Carlton," bestowing upon it this name from the terrace where the club was originally held. In the April of the above year we find the following entry in Mr. Raikes's " Journal:"—" A new Tory club has just been formed, for which Lord Kensington's house in Carlton Gardens has been taken. . . . The object is to have a counterbalancing meeting to ' Brooks's,' which is purely a Whig *réunion*; ' White's,' which was formerly devoted to the other side, being now of no colour, and frequented indiscriminately by all (parties)."

The club-house, built from the designs of Mr. Sydney Smirke and his brother, Sir Robert, was finished about 1856. It bears upon its exterior a degree of richness almost unprecedented in the metropolitan architecture. The façade in Pall Mall is upwards of 130 feet in length, with nine windows on a floor; between each of the windows are columns of highly polished red Peterhead granite. The design is said to be founded on the east front of the Library of St. Mark's at Venice.

The Carlton is the head-quarters of Conservative, as the Reform Club is of Liberal politics. The Conservative Club in St. James's Street was started for the reception of the Tory rank and file, but in Pall Mall congregate the leading men of the party. Here are concerted the great political " moves " which are to upset a Whig or Liberal Administration; here the grand mysterious tactics of a general election are determined upon, and here are the vast sums subscribed which are to put the whole forces of the party in motion in the country boroughs. This club still retains its original name, though removed from the lordly terrace which gave rise to it, to the " shady side of Pall Mall." Passing to what may be called the " inner life " of the club, we may state that the first head of its *cuisine* was a French " artist " who had lived with the Duc d'Escars, chief *maître d'hôtel* to Louis XVIII., and who is said to have made that famous *pâté* which killed his master.

The " Reform," which is situated between the " Carlton " and the " Athenæum," was built from the designs of the late Sir Charles Barry, R.A., and was for a long time considered one of the " lions " of the metropolis. The style is purely Italian, and partakes largely of the character of many of the celebrated palaces in Italy. The building is chiefly remarkable for simplicity of design, combined with grandeur of effect, as well as for the convenience and elegance of its internal arrangements. It differs from most of the other club-houses, in having two ranges of windows above the ground floor instead of a single range. The latter feature has been regarded as rendering the metropolitan club-houses eminently characteristic of their purpose, and highly favourable to architectural dignity.

On the first establishment of the "Reform" by the Liberal party, Gwydyr House, in Whitehall, was hired, and in that mansion the club was located until the present club-house was erected. This, although of severe simplicity, by the utter absence of exterior ornament, is nevertheless an imposing structure. Some critics, indeed, have compared it to an inverted chest of drawers; but the chief beauty of the Reform Club is *ab intra*. On entering the vestibule one is immediately struck by the splendid proportions of the hall and the elegance of the staircase, reminding one of the magnificent *salles* of Versailles and of the glories of the Louvre. In the upper part of the building are a certain number of "dormitories" set apart for those who pass their whole existence amid club gossip and politics—one of the peculiarities of the establishment.

The author of "The London Clubs" writes— "It is in the lower regions, where Soyer reigns supreme, that the true glories of the Reform Club consist; and here the divine art of cookery—or, as he himself styles it, gastronomy—is to be seen in all its splendour. Heliogabalus himself never gloated over such a kitchen; for steam is here introduced and made to supply the part of man. In state the great dignitary sits, and issues his inspiring orders to a body of lieutenants, each of whom has pretensions to be considered a *chef* in himself. 'Gardez les rôtis, les entremets sont perdus,' was never more impressively uttered by Cambacérès, when tormented by Napoleon detaining him from dinner, than are the orders issued by Soyer for preparing the refection of some modern attorney; and all the energies of the vast establishment are at once called into action to obey them—steam eventually conducting the triumphs of the cook's art from the scene of its production to a recess adjoining the dining-room, where all is to disappear.

"Soyer is, indeed, the glory of the edifice—the *genus loci*. Peers and plebeian *gourmands* alike penetrate into the recesses of the kitchen to render him homage; and, conscious of his dignity, —or, at least, of his power—he receives them with all the calm assurance of the *Grand Monarque* himself. Louis XIV., in the plenitude of his glory, was never more impressive; and yet there is an aspect—we shall not say assumption—of modesty about the great *chef*, as he loved to be designated, which is positively wondrous, when we reflect that we stand in the presence of the great 'Gastronomic Regenerator'—the last of his

titles, and that by which, we presume, he would wish by posterity to be known. Soyer, indeed, is a man of discrimination, and taste, and genius. He was led to conceive the idea of his immortal work, he tells us, by observing in the elegant library of an accomplished nobleman the works of Shakespeare, Milton, and Johnson, in gorgeous bindings, but wholly dust-clad and overlooked, while a book on cookery bore every indication of being daily consulted and revered. 'This is fame,' exclaimed Soyer, seizing the happy inference; and forthwith betaking himself to his chambers and to meditation, his divine work on Gastronomic Regeneration was the result."

The breakfast given by the Reform Club on the occasion of the Queen's coronation obtained for Soyer high commendation; and in his O'Connell dinner, the "soufflés à la Clontarf" were considered by gastronomes to be a rich bit of satire. The banquet to Ibrahim Pacha, in 1846, was another of Soyer's great successes, when "Merlans à l'Égyptienne," "La Crême d'Égypte," and "à l'Ibrahim Pacha," mingled with "Le Gâteau Britannique à l'Admiral (Napier)." Another famous banquet was that given to Admiral Sir Charles Napier, in March, 1854, as Commander of the Baltic Fleet; and the banquet given in July, 1850, to Viscount Palmerston, who was a popular leader of the Reform, was, gastronomically as well as politically, a brilliant triumph. It was upon this occasion that Mr. Bernal Osborne characterised the Palmerston policy in this quotation:—

"Warmed by the instincts of a knightly heart,
    That roused at once if insult touched the realm,
He spurned each state-craft, each deceiving art,
    And met his foes no visor to his helm.
This proved his worth, hereafter be our boast—
    Who hated Britons, hated him the most."

The following description of the kitchen of the Reform Club is from the pen of Viscountess de Malleville, and appeared originally in the *Courrier de l'Europe:*—"It is spacious as a ball-room, kept in the finest order, and white as a young bird. All-powerful steam, the noise of which salutes your ear as you enter, here performs a variety of offices. It diffuses a uniform heat to large rows of dishes, warms the metal plates upon which are disposed the dishes that have been called for, and that are in waiting to be sent above; it turns the spit, draws the water, carries up the coal, and moves the plate like an intelligent and indefatigable servant. Stay awhile before this octagonal apparatus, which occupies the centre of the place. Around you the water boils and the stew-pans bubble, and a little further on is a movable furnace, before which pieces of meat are converted into savoury *rôtis:* here are sauces and gravies, stews, broths, soups, &c.　In the distance are Dutch ovens, marble mortars, lighted stoves, iced plates of metal for fish, and various compartments for vegetables,

as a whole, and in their relative bearings to one another, all are so intelligently considered, that you require the aid of a guide to direct you in exploring them, and a good deal of time to classify in your mind all your discoveries.　Let all strangers

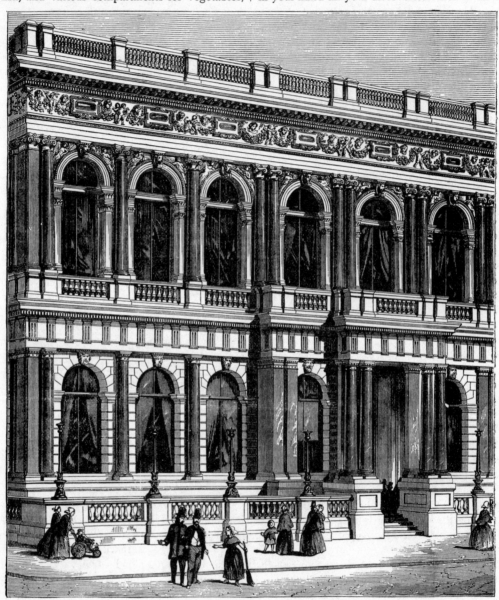

ENTRANCE TO THE CARLTON CLUB.　(*See page* 148.)

fruits, roots, and spices.　After this inadequate, though prodigious, nomenclature, the reader may perhaps picture to himself a state of general confusion—a disordered assemblage, resembling that of a heap of oyster-shells.　If so, he is mistaken; for, in fact, you see very little or scarcely anything of all the objects above described.　The order of their arrangement is so perfect, their distribution

who come to London for business, or pleasure, or curiosity, or for whatever cause, not fail to visit the Reform Club.　In an age of utilitarianism and of the search for the comfortable like ours, there is more to be learned here than in the ruins of the Coliseum, of the Parthenon, or of Memphis."

Thackeray was a member of the Reform, the Athenæum, and Garrick Clubs—perhaps of others,

LIBRARY OF THE REFORM CLUB. (*See page* 148.)

but it was in those here named that his leisure was usually spent. "The afternoons of the last week of his life," writes one of his biographers, "were almost entirely passed at the Reform Club, and never had he been more genial or in such apparently happy moods. Many men sitting in the libraries and dining-rooms of these clubs have thought this week of one of the tenderest passages in his early sketches—'Brown the Younger at a Club'—in which the old uncle is represented as telling his nephew, while showing him the various rooms in the club, of those who had dropped off—whose names had appeared at the end of the club list, under the dismal head of 'members deceased,' in which (added Thackeray) 'you and I shall rank some day.'"

Among the latest additions to the batch of clubs that line Pall Mall are the "Junior Carlton" and the "Marlborough." The former, which was established in 1864, numbers about 1,500 members. It is a political club, in strict connection with the Conservative party, and designed to promote its objects. The "Marlborough"—so named in honour of the Prince of Wales—was started about 1868, and numbers among its members the Prince of Wales and several of the aristocratic patrons of the turf.

The "Century Club" has its abode at 6, Pall Mall Place, and there is a tradition that the premises were once inhabited by Nell Gwynne.

Whatever may have been the "rules and regulations" of the now defunct species of club of the last century—such as the "Essex Street," the "Literary," and others of which we have spoken in the previous volume—a wide difference exists between them and those of the present day in the matter of bacchanalian festivities. It may with truth be said that high play and high feeding are no longer the rules; in fact, clubs are to many persons even dull and unsociable. In most of the clubs of the Johnsonian period, the flow of wine or other liquor was far more abundant than that of mind, and the conversation was generally more easy and hilarious than intellectual and refined. The bottle, or else the punch-bowl, played by far too prominent a part, and sociality too frequently took the form of revelry—or, at least, what would be considered such according to our more temperate habits. Though in general the elder clubs encouraged habits of free indulgence as indispensable to good fellowship and sociality, the modern clubs, on the contrary, have done much to discourage them, as low and ungentlemanly. "Reeling home from a club" used formerly to be a common expression, whereas now inebriety, or the symptom of it, in a club-house, would bring down disgrace upon him who should be guilty of such an indiscretion.

The pleasures and comforts of clubs and club-life to the bachelor whose means and position allow of such luxuries have been often graphically and humorously described in serious and ephemeral publications for the past century and a half, but nowhere in a more amusing manner than in the "New Monthly Magazine," in 1842; and it has been wittily observed by Mrs. Gore in one of her novels that, "after all, clubs are not altogether so bad a thing for family-men; they act as conductors to the storms usually hovering in the air. There is nothing like the subordination exercised in a community of equals for reducing a fiery temper."

CHAPTER XIII.

ST. JAMES'S STREET.—CLUB-LAND (*continued*).

"The Campus Martius of St. James's Street,
Where the beaux' cavalry pace to and fro,
Before they take the field in Rotten Row."—*Sheridan.*

Origin of "Brooks's Club"—Hazard-playing—St. James's Coffee-house—The "Thatched House" Tavern—An Amusing Story about Burke and Dr. Johnson—Origin of Goldsmith's Poem, "Retaliation"—The "Neapolitan Club"—The Dilettanti Society—The "Civil Service," now the "Thatched House" Club—The "Conservative"—"Arthur's"—The "Old and Young Club"—The "Cocoa Tree"—Dr. Garth and Rowe, the Poet—Familiarity of Menials—"Brooks's"—How Sheridan was elected a Member—The "Fox Club"—The "New University"—The "Junior St. James's"—The "Devonshire"—"Crockford's"—"White's"—The Proud Countess of Northumberland—Lord Montford's "important Business" with his Lawyer—Colley Cibber at "White's Club"—Lord Alvanley—A Waiter at "White's" elected M.P.—"Boodle's"—Michael Angelo Taylor and the Earl of Westmorland.

THE spread and increase of our clubs are remarkable signs of the times; their uses and advantages are such as to make one wonder not only why such things were not established very much earlier than they were, but how "men about town" existed without them. "White's," "Brooks's," and "Boodle's" were *the* clubs of London for many years; "White's" being the oldest, and famous as a "chocolate-house" in the time of Hogarth. The origin of "Brooks's" was the "blackballing" of

Messrs. Boothby and James, at "White's;" they established it as a rival, and it was at first held at "Almack's." Sir Willoughby Aston subsequently originated "Boodle's;" but these clubs were clubs of amusement, politics, and play, not the matter-of-fact meeting-places of general society, nor did they offer the extensive and economical advantages of breakfast, dinner, and supper, now afforded by the present race of establishments. And, connected with this subject in some degree, what a wonderful change in the state of affairs has taken place since it was the custom of the king to play "hazard" publicly at St. James's Palace, on Twelfth Night! In the *Gentleman's Magazine* for 1753 is the following account of the result of this annual performance for that year:—

"*Saturday, Jan.* 6.—In the evening his Majesty played at hazard for the benefit of the groom-porter; all the Royal Family who played were winners — particularly the duke, £3,000. The most considerable losers were the Duke of Grafton, the Earl of Huntingdon, the Earls of Holderness, Ashburnham, and Hertford. Their Royal Highnesses the Prince of Wales and Prince Edward, and a select company, danced in the little drawing-room till eleven o'clock, when the Royal Family withdrew."

The custom of hazard-playing was discontinued after the accession of George III.; but it is odd, looking back scarcely a century, to find the sovereign, after attending divine service with the most solemn ceremony in the morning, doing that in the evening which, in these days, subjects men to all sorts of pains and penalties, and for the prohibition and detection of which a bill has been passed through Parliament, arming the police with the power of breaking into the houses of Her Majesty's lieges at all hours of the day and night.

It is obvious that the gradual improvement of the club-houses, together with the changes which passed over West-end society, would almost of its own accord develop the club system out of that which preceded it. There is, therefore, little need for dwelling on the subject, in the way of explanation, and so we will at once pass on up St. James's Street.

At the south-west corner of St. James's Street, next door to the corner house, and commanding the view up Pall Mall, was the "St. James's Coffee-house," the great rendezvous of the Whig party for nearly a hundred years, beginning with the reign of Queen Anne. Its very name has become classical, and indeed immortal, by being so repeatedly mentioned in the pages of the *Spectator, Tatler*, &c. Thus we find, in a passage already quoted by us

from the first number of the *Tatler*—"Foreign and domestic news you will have from the St. James's Coffee-house;" and thus Addison, in one of his papers in the *Spectator* (No. 403), remarks—'That I might begin as near the fountain-head [of information] as possible, I first of all called in at the St. James's, where I found the whole outward room in a buzz of politics. The speculations were but very indifferent towards the door, but grew finer as you advanced to the upper end of the room; and were so much improved by a knot of theorists who sat in the inner rooms, within the steams of the coffee-pot, that I heard there the whole Spanish monarchy disposed of, and all the line of the Bourbons provided for, in less than a quarter of an hour." This house was much frequented by Swift, who here used to receive his letters from "Stella," and who tells us in his "Journal to Stella," how in 1710 he christened the infant of its keepers, a Mr. and Mrs. Elliot, and afterwards sat down to a bowl of punch along with the happy parents. Being so close to the palace it was also frequented by the officers of the household troops, who, it is said, would lounge in to listen to the learned Dr. Joseph Warton, as he sat at breakfast in one of the windows. Mr. John Timbs reminds us that, "in the first advertisement of the 'Town Eclogues' of Lady Mary Wortley Montagu, they were stated to have been read over at the St. James's Coffee-house, where they were considered by the general voice to be the productions of a lady of quality."

In 1665 there appeared a poem with the title of "The Character of a Coffee House, wherein is contained a description of the persons usually frequenting it, with their discourse and humours, as also the admirable virtues of coffee; by an Ear and Eye Witness." It begins thus:—

> "A coffee-house the learned hold,
> It is a place where coffee's sold;
> This derivation cannot fail us,
> For where ale's vended, that's an alehouse."

It is evident from what follows that these coffee-houses soon became places of general resort—

> "—— of some and all conditions,
> E'en vintners, surgeons, and physicians,
> The blind, the deaf, the aged cripple,
> Do here resort, and coffee tipple."

At the door of the St. James's Coffee-house, a globular oil-lamp, then described as "a new kind of light," was first exhibited in 1709, by its inventor, Michael Cole. To this house, in early life, the elder D'Israeli, as his son tells us, would repair to read the newspapers of the day, returning to his home at Enfield in the evening, sometimes "laden with journals."

The St. James's Coffee House continued to exist for some few years into the present century, when, its Whig friends having deserted its doors, it passed quietly away, superseded, no doubt, in a great degree, by Brooks's Club.

The "Thatched House Tavern," the name of which implies a very humble and rural origin, was probably an inn which had existed in the days when St. James's was a veritable hospital and not a palace. It stood near the bottom, on the western side of the street. When the Court settled at St. James's, it was frequented by persons of fashion, and grew gradually in importance, as did the suburb of which it formed part. We should like to have seen it in the days when the frolicsome maids of honour of the Tudor and Stuart days ran across thither from the Court to drink syllabub and carry on sly flirtations. In the absence of documents, it is impossible to trace its growth down to the days of Swift, who speaks in his "Journal to Stella," in 1711, of "having entertained our society at dinner at the Thatched House Tavern;" it was, however, a small hotel at that date, for the party were obliged to "send out for wine, the house affording none." It was possibly on account of this and other proofs of its earlier stage of existence, that even when the "Thatched House" had grown into a recognized rendezvous of wits, politicians, and men of fashion, Lord Thurlow alluded to it during one of the debates on the Regency Bill as the "ale-house." By the time of Lord Shelburne, or at all events in the days of Pitt and Fox, it had become one of the chief taverns at the West-end, and had added to its premises a large room for public meetings.

Here the Earl of Sunderland, the great Duke of Marlborough's son-in-law, having shaken off the cares of state, would dine off a chop or steak, in a quiet way, along with Lord Townshend, or his constant companion, Dr. Monsey. The tavern was for many years the head-quarters of the annual dinners or other convivial meetings of the leading clubs and literary and scientific associations. Mr. Timbs gives the following as the list of such gatherings in 1860, on the authority of the late Admiral W. H. Smyth—The Institute of Actuaries, the Catch Club, the Johnson Club, the Dilettanti Society, the Farmers', the Geographical and the Geological, the Linnæan and Literary Societies, the Navy Club, the Philosophical Club, the Club of the Royal College of Physicians, the Political Economy Club, the Royal Academy Club, the Royal Astronomical Society, the Royal Institution Club, the Royal London Yacht Club, the Royal Naval Club, the Royal Society Club, the St. Alban's Medical Club, the St. Bartholomew's Cotemporaries, the Star Club, the Statistical Club, the Sussex Club, and the Union Society of St. James's.

The Literary Society (or Club) was limited to forty members, and its meetings in 1820 were held here. At that time Canning was a member of it ; so were Sir William Scott (Lord Stowell), Sir William Grant, and Mr. J. H. Frere.

Mr. Cradock tells us in his "Memoir," that one evening he dined with the club, being introduced by Dr. Percy, and met, *inter alios*, Edmund Burke and Oliver Goldsmith. "The table that day was crowded, and I sat next Mr. Burke ; but as the great orator said very little, and as Mr. Richard Burke talked much, I was not aware at first who my neighbour was." He adds an amusing story which brings in both Burke and Johnson, and may therefore well bear telling here :—" One of the party near me remarked that there was an offensive smell in the room, and thought it must proceed from some dog that was under the table ; but Burke, with a smile, turned to me and said, ' I rather fear it is from the beef-steak pie that is opposite us, the crust of which is made of some very bad butter which comes from my country. Just at that moment Dr. Johnson sent his plate for some of it ; Burke helped him to very little, which he soon dispatched, and returned his plate for more ; Burke, without thought, exclaimed, ' I am glad that you are able so well to relish this beef-steak pie.' Johnson, not at all pleased that what he ate should ever be noticed, immediately retorted, 'There is a time of life, sir, when a man requires the repairs of a table.'

" Before dinner was finished, Mr. Garrick came in, full-dressed, made many apologies for being so much later than he intended, but he had been unexpectedly detained at the House of Lords ; and Lord Camden had absolutely insisted upon setting him down at the door of the hotel in his own carriage. Johnson said nothing, but looked a volume.

" During the afternoon some literary dispute arose ; but Johnson sat silent, till the Dean of Derry very respectfully said, ' We all wish, sir, for your opinion on the subject.' Johnson inclined his head, and never shone more in his life than at that period. He replied, without any pomp ; he was perfectly clear and explicit, full of the subject, and left nothing undetermined. There was a pause ; and he was then hailed with astonishment by all the company. The evening in general passed off very pleasantly. Some talked perhaps for amusement, and others for victory. We sat very late ; and the conversation that at last ensued was the direct cause of my friend Goldsmith's poem, called ' Retaliation.' "

Here, in the beginning of the present century, the "Neapolitan Club" used to dine, the Prince of Wales or the Duke of Sussex taking the chair. Beckford was frequently a guest, and so were " Beau" Brummell, Sir Sidney Smith, Richard Brinsley Sheridan, and Tommy Moore, then quite a young man. Here, too, the members of the Old Royal Naval Club—not a club in the modern West-end sense, but a charitable institution for the dispensing of charity among old " salts" and their families—used to dine on the anniversary of the battle of the Nile.

At the " Thatched House Tavern " were formerly held, on Sunday evenings during the London season, the dinners of the Dilettanti Society, the portraits of whose members—many of them painted by Sir Joshua Reynolds—adorned the walls of a room which was devoted exclusively to their accommodation.

This society, composed of lovers of the fine arts, was founded in 1734 by some gentlemen who had travelled in Italy, and who thought that that fact, coupled with a taste for the beautiful and for the remains of antiquity, was a sufficient bond of union. The members, though they have enjoyed a "name" for a century and a half, have never had a "local habitation." They met originally at Parsloe's, in St. James's Street, but removed to the "Thatched House Tavern" in 1799. By the time that the society was thirty years old, its finances were found to be so prosperous, that its members resolved to send out properly-qualified persons to the East, in order to collect information as to such antiquities as the hands of time and of man had spared, and to bring back their measurements, and correct drawings and elevations. The first persons so sent abroad were Mr. Chandler, a Fellow of Magdalen College, Oxford, an architectural draughtsman named Rivett, and Mr. J. Stuart, whose name will long be remembered as the author of " The Antiquities of Athens." This noble work, published under the auspices of the Dilettanti Society, in instalments, had the effect of rescuing Grecian architecture and art from the contempt into which it had fallen, and to revive a taste for the majestic and beautiful. This book was followed, at distant intervals, by similar works, magnificently illustrated; among these were "Specimens of Sculpture, Egyptian, Etruscan, Greek, and Roman," published in 1809; "The Unedited Antiquities of Attica," in 1817; a large treatise on "Ancient Sculpture," in 1835; and Professor Cockerell's elaborate work on "The Temples of Jupiter in Ægina, and of

Bacchus at Phigaleia," published in 1860. It was, no doubt, the interest excited by the early meetings of the Dilettanti Society which first woke up the Earl of Aberdeen, or, to give him Lord Byron's title—

" The travell'd Thane, Athenian Aberdeen,"

to write and publish his " Enquiry as to the Principles of Beauty in Grecian Architecture ; " Sir William Gell to explain the Troad, Argolis, and Ithaca ; whilst the Earl of Elgin, our ambassador at Constantinople, rescued from destruction and sent over to England that collection of Athenian sculpture which is known to every visitor to the British Museum as the Elgin Marbles. Among the best-known members of the Dilettanti Society, besides those above-mentioned, were Sir William Chambers, Mr. John Towneley, the Marquises of Northampton and Lansdowne, Sir Richard Westmacott, Henry Hallam, the Duke of Bedford, Mr. H. T. Hope, Sir Martin Archer Shee, Mr. Richard Payne Knight, the Earl of Holderness, Sir Bourchier Wrey, Sir Henry Englefield, and Lord Le Despencer (better known by his former name of Sir Francis Dashwood), Lord Northwick, George Selwyn, Charles James Fox, Garrick, Colman, Lord Holland, Lord Fitzwilliam, Sir William Hamilton, and the Duke of Dorset.

Mr. Peter Cunningham says that the original "Thatched House Tavern" stood on the site of the present Conservative Club, to build which it was pulled down in 1843, when it was moved to another house a few doors nearer to the gate of the palace. When he wrote, in 1850, the Dilettanti still numbered fifty members, and continued to hold their Sunday evening meetings. Horace Walpole, in 1743, had described it in one of his letters to Sir H. Mann, as " a club for which the nominal qualification is having been in Italy, and the real one, being drunk ; the two chiefs," he adds, " are Lord Middlesex and Sir Francis Dashwood, who were seldom sober the whole time they were in Italy." Mr. Cunningham, however, assures us, that in the middle of the present century " the character of the club was considerably altered "— it may be hoped and believed for the better. If Horace Walpole's words are true, it could not well be for the worse.

An interesting account of the Dilettanti Society will be found in the *Edinburgh Review*, vol. 107. Since the demolition of their old house, the Dilettanti have held their weekly festive gatherings at Willis's Rooms, where the pictures belonging to the society now grace the walls. Their publications, however, are no longer such as those which were produced under their auspices in the last century.

The original "Thatched House Tavern" was taken down in 1814. "Beneath its front," says Mr. John Timbs, "was a range of low-built shops, including that of Rowland, the fashionable *coiffeur* of 'Macassar fame.' Through the tavern was a

Adjoining the "Thatched House Club," on the south, is one of the most recent additions to club-land, the "United Eton and Harrow Club." It occupies a portion of the house No. 87.

Higher up, at the corner of Little St. James's

THE "THATCHED HOUSE" TAVERN. (*See page* 154.)

passage to the rear, where, in Catharine Wheel Alley, in the last century, lived the widow Delaney, some of whose fashionable friends then resided in Dean Street, Soho.

On the site of the new "Thatched House Tavern" was built, in 1865, the "Civil Service Club," which was modified in 1873, and changed its name to the "Thatched House Club." It is still, however, mainly recruited from the Civil Service of the Crown, including county magistrates, ex-high sheriffs, and deputy-lieutenants.

Street, stands the "Conservative Club." This was established in 1840, in order to supply accommodation for those who could not procure admission into the "Carlton." The building was erected from the designs of Messrs. Basevi and Sydney Smirke. It is at once ornate and stately in its external appearance, and the interior is well arranged, but the club is not rich in anecdote or in incident.

On the same side of the street, only two or three houses intervening, is "Arthur's Club House." This club was so named after its founder, who was also, at one time, the keeper of "White's." Dr. King, in his "Anecdotes of his Own Times," alludes to these two clubs in the following terms, which imply that they were both addicted to high play :—"If I were to write a satire against gaming, and in the middle of my work insert a panegyric on the clubs at 'Arthur's,' who would not question the good intention of the author, and who would not condemn the absurdity of such a motley

Some of Horace Walpole's dilettante friends at Strawberry Hill once beguiled a dull and wet day by devising for this club a satirical coat of arms. The shield was devised by Walpole, Sir C. H. Williams, George Selwyn, and the Hon. R. Edgecumbe, and drawn by the last. The drawing formed a lot in the Strawberry Hall sale ; and a copy of it, with an explanation of its punning or "canting" allusions to card-playing, the great end

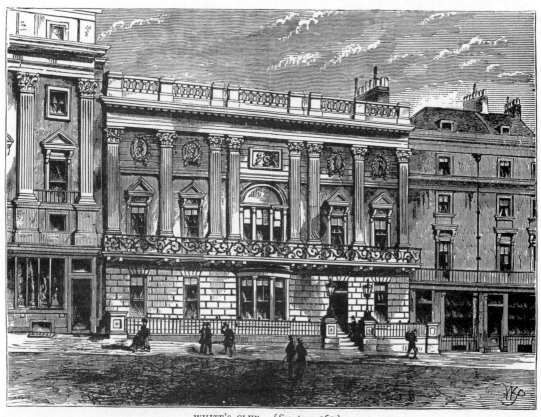

WHITE'S CLUB. (*See page* 161.)

piece ?" Here used to meet an inner club—an *imperium in imperio*—called "the Old and Young Club." Lady Lepel Hervey gives a clue to its name when she laments, in a letter dated 1756, that "luxury increases. All public places are full, and 'Arthur's' is the resort of old and young, courtiers and anti-courtiers—nay, even of ministers." By way of a sneer at the wide-spread habit of presenting civic freedoms to Mr. Pitt and his colleagues in office, this same Lady Hervey writes, under date 1757, "I hear Mr. George Selwyn has proposed to the old and new clubs at 'Arthur's' to depute him to present the freedom of each club in a dice-box to the Right Hon. William Pitt, and the Right Hon. Henry Bilson Legge. I think it ought to be inserted in the newspapers."

and object of the club, will be found in Chambers' "Book of Days."

"Arthur's Club" has always embraced a goodly list of members of the titled classes and the heads of the chief county families, though less aristocratic than "White's" or "Brooks's." A most painful circumstance, however, took place within it in the year 1836. To use the words of Captain Gronow's "Reminiscences," "A nobleman of the highest position and influence in society was detected in cheating at cards, and after a trial, which did not terminate in his favour, died of a broken heart."

At No. 64, on this side of the street, is the "Cocoa Tree Club." In the reign of Queen Anne there was a famous chocolate-house known as the "Cocoa Tree," a favourite sign to mark that new and fashionable beverage. Its frequenters were Tories of the strictest school. De Foe tells us in his "Journey through England," that "a Whig will no more go to the 'Cocoa Tree' . . . . than a Tory will be seen at the Coffee House of St. James's." In course of time, the "Cocoa Tree" developed into a gaming-house and a club. In its former capacity, Horace Walpole, writing in 1780, mentions an amusing anecdote connected with it :—"Within this week there has been a cast at hazard at the 'Cocoa Tree,' the difference of which amounted to an hundred and fourscore thousand pounds. Mr. O'Birne, an Irish gamester, had won £100,000 of a young Mr. Harvey, of Chigwell, just started from a midshipman into an estate by his elder brother's death. O'Birne said, ' You can never pay me.' ' I can,' said the youth ; ' my estate will sell for the debt.' ' No,' said O'Birne, ' I will win ten thousand, and you shall throw for the odd ninety thousand.' They did, and Harvey won." It is to be hoped that he left the gaming-house a wiser man thenceforth.

The anecdotes connected with the "Cocoa Tree" when it was really " the Wits' Coffee House," would fill a volume. One of them may be quoted here. Dr. Garth, who used often to appear there, was sitting one morning in the coffee-room conversing with two persons of " quality," when the poet Rowe, who was seldom very attentive to his dress and appearance, though fond of being noticed by great people, entered the door. Placing himself in a box nearly opposite to that in which the doctor sat, Rowe looked constantly round with a view to catch his eye, but not succeeding, he desired the waiter to ask him for the loan of his snuff-box, which he knew to be a very valuable one, set with diamonds, and the gift of royalty. After taking a pinch he returned it, but again asked for it so repeatedly that Garth, who knew him well, and saw through his purpose, took out a pencil and wrote on the lid two Greek characters, Φ and P, "Fie! Rowe." The poet's vanity was mortified, and he left the house.

As an instance of the familiarity that would some-times show itself between the menials and the aristocratic visitors at these fashionable rendezvous, this anecdote may be given. A waiter named Samuel Spring having on one occasion to write to George IV., when Prince of Wales, commenced his letter as follows :—" Sam, the waiter at the Cocoa Tree, presents his compliments to the Prince of Wales," &c. His Royal Highness next day saw Sam, and after noticing the receiving of his note, and the freedom of the style, said, "Sam, this may be very well between you and me, but it will not do with the Norfolks and Arundels."

As a club, the "Cocoa Tree" did not cease to keep up its reputation for high play. Although the present establishment bearing the name dates its existence only from the year 1853, the old chocolate-house was probably converted into a club as far back as the middle of the last century. Lord Byron was a member of this club ; and so was Gibbon, the historian.

"Brooks's," pre-eminently the club-house of the Whig aristocracy, occupies No. 60 on the west side of the street. It was originally established at "Almack's," in Pall Mall, in 1764, by the Duke of Portland, Charles James Fox, and others. They afterwards removed it to St. James's Street, and the club-house, designed by Holland, was opened in 1778. The early history of this club, so long the head-quarters of the leaders of the old Whig party, is thus told in the "Percy Anecdotes :"—"When the Whigs, with Mr. Fox for their leader, commenced their long opposition to the Tory party under Pitt, they formed themselves into a club at 'Almack's,' for the joint purpose of private con-ference on public measures, and of social inter-course. In 1777, a Mr. Brooks built, in St. James's Street, a house for the accommodation of the club, and had the honour of conferring on it the name by which it has ever since been known. The number of members is limited to four hundred and fifty. . . . . A single black ball is suf-ficient to exclude. The members of the club are permitted by courtesy to belong to the club at Bath, and also to 'Miles's' and other respectable clubs, without being balloted for. The subscription is eleven guineas a year. Although, strictly speak-ing, an association of noblemen and gentlemen for political objects, gaming is allowed. . . . It was in the bosom of this club that Fox may be said to have spent the happiest hours of his life. Here, when the storm of public contention was over, would the banished spirit of true kind-heartedness return to its own home. Here, with Sheridan, Barré, Fitzpatrick, Wilkes, and other men of the same stamp, did his spirit luxuriate in its natural simplicity ; and hence, after a night of revelry, he would hasten off to the shades of St. Anne's Hill, near Chertsey, and with a pocket Horace—his favourite companion—bring back his mind to con-templative tranquillity."

If we may trust Captain Gronow's "Anecdotes and Reminiscences," at "Brooks's," for nearly half a century, the play was of a more gambling character than at "White's." Faro and macao were indulged in to an extent which enabled a man to win or to lose a considerable fortune in one night. It was here that Charles James Fox, Selwyn, Lord Carlisle,

Lord Robert Spencer, General Fitzpatrick, and other great Whigs won and lost hundreds of thousands, frequently remaining at the table for many hours without rising. On one occasion Lord Robert Spencer contrived to lose the last shilling of his considerable fortune given him by his brother, the Duke of Marlborough. General Fitzpatrick being much in the same condition, they agreed to raise a sum of money, in order that they might keep a faro bank. The members of the club made no objection, and ere long they carried out their design. As is generally the case, the bank was a winner, and Lord Robert bagged, as his share of the proceeds, one hundred thousand pounds. He retired, strange to say, from the fetid atmosphere of play, with the money in his pocket, and never again gambled. George Harley Drummond, of the famous banking-house at Charing Cross, played once only in his whole life at "White's" at whist, on which occasion he lost twenty thousand pounds to Brummell. This event caused him to retire from the banking-house of which he was a partner. Lord Carlisle was one of the most remarkable victims amongst the players at "Brooks's," and Charles Fox was not more fortunate, being subsequently always in pecuniary difficulties.

The membership of "Brooks's Club," in the days of Pitt and Fox, was a sort of crucial test by which the members of the Whig party of the time were distinguished. It was a passport to Holland and Devonshire House, and also to Carlton House, while the Prince of Wales was at war with his father and his ministers. Hence, on Sheridan's entrance into the House of Commons, in 1789, one of the first objects of Fox and his friends was to procure his admission inside the doors of "Brooks's." But he was, personally, most unpopular with two of the leaders of the Whig *coterie*, George Selwyn and Lord Bessborough, who were resolved to keep him out. As one black ball at that time excluded a candidate, the Foxites resolved to get him in by a *ruse*. Aided by Georgiana, Duchess of Devonshire, the presiding genius of the Whig party, when the time for the ballot came on, they sent false messages, conveying alarming news of the illness of near relatives, to both of the dissentients. The bait took in both cases, each no doubt supposing that the other would be in his place to give the black ball; and the result was the election of Richard Brinsley Sheridan, wit, dramatist, orator, and statesman in one.

Even after he had published the first volume of his " History," Gibbon observes that his forced residence in London was sad and solitary. "The many forgot my existence when they saw me no longer at ' Brookes's,' and the few who sometimes had a thought on their friend were detained by business or pleasure ; and I was proud if I could prevail on my bookseller, Elmsley, to enliven the dulness of the evening."

Unlike his proud and haughty rival Pitt, it was in the nature of Fox to unbend in social intercourse. The latter, when away from London or from his club, found his home at St. Anne's Hill, at Chertsey, where he derived amusement from his library, from his garden, from conversation, and from a variety of domestic and literary avocations.

Here, William, the fifth Duke of Devonshire, would spend his evenings, at whist or faro, whilst his Duchess, the beautiful Georgiana, was laying down the law to her political allies in the saloons of Devonshire House. At one time O'Connell was a member ; but he was not at all a man after the hearts of the old English Whigs, who on one occasion, if we may believe Mr. Raikes' " Journal," had serious thoughts of expelling him.

Mr. Raikes, under date of 1832, recording the defeat of the Reform Bill in the House of Lords, and the refusal of the king to create fresh peers, writes : " ' Brooks's ' is full of weeping and of gnashing of teeth, so little was the Whig party prepared for this sudden catastrophe." " In the evening," he adds, " there was a most violent meeting of Whigs at ' Brooks's,' where the virulence of the speeches, and especially that of Mr. Stanley, the Irish secretary, who got on the table, showed the exasperated feelings of the party." This Mr. Stanley, it may be added, is the same individual who became afterwards the Tory premier, as the Earl of Derby.

Like " Arthur's Club," of which we have spoken above, " Brooks's " contains a sort of *imperium in imperio* in the " Fox Club," an association of the admirers of the statesman whose name it perpetuates. The members of the Fox Club dine together constantly during the London season. Though nearly eighty years have passed away since the death of Charles James Fox, in the upper room at Chiswick House, yet his name and memory are fresh among the sons and grandsons of his old personal and political friends. It may be asked why there is not still equally green and fresh amongst us a " Pitt Club," as once there was ? Englishmen as a rule are " conservative " as well as " progressive " in their tastes and likings ; but, as a matter of fact, the " Pitt Club" is particularly extinct, while that named after the great Premier's rival, Fox, still exists. Can the reason be after all that while Pitt was stern and haughty, Fox was pleasant and genial, and made friends instead of repelling them ? If so, it is good to know that amiable traits of character are not soon forgotten.

"Brooks's Club," according to Mr. Rush, the American Minister, at the time of the Regency, consisted of 400 members.

A little below Bennett Street is the "New University Club," founded in 1864. The house, which is semi-Gothic in its style of architecture, reaches back into Arlington Street. It consists mainly of the younger members of the Universities of Oxford and Cambridge.

At the corner of Bennett Street, the house No. 54 has been, since 1871, successively the "Junior St. James's" and the "Verulam;" and next door, occupying part of the building formerly known as "Crockford's," is the "Devonshire Club." Like its neighbour, this club is of recent origin (1874), but it nevertheless numbers among its members most of the *élite* of the Liberal party. It was at one time proposed that its name should be altered to the "Liberal," so as to place it in direct antagonism to the "Conservative," but this proposal was ultimately negatived. Whenever the club begins to build, it will probably take the site hitherto occupied by the late Duke of Buckingham's house on the south side of Pall Mall adjoining to the War Office, and at present used for some of the clerks of that department.

Lord Hartington was chosen as the first chairman of the "Devonshire Club," so called after his father. Among its trustees and members of its committee appeared the names of the Duke of Westminster, Lords Huntly, Cork, Wolverton, Kensington, and Lansdowne; Mr. Gladstone and Mr. John Bright; the Right Hons. W. F. Cogan, H. C. E. Childers, and W. P. Adam; Sir Henry James, Q.C., Mr. A. D. Hayter, Sir William Drake, and several leading members of Parliament.

"Crockford's Club-house," at which we have now arrived, was built for its founder, the late Mr. John Crockford, in 1827, by Wyatt. It was erected at a vast cost, and in the grand proportions and palatial decorations of the principal floors, "had not been surpassed in any similar building in the metropolis." On the ground floor are the entrance-hall and inner-hall opening into a grand suite of rooms of noble proportions; on the principal floor are a suite of very lofty and splendid reception-rooms, gorgeously decorated *à la Grand Monarque*, approached from a superb staircase, itself an architectural triumph, and a great feature of the building.

This club was founded by Mr. John Crockford, of whom we have already made mention in speaking of the shop just outside Temple Bar,

where his money was made; and during the last twenty years of his life-time it was frequented by wealthy and aristocratic gentlemen. It lost its character at his death in 1844, and soon afterwards was closed. It was re-opened, after a few years' interval, as the "Naval, Military, and Civil Service Club;" it then was converted into a dining-room, called the "Wellington;" and, lastly, it was taken by a Joint-Stock Company as an auction-room.

The death of Mr. Crockford, in May, 1844, is thus mentioned in the "Journal" of Mr. T. Raikes:—"That arch-gambler Crockford is dead, and has left an immense fortune. He was originally a low fishmonger in Fish Street Hill, near the Monument, then a 'leg' at Newmarket, and keeper of 'hells' in London. He finally set up the club in St. James's Street, opposite to 'White's,' with a hazard bank, by which he won all the disposable money of the men of fashion in London, which was supposed to be near two millions."

At the time of his decease Mr. Crockford was worth £700,000, if we may trust the above-mentioned authority, though he had lost as much more in mining and other speculations. His death was accelerated by anxiety about his bets on the Derby; a proof of the inconsistency of human nature, which seeks the acquisition of wealth at the risk even of life and health, without which all is valueless.

In a work entitled "Doings in London," with illustrations by Cruikshank, it is not obscurely hinted that Mr. Crockford made his fortune by keeping a "hell" in King Street, St. James's, and that the fashionable club called after his name was in reality little or no better. No doubt very high play was carried on there, and the exact limits of a house so called have never, that we know of, been strictly defined.

Many stories are told about "Crockford's," and most of them certainly not to the credit of its owner. For instance, Mr. B. Jerrold tells us that in 1847 the proprietor of "Crockford's" "was compelled to return to Prince Louis Napoleon £2,000, which a cheat had endeavoured to extort from him inside his walls." It is almost a satisfaction to read the fact which has been stated, that this same proprietor of "Crockford's" became afterwards so reduced in circumstances that in 1865 he begged money of the emperor, at whose "fleecing" he had at all events connived.

Mr. Raikes writes in his "Journal" from Paris, in 1835—"Had a letter from G——, with a detail of what is going on in London society, where the gaming at 'Crockford's,' is unparalleled. Alea quando hos animos?"

"White's Club," near the top of the street, on the east side, occupies the site of the town-house of Elizabeth, Countess of Northumberland, daughter of Theophilus, Earl of Suffolk. Here she lived in her widowhood, if we may trust Horace Walpole, whose information came from the lady's niece by marriage. She was "the last lady who kept up the ceremonious state of the old peerage. When she went out to pay visits, a footman, bareheaded, walked on each side of her coach, and a second coach with her women attended her. I think," adds Horace Walpole, "Lady Suffolk told me that her daughter-in-law, the Duchess of Somerset, never sat down before her without her leave to do so. I suppose old Duke Charles, the 'proud' Duke of Somerset, had imbibed a good quantity of his stately pride in such a school."

"White's" originally stood at the bottom of St. James's Street, on the eastern side, nearly opposite to where are now the Conservative and Thatched House Clubs. Gay, in his "Trivia," thus brings to the mind's eye the scene which in former times might here be witnessed—in the winter, of course :—

"At ' White's ' the harness'd chairman idly stands,
And swings around his waist his tingling hands."

The history of the establishment of this club is related as follows in the "Percy Anecdotes :"—"When 'Brooks's' became the head-quarters of the Foxite party, their opponents formed on the other side of the street a club which, from the name of its first steward, took the name of 'White's.' Here those measures which were to agitate Europe were submitted to the country gentlemen, whilst the spirit of resistance to the minister's power and ambition was cherished and fed at the other club. In the morning they met to organise and train their opposing forces; at night, when debate was over, each party retired, the one to 'White's,' and the other to 'Brooks's,' to talk over triumphs achieved, or to sustain disappointed hopes by new resolves and new projects."

"White's" was the great Tory club, and in the days of the Regency, when Whig and Liberal peers could almost be counted on the fingers, it embraced two-thirds, if not three-fourths, of the "upper ten thousand" among its members. Being so fashionable, it is not a matter of wonder that it should have been extremely difficult to gain entrance to it. Its doors were shut against anybody, however rich, who had made his money by mercantile industry. Its large bow window, looking down into St. James's Street, during the season, was very frequently filled by the leading dandies and beaux, who preferred lounging to politics: such as the Marquis of Worcester, the Duke of Argyll, Lord Alvanley, Lord Foley, Mr. G. Dawson Damer, Hervey Aston, "Rufus" Lloyd, &c.

Mr. Rush, the American ambassador, speaks of "White's" as the Tory Club established in the reign of Charles II., and consisting of five hundred members. He adds that it was generally so full that there was great difficulty in gaining admission; and that the place of head-waiter was said to be worth five hundred pounds a year. The club was a great place of resort among the "upper ten thousand." "Whenever I lose a friend," said George Selwyn, "I go to ' White's,' and pick up another."

This club was originally one of the head-quarters of the Tories of the old school, who here, in 1832, discussed the advisability of throwing out the first Reform Bill. But from and after that day it adopted a neutral tint, being frequented by members of both sides of the house.

The records of "White's" are said to be perfect from 1736. It may be questioned whether any entry on the books of "this famous academy" (as Swift once described it) has more interest than that which records an event in the year 1854—viz., when the leading members of the club gave a complimentary dinner to their fellow-member, the Duke of Cambridge, on his departure to take a command in the military expedition about to proceed to the East.

To this club belonged Sir Everard Fawkner, an official high in the Post Office department, who was celebrated for playing cards for high stakes, and very badly too. In allusion to his office, George Selwyn used to say, that some one who played with him was "robbing the mail."

At this club, on the last night of the year 1754, the first Lord Montfort supped and played at cards, as usual, and on leaving told the waiter to send his lawyer to wait on him the next day at eleven, as he had important business to transact. The important business was simply the work of blowing out his brains with a horse-pistol. Lady Hervey says that the sole cause of this rash act was a *tædium vitæ*, quite unaccountable in a man who had enjoyed all the success of public life.

Colley Cibber, "player, poet, and manager," not only an excellent actor, but the author of a treatise on the stage, which Horace Walpole terms "inimitable," was a member of "White's Club." Davies, in his "Life of Garrick," tells us the following story about him :—"Colley, we are told, had the honour to be a member of the great club at 'White's;' and so, I suppose, might any other man who wore good clothes, and paid his money when he lost it. But on what terms did Cibber live with this society ?

Why, he feasted most sumptuously, as I have heard his friend Victor say, with an air of triumphant exultation, with Mr. Arthur and his wife, and gave a trifle for his dinner. After he had dined, when the club-room door was opened and the laureate was introduced, he was saluted with a loud and joyous acclamation of ' O, King Coll!' 'Come in, King Coll!' and 'Welcome, welcome, King Colley!' And this kind of gratulation Mr. Victor thought was very gracious and very honourable."

garded as the author of the chief witticisms in the clubs after the abdication of the throne of dandyism by Brummell, who, before that time, was always quoted as the sayer of good things, as Sheridan had been some time before. Lord Alvanley had the talk of the day completely under his control, and was the arbiter of the " school for scandal " in St. James's. A *bon mot* attributed to him gave rise to the belief that Solomon caused the downfall and disappearance of Brummell ; for on some friends of

CROCKFORD'S CLUB ABOUT 1840. (*See page* 160.)

" White's Club " is more than once alluded to by Pope, as a place where high play and loose morality prevailed in his day. In one of Walpole's letters occurs the following rich bit of satire on the folly of betting, which we may imagine was here indulged in to a very large extent:—"Sept. 1st, 1750. —They have put in the papers a good story made at 'White's.' A man dropped down dead at the door, and was carried in; the club immediately made bets whether he was dead or not; and when they were going to bleed him, the wagerers for his death interposed, and said it would affect the fairness of the bet."

By common consent, as it would appear from Captain Gronow, the late Lord Alvanley was re-

the prince of dandies observing that if he had remained in London something might have been done for him by his old associates, Alvanley replied, " He has done quite right to be off: it was Solomon's judgment."

Of "White's Club," Lord Russell tells in his " Recollections " an amusing story. "A noble lord, who owned several 'pocket boroughs' in the good old days of Eldon and Perceval, was asked by the returning officer whom he meant to nominate. Having no 'eligible' candidate at hand, he named a waiter at 'White's,' one Robert Mackreth; but as he did not happen to be sure of the Christian name of his nominee, the election was declared void. Nothing daunted, his lordship persisted in

1. ARTHUR'S CLUB. (See p. 156.) 2. BROOK'S CLUB. (See p. 158.)

his nomination. A fresh election was therefore held, when the name of the gentleman having been ascertained, he was returned as a matter of course, and took his seat in St. Stephen's." In order to do this, he must at that time have been qualified by his patron with freehold land to the value of £300 a year ! Such was the representation of England in the good old days before the first Reform Bill !

About the year 1870 this club was offered for auction, and changed hands, becoming the property of Mr. T. Percivall, of Wansford, in Northampton-shire. Since this period there has been, it is stated, a great falling off in the number of members proposed for election ; and after being so many years the great resort of the dandies, it is rapidly becoming the stronghold of what may be called "fogeydom." This is supposed to be the result of the establishment of the Marlborough Club, which has special attractions for the rising young men of the day. The club nevertheless still counts a goodly number of the wealthy portion of the aristocracy among its members, including the Prince of Wales and the Duke of Edinburgh.

"Boodle's" is the last of the three surviving clubs which have been identified with the names of individuals ; it was so called after its first founder, of whom, however, little or nothing is known. It is still the property of his representatives, though governed by a committee. Like "White's," it has a very modest and unpretending aspect when compared with some of the lordly edifices in its neighbourhood ; but it is said to be marked by most agreeable and comfortable arrangements within. It is frequented mainly by elderly country gentlemen, chosen indifferently from both of the two great political parties. Hence this club has never been identified with politics. It has been sarcastically said to be sacred to Bœotian tastes, but it has had distinguished persons on its list of members— Edward Gibbon, for instance, whose waddling gait and ugly visage convulsed with laughter not merely such fast friends as Lord and Lady Sheffield, but many of his literary friends and compeers.

Among the eccentric members of this club were the late Mr. Michael Angelo Taylor, M.P., and John, tenth Earl of Westmorland. The former was a notorious gossip and retailer of news and small talk ; in fact, quite a "Paul Pry" in his way : the latter was as thin as a lath. Coming in one day, Taylor found Lord Westmorland, who had just dined off a roast fowl and a leg of mutton. "Well, my lord," said Taylor, "I can't make out where you have stowed away your dinner, for I can see no trace of your ever having dined in your lean body." "Upon my word," replied Lord Westmorland, "I have finished both, and could now go in for another helping." His lordship, slim as was his figure, was remarkable for a prodigious appetite : in fact, it is said that he thought nothing of eating up a respectable joint or a couple of fowls at a single meal.

The original name of this club was the "Savoir vivre," and along with "Brooks's" and "White's," it formed a trio of nearly coeval date. In its early years it was noted for its costly gaieties, and its epicurism is thus commemorated in the "Heroic Epistle to Sir William Chambers : "—

"For what is Nature ? Ring her changes round,
    Her three flat notes are water, plants, and ground ;
Prolong the peal, yet, spite of all your chatter,
    The tedious chime is still ground, plants, and water.
So, when some John his dull invention racks,
    To rival Boodle's dinners, or Almack's,
Three uncouth legs of mutton shock our eyes,
    Three roasted geese, three buttered apple-pies."

A variety of clubs, past and present, have not been mentioned in this or the previous chapter : these, however, will be dealt with as we come to them in our future account of St. James's Square, Piccadilly, and other parts of the West-end of "Modern Babylon."

It may be remarked, by way of a conclusion to the present chapter, that there were from the first too many aristocratic clubs and private mansions in St. James's Street to leave much room for plebeian inns and hostelries on either side of so highly respectable a thoroughfare. Still, Mr. Jacob Larwood is at the pains of reminding us, in his very amusing and entertaining "History of Sign-boards," that, in the seventeenth century, there was in this street an inn known as "The Poet's Head." He adds, however, "Who the poet was, it is impossible to say now ; perhaps it was Dryden, since the trade's tokens represent a head crowned with bays." The "poet," as such, has not been a favourite as the sign of an inn, though we fail to see why such should be the case if there be truth in the old saying of Horace, that "no poems will last or live that proceed from the pens of water-drinkers."

CHAPTER XIV.

ST. JAMES'S STREET AND ITS NEIGHBOURHOOD.

"Come, and once more together let us greet
The long-lost pleasures of St. James's Street."—*Tickell.*

Original Name of St. James's Street—The Royal Mercatorium—Anecdote of George Selwyn—"Jack Lee" and George, Prince of Wales—Beau Brummell's Quarrel with the Prince—"Hook and Eye"—Manners of the Court Region a Century and a-half ago—Colonel Blood's Attack on the Duke of Ormonde—Dangers of the Streets in the Reign of Charles II.—The Wig Riots—Noted Residents in St. James's Street—Gillray, the Caricaturist—Pero's Bagnio—"Political Betty"—Sams' Library—Louis Napoleon's Residence at Fenton's Hotel—Arlington Street—Park Place—Society for the Propagation of the Gospel in Foreign Parts—"Mother Needham"—Lepel, Lady Hervey—Lord Guildford—Sir Francis Burdett—Robert Smith, Lord Carington—A Jovial Supper Party—Sir Richard Philipps—Samuel Rogers, the Poet—The Public Schools Club—Spencer House—Cleveland Row—Bridgewater House—The Green Park—Peace Illuminations of 1749 and 1814—Constitution Hill.

HAVING in the preceding chapter given an account of the various clubs in St. James's Street, we shall now proceed to notice what may be called the historical memories of the place, then pass rapidly through the various thoroughfares on its western side, and extend our perambulation into the Green Park.

Two centuries ago St. James's Street was called "the long street." Old Strype describes it as "beginning at the palace of St. James's, and running up to the road against Albemarle Buildings; the best houses, at the upper end, having a terrace-walk before them;" a little more than half a century later, the parish of St. James's was described as including "all the houses and grounds comprehended in a place heretofore called St. James's Fields, and the confines thereof." St. James's Street dates from the middle of the seventeenth century; and we read in "Hunter's History of London" that "the road from Petty France to St. James's Palace, that which afterwards became St James's Street," was first paved in the year after the Restoration. The old buildings have nearly all been swept away to make room for the more stately club-houses and hotels of modern times; and of these the western side of the street in the present day is chiefly composed. The east side, with the exception of "Boodle's" and "White's" Clubs, consists mainly of elegant shops, one of which, at the beginning of the present century, was fitted up as a bazaar, and rejoiced in the name of the "Royal Mercatorium." The busy tenants of this establishment were summoned before the magistrate at the Queen Square Police Office, for "hawking" their goods without a licence; but the summons was dismissed, it being decided that the occupants of the bazaars did not come under the Hawkers' Act.

For upwards of a century this noble thoroughfare—for such it really is—has maintained its character as an aristocratic lounge, and a place where only the privileged classes have a right to be seen. To what extent this privilege was carried in former times may be judged from the following anecdote :—

George Selwyn happening to be at Bath when it was nearly empty, was induced, from the necessity of having somebody to associate with, to make the acquaintance of an elderly twaddling gentleman whom he invariably met in the rooms. In the height of the following season Selwyn encountered his old associate here, in St. James's Street, and endeavoured to pass him unnoticed, but in vain. "What, sir," asked the *cuttee*, holding out his hand, "don't you recollect me? We became acquainted at Bath." "I know we did," returned Selwyn, declining the proferred hand, "and when I next go to Bath I shall be happy to know you again—but not till then."

It was in walking up this street one day, and meeting "Jack Lee" arm-in-arm with George, Prince of Wales, that Beau Brummell sarcastically asked him, "Jack, who's your fat friend?" pretending not to recognise his Royal Highness, with whom he had quarrelled at Carlton House a few days previously. Tommy Moore, in his "Twopenny Post Bag," immortalises the quarrel in a parody on a letter from the Prince to the Duke of York, in which his Royal Highness is made to say—

"I indulge in no hatred, and wish there may come ill
To no mortal, except, now I think on't, Beau Brummell,
Who declared t'other day, in a superfine passion,
He'd cut me and bring the old king into fashion."

Such attacks as these must have turned the warm friend, though a prince of the blood, into a bitter enemy; and it must be said in "Beau" Brummell's behalf, that it was at Carlton House that he was led to indulge in those gambling tastes and in that dangerous familiarity with royalty which in the end proved his ruin.

Theodore Hook figured once, and once only, in the celebrated "H. B. Sketches" of the elder Doyle. He is represented walking down St. James's Street, arm-in-arm with the then Speaker, Mr. Manners Sutton (afterwards Viscount Canterbury), who—otherwise a fine-looking man—had a notable squint; hence the title of the engraving—"Hook and Eye!"

"St. James's, in Westminster," observes the witty author of the "Town Spy," "has a very large share of the nobility and gentry; yet a person of indifferent rank may find a vacant seat in the church on Sunday. The 'quality,' who fly about in their sumptuous equipages, imagine themselves to be the admiration of the vulgar sort, but, on the contrary, they are only the objects of their ridicule, they being too well acquainted with their most private affairs." No man, as we all know, is a hero in the eyes of his valet; and no doubt the morals of the age in which the "Town Spy" was written (1755), and especially in the neighbourhood of St. James's, were such as often would serve to illustrate the assertion.

Thackeray, in one of his "Lectures on English Humorists," describes in minute detail the manners of the Court region a century and a half ago, when a lady of fashion would joke at table with her footmen, and noble lords call out to the waiters, before ladies, "Hang expense, bring us a ha'porth of cheese." "Such," he adds, "were the ladies of St. James's; such were the frequenters of White's Chocolate-house, when Swift used to visit it, and Steele described it as the centre of pleasure, gallantry, and entertainment."

It is often said that London is more like a country made up of several states than an individual city; and it is in keeping with this idea that Addison, in the *Spectator* (No. 340), speaks of the metropolis as composed of different races, instead of being made up, like a town, of one cognate family. "When I consider this great city," he writes, "in its several quarters, or divisions, I look upon it as an aggregate of various nations, distinguished from each other by their respective customs, manners, and interests. The courts of two countries do not differ so much from one another as the Court and the City of London in their peculiar ways of life and conversation. In short, the inhabitants of St. James's, notwithstanding they live under the same laws, and speak the same language, are a distinct people from those of Cheapside, by several climates and degrees, in their ways of thinking and conversing together." If such was the essayist's opinion in the reign of Queen Anne or George I., what, we may fairly ask, would he have said stronger on the subject, had he lived on into the reign of Victoria?

It was in this street that, on a cold December morning in 1670, Colonel Blood—whose name is notorious for his attempt to rob the Tower of the regalia of England—set upon the great Duke of Ormonde, aided by four ruffians, and attempted to assassinate him on his way to Clarendon House,

which stood facing the top of the street, upon the site of what is now Albemarle Street. The duke was dragged out of his carriage by Blood and his associates, tied to one of them on horseback, and carried along Piccadilly towards Tyburn, where it was their intention to have hung him, in revenge, it is said, for a punishment inflicted upon some companions of theirs in Ireland during the duke's administration of that country. The alarm being given at Clarendon House, the servants followed, and recovered his grace from a struggle in the mud with the man to whom he was tied, and who, on regaining his horse, fired a pistol at the duke, and escaped. In the "Historian's Guide" (1688), it is stated that there were "six ruffians mounted and armed," and that the duke's six footmen, who usually walked beside his carriage, were absent when the attack was made—probably having dropped in at a sideway hostelry, in quest of "something to keep out the cold."

As to the dangers of the streets at the West-end at the period in which the above incident occurred, we are not left in the dark by Macaulay. He writes:—"When the evening closed in, the difficulty and danger of walking about London became serious indeed. The garret windows were opened and pails were emptied, with little regard to those who were passing below. Falls, bruises, and broken bones were of constant occurrence; for, till the last year of the reign of Charles II., most of the streets were left in profound darkness. Thieves and robbers plied their trade with impunity; yet they were hardly so terrible to peaceful citizens as another class of ruffians. It was a favourite amusement of dissolute young gentlemen to swagger by night about the town, breaking windows, upsetting sedans, beating quiet men, and offering rude caresses to pretty women. Several dynasties of these tyrants had, since the Restoration, domineered over the streets. The 'Muns' and 'Tityre Tus' had given place to the 'Hectors,' and the 'Hectors' had been recently succeeded by the 'Scourers.' At a later period arose the 'Nicker,' the 'Hawcubite,' and the yet more dreaded name of 'Mohawk,' as we learn from Oldham's 'Imitation of the Third Satire of Juvenal' (1682), and Shadwell's 'Scourers' (1690). Many other authorities will readily occur to all who are acquainted with the popular literature of that and the succeeding generation. It may be suspected that some of the 'Tityre Tus,' like good Cavaliers, broke Milton's windows shortly after the Restoration. I am confident that he was thinking of those pests of London when he dictated the noble lines—

' And in luxurious cities, where the noise
    Of riot ascends above their loftiest towers,
    And injury and outrage, and when night
    Darkens the streets, then wander forth the sons
    Of Belial, flown with insolence and wine.' "

"There were," writes Macaulay, "at the end of Charles II.'s reign, houses near St. James's Park, where fops congregated, their heads and shoulders covered with black or flaxen wigs, not less ample than those which are now worn by the Lord Chancellor and the Speaker of the House of Commons." He adds, "that the wigs and most of the dress of these fops came from Paris, and that they spoke a peculiar and affected dialect, called a 'Lord' a 'Lard.'"

In the year 1764, owing to changes in the fashion, people gave over the use of that very artificial appendage, the wig, and wore their own hair, when they had any. In consequence of this, the wig-makers, who were very numerous in London, were suddenly thrown out of work, and reduced to great distress. For some time, we are told, both town and country rang with their calamities, and their complaints that men should wear their own hair instead of perukes; and at last it struck them that some legislative enactment ought to be at once procured in order to oblige gentlefolks to wear wigs, for the benefit of the suffering wig-trade. Accordingly they drew up a petition for relief, which, on the 11th of February, 1765, they carried to St. James's to represent to his Majesty George the Third. As they went processionally through the town, it was observed that most of these wig-makers, who wanted to force other people to wear them, wore no wigs themselves; and this striking the London mob as something monstrously unfair and inconsistent, they seized the petitioners, and cut off all their hair *par force*. Horace Walpole, who alludes to this ludicious petition, in his Letters to the Earl of Hertford, asks, with his usual wit, "Should one wonder if carpenters were to remonstrate, that since the peace their trade decays, and that there is no demand for wooden legs?"

St. James's Street in its time has had many distinguished residents. Waller, the poet, as Mr. John Timbs tells us, lived on the west side from 1660 until 1687, when he died at Beaconsfield, in Buckinghamshire. Pope lodged "next door to ye Golden Ball, on ye second terras." Gibbon, the historian, died in January, 1794, at No. 76, then Elmsley's, the bookseller's. Horace Walpole says: "I was told a droll story of Gibbon the other day. One of those booksellers in Paternoster Row, who publish things in numbers, went to Gibbon's lodgings in St. James's Street, sent up his name,

and was admitted. 'Sir,' said he, 'I am now publishing a History of England done by several good hands. I understand you have a knack of these things, and should be glad to give you every reasonable encouragement.' As soon as Gibbon had recovered the use of his legs and tongue, which were petrified with surprise, he ran to the bell, and desired his servant to show this encourager of learning down stairs."

At his residence in this street, in February, 1723, died Sir Christopher Wren, the architect of St. Paul's; in 1811, Lord Byron was living in lodgings at No. 8, just after attaining his majority.

At No. 29, next door to Boodle's Club, lived the caricaturist Gilray, who here committed suicide, in 1815, by throwing himself from the window on to the pavement below. The shop was well known as that of Miss Humphrey, the caricature print-seller, sister of the conchologist, and the vendor of his works. Gilray was first the pupil of Mr. Ashby, the celebrated writing engraver; but afterwards studied under Bartolozzi. The author of the "Book for a Rainy Day" says that Gilray engraved several portraits and other subjects in a steady mechanical way, but soon followed the genuine bent of his genius, though, it must be acknowledged, it was too often at the expense of honour and even common honesty. "He would, by his publications, either divulge family secrets which ought to have been ever at rest, or expect favours for the plates which he destroyed. This talent, by which he made many worthy persons so uneasy, was inimitable; and his works, though time may destroy every point of their sting, will remain specimens of a rare power, both for character and composition." Among numerous instances, he suffered himself to bear evidence against Samuel Ireland, the publisher of the pretended Shakespeare papers. Ireland had given away an etching, a portrait of himself. This print Gilray copied, and offered a few impressions publicly for sale in Miss Humphrey's shop-window, in December, 1797. Gilray, it may be remarked, lies buried in the churchyard of St. James's, Piccadilly.

At the commencement of the last century, Peyrault's, or Pero's, "Bagnio," in this street, was high in fashion. It occupied the site of what is now Fenton's Hotel, on the west side of the street; this was a bagnio of old standing, as appears by the title of a catalogue of the "valuable collection of pictures, the property of the late Mr. Bartrum Aumailkey, *alias* Pero, who kept the bagnio previous to 1714." Next door to the above establishment was a tavern bearing the sign of the "Bunch of Grapes," where, as we learn from the newspapers

ST. JAMES'S STREET IN 1750. (*From an Original Drawing in Mr. Crace's Collection.*)

of 1711, "was sold extraordinary good cask Florence wine, at 6s. per gallon."

The next house of notoriety is now No. 62, some time occupied by Lauriere, the jeweller. It was formerly held by an old lady well known under the appellation of "Political Betty," and was famous in Horace Walpole's time.

At the corner opposite the Palace, the shop which is now occupied by a firm of booksellers was, until recently, well known in the fashionable and

year 1827, was for some time published at Sams' Library, and called "Sams' Peerage."

In 1838-9, Louis Napoleon, then in exile, between the "affair" of Boulogne, and the "affair" of Strasburg, took up his quarters for a time at Fenton's Hotel, leading the life of a young man of fashion. From Fenton's he removed with a suite of seventeen friends and servants into Waterloo Place, and thence to Carlton Terrace and Carlton Gardens, where we have already mentioned him.

ST. JAMES'S PLACE. (*See page* 170.)

aristocratic circles as "Sams' Library." Mr. W. H. Sams, who died in 1872, had here for some time carried on his father's business as librarian and publisher. In former times its windows were often crowded with gazers at the caricatures of well-known political and other celebrities, before the days when Sig. Pellegrini made *Vanity Fair* famous.

　"There, where you stop to scan the last 'H. B.',
　　Swift paused and muttered, 'Shall I have that see?'"

wrote Lord Lytton in the "New Timon;" and, in truth, upon the site of Sams' shop the great satirist, coming out of St. James's Palace, might often have stood and quieted his fervid indignation at the baseness of the Court of Queen Anne. "Lodge's Peerage," the first edition of which appeared in the

It was in 1843-44, whilst residing in chambers at 88, St. James's Street, close to where now stands the Conservative Club, that Thackeray began and finished "The Luck of Barry Lyndon," which many consider the most original of his earlier writings.

Branching off from the west side of St. James's Street are Bennett Street, Park Place, St. James's Place, and Little St. James's Street. The highest and northernmost of these turnings leads into Arlington Street, a thoroughfare running at right angles with Piccadilly. This street has always been inhabited by statesmen and public men. The first house on the west side was for many years the house of the Duke of Beaufort, and then of the Duke of Hamilton, before it passed into the hands of

Lord Wimborne. It has on the ground floor a magnificently-carved ceiling, painted with the heraldic insignia of the house of Somerset.

In this street was for many years the town residence of the Dukes of Rutland. It was lent by the then Duke, in 1826, to the Duke of York, who died there quite suddenly in his arm-chair, on one of the first days of the following year. His body was removed to St. James's Palace, where it lay in state, and was buried in St. George's Chapel, at Windsor, on the 20th of January, 1827.

In 1708 the Duke of Richmond, Lord Cholmondeley, Lord Kingston, and Guildford Brooke were living in this street. In 1745 the first Earl of Orford, the great Sir Robert Walpole, died here. Here the old Marchioness of Salisbury, one of the leaders of "society" in the reign of George IV., used to hold her Sunday evening receptions, of which we find many notices in "Raikes's Journal," and other books of cotemporary anecdote. They were frequently attended by royalty, ambassadors, &c. The Marchioness was burnt to death at Hatfield House, in December, 1834.

Lord Carteret was living in this street both before and after he was promoted to an earl's coronet, as Lord Granville.

The writer of "A New Review of the Public Buildings, &c.," in the reign of George II., is enthusiastic in his praises of the side of Arlington Street which faces the Green Park, as "one of the most beautiful situations in Europe for health, convenience, and beauty, and combining together the advantages of town and country." The only fault that he can find with the mansions is the "want of uniformity."

In Park Place, in 1835, Vernon House, now the residence of Lord Redesdale, was occupied by Lord William Bentinck, some time Governor-General of India. Close by it are the offices and head-quarters of the Society for the Propagation of the Gospel in Foreign Parts, which was founded in 1701. This institution was formerly in Pall Mall, as we have mentioned. Its aim is to establish and support bishops and clergy of the Church of England abroad, and chiefly in our own colonies. There also is the office of the Colonial Bishoprics Fund, which was established in 1861 for founding and endowing additional Colonial bishoprics.

As a set-off to the good work carried on by the society above mentioned, we may state that in the early part of the last century the noted "Mother Needham" was "convicted of keeping a lewd and disorderly house in Park Place; she was fined one shilling, to stand twice in the pillory, and find sureties for her good behaviour for three years."

The memory of this woman is perpetuated by a couple of lines in the "Dunciad;" and a note on the passage says she was "a matron of great fame, and very religious in her way; whose constant prayer it was, that she might get enough by her profession to leave it off in time, and make her peace with God. This, however, was not granted to her, as she died from the effects of her exposure in the pillory."

No. 4 is the home of the Road Club, which was established here in 1874, by a number of gentlemen who take an interest in figuring as amateur "Jehus."

St. James's Place dates from about the year 1694. At the present time it forms the headquarters of bachelor members of Parliament, almost every other house being let out in apartments; it has been in past time also the abode of several individuals whose names have become as familiar as "household words." Here, in 1712, Addison had lodgings; and a few years later we find John Wilkes living here in "very elegant lodgings." Here, too, resided Parnell, the poet, Mr. Secretary Craggs, Bishop Kennett, the antiquary, and Mrs. Robinson (Perdita), the actress, already mentioned by us in speaking of Carlton House.

At the western end of St. James's Place, overlooking the Green Park, the learned Lepel, Lady Hervey, in 1748, built a house, which was subsequently occupied by Lord Hastings, and ultimately divided into two. Lady Hervey speaks of its windows as commanding a view towards Chelsea and the country, as also of the Duke of Devonshire's house, when the dust in Piccadilly permitted it. Within its walls Lord Chesterfield and other wits and learned persons used to meet constantly.

Lord John Hervey, who in 1720 married the "fair Lepel," one of the maids of honour to the Princess of Wales, was the eldest son of the first Earl of Bristol, and was early attached to the court of the Prince and Princess at Richmond. His marriage was signalised by Pulteney and Lord Chesterfield by a ballad in honour of both bride and bridegroom, in which the noble poets declared that never had been seen—

> "So perfect a beau and a belle,
> As when Hervey the handsome was wedded
> To the beautiful Molly Lepel."

His connection both with the world of politics and with that of poets is known to every reader of his memoirs, and of the life of Pope, who cruelly satirised him under the name of "Sporus."

At No. 25 lived Lord Guildford, who, as John Timbs tells us in his "Curiosities of London," "had his library lined with snake-wood from Ceylon, of which island he was at one time governor." The next tenant was Sir Francis Burdett, so many years the popular member for Westminster, who resided here from about 1820 to his death in 1844.

The life of Sir Francis Burdett affords a remarkable illustration of the political vicissitudes a popular man may encounter. Every reader of the political events of the present century will know how he was idolised by the people during the reign of George III.; and the story of his standing a siege of horse and foot for two days in his house in London, before the warrant could be executed, rather than surrender to the warrant officer who came to convey him to the Tower of London on a charge of libelling the House of Commons, stands out in strong contrast to the staunch Conservatism which marked the later years of his life.

Mr. Raikes, in his "Journal," tells the following anecdote of Sir Francis Burdett :—" Early in life he passed three years in France, at the outbreak of the Revolution, when he attended the meetings of the National Assembly and the Political Clubs, which, during that period of public agitation, were so numerous. When he returned home in 1793, dazzled by the political doctrines he had imbibed, he became a notorious reformer in Parliament, and married the second daughter of Thomas Coutts, the wealthy banker. He was a votary of Horne Tooke; and through the Radical interest of Westminster was elected member for that borough, without a shilling of expense to himself, in 1807, as the man of the people. He was imprisoned in the Tower in 1810, by order of the House of Commons, for addressing a printed letter to his constituents on the commitment of Mr. Gale Jones. Having seen the favourite object of Parliamentary Reform carried by the Whigs, and probably the inefficiency of his former wild theories to confer real happiness on his country, he gradually moderated his views on national politics, and settled down into a good Conservative, which brought upon him the abuse and obloquy of his own party, who then gave him the name of ' Old Glory.' It was a singular coincidence, that he died ten days after his wife, Lady Burdett, to whom he was most tenderly attached. Sir Francis was a great fox-hunter, and a type of the ' fine old English gentleman,' of which he preserved to the last the characteristic dress—leather-breeches and top-boots. When young, he was for a long time the notorious lover of Lady Oxford—cum multis aliis. He had a very large fortune, which goes to his eldest son Robert. His daughter, who inherited the Coutts's fortune, is the richest heiress in all England. He had once a dispute with Mr. Paul about the Westminster election after the death of Mr. Fox, which terminated in a duel, in which both parties were severely wounded ; and there being no medical persons present, and but one carriage on the spot, it became necessary to remove both the combatants to town in the same vehicle."

The death of Sir Francis was as pathetic as his parliamentary life had been famous. His wife was a daughter of Mr. Coutts, the celebrated banker, and for the long period of fifty years they lived happily together ; and when death took away Lady Burdett, in January, 1844, her husband, then in his seventy-fourth year, became inconsolable, and felt that he had nothing left to live for. Wrapping himself up in his sorrow, he refused all consolation and all nourishment. In spite of the most earnest entreaties he would taste no food, and at last nature gave way, and he died on the 23rd of the same month ; and the husband and wife were buried at the same hour, on the same day, in the same vault, in Ramsbury Church, Wiltshire. The above-mentioned daughter of Sir Francis Burdett, Angela Georgina, assumed in 1837 the additional surname and arms of Coutts, under the will of her grandfather's widow, Harriet (afterwards Duchess of St. Albans). Miss Burdett Coutts was raised to the peerage in 1871, by having conferred upon her the title of a Baroness, in recognition of her large-hearted charity and general philanthropy.

In 1790 one of the fine houses on the west side of St. James's Place was occupied by Mr. Robert Smith, a London banker, and M.P. for Nottingham, who, most reluctantly on the part of George III., was created a peer as Lord Carington. This was the first instance in which a peerage was ever bestowed on the moneyed interest as distinct from the ownership of broad acres ; and it was believed, not only by Pitt's enemies but by his friends, that the bestowal of the coronet in this case was the discharge of some pecuniary obligations of the Premier, who forced the King to sign the patent.

Readers of Mr. Harrison Ainsworth's historical romance of "St. James's" will scarcely need to be reminded of two chapters in the early part of that work, in which he gives us a picture of a jovial supper party at St. John's residence in this street, at which Wycherley, Congreve, Tickell, Mrs. Bracegirdle, Mrs. Oldfield, Addison, Vanbrugh, Steele, Rowe, Tom D'Urfey, Dr. Garth, Kneller, Harley, Mr. Markam, Mrs. Manley, and the other wits, poets, and painters of that truly Augustan era, were present, when Mrs. Oldfield and Mrs. Bracegirdle settled a quarrel as to which should sing first, by pistols—not, however, after the way of a duel, but by trying to snuff a candle by a shot at twelve paces. We should like to have been present at the break-up of the party at early dawn, and to have seen the ladies' chairs arrive, and take their departure ; Mrs. Bracegirdle escorted home by Congreve, Mrs. Old-field by Maynwaring, and Mrs. Centlivre by Prior, who persisted in calling her " Chloe " all the way ; whilst Steele and Wycherley, walking along by Mrs. Manley's chair, and being rather excited by St. John's port wine, assaulted the watch, and for their pains were arrested by the " Charlies," and lodged in the St. James's Round House.

Sir N. W. Wraxall, in his gossiping " Memoirs of his own Time," tells the following amusing story about one of the residents of St. James's Place towards the close of the last century :—

" Sir Richard Phillipps, a Welsh baronet of ancient descent, when member for Pembrokeshire, in the year 1776, having preferred a request to his Majesty, through the first Minister, Lord North, for permission to make a carriage-road up to the front of his house, which looked into St. James's Park, met with a refusal. The king, apprehensive that if he acceded to Sir Richard's desire, it would form a precedent for many similar applications, put a negative on it ; but Lord North, in delivering the answer, softened it by adding, that if he wished to be created an Irish peer, no difficulty would be ex-perienced. This honour being thus tendered him, he accepted it, and was forthwith made a baron of that kingdom by the title of Lord Milford. His intimate friend and mine, the late Sir John Stepney, related this fact to me not long after it took place."

At No. 22, a house built by James Wyatt, R.A., lived from 1808 until his death in December, 1855, Samuel Rogers, the poet. Here Sheridan, Lord Byron, Sir James Mackintosh, Thomas Moore, Macaulay, Sharp, and almost all the other literary celebrities of the first half of the present century, were often guests. The house, which is com-paratively small, and is distinguished by its bow windows, fronting the Green Park, contained a choice collection of pictures, Etruscan vases, sculp-ture, antique bronzes, and literary curiosities, and a variety of lesser objects of art—all distinguished for rare excellence ; some of the pictures were be-queathed to the nation, and the remainder of the collection was ultimately disposed of. Among the most valued treasures in the house there was to be seen framed and hung on one of the walls of his library, the original agreement by which Milton assigned to the publisher, Symons, his poem of " Paradise Lost," for the sum of five pounds. This historical document bears the undoubted autograph signature of the poet.

Samuel Rogers was a banker as well as a poet ; he knew how to spend his wealth, and his name will live as at once a poet and as a patron of litera-ture. Born in the year 1763, he lived to the great age of ninety-two. His first publication was his " Ode to Superstition, and other Poems," which appeared in 1787 ; five years later he published his " Pleasures of Memory," the work by which his fame as a poet was established, and by which his name came to be most widely and permanently known. In 1798 he gave to the world his " Epistle to a Friend, and other Poems ;" in 1814, appeared his " Vision of Columbus and Jacqueline ;" in 1819, " Human Life ;" and in the following year the first part of his " Italy," on the printing and illustrating of which he is said to have spent not less than £10,000.

The Rev. A. C. Coxe, of the United States, in his " Impressions of England," writes :—" Among the authors of England, I had desired to see especially Mr. Samuel Rogers, who is now the last survivor of a brilliant literary epoch, and whose long familiarity with the historical personages of a past generation would of itself be enough to make him a man of note, and a patriarch in the republic of letters. Though now above ninety years of age, he still renders his elegant habitation an attractive resort, and I was indebted to him for attentions which were the more valuable, as he was at that time suffering from an accident, and hence pecu-liarly entitled to deny himself entirely to strangers. His house, in St. James's Street, has been often described, and its beautiful opening on the Green Park is familiar from engravings. Here every Englishman of literary note, during the last half century, has been at some time a guest ; and if its walls could but *Boswellise* the wit which they have heard around the table of its hospitable master, no collection of *Memorabilia* with which the world is acquainted could at all be compared with it. Here I met the aged poet at breakfast ; Sir Charles and Lady Lyell completing the party. He talked of the past as one to whom the present was less a reality, and it seemed strange to hear him speak of Mrs. Piozzi, as if he had been one of the old circle at Thrale's. When a boy, he rang Dr. Johnson's bell, in Bolt Court, in a fit of ambition to see the literary colossus of the time, but his heart failed him at the sticking point, and he ran away before the door was opened. Possibly the old sage himself responded to the call, and as he retired in a fit of indignation, moralising on the growing impertinence of the age, how little did he imagine that the inter-ruption was a signal tribute to his genius, from one who, in the middle of the nineteenth century, should be himself an object of veneration as the Nestor of Literature!"

But it must be owned, with every wish to speak well of those who are gone, that Samuel Rogers was not a man gifted with such qualities as to make real friends. Acquaintances and hangers-on he numbered by scores; but of friends he had very few. He was full of spleen and sarcasm, though the sun of fortune had smiled on him through life, and accordingly, if he had been a poor man, he would have had many enemies. The following passage from Mr. William Jerdan's "Men I have Known" will serve to illustrate our meaning, though an admission to Mr. Rogers's breakfasts was one of the greatest privileges accorded to men of literary tastes and abilities, who wished to get on in London :—

"Rogers was reputed a wit, and did say some good things; but many of the best were said by others, and fathered upon him (as the use is), especially when there was any bitterness in the joke, which was his characteristic. His going to Holland House by the Hammersmith stage-coach (in the days when cabs and omnibuses were unknown), and asking the loitering driver what he called it, is not one of his worst : being answered 'The Regulator,' he observed that it was a very proper name, as all the rest *go by it*. Luttrell and Rogers were intimate friends and rival wits, and disliked each other accordingly. I have used the word 'friend,' but it did not appear that the nonogenarian (whatever he might have enjoyed half a century before) had any friends. I never saw about him any but acquaintances or toadies. Had he outlived them? No; he was not of a nature to have friends. He was born with the silver spoon in his mouth, and had never needed a friend in his long, easy journey through life. The posthumous laudation lavished upon him by his political cronies was purely of the *de mortuis nil nisi bonum* kind. He never received that coin when alive; for, if the truth be told, his liberality and generosity were small specks which could not bear blazon, and he was radically ill-tempered. Now, nobody can love a cantankerous person, even though placed in such fortunate circumstances as not to be always offensive. His whole career was too sunny. There were neither clouds nor showers to nourish the sensitive plants which adorn humanity—nothing but showy sunflowers. No lovely dew-dipped blossoms; no sweet buddings of refreshing scent; no soft green tufts sending up grateful incense, as when varying seasons produce their beneficial influence, and the breezes and the rains (ay, the storms) from heaven serve but to root and expand the spirit's growth.

"Few men who have had nothing but an even tenor of their way, are duly touched with feeling for the distresses of their fellow-creatures, which they have never experienced. In the absence of any higher motive to benevolence, there was not even a trace of *bonhomie* about Rogers. Sarcasm and satire were his social weapons. Kindness and geniality do not crop out in any account of him that I have seen; and this negative describes the individual, of whom I did not care to know much. The constant little bickering competitions between him and Luttrell were very entertaining to some minds. They met once, and did not squabble. It was in the Crystal Palace in Hyde Park, into which they were both wheeled in chairs, when no longer able to walk!"

On one occasion the venerable poet was visited by Wordsworth and Haydon the painter. They had been to Paddington together, and had afterwards walked across the Park to Rogers's house. He had a party to lunch, so Haydon went into the pictures, and studied Rembrandt, Reynolds, Veronese, Raffaelle, and Tintoretto. Wordsworth remarked, "Haydon is down-stairs." "Ah," said Rogers, "he is better employed than chattering nonsense up-stairs." As Wordsworth and Haydon crossed the Park, the latter remarked, "Scott, Wilkie, Keats, Hazlitt, Beaumont, Jackson, Charles Lamb are all gone—we only are left." He said, "How old are you?" "Fifty-six," replied the painter; "how old are you?" "Seventy-three," said Wordsworth, "in my seventy-third year; I was born in 1770." "And I in 1786." "You have many years before you." "I trust I have; and you, too, I hope. Let us cut out Titian, who was ninety-nine." "Was he ninety-nine?" said Wordsworth. "Yes," said his friend, "and his death was a moral; for as he lay dying of the plague, he was plundered, and could not help himself."

"Eminent as he was, both by position and genius," says his biographer, "Rogers's opinion was frequently sought by authors and by artists. He was shy of praise—shy of censure. In an age when almost every poet of any name was a reviewer, Rogers was *not* a reviewer. When in the presence of the painter of any picture, he had constant recourse to the safe and general criticism of Sir Joshua : 'Pretty, very pretty,' were the words that conveyed satisfaction to the eager ears of many a clever artist." The critic who annoyed Mr. Rogers in the *Quarterly Review* was never more in the wrong than when he asserted that his author was a hasty writer. A man of letters and of fortune from his birth, whose literary life extended over sixty years, cannot be called a hasty writer when the produce of his life can be placed with ease in an ordinary pocket volume, for such is the shape his works assume in the latest edition. The fact is, that his were hard-bound brains, and not a line he ever wrote was produced at a single

Mr. Rogers with which he had nothing whatever to do. In the early days of the *John Bull* newspaper, "Sam Rogers" had fathered on him many a smart saying, and many a clever and many a stupid jest. Once, when a certain M.P. wrote a review of his poems, and said he wrote very

SAMUEL ROGERS. (*From a Portrait taken shortly before his death.*)

sitting. This was well exemplified in a favourite saying of Sydney Smith : "When Rogers produces a couplet he goes to bed, the knocker is tied, and straw is laid down, and the caudle is made, and the answer to inquiries is, that Mr. Rogers is as well as can be expected." How many smart sayings have been assigned to Sheridan and Selwyn, to Jekyll and Rose, to Walpole and others of Walpole's contemporaries, which in truth they never uttered! Many were, and still are, assigned to

well for a banker, Rogers wrote, in return, the following :—

" They say he has no heart, and I deny it :
He has a heart, and—gets his speeches by it."

The principal front of the house once tenanted by Samuel Rogers overlooks the Green Park, where it forms a conspicuous object by the side of Spencer House. "Within that house," writes Mr. Miller in 1852, "every distinguished literary man of the last century has been a guest. Here Scott,

Byron, Shelley, Coleridge and Campbell have many a time discoursed with the venerable poet. What a rich volume would that be, were it possible to write it, that contained all the good sayings that have been uttered beneath that roof! Here I first sat as a guest, roaring with laughter at the wit of received, would require the hand of another Horace Walpole to illustrate it. The name of Samuel Rogers," he adds, "alone would save the Green Park from oblivion, and give it a popularity which, but for him, it would never have possessed."

About the year 1863 was established, at No. 17

SAMUEL ROGERS' HOUSE, GREEN PARK FRONT. (*See page* **174**)

Sydney Smith; here also I have listened 'with bated breath' to the music murmured by the lips of Tommy Moore. Within those walls I first saw that true poetess and much-injured lady, Caroline Norton, and from the host himself in my early career as an author received that kindness and encouragement without which I might have 'fallen on the way.' A description of this celebrated house, of all it contains, and of all the guests it has in St. James's Place—previously the residence of Lord Lyttelton—the Public Schools Club; which, however, had but a transient existence. Its name was subsequently changed to the Phœnix, but the club does not appear to have been more flourishing under its new name, and in a short time it ceased altogether, and the premises were converted into a private hotel.

The mansion of Earl Spencer, which stands at

the south-west angle, with one front facing the Green Park, is by some considered one of the finest designs of Inigo Jones; by others it is said to have been built by Vardy, a scholar of Kent, and architect of the Horse Guards. It consists of an admixture of the Grecian style of architecture, and is highly, though not profusely, ornamented. The principal ornament of the interior is the library, an elegant room, containing one of the finest collections of books in the kingdom. This noble and even palatial edifice was built for John, first Lord Spencer, who died in 1783. The front towards the Park, which is of Portland stone, with attached columns, is surmounted by a pediment adorned with statues and vases, very tastefully disposed.

Retracing our steps into St. James's Street, we now descend towards the Palace gates and Cleveland Row. How different now is the scene to be witnessed here from what it was before the introduction of coaches or even of sedan-chairs. On the happiness of those days, Gay thus descants in his "Trivia:"—

" Thus was of old Britannia's city bless'd
　Ere pride and luxury her sons possess'd;
　Coaches and chariots yet unfashion'd lay,
　Nor late-invented chairs perplex'd the way:
　Then the proud lady tripp'd along the town,
　And tucked up petticoats, secur'd her gown;
　Her rosy cheek with distant visits glow'd,
　And exercise unartful charms bestowed;
　But since in braided gold her foot is bound,
　And a long trailing manteau sweeps the ground,
　Her shoe disdains the street; the lazy fair
　With narrow step affects a limping air."

At the time of which Gay speaks, of course it was but a rare thing for a country dame to be seen in London. Lord Clarendon tells us that his mother, though she was the daughter of a peer, and though her husband had been a member of Parliament, was never in London in her life, " the wisdom and frugality of that time being such that few gentlemen made journeys to London, or any other expensive journeys, but upon important business, and their wives never."

A very different state of things is this from that which meets our eyes in the reign of Victoria, when every nobleman and country gentleman who has a wife and family brings them up yearly to London, for the whole, or at least for a part, of the " season." Young ladies a century ago, as Mr. Cradock observes in his amusing " Library Memoirs," were "not so deeply read as at present;" and " if, when married, they went once a year up to London to see the fashions and attend the theatres, it was thought sufficient. They neither wished to be presented at court, nor to retain a box at the opera-house."

Mr. F. Locker in the following lines gives us an imaginary picture of St. James's Street and Place in those " good old times:"—

" At dusk, when I am strolling there,
　　Dim forms will rise around me;
　Lepel flits by me in her chair,
　　And Congreve's airs astound me.

" And once Nell Gwynne, a frail young sprite,
　　Looked kindly when I met her;
　I shook my head, perhaps—but quite
　　Forgot to quite forget her."

It has been said that Campbell's " Last Man " owed its composition to a chance conversation in St. James's Street. With reference to this " moot point," Cyrus Redding writes in his " Recollections:"—" I had a singular dispute with Campbell, who, if he once adopted an idea, was very difficult to convince of being in error. He had written a letter to the editor of the *Edinburgh Review*, in consequence of the reviewer having stated that his poem of the 'Last Man' had been suggested by Byron's 'Darkness.' He stated that in a conversation with Byron, in St. James's Street, he had mentioned the subject of the extinction of the creation and of the human species to Byron, as a fit subject for a poem. I happened to know that Byron and Shelley were once standing together looking at the splendid view of the Alps across the Leman, and Shelley remarked—' What a thing it would be if all were involved in darkness at this moment—the sun and stars to go out. How terrible the idea!' Such a thought was likely to arise in the minds of more persons than one. Barry Cornwall had told Campbell that some friend of his thought of writing a poem on that subject. The date of the conversation of Shelley and Byron I cannot state exactly, but I know it was years before the 'Last Man' of Campbell appeared. I told the poet this, and contended that the idea was not new."

Extending towards the Green Park, from the south-west corner of St. James's Street, is Cleveland Row. Here Lord Stowell resided when known as Sir William Scott, the honoured M.P. for the University of Oxford. Theodore Hook lived here from 1827 till he removed to Fulham, in 1831. His residence was handsome, and extravagantly too large for his purpose. He was admitted a member of divers clubs; shone the first attraction of their house-dinners; and in such as allowed of play he might commonly be seen in the course of his protracted evening. Presently he began to receive invitations to great houses in the country, and, for week after week, often travelled from one to another such scene, to all outward appearance in the style of an idler of high condition. In a word, he had soon entangled himself with habits and connections which implied much curtailment of the time for labour at the desk, and a course of expenditure more than sufficient to swallow all the profits of what remained from his editorial salary and literary gains. We shall have more to say of him when we come to Fulham.

But the spot we are upon has earlier associations. In the spring of the year 1668 Lady Castlemaine, who had just before made up a quarrel with the King, became possessed, by royal gift, of Berkshire House, to the north-west of the Palace Gate, which had been the town residence of the first two Earls of Berkshire, and subsequently occupied by Lord Clarendon. Adjoining the house was a large walled-in Dutch garden, with a summer-house in the north-western corner, in the rear. At the time of which we write it was really a country house, standing quite isolated in its own grounds. The site of the property is now bounded on the south by Cleveland Row and Cleveland Square; on the east by St. James's Street: on the north and west its limits were defined by Park Place and the edge of the Green Park. The house is shown in Faithorne's map of London and Westminster in 1658. The furnishing of the mansion in a style suited to the caprice of the haughty mistress must have been a severe trial for the purse-strings of even a king, for we are told that Berkshire House was most lavishly and sumptuously adorned and decorated.

The dining-room of one of the houses in Cleveland Row, occupied in the reigns of George I. and George II. by Lord Townshend, witnessed the memorable and not very dignified quarrel between its owner, then Secretary of State, and the Premier, Sir Robert Walpole. The two combatants are said by Sir N. Wraxall to have seized each other by the throat—a scene which Gay portrayed in the *Beggar's Opera*, under the characters of "Peachum" and "Lockitt."

At the western end of Cleveland Row stands Bridgewater House, the town residence of the Earl of Ellesmere. Erected in 1847-50, from the designs of the late Sir Charles Barry, the mansion occupies the site of what was formerly Berkeley House, which Charles II. presented to the Duchess of Cleveland. Jarvis, the portrait-painter, died in the old house in 1739. Afterwards, when Berkeley House was named Cleveland Court, it was occupied by Mrs. Selwyn, mother of George Selwyn. It is said of George Selwyn, who died here in 1791,

aged seventy-two, that "he lived for society, and continued in it until he looked like the waxwork figure of a corpse."

The plan of Bridgewater House approaches a square, the south front being about 140 feet in length, and the west 120 feet; and there are two small courts within the mass to aid in lighting the various apartments. The ground-plan itself comprises a perfect residence—drawing-room, dining-room, ladies' rooms, chamber, dressing-rooms, &c. The first floor is, with a small exception, appropriated to state-rooms, dining-room, drawing-room, the splendid picture-gallery, &c. The gallery occupies the whole of the north side of the house, and is carried out a few feet beyond the east wall. The building, in both interior and exterior decoration, is worthy of the splendid collection of works of art which are here brought together. The main portion of this collection, so well known as the "Bridgewater Gallery," was made by the Duke of Bridgewater, who, dying in 1803, left his pictures, valued at £150,000, to his nephew, the first Duke of Sutherland (then Marquis of Stafford), with remainder to the marquis's second son, Francis, afterwards Earl of Ellesmere. This gallery of paintings is in many respects the most valuable in this country; in no gallery is the school of Carracci so well represented. One of the gems of Lord Ellesmere's gallery is the "Chandos" portrait of Shakespeare, which is believed to have belonged once to Sir William Davenport, and then to Betterton, the actor, and while in the possession of the latter was copied by Sir Godfrey Kneller for Dryden, who considered it an original likeness, and who has thus celebrated the copy :—

"Shakespeare, thy gift I place before my sight:
With awe I ask his blessing ere I write,
With reverence look on his majestic face,
Proud to be less—but of his godlike race."

The portrait was bought by the first Lord Ellesmere, at the Stowe sale, for 355 guineas.

The Green Park, which we now enter, is separated from St. James's along part of its southern side by the Mall, and covers a large triangular piece of ground, extending westwards as far as Hyde Park Corner, the line of communication from the end of the Mall being by Constitution Hill. It was formerly called Little or Upper St. James's Park, and was reduced in extent in 1767, by George III., in order to add to the gardens of Buckingham House. Old maps of London show us that the spot of ground situated between the wall of St. James's Palace, and "the way to Reading," as Piccadilly was formerly called, was before the Restoration merely a piece of waste ground—in fact, a meadow. It is represented in those maps as planted with a few willow-trees, and intersected with ditches, among which must have been "the drie ditch-bankes about Pikadilla," in which old Gerarde, the author of "The Herbalist" (1596), used to find the small buglosse or ox-tongue. In October, 1660, as stated in Rugge's "Diurnal," ice-houses were built in Upper St. James's Park, "as the mode is in some parts of France and Italy, and other hot countries, for to cool wines and other drinks for the summer season." Old plans show that these ice-houses were situated in the middle of what is now called the Green Park, and here they remained till the beginning of the present century. At the western extremity, close to the road leading into Hyde Park, Charles II. formed a deer-harbour.

We read that when, in 1642, it was resolved by the Parliament to fortify the suburbs of the metropolis, "a small redoubt and battery on Constitution Hill" were among the defences ordered to be erected.

Dr. King, in his "Anecdotes of his Own Time," tells an amusing story about the "witty monarch" and his saturnine brother James, which we may as well tell in this place :—"King Charles II., after taking two or three turns one morning in the Park (as was his usual custom), attended only by the Duke of Leeds and my Lord Cromarty, walked up Constitution Hill, and from thence into Hyde Park. But just as he was crossing the road, the Duke of York's coach was nearly arrived there. The duke had been hunting that morning on Hounslow Heath, and was returning in his coach, escorted by a party of the guards, who, as soon as they saw the king, suddenly halted, and consequently stopped the coach. The duke, being acquainted with the occasion of the halt, immediately got out of his coach, and, after saluting the king, said he was greatly surprised to find his Majesty in that place with such a small attendance, and that he thought his Majesty exposed himself to some danger. 'No danger whatever, James,' said Charles, 'for I am sure that no man in England would take my life to make you king.'"

Like most other lonely places a little distance out of London, it soon became a favourite spot for the gentlemanly diversion of duelling. On Saturday night, January 11, 1696, Sir Henry Colt having been challenged by "Beau" Fielding, these two gentlemen here fought a duel. The spot chosen for this little passage of arms was at the back of Cleveland Court, which, as above stated, stood on the site of what is now Bridgewater House. This place was chosen, it is said, because the "Beau,"

like the knights of old, wished to fight under the beautiful eyes of his mistress and future wife, the notorious Duchess of Cleveland. It was stated at the time that Fielding, whose courage was none of the brightest, ran Sir Henry through the body before he had time to draw his sword ; but the baronet disarmed him, notwithstanding this wound, and so the fight ended.

From the "Foreigner's Guide to London," published in 1729, we learn that early in the last century Constitution Hill had become as much frequented for the purpose of fighting duels as the favourite little spot at the back of Montague House. The year after this was written, there occurred another duel in this park, which occasioned a great noise. The combatants were William Pulteney (afterwards Earl of Bath) and John, Lord Hervey—the "Sporus" of Pope—

"—— that thing of silk,
Sporus, that mere white curd of asses' milk."

The latter, it appears, had written several defences of Sir Robert Walpole, in answer to attacks on him in the *Craftsman*. To one of these Pulteney published an answer, entitling it "A Proper Reply to a late Scurrilous Libel." The "Reply," it must be owned, was grossly personal ; Hervey therefore challenged his rival, and they fought with swords in St. James's Park. The duel took place on Monday, January 25, 1730, between three and four o'clock in the afternoon, behind Arlington Street, Mr. Fox and Sir John Rushout acting as seconds. The "affair of honour," however, turned out to be a bloodless one ; no serious bodily harm ensued to either combatant, and Lord Hervey was left to the vengeance of Pope's satire. The germ of Pope's "Sporus" will be found in these party pasquinades out of which the duel arose.

One evening in May, 1771, a duel was fought here between Edward, Viscount Ligonier, nephew of the celebrated general, and Count Alfieri, the Italian poet, in which the latter was slightly wounded.

"Queen Caroline, who made so many useful improvements in Hyde Park," says Mr. Larwood, in his "History of the London Parks," "also extended her patronage to the Green Park. In February, 1730, the Board of Works received orders to prepare a private walk in Upper St. James's Park, for the Queen and the royal family to divert themselves in the spring. This walk extended along the row of mansions at the eastern extremity of the Park ; but that plan never came to anything farther than the erection of a sort of pavilion, called the 'Queen's Library.' Indeed, her Majesty's death was caused by her partiality for this spot. On the

9th of November, 1737, she walked to the 'Library' and breakfasted there. On that occasion she caught such a severe cold that she had to retire to her bed immediately on her return to the palace : ten days after she was a corpse." All traces of this "Library," and of a curious fountain which was once here, have long since passed away.

In 1749, on the publication of the Peace of Aix-la-Chapelle, the centre of the Green Park was selected for an exhibition of fireworks, which in grandeur could not have been surpassed in the last century. A huge and substantial building was constructed, running from north to south, with a solid centre and wings ; if we may judge from a rare print of the time, it must have been upwards of 400 feet in length : it contained pavilions for the Engineers, ten "arcades for planting the cannon," a grand musical gallery in the centre, surmounted by the arms of the Duke of Montague, at whose cost, in all probability, it was put up. Over the music-gallery was an allegorical figure of Peace attended by Neptune and Mars, and above, a grand basso-relievo, representing the King in the act of giving peace to Britannia. This was illuminated in the evening, and on a pole at the top of all was an illumination representing the sun, which burnt nearly all the night long. The print shows Buckingham House surrounded with a long square wall, extending westwards to Chelsea College. The ground is all open up to Hyde Park Corner, where St. George's Hospital and "Lord Chesterfield's new house" figure as almost the only buildings ; a carriage and pair, with outriders, is making its way up an open road marked as "Constitution Hill" towards the spot where now stands Apsley House.

Thursday, the 27th of April, was the grand day appointed for the fireworks. All the entrances into the Green Park were opened, and a breach of fifty feet was made into the Park wall on the Piccadilly side in order to give admittance to the vast concourse of spectators. A gallery was erected for the Privy Council, the Peers, the House of Commons ; and the rest of the places were given to the Lord Mayor. The King, who had in the fore-part of the day reviewed the three regiments of Foot-guards from the garden wall of St. James's, witnessed the fireworks from a pavilion in the Park which had been erected for his reception. The Prince and Princess of Wales, who were on bad terms with the King, kept aloof, and saw the display from the house of the Earl of Middlesex, in Arlington Street. The performance began with a grand military overture, composed by Handel, in which "one hundred cannon, fired singly with the music," formed

a distinctive feature. Shortly after the commencement of the fireworks, the temple accidentally took fire, and part of it was consumed.

During the peace *fêtes* of 1814, the Green Park was again chosen for the scene of a grand pyrotechnic display. Near Constitution Hill a building was erected from the design of Sir William Congreve (of rocket celebrity), which, with all its palings, and the cordon of sentries round it, covered one-third of the Green Park. This building received the name of the Temple of Concord. The materials of this structure, and of the other erections set up on that occasion, were sold afterwards by auction, and fetched only about £200.

Coming down to more recent times, we may state here that on Constitution Hill, near Buckingham Palace, three diabolical attempts have been made to shoot Her Majesty, Queen Victoria. In June, 1840, a lunatic, named Edward Oxford, deliberately fired twice at Her Majesty as she was riding past in her carriage, in company with Prince Albert. Oxford was tried at the Central Criminal Court, when a verdict was returned of "Guilty, but insane," and the prisoner was accordingly removed to be "confined during Her Majesty's pleasure." The second attempt on the life of the Queen was made by Francis, another lunatic, in May, 1842 ; and the third by an idiot, named Hamilton, in 1849.

On the 29th of June, 1850, at the upper end of Constitution Hill, Sir Robert Peel was thrown from his horse, and very severely injured. He died at his house, in Whitehall Gardens, about three days afterwards.

The rest of the history of the Green Park is soon told. In 1829 the Chelsea Waterworks Company constructed an immense reservoir in the north-east corner of the park, opposite Stratton Street ; it was capable of containing 1,500,000 gallons. This reservoir was removed about 1855, and the entrance close by was at the same time considerably widened. "Amidst all the improvements of late years," writes Walker in "The Original," in 1835, "it is much to be lamented that the Green Park has been so much neglected, seeing that it is most conspicuously situated, and, notwithstanding its inferior size, is by much the most advantageously disposed as to ground. There was some years ago a talk of its being terraced in part, and wholly laid out in a highly ornamental style ; which, by way of variety, and with reference to its situation, seems a judicious plan. I would that his Majesty would give orders to that effect ; and then, as its present name would become inappropriate, it might be called after its royal patron. It is to be hoped that, whenever the opportunity occurs, the Ranger's house will not be allowed to stand in the way of the very great improvement which its removal would cause both to the park and to Piccadilly. I do not believe that anything would add so much to the ornament of London as

As Thomas Miller remarks in his "Picturesque Sketches of London," the Green Park "possesses but little to interest, beyond a walk beside the gardens which run up in a line with St. James's Street." But those who know the locality will not

BRIDGEWATER HOUSE. (*See page* 177.)

the embellishment of the Green Park to the extent of which it is capable."

The Ranger's lodge spoken of above stood near the north-west corner, and was removed about the year 1847. The two stags from the pillars at the entrance now adorn the Albert Gate, Hyde Park. The entire park had a few years previously been drained, and the surface re-laid and planted. The Rangership of the Green Park is at present, together with the rangership of St. James's and Richmond Parks, held by the Duke of Cambridge.

pass without gazing at one residence (a little above Spencer House), conspicuous by its large bow-windows, the upper one of which is encircled by a gilt railing. This was the house of the banker-poet, Samuel Rogers, of whom we have already spoken. The gardens of the several houses on this side of the park are leased of the Crown. Owing to its happy site on a sloping ground, the view from the upper walk is very extensive; and whenever the atmosphere is unobscured by fog or smoke, a lovely panorama presents itself.

An Horizontal View of the PUBLIC FIREWORKS ordered to be exhibited on occasion of the GENERAL PEACE conducted at Aix le Chapelle on November 7ᵗʰ 1748.

THE EXPLANATION.

From A to A is the full length of the scheme including, 1 Pavilions or store Houses for the Engineers use. 2 Arcades for planting the Cannon. 3 Flight of 3 steps ascending to the Music. Gallery. 4 The grand Area or Music Gallery. N.B. over the Entrance is the D. of Montagu's Arms: above the Music is PEACE attended by Neptune and Mars, higher is a grand Bass. Relievo to be illuminated, in which the King is rᵖresented giving PEACE to BRITANNIA: over all is the King's Arms, from whence rise 50 feet high, with a Jun 40 foot 32 feet diameter, which will burn some hours. 5 The passage from the Mall on St James's Park into the Green Park. 6 Constitution Hill. 7 Hide Park Corner. 8 The 6 of Chesterfields New House. 9 St Georges Hospital. 10 The Patheon. 11 Chelsea Colleege. 12 Chelsea Church. 13 Surry Hills. 14 Buckingham House. 15 piece of Water in the Green Park.
N.B. This Prospect is taken from the Library at St James's Palace.

THE PEACE REJOICINGS IN THE GREEN PARK. *From a Contemporary Print.* (*See page 179*)

CHAPTER XV.

ST. JAMES'S SQUARE AND ITS DISTINGUISHED RESIDENTS.

" The lordly region of St. James's Square."

Character of the Square in the Seventeenth and Eighteenth Centuries—Patriotism of Dr. Johnson and Savage—Ormonde House—The Duke and the Irish Peer—Romney House—The Fireworks at the Peace of Ryswick—Distinguished Residents—Norfolk House—"Jockey of Norfolk "—" All the Blood of all the Howards "—A Duke over his Cups—The Residence of the Bishop of London—The Bishop of London's Fund—Allen, Lord Bathurst—The Roxburgh Club—The Windham Club—The London Library—The "Lichfield House Compact" —The Residence of Mrs. Boehm—Receipt of News of the Victory of Waterloo—The East India United Service Club—Lady Francis and Queen Caroline—" Jack Robinson " and Lord Castlereagh—The Copyhold, Inclosure, and Tithe Commission.

STANDING as it does so near to "our palace of St. James," St. James's Square was for many years the most fashionable square in London, and though fashion is now fast migrating—perhaps has already migrated—to Belgravia, still it retains much of its long-established character. In the last century its claim was undisputed, as may be gathered from some lines which were favourites of Dr. Johnson—

> " When the Duke of Leeds shall married be
> To a fine young lady of quality,
> How happy that gentlewoman will be
> In his Grace of Leeds' good company !
> She shall have all that's fine and fair,
> And ride in a coach to take the air,
> And have a house in St. James's Square."

This square is mentioned in the comedies of the time of George I. as the *ne plus ultra* of fashion. Thus Shadwell, in his *Busy Fair*, writes, "We call it London, and it outdoes St. James's Square and all the squares in dressing and breeding."

This square is built on the site of the old "St. James's Fields," and the surrounding streets were named, with the usual loyalty of the time, after King Charles II. and his royal brother, the Duke of York (afterwards James II.), namely, King Street, Charles Street, Duke Street, and York Street. On account of their central situation, most of the houses in these side streets are occupied as hotels, or let out in furnished apartments for gentlemen who live mainly at their clubs.

There was a time, however, when the square was not as yet known to the leaders of fashion. "St. James's Square," says Macaulay, "in 1685 was a receptacle for all the offal and cinders, and for all the dead cats and dogs of Westminster. At one time a cudgel-player kept the ring there. At another time an impudent squatter settled himself there, and built a shed for rubbish under the windows of the gilded *salons* in which the first magnates of the realm, Norfolk, Ormond, Kent, and Pembroke, gave banquets and balls. It was not till these nuisances had lasted through a whole generation, and till much had been written about them, that the inhabitants applied to Parliament for permission to put up rails and plant trees."

It would appear, by the few notices of the time that can be found, that the central area of the square was but little cared for even in the last century; indeed, it may be justly remarked that it must have presented in 1773 much the same appearance which all London noticed in Leicester Square as lately as 1873. The Chevalier David in 1721 endeavoured, but in vain, to collect a sum of £2,000 towards erecting in its centre an equestrian statue of George I., which, most disinterestedly of course, he hoped to be commissioned to execute; but an adequate sum was not collected, and the project fell through. Four years later, according to a statement laid before Parliament, the surface of the interior of the square was still a "common laystall for dust, and for the refuse of kitchens and dead animals;" and, worse than all, because less easily dispossessed, we are told that a coachmaker had the audacity to put up a shed some thirty feet in length, and to pile a stack of wood in the area. Under these circumstances, at last it became necessary "to do something;" and accordingly the courtly and, for the most part, titled personages who lived on the north, east, and west sides of the square asked, and obtained, permission to tax themselves for the common benefit, in order to cleanse and improve the square.

From Sutton Nichols' print of the square, published in 1720, it appears that there was in the centre of the area a small lake or reservoir, and a fountain which played to about the height of fifteen feet; as also that there was a pleasure-boat on the water, and that numerous posts were placed at a small distance from the houses all round the square. Another print dated 1773 shows the enclosure of iron rails to have been octagonal, and the interior of it to have been still occupied by a circular pond, edged round with stone. It is described by Northouck, who wrote at the same date, as "the most pleasing square in all London;" and he instances as an example of "true taste" the contrast between the square formed by the houses and the circular nature of the enclosed area. He says, however, that the houses in it are grand individually rather than collectively, each being built on a scale and plan of its own. He writes: "The largest house is Norfolk House, at the south-east corner, a building which gives great offence to a late critic, who observes that in such mansions we expect something beyond roominess and convenience, the mere requisites of a packer or a sugar-baker. Would any foreigner, beholding an insipid length of wall broken with a regular row of windows, ever figure from thence the residence of the first duke of England ?"

In a like spirit the author of "A New Critical Review of the Public Buildings, &c.," observes, too, that this square is superior in grandeur of appearance to any other, though it has not in it a single "elegant" house; he bitterly complains of the irregularity of the southern side, and the want of a statue or obelisk in the middle of the large oval basin of water which, as we have said, then occupied the centre. This sheet of water, which was six or seven feet in depth, had subsequently placed in its centre a fine equestrian statue of William III. According to Lambert's "History of London," the basin was 150 feet in length. Into the water in this lake the mob in the "Gordon Riots" of 1780 threw the keys of Newgate, which they had broken open and burnt. They were not found for several years afterwards. Mr. John Timbs tells us that "a pedestal for the statue was erected in the centre of the square in 1732; but the statue, cast in brass by the younger Bacon, was not set up until 1808; the bequest in 1724 for the cost having been forgotten, until the money was found in the list of unclaimed dividends."

Such must have been the appearance of the square at the time that Dr. Johnson and his friend Savage, in early life, when friendless and penniless, spent a summer night walking round the enclosure, now and then resting on a stray cart or friendly bench, and bellowing out all sorts of wild denunciations of the then Government. To use Boswell's own words, "They were not at all depressed by their situation; but in high spirits, and brimful of patriotism, they traversed the square for several hours, inveighed against the Minister, and resolved that they would stand by their country." By prudence and perseverance, and the help of friends, Johnson lived to rise above this obscurity; whilst Savage, although perhaps endowed with even more genius, only sank lower and lower. When he was employed upon his tragedy of *Sir Thomas Overbury*, "he was," says Johnson, "often without lodgings and often without meat, nor had he any other conveniences for study than the fields or the streets allowed him. There he used to walk, and form his speeches, and afterwards step into a shop, beg

for a few moments the use of pen and ink, and write down what he had composed upon paper which he had picked up by accident."

But it is time to pass from these general remarks on the square to a more detailed account of its houses and its residents.

In 1684, the Duchess of Ormonde died at her residence, Ormonde House, on the north side of the square. The Duke of Ormonde, who was living here in the reign of Queen Anne and George I., was said to have been the best bred man of his day. He entertained largely and liberally, but he allowed the bad practice of his servants taking money from his guests. Dr. King tells the following story in his "Anecdotes of his Own Times :"—"I remember a Lord Poer, a Roman Catholic peer of Ireland, who lived upon a small pension which Queen Anne had granted him : he was a man of honour, and well esteemed; and had formerly been an officer of some distinction in the service of France. The Duke of Ormonde had often invited him to dinner, and he as often excused himself. At last the duke kindly expostulated with him, and would know the reason why he so constantly refused to be one of his guests. My Lord Poer then honestly confessed that he could not afford it ; 'but,' says he, 'if your Grace will put a guinea into my hands as often as you are pleased to invite me to dine, I will not decline the honour of waiting on you.' This was done ; and my lord was afterwards a frequent guest in St. James's Square."

From the *Post Boy*, No. 411, published in 1698, it appears that the house was taken for the Count de Tallard, the French ambassador. The rent paid by the Count is stated to have been no less than £600 per annum, a large rental in those days, even for a house in the very centre of the fashionable world. Ormonde House stood on the east side of James Street, in the north-east corner of the square. In the rear of the houses which at present cover its site is Ormonde Yard, now a mews. Romney House was also on the north side of the square; and here in 1695 and again in 1697, as we learn from the *Flying Post*, the *Post Boy*, and the *Post Man*—the fashionable papers of the day—King William III. visited the Earl of Romney to witness the fireworks in the square; and in 1697, on the conclusion of the treaty of peace of Ryswick, the Dutch Ambassador made before his house a bon-fire of 140 pitch-barrels, and wine was "kept continually running among the common people." We learn accidentally, from an anecdote in Joe Miller's "Jest Book," that the author of these fireworks being in company with some ladies, was highly commending the epitaph just then set up in the

Abbey on Mr. Purcell's monument—" He has gone to that place where only his own harmony can be exceeded." " Well, Colonel," said one of the ladies, " the same epitaph might serve for you by altering one word only : ' He has gone to that place where only his own fireworks can be exceeded.' "

In 1708 the following noblemen resided in this square—namely, the Dukes of Norfolk, Northumberland, and Ormonde ; and Lords Ossulston, Kent, Woodstock, and Torrington. The Earl of Sunderland (one of the Chief Secretaries of State), the Duke of Kent, and Lord Bathurst were living there in 1724. No. 2 is still Lord Falmouth's town residence. " The street-posts," Mr. John Timbs tells us in his " Curiosities of London," are made of cannon captured by Lord Falmouth's ancestor, Admiral Boscawen, off Cape Finisterre."

In one of the houses in this square, in the reign of Queen Anne, was living Lord Pembroke, whom Pope celebrates as a connoisseur in such matters as " statues, dirty gods, and coins." The house No. 6, on the north side, the town-house of the Marquis of Bristol, has been the residence of his ancestors, the Herveys, since the first laying out of the square in the reign of Charles II. It is not often, however, that the family of any nobleman, except of a Duke like their Graces of Norfolk and Northumberland, has owned one and the same town-house for two centuries without a break. It was of this " noble family "—who are stated to have produced so many eccentric characters—that the Dowager Lady Townshend remarked, a century or more ago, that " God had created three races of bipeds —men, women, and Herveys ! "

The Earl of Radnor—the handsome Sydney of De Grammont's Memoirs—who died in 1723, had his mansion enriched with paintings by Vanson over the doors and chimney-pieces ; the staircase was painted by Laguerre, and the various apartments hung with pictures by many of the celebrated masters. An advertisement in the *Postman*, of August, 1703, offers a reward of two guineas for the detection of a thief who had mischievously cut down and carried off one of the trees in front of Lord Radnor's house. Here afterwards lived Josiah Wedgwood, and here his stock of classic pottery was dispersed by auction. The building was afterwards converted into a club, called the Erectheum, and celebrated for its good dinners. About 1854 the club was joined to the Parthenon in Regent Street, and the house was taken as the office of the Charity Commissioners. It is now the Junior Oxford and Cambridge Club.

Among the other notable personages who have lived here at various times may be mentioned Lewis, Earl of Faversham ; Lawrence Hyde, Earl of Rochester ; Arabella Churchill, the mistress of James, Duke of York, and mother by him of the Duke of Berwick ; Sir Allen Apsley, at whose house the Duke of York put up on his sudden return from Brussels ; Barillon, Ambassador from the Court of France, the same (says Mr. P. Cunningham) " whose despatches to Louis XIV. revealed the bribes received by Charles II. and his ministers, and even by a patriot so professedly pure as Algernon Sydney ;" Aubrey de Vere, the twentieth and last Earl of Oxford of the old line of that illustrious name ; Lord Chancellor Thurlow ; the Countess of Warwick, 1676 ; and Lord Halifax, 1676.

The west side of the square, when first built, does not appear to have been very respectably tenanted. At all events, in 1676, we find the houses occupied by three titled personages, Lord Purbeck, Lord Halifax, and Sir Allen Apsley, and by two notorious ladies, " Moll Davis," one of the King's mistresses, and Madame Churchill, mistress of James, Duke of York, and mother of the Duke of Berwick. In later times, however, and more especially within the last century, some of the houses on this side have got a little better reputation, having been held by different members of the aristocracy ; one being the residence of the Duke of Cleveland, Sir Watkin Williams-Wynn, Bart., and another the town residence of the Bishop of Winchester. The latter was sold in 1875, for the purpose of raising a sum for founding the new Bishopric of St. Albans.

In the house of the Duke of Cleveland is the well-known original portrait of the beautiful Duchess of Cleveland, by Sir Peter Lely ; and the mansion of the late Earl De Grey, afterwards that of the Dowager Countess of Cowper (No. 4), is mentioned by Dr. Waagen as containing a fine gallery of portraits by Vandyke, Salvator Rosa, Titian, Vandevelde, and other foreign masters.

The large house in the south-eastern corner of the square has been since 1684 the residence of the Dukes of Norfolk, who migrated hither from the Strand. The old house which they occupied, which was tenanted by Frederick, Prince of Wales, and in which George III. was born in 1738, is still standing in the rear of the present mansion, which was built by Mr. R. Brittingham, and dates from 1742. The portico was added in 1824. The old mansion—which occupies part of the site of the residence of Henry Jermyn, Earl of St. Albans —formerly had in front of it a court-yard. It is a plain, dull, heavy building, of no architectural pretensions, and is now used as a lumber-house and a laundry. The room in which the future king was born is on the first floor. It is a spacious apartment with a roof slightly arched, and divided into compartments or panels, on which some remnants of the ornamental colouring are still visible.

The house of Norfolk has stood for nearly four centuries at the head of the peers of England, since its ancestor, " Jockey of Norfolk," who fell at Bosworth Field, was raised to the dukedom by Richard III., and during that time its members have held or still hold no less than twenty-five patents of creation to separate peerages, such as the Earldoms of Surrey, Suffolk, Northampton, Stafford, Effingham, and Carlisle. Though its founder was only a lawyer, it has produced statesmen, generals, admirals, and also poets, including that flower of chivalric grace, the Earl of Surrey. With one or two temporary breaks, its head and most of its members have adhered steadily to the Roman Catholic religion ; and Henry, Earl of Surrey, the only son of the third duke, had the honour of laying his head on the block and seeing an attainder passed upon his coronet by the tyrant, Henry VIII.

Charles, the eleventh duke, finding himself excluded on account of his hereditary faith from his seat in the Legislature, professed himself a member of the Established Church, and sat in Parliament first as Earl of Surrey in the Commons, and afterwards in the Upper House as Duke. Sir N. W. Wraxall, who comments in terms of surprise at the spectacle, new to the House of Peers—namely, a Protestant Duke of Norfolk taking an active part in the legislative proceedings of that body—describes him as " cast in Nature's coarsest mould, and with a person so clumsy that he might have been mistaken for a grazier or a butcher." He tells about him many anecdotes, which show that he could play to perfection the part of a Tribune of the People. He lived mainly in clubs and coffee-houses, and was never so happy as when dining at the " Beefsteaks " or the " Thatched House," or breakfasting or supping at the " Cocoa Tree," in St. James's Street. When under the influence of wine, he would say that, "in spite of his having swallowed the Protestant oath, there were, at all events, three good Catholics in Parliament, Lord Nugent, Gascoyne, and himself ; " so little store did he set on religion. This duke, who really deserved the title of a " Jockey " far more than his ancestor, was remarkable for the amount of wine which he could swallow. He would spend the whole night in excesses of every kind. Sir N. W. Wraxall, who knew him well, and constantly met him at his midnight revels, tells us that " when drunk he would lie down to sleep in the streets or on a block of wood." For personal uncleanliness he was nearly as remarkable as for his drunken habits, "carrying his neglect of his person so far that his servants were accustomed to avail themselves of his fits of intoxication for the purpose of washing him, and to strip him as they would a corpse in order to perform the necessary ablutions. Nor did he change his linen more frequently than he washed himself. One day he complained to Dudley North that he was a martyr to the rheumatism, and had ineffectually tried every remedy for its relief. ' Pray, my lord,' was North's reply, ' did you ever try a clean shirt ? ' " It is to be hoped that such a specimen of humanity must not be regarded as a fair sample of our hereditary legislators a hundred years ago ; and it is only right to add that the duke had many good and amiable qualities to compensate for his follies and vices.

Very naturally, his Grace was proud of his undisputed headship of "all the blood of all the Howards." When sitting at breakfast with him at the "Cocoa Tree Coffee-house" one day, his Grace told Sir N. W. Wraxall that he purposed in the year 1783 to commemorate the " ter-centenary " anniversary of the creation of his dukedom by giving a dinner at his house in St. James's Square to every person whom he could ascertain to be descended in the male line from the loins of the first duke. " But having discovered already," he added, " nearly six thousand persons sprung from him, a great number of whom are in very obscure or indigent circumstances, and believing, as I do, that as many more may be in existence, I have abandoned the design." It is to be feared that even the hall and long suite of rooms in Norfolk House would scarcely have contained such a " family party."

The above-mentioned duke, whose name figures so prominently in the political history of the reign of George III., and who was so frequent a speaker at public meetings at the " Crown and Anchor Tavern," and was deprived of his command of a militia regiment for proposing as a toast, " The People, the Source of Power," was the first member of the House of Lords who laid aside the " pig-tail " and hair powder, which remained so long in use as a relic of the old court dress. His Grace's object, no doubt, was to identify himself with the principles of the French encyclopædists. It was probably this duke who is the hero of a ludicrous story told as follows in the pages of Joe Miller's "Jest Book :"— " Mr. Huddlestone, whose name was admitted to be a corruption of Athelstone, from whom he claimed descent, often met the Duke of Norfolk over a bottle, to discuss the respective pretensions of their pedigrees ; and on one of these occasions, when Mr. Huddlestone was dining with the duke, the discussion was prolonged till the descendant of the Saxon kings fairly rolled from his chair upon the floor. One of the younger members of the family hastened by the duke's desire to re-establish him ; but he sturdily repelled the proffered hand of the cadet. 'Never,' he hiccuped out, 'shall it be said that the head of Huddlestone was lifted from the ground by

with the Church of England societies for the relief of the spiritual destitution of the metropolis, and to distribute the fund through such agencies and in such manner as may be deemed desirable, as well as by sending earnest and active men to labour among the masses, by opening new churches and schools, and, where necessary, by originating efforts of a strictly missionary character.

The mansion adjoining London House on the

THE FOUNTAIN IN THE GREEN PARK, 1808. (*See page* 179.)

a younger branch of the house of Howard.' 'Well, then, my good old friend,' said the good-natured duke, 'I must try what I can do for you myself. The head of the house of Howard is too drunk to pick up the head of the house of Huddlestone, but he will lie down beside him with all the pleasure in the world ;' so saying, the duke also took his place on the floor."

Next to Norfolk House is the official town residence of the Bishops of London. It was rebuilt about the year 1820. Here was started by Bishop Blomfield the "Bishop of London's Fund," for providing for the spiritual wants of the metropolis. The raising of this fund is entrusted to a board, with the Bishop of London as its president, with authority to direct its investment, and co-operation

north side, at the corner of Charles Street, is the town residence of the Earl of Derby.

In St. James's Square was residing the French ambassador, Barillon, during the autumn of 1688, when the popular frenzy broke out against the Catholics, and in which the representatives of the great Catholic powers of Europe were insulted and assaulted by a mob that showed but slight respect for the law of nations. Macaulay tells us in his "History" that though an excited multitude collected before his doors, yet Barillon fared better than some of his brother ambassadors, "for, though the Government which he represented was held in abhorrence, his liberal housekeeping and exact payments had made him personally popular. Moreover, he had taken the wise precaution of asking for

ST. JAMES'S SQUARE IN 1773. (*See page* 182.)

a guard of soldiers, and, as several men of rank who lived near him had done the same thing, a considerable force was collected in the square. The rioters, therefore, when they were assured that no arms or priests were concealed under his roof, left him unmolested."

In this square resided Pope's friend, Allen, Lord Bathurst, who was created a peer by Queen Anne in 1711, and who, living for sixty years longer, was the last of that great knot of men of wit and genius who rendered illustrious in one way the short but inglorious ministry of Oxford and Bolingbroke. Pope addressed to him the Third Epistle of his "Moral Essays;" and it is to him, in conjunction with the famous architect, Lord Burlington, that the poet alludes when he asks—

" Who then shall grace, or who improve the soil?
Who plants like Bathurst, or who builds like Boyle?"

Lord Bathurst lived to a patriarchal age, in possession of all his faculties, passing the evening of his life among those woods and in those shades which he had reared with his own hand, at Oakley, near Cirencester, and which Pope has immortalised, and enjoying the rare felicity of seeing his son Lord Chancellor.

The house, No. 10, on the north-west side of the square, was in 1880 opened as the Salisbury Club.

No. 11, now the Windham Club, was formerly the residence of John, third Duke of Roxburgh, the bibliophilist (not to say biblio-maniac) of his time. After his death the sale of his books in May, 1812, occupied no less than forty-two days. Many rare specimens of printing, an early Shakespeare, a few Caxtons and Wynkyn de Wordes, wonderful and unique editions of works on theology, poetry, philosophy, and the drama, were fought for with spirit and even recklessness, as one by one they fell beneath the hammer of the auctioneer, Mr. Evans. At last, what Dr. Dibdin calls "the Waterloo of book battles" commenced when Boccaccio's "Decameron," printed at Venice in 1471, was put up. The volume had been bought by the duke for a hundred guineas, and, after a fierce and spirited competition with Lord Spencer, it was knocked down to the Marquis of Blandford for £2,260. Seven years later, the noble purchaser was glad to part with his treasure for £918, and it now forms one of the treasures of the library of his old antagonist, Lord Spencer, at Althorp. It may be added, that on the evening after the sale of the duke's library, some sixteen of the leading bibliophilists or "biblio-maniacs" of the day dined together at the "St. Alban's Tavern" to celebrate the battle. Lord Spencer, the defeated bidder,

occupied the chair, and Dr. Dibdin acted as croupier. At this dinner was originated the Roxburgh Club. This Club may justly be said to have suggested the publishing societies of the present day; as the "Camden," "Shakespeare," "Percy," &c. Among the club were several noblemen, who, we are told, in other respects, were esteemed men of sense. Their rage was to estimate books not according to their intrinsic worth, but for their rarity. Hence any volume of trash, which was scarce merely because it never had any sale, fetched fifty or a hundred pounds; but if it were only one out of two or three known copies, no limits could be set to the price. Books altered in the title-page, or in a leaf, or in any trivial circumstance which varied a few copies, were bought by these *soi-disant* maniacs at one, two, or three hundred pounds, though the copies were not really worth more than threepence per pound. Specimens of first editions of all authors, and editions by the first clumsy printers, were never sold for less than £50, £100, or £200. To gratify the members of this club, *fac-simile* copies of clumsy editions of trumpery books were reprinted; and, in some cases, it became worth the while of more ingenious people to play off forgeries upon them. This mania after a while abated, and in future ages it will be ranked with the tulip mania, during which estates were given for single flowers.

The Roxburgh Club, however, became less celebrated for its publications than for its dinners, which were held at Grillon's, at the St. Alban's, and at the Clarendon Hotels. Some particulars of these feasts, with their bills of fare, were published in the *Athenæum*, from an account of one of its members. On one occasion the bill was above £5 10s. per head, and the list of toasts included the "immortal memory" not only of John, Duke of Roxburgh, but of William Caxton, Dame Juliana Berners, Wynkyn de Worde, Richard Pynson, the Aldine family, and "the cause of Bibliomania all over the world." In one year, when Lord Spencer presided over the feast, the account above mentioned thus records the fact: "Twenty-one members met joyfully, dined comfortably, challenged eagerly, tippled prettily, divided regretfully, and paid the bill most cheerfully."

The mansion of the Duke of Roxburgh had previously been the residence of William Windham; after the death of the duke it was occupied for some time by Lord Chief-Justice Ellenborough, and at a later date by the Earl of Blessington, who possessed a fine collection of pictures. The Windham Club, which was afterwards established here, was founded by the late Lord Nugent for gentlemen " connected with each other by a common bond of literary or personal acquaintance."

Adjoining the Windham Club is the mansion once tenanted by Lord Amherst, when Commander-in-Chief, and formerly known as Beauchamp House. It is now the London Library. This library, which dates its origin from 1840, is conducted upon the subscription and lending plan, and its books may be borrowed by subscribers and taken to their homes. It embraces every department of literature and philosophy. The library was opened on the 3rd of May, 1841, with a collection of about 3,000 volumes, which, by the following March, when the first catalogue was published, had increased to 13,000. "The additions of subsequent years," as we learn from the report published in 1870, "have raised the number of volumes in the library to more than 80,000. Purchased on the most advantageous terms, there has been brought together in the course of thirty years, by the expenditure of little more than £20,000, a noble collection of books, offering to members of the library a choice of standard works in all the various departments of literature." It may be added that its contents have since continued to increase. A striking proof of the success with which the library has fulfilled and continues to fulfil the purpose for which it was created, will be found in the names of the many illustrious writers which appear in the various published lists of its members, and in the use they have made of its treasures. In addition to this silent testimony to the usefulness of the institution, may be quoted the opinion of M. Guizot, given in evidence before a Committee of the House of Commons on Public Libraries in 1849, an opinion which is supported by that of many other participants in the benefits of the library. "If the London Library," says M. Guizot, "had not existed, I should have felt great inconvenience. It is a very useful library : there are a great many excellent books about English history which I have found there. It is a great inconvenience to me to be obliged to go to the British Museum, and not to be able to work in my own room with my own books ; that is a great part of the pleasure of working."

Here also the Statistical Society of London and the Institute of Actuaries hold their meetings periodically.

The house No. 13, formerly the residence of the Earl of Lichfield, when Postmaster-General in Lord Melbourne's Ministry, was the scene of the "Lichfield House Compact," as the friendly understanding between the Whigs of that day and Daniel O'Connell was often jestingly styled.

The house two doors beyond the London Library, in the direction of King Street, was at the beginning of the present century in the occupation of Mrs. Boehm. Here the Prince Regent, Lord Castlereagh, and many of the leading politicians of the day, were dining, on the 21st of June, 1815, when the news was brought of the victory of Waterloo, thus putting an end to and confirming the rumours by which London had been kept in suspense for more than twenty-four hours. The scene is thus described by Lady Brownlow in her "Reminiscences of a Septuagenarian : "—

" Never shall I forget that evening. . . . I was sitting quietly alone at Lord Castlereagh's, when suddenly there came the sound of shouting and the rush of a crowd ; and on running to the window to discover the cause of all this noise, I saw a post-chaise and four, with three of the French eagles projecting out of its windows, dash across the square to Lord Castlereagh's door. In a moment the horses' heads were turned, and away went the chaise to Mrs. Boehm's."

It was, of course, the work of a few minutes for Lady Brownlow to dress and join Lady Castlereagh at Mrs. Boehm's house. She continues thus : —"The ladies had left the dining-room, and I learnt that Major Henry Percy had arrived, the bearer of despatches from the Duke of Wellington, with the intelligence of a glorious and decisive victory of the Allies over the French army, commanded by Buonaparte in person. The despatches were being then read in the next room to the Prince, and we ladies remained silent, too anxious to talk, and longing to hear more. Lord Alvanley was the first gentleman who appeared, and he horrified us with the list of names of the killed and wounded. . . . What I heard stupefied me ; I could scarcely think or speak. The Prince presently came in, looking very sad, and he said, with much feeling, words to this effect : 'It is a glorious victory, and we must rejoice at it ; but the loss of life has been fearful, and I have lost many friends;' and, while he spoke, the tears ran down his cheeks. His Royal Highness remained but a short time, and soon after the party broke up."

With reference to Mrs. Boehm, Captain Gronow, in his "Anecdotes and Reminiscences," says :—"This lady used to give fashionable balls and masquerades, to which I look back with much pleasure. The Prince Regent frequently honoured her *fêtes* with his presence. Mrs. Boehm, on one occasion, sent invitations to one of her particular friends, begging him to fill them up, and tickets were given by him to Dick Butler (afterwards Lord Glengall) and to Mr. Raikes. Whilst they were deliberating in what character they should go, ' Dick Butler '—for by that name he was only then known—proposed that Raikes should take the part of Apollo, which the latter agreed to, provided Dick should be his ' lyre.' The noble lord's reputation for ' stretching the long bow' rendered this repartee so applicable that it was universally repeated at the clubs."

This house is now the home of the East India United Service Club, which was established here about the year 1860.

The next house (No. 15) was once the property of Lady Francis, the widow of Sir Philip Francis, to whom the "Letters of Junius" are usually attributed. Lady Francis lent this house to the unfortunate Queen Caroline, in the month of August, 1820; and it was from its doors that her Majesty proceeded every day in state to the House of Peers during the progress of the attempted Bill of " Pains and Penalties."

In this square lived Mr. Robinson—"Jack Robinson"—the Secretary of the Treasury under Lord North. He is described by Sir N. W. Wraxall as knowing the secrets of ministerial and political affairs better than any man of his day.

Lord Castlereagh was residing at No. 16 in December, 1813, when dispatched abroad to enter into negotiations with Napoleon. In March, 1816, during the riots at the West-end, on account of the rejection of the Corn-Law Alteration Bill, his lordship's house was attacked by the mob, together with that of Mr. Robinson, from the parlour window of which shots were fired, which proved fatal to two innocent persons. The cavalry appearing, the rioters desisted and retired, to vent their fury by damaging the mansions of Lord Bathurst, Lord King, &c. The riots continued more or less to the latter end of the week.

Lady Brownlow records an instance of the coolness and self-possession of Lord Castlereagh. One night, when an excited mob attacked his house in this square, and paving-stones were being thrown at his windows, he quietly mixed with the crowd outside, till some one whispered to him, " You are known ; you had better go in." He did so, and then went to the drawing-room, and, with the utmost composure, closed the shutters while a shower of stones fell all around him. " When I called next day," adds her ladyship, "I found him on the point of walking out, and as I knew that he would have the mob to encounter, I with difficulty persuaded him to let me take him in my carriage."

Lord Castlereagh was always unpopular with the mob. In 1819, Mr. Rush, in his " Diary of a Residence at the Court of London," speaks of several official interviews which he had here with Lord Castlereagh, then Secretary of State for Foreign Affairs, and describes the mansion as having lately suffered much, especially in its windows, from the effects of the violence of the mob in a late Westminster election.

Lord Castlereagh played a foremost part in effecting the union of Ireland with England, and in 1801 entered the first Imperial Parliament as member for County Down. He held the post of President of the Board of Control during Mr. Addington's administration, and Secretary of State for War and the Colonies in the ministries of Mr. Pitt and the Duke of Portland. In 1809, the year of the Walcheren expedition, occurred his duel with Canning, then Foreign Secretary. In this affair Canning was wounded, and both the duellists resigned their offices. Before the end of the year, however, Lord Castlereagh succeeded his antagonist as Secretary for Foreign Affairs, an office which he retained till his death, in 1822. His remains were buried in Westminster Abbey, between Pitt and Fox. Mr. Rush, in the work above mentioned, avers of him that " no statesman ever made more advances, or did more in fact towards placing the relations of England and America on an amicable footing ;" and in his description of the funeral he adds, " Nor did I ever see manly sorrow more depicted on any countenance than that of the Duke of Wellington, as he took a last look of the coffin when lowered down into the vault."

Near the north-east corner of the square are the offices of the Copyhold, Inclosure, and Tithe Commission. The Tithe Commissioners for England and Wales were appointed in 1836 to provide the means for an adequate commutation and compensation for the tithes payable to the clergy of the Established Church. The Copyhold Commissioners were appointed in 1841, and the Inclosure Commissioners some four years later. The duties of the commissioners are " to facilitate the enclosure and improvement of all lands subject to any rights of common whatsoever, and the exchange of lands inconveniently intermixed or divided ; and to provide remedies for the incomplete execution of powers of enclosure made under local and general Enclosure Acts."

Nearly the whole of the south side of the square is occupied by an uneven row of houses, the fronts of which face Pall Mall; and a considerable part is taken up by the back of the Junior Carlton Club, which we have already described in our chapter on Pall Mall.

CHAPTER XVI.

THE NEIGHBOURHOOD OF ST. JAMES'S SQUARE.

> " John his dull invention racks,
> To rival Boodle's dinners, or Almack's."
>
> *Heroic Epistle to Sir W. Chambers.*

King Street—Nerot's Hotel—St. James's Theatre—*Début* of John Braham—An Amusing Story of him—Mr. Hooper opens the St. James's Theatre—Mr. Bunn and German Opera—The Name of the Theatre changed to "The Prince's"—The Theatre opened with English Opera—Willis's Rooms—"Almack's"—The Dilettanti Society and their Portraits—Curious Comments on Quadrilles—A Ball in Honour of the Coronation of George IV.—Christie and Manson's Sale-rooms—Famous Residents in King Street—Louis Napoleon—Crockford's Bazaar—Duke Street and Bury Street—A Famous Lawyer and his Will—Steele—Swift and Crabbe—Yarrell, the Naturalist—York Street and its Foot Pavement—Charity Commission Offices—Jermyn Street—A Strange Story of a Truant Husband—The Brunswick Hotel—The Museum of Practical Geology—The Society for the Prevention of Cruelty to Animals—The Turkish Bath—An Artists' Quarter—"Harlequin's" Account of the Neighbourhood.

EXTENDING from the west side of the square to St. James's Street, parallel with Pall Mall and Jermyn Street, runs a thoroughfare to which the loyalty of the Stuart times gave the name of King Street. On the south side of this street, on the site now occupied by the St. James's Theatre, formerly stood a large building, long known as Nerot's Hotel. The premises were old, probably dating from the time of Charles II.; it had a large heavy staircase, carved after the fashion of the time, its panels being adorned with a series of mythical pictures of Apollo and Daphne and other heathen deities. The front of the house was pierced with no less than twenty-four windows.

The St. James's Theatre, like the New Royalty, owes its existence to one of those unaccountable infatuations which stake the earnings of a lifetime upon a hazardous speculation. It was built in 1835, from a design by Mr. Beazley, and at a cost of £26,000, by the celebrated John Braham, then sixty years of age. The great tenor, who was of Jewish origin, having from childhood developed remarkable vocal powers, made his *début* at the old Royalty Theatre in 1787, at the age of thirteen, as a pupil of Leoni; in the bills he is called "Master Abrahams." Here he is said to have attracted the notice of the wealthy Abraham Goldschmidt, who placed him under the tuition of Rauzzini, the director of the Bath concerts, in which city Braham first established his reputation as a vocalist. He returned to London in 1796, and made his appearance in Storace's opera of *Mahmoud.* Subsequently he proceeded to Italy, where he completed his musical studies, and returned to England in 1801, from which time he pursued his professional career with uninterrupted success. His delivery of the recitative "Deeper and deeper still," from Handel's *Jephthah,* is said to have been one of the finest specimens of tragic vocalisation ever heard. Charles Lamb says of him:—"There is a fine scorn in Braham's face. . . . . . The Hebrew spirit is strong in him, in spite of his proselytism. He cannot conquer the shibboleth: how it breaks out when he sings 'The children of Israel passed through the Red Sea!' The auditors for the moment are as Egyptians to him, and he rides over our necks in triumph. The foundation of his vocal excellence is sense." Henry Russell relates the following amusing story of him:—"His father's name was Abraham, and as he was short and stout, his neighbours nicknamed him 'Aby Punch.' Braham on one occasion was performing in an absurd *pasticcio* with Mrs. Crouch, Mrs. Bland, Kelly, and Jack Bannister. The scene represented the interior of an old country inn. [*Enter Braham with a bundle slung to a stick on his shoulder.*] ' I have been traversing this desolate country for days with no friend to cheer me. [*Sits.*] I am weary—yet no rest, no food, scarcely life. O Heaven, pity me! Shall I ever realise my hopes? [*Knocks on the table.*] What ho there, house! [*Knocks again.*] Will no one come!' [*Enter Landlord.*] 'I beg pardon, sir, but—[*starts*]. I know that face [*aside*]. What can I do for you, sir?' *Braham:* 'Gracious Heaven! 'tis he — the voice, the look — the — [*with calmness*]—Yes; I want food.' *Landlord:* 'Tell me, what brings one so young as thou appearest to be through this dangerous forest?' *Braham:* 'I *will.* For days, for months, oh! for years, I have been in search of my father.' *Landlord:* 'Your father!' *Braham:* 'Yes; my father. 'Tis strange—but that voice—that look—that figure —tell me that *you* are my father.' *Landlord:* 'No, I tell thee, no; I am *not* thy father.' *Braham:* 'Heaven protect me! Who, tell me, WHO IS MY FATHER?' Scarcely had Braham put this question when a little Jew stood up in an excited manner in the midst of a densely-crowded pit, and exclaimed, 'I knowed yer father well. His name was Abey Punch!' The performance was suspended for some minutes by the roars of laughter which followed this revelation."

Braham's theatre opened under the most favourable auspices on the 14th of December, 1835, with an original operatic burletta by Gilbert A'Beckett, entitled *Agnes Sorel*, in which the principal parts were sustained by Messrs. Braham and Morris Barnett, and the Misses Glossop and P. Horton.

nist, were engaged at the St. James's Theatre during Lent, 1836, Mrs. Honey appearing in the parts of "Captain Macheath," in the *Beggar's Opera*, and "Kate O'Brien," in *Perfection*. It seems rather ominous of the future that the first season of the

ST. JAMES'S THEATRE. (*See page* 191.)

An original interlude, *A Clear Case*, followed the opera, and an original farce, *A French Company*, concluded the performances. Braham appears to have been a liberal patron of dramatic writers, as we find an unusual number of "new and original" pieces produced at this theatre during his too brief reign, although far more numerous audiences assembled on the nights when he performed in his famous parts of "Fra Diavolo" and "Tom Tug," in *The Waterman*. Mrs. Honey and Love, the polypho-

new theatre lasted little more than three months, when Braham was glad to let it to Madame Jenny Vertpré for French plays, which commenced April 8th, 1836, and in which Mdlle. Plessis appeared. Braham re-opened his theatre on September 29th, 1836, with the somewhat pompous announcement that "The theatre having been, during the recess, perfected in all parts, was now admitted to be the most splendid in Europe!" The performances commenced on this occasion with *The Strange*

Gentleman, by "Boz," followed by *The Sham Prince*, by John Barnett, concluding with *The Tradesmen's Ball*, all three being burlettas, and all "new and original." Dr. Arne's operetta of *Artaxerxes* was produced the following month, with Miss Rainforth as "Mandane," and Braham as

run of more than fifty nights, while the former disappeared from the bills after fifteen representations. By this time Wright and Mrs. Stirling had joined the already powerful company; yet, in spite of the combination of talent which he had assembled in his elegant little theatre, the unfortunate proprietor

WILLIS'S ROOMS. (*See page* 196.)

"Artabanes." "Boz" again appears in December, 1836, as the author of the libretto of *The Village Coquettes*, the music being by John Hullah, in which the chief performers were Miss Rainforth and Messrs. Braham, Morris Barnett, Harley, and John Parry—a strong caste, indeed, and one which might have been supposed to ensure the success of any piece of average merit. *The Village Coquettes* seem, however, to have met with less favour than *The Strange Gentleman*, the latter having had a

found himself at the close of the season of 1838 a ruined man, forced, at the age of sixty-four, to seek a maintenance in America by the exercise of his profession. Here he achieved as great a popularity as he had enjoyed in England, and on his subsequent return a few years later to his native land, his old age was made happy by the dutiful affection of his daughter, the Countess Waldegrave. He died in 1856, in his eighty-third year, leaving a name which will always be remembered as one of the greatest of English singers. His fame did not rest solely upon his remarkable skill as a scientific vocalist in operas and oratorios, but upon his exquisite and most pathetic rendering of the homely ballads and patriotic songs so dear to the heart of the people of every country, and to an especial degree of the people of England.

But to return to the history of the St. James's Theatre, which was opened by Mr. Hooper in 1839, with a company comprising Messrs. Dowton, Wrench, Alfred Wigan, Mdmes. Glover, Honey, Nisbett, and several other excellent performers from the Haymarket Theatre. As he was a sufficiently wise man in his generation to profit by the unfortunate experience of his predecessor, Hooper resolved not to depend upon talent alone for success. Van Amburgh, the lion-tamer, with his formidable *troupe* of wild beasts, had at this time gained such a triumph over Macready and the legitimate drama at Drury Lane, that, as Mr. Bunn, the lessee, tells us, whereas the latter had been playing (at £16 a night) to comparatively empty benches, the former now nightly exhibited his intrepidity before crowded audiences, including on several occasions the young Queen, who highly eulogised this fascinating exhibition ! Mr. Hooper therefore announced that the St. James's Theatre would re-open on the 4th of February, 1839, with three new pieces, and a dozen lions and tigers of extraordinary size. The three new pieces consisted of a burletta, *Friends and Neighbours*, by Haynes Bayley ; *The Young Sculptor*, by Henry Mayhew ; and *The Troublesome Lodger*, by Bayley and Mayhew. Dowton, although at that time the oldest actor on the stage, having passed his seventieth year, was a universal favourite, as also were both Wrench and Mrs. Glover ; but the manager soon found that the taste of the day gave four-legged performers so decided a preference over bipeds, that he started off to Paris and obtained the services of a *troupe* of highly-trained monkeys, dogs, and goats. The event proved his sagacity ; the attraction was irresistible, and all the rank and fashion of the metropolis crowded to witness the antics of " Madame Pompadour, Mademoiselle Batavia, Lord Gogo, and his valet Jacob !" So, at least, says Theodore Hook, in an essay written during this year upon " The Decline of the Drama :"—

"Perhaps as great an alteration as any which has occurred during the present generation is to be found in the theatrical taste of the people—not to go back to the theatrical reign of Garrick, which terminated in 1811, during which the acceptance or rejection of a comedy formed the subject of general conversation. Then there were but two theatres, the seasons of which were limited from the 15th of September to the 15th of May. Then each theatre had its destined company of actors, a change in which, even in an individual instance, created a sensation in society. Theatrical representations had a strong hold upon the public, up to a much later period—in fact, until that which modern liberality denounced as a gross monopoly was abolished, and theatres sprung up in almost every street of the metropolis. The argument in favour of this extension was that the population of London and the suburbs had so much increased, that the demand for playhouses was greater than the supply, and that ' more theatres ' were wanted. We have the theatres, but where are the authors and the actors to make them attractive? Monkeys, dogs, goats, horses, giants, lions, tigers, and gentlemen who walk upon the ceiling with their heads downwards, are all very attractive in their way, and they will sometimes, not always, fill the playhouses. But as to the genuine drama, the public taste has been weaned from it, first by the multitude of trashy diversions scattered all over the town, and, secondly, by the consequent scattering of the theatrical talent which really does exist. At each of these minor theatres you find some three or four excellent actors, worked off their legs, night after night, who if collected into two good companies, as of old, would give us the legitimate drama well and satisfactorily."

On the marriage of Her Majesty with Prince Albert, in February, 1840, a scheme was set on foot for the establishment of a German opera in London. An arrangement was effected with Herr Schuman, director of the opera at Mayence, and the St. James's Theatre, of which Mr. Bunn had become the lessee, was selected as a suitable *locale* for the purpose, and its name changed to "The Prince's Theatre," in honour of the illustrious bridegroom. Public expectation was wrought up to the highest pitch : a new entrance was made for Her Majesty and the Queen Dowager through Mr. Braham's private house ; the Duke of Brunswick engaged the box next to that of the Queen for the season, and long before the opening night every box and stall had been disposed of. The German company, headed by their director, Herr Schuman, duly arrived in London, and the procession of carriages and baggage wagons, containing the stage wardrobes, decorations, and other articles, resembled, said the *Era*, " a troop of soldiers rather than a *troupe* of actors ; it was, indeed, more like a military than a Thespian corps."

With all this flourish of trumpets, and under this distinguished patronage, " The Prince's " opened on the 27th of April, 1840. "Never was it our lot," says one of the weekly papers of that date, "to witness such a fashionable and crowded audience in the walls of any theatre. Many families of the highest rank were obliged to be contented with seats in the public and upper boxes, while the private ones were filled by their noble subscribers, including the Cambridge family, and a portion of that of the Queen Dowager. The two queens were prevented from attending by the death of the Countess of Burlington." The well-known and ever-popular *Der Freischütz*, by Weber, was judiciously chosen for the opening performance. Among the operas subsequently produced at this theatre were Spohr's *Jessonda;* his *Faust,* of which it was remarked that "the opera of *Faust* might be set to the text of the oratorio of *The Day of Judgment,* and would be as much in character with the one as with the other;" Weber's *Euryanthe,* said, on account of its dulness, to have been nicknamed in Germany *Ennuianthe;* Glück's *Iphigenia in Tauris;* and Beethoven's *Fidelio.*

The German singers were not generally admired. The *Era* remarks, *apropos* of the performance of Weber's *Euryanthe:* "Herr Poeck sang with great spirit and power, Schmerzer was good in some parts of the opera; but the ladies, whom out of gallantry we ought to praise, can only claim it on that head. If they had but moderate execution, and could but sing tolerably in tune, we would willingly excuse their badness of school, for we should at least hear the composer without being offended; but really (and the ladies must pardon us for saying so) such singers as Madame Fischer Schwartzböck and Madame Michalesi are sufficient to destroy the effect of any opera, however fine it may be." In spite of these trifling drawbacks, the Prince's Theatre continued to be both fashionably and fully attended up to the close of the season, and Herr Schuman, previous to his departure, is said to have expressed himself "confident that he had laid the foundation of a permanent German opera in England, and that he should return the following year, this, his experimental season, having proved that it would be worth his while to bring over the *élite* of the German singers."

These "great expectations" were never destined to be fulfilled. The late German opera-house re-opened in November, 1840, under the management of Mr. Morris Barnett, with *Fridolin,* a new opera by Frank Romer, which, not proving a success, terminated the winter season before Christmas, and with it ended the career of this theatre as "The Prince's." In 1841 we find it was taken by Mr. Mitchell, and opened for French plays, in its old name of the St. James's, which it has ever since retained. Under the lesseeship of Mr. Mitchell, which lasted twelve years, the English public had an opportunity of witnessing the best works of the French dramatists, represented by the best native artists, such as the veteran Perlet, Achard, Ravel, Levasseur, Lemaitre, Mdlle. Plessy, the famous Dejazet, and the gifted Rachel, who, to use the fashionable cant, "created" the parts of "Adrienne Lecouvreur," of Racine's *Phèdre,* and of Corneille's "Camille" in *Les Horaces.* At the close of each of his last two seasons of French plays Mr. Mitchell essayed the experiment of a brief series of German dramas, but with no encouraging result. In 1855, the St. James's Theatre, then under the management of Mrs. Seymour, produced the lyrical drama of *Alcestis,* adapted from the Greek of Euripides, set to music by Glück, the choruses, &c., being under the direction of Sir Henry Bishop. This scarcely classical entertainment was lightened by two after-pieces, *Abon Hassan,* an extravaganza, and *The Miller and his Men. Alcestis* was not appreciated by the public, and was withdrawn after a few nights.

In June, 1859, an English opera by Edward Loder, entitled *Raymond and Agnes,* was brought out at this theatre, under the management of Augustus Braham, a son of the great tenor. The principal parts were sustained by Hamilton Braham, George Perren, Mdmes. Rudersdorf and Susan Pyne. But the St. James's Theatre would seem to have been the evil genius of the Braham family; for, although the opera was highly commended by musical authorities, and the caste unobjectionable, *Raymond and Agnes* proved an utter failure, and after being performed five nights to nearly empty benches disappeared on the sixth, to be seen and heard no more. From 1859 to 1863 the St. James's was successively leased to Messrs. F. B. Chatterton, Alfred Wigan, Frank Matthews, and B. Webster, the short tenure of each lease proving that the speculation was in no case satisfactory. The company during the greater part of the time comprised the two clever couples, Mr. and Mrs. Alfred Wigan and Mr. and Mrs. Frank Matthews, Miss Rainforth, and Miss Herbert. The last-named lady became lessee of the theatre in 1864, but, although an elegant and highly popular actress, she, like her predecessors, failed to make a fortune out of the proverbially unfortunate place. In 1868 the management was assumed by Mrs. John Wood, a lively lady, whose piquant performance of "La Belle Sauvage" was the great hit of the season of 1869. In 1874, the St. James's acquired an unenviable notoriety from the nature of the entertainment offered, which fell under the ban of the Lord Chamberlain; but its character has improved of late years, under the joint management of Messrs. Kendal and Hare.

We learn casually from Forster's "Life of Charles Dickens," that when in 1846 the idea of giving readings from his published works first came into his head, he at first proposed to take the St. James's Theatre for that purpose.

Apropos of Mr. Braham's management of the St. James's, a story is told, which may be worth repeating here. Mr. Bunn was passing through Jermyn Street late one evening, and seeing Kenney at the corner of St. James's Church, swinging about in a nervous sort of manner, he inquired the cause of his being there at such an hour. He replied, "I have been to the St. James's Theatre, and, do you know, I really thought Braham was a much prouder man than I find him to be." On asking why, he answered, "I was in the green-room, and hearing Braham say, as he entered, 'I am really proud of my pit to-night,' I went and counted it, and there were but seventeen people in it!"

Close by the St. James's Theatre are "Willis's Rooms," a noble suite of assembly-rooms, formerly known as "Almack's." The building was erected by Mylne, for one Almack, a tavern-keeper, and was opened in 1765, with a ball, at which the Duke of Cumberland, the hero of Culloden, was present. Almack, who was a Scotchman by birth, seems to have been a large adventurer in clubs, for he at first "farmed" the club afterwards known as "Brooks's." The large ball-room is about one hundred feet in length by forty feet in width, and is chastely decorated with columns and pilasters, classic medallions, and mirrors. The rooms are let for public meetings, dramatic readings, concerts, balls, and occasionally for dinners. Right and left, at the top of the grand staircase, and on either side of the vestibule of the ball-room, are two spacious apartments, used occasionally for large suppers or dinners.

In these rooms are held the re-unions of the Dilettanti Society. This society, as we have stated in a previous chapter, was established in the year 1734, and originally met at the "Thatched House" Tavern, St. James's Street, its object being "the promotion of the fine arts, combined with friendly and social intercourse." The members of this association dine nere every fortnight during the "London season." The walls of the apartment are still hung with the portraits of the members, most of which were removed hither on the demolition of the old "Thatched House." Many of the

portraits are in the costume familiar to us through Hogarth, others are in Turkish or Roman dresses, and several of them are so represented as to show the convivial nature of the gatherings for which they were famous: for instance, Sir Francis Dashwood, afterwards Lord Le Despenser, who figures as a monk at his devotions—the object on which his gaze is intently fixed, however, is *not* a crucifix, nor an image of "Our Lady;" Charles Sackville, Duke of Dorset, appears as a Roman soldier. The three principal pictures in the room are those by Sir Joshua Reynolds, who was himself a member of the Dilettanti Society: one of these represents a group containing portraits of the Duke of Leeds, Lord Dundas, Lord Mulgrave, Lord Seaforth, the Hon. Charles Greville, Charles Crowle, Esq., and Sir Joseph Banks; another is a group treated in the same manner, containing portraits of Sir William Hamilton, Sir Watkin W. Wynn, Mr. Richard Thomson, Sir John Taylor, Mr. Payne Gallwey, and Mr. Spencer Stanhope; the third is a portrait of Sir Joshua himself, attired in a loose robe, and without the addition of his customary wig. There are also portraits of the late Lord Broughton (better known as Sir John Cam Hobhouse), and Lord Ligonier, and, in fact, nearly every man of note in the early part of the present century. The latest addition to the collection is the portrait of Sir Edward Ryan, who died in August, 1875.

"Almack's" was already established as a place of public amusement as far back as 1768, for in the *Advertiser* of November 12th, in that year, we find the following notice:—"Mr. Almack humbly begs leave to acquaint the nobility and gentry, subscribers to the Assembly in King Street, St. James's, that the first meeting will be Thursday, 24th inst. N.B. Tickets are ready to be delivered at the Assembly Room."

In a satire on the ladies of the age, published in 1773, we read—

> "Now lolling at the Coterie and 'White's,'
> We drink and game away our days and nights.
>
> *   *   *   *   *
>
> No censure reaches them at Almack's ball;
> Virtue, religion—they're above them all."

The assembly which bore the title of "Almack's" was in its palmy days under the regulation of six lady patronesses, of the first distinction, whose fiat was decisive as to admission or rejection of every applicant for tickets, and became a most autocratic institution—quite an *imperium in imperio*. In fact, the *entrée* to "Almack's" was in itself a passport to the highest society in London, being almost as high a certificate as the fact of having been presented at Court.

Lady Clementina Davies writes in her "Recollections of Society:"—"At 'Almack's,' in 1814, the rules were very strict. Scotch reels and country dances were in fashion. The lady patronesses were all powerful. No visitor was to be admitted after twelve o'clock, and once, when the Duke of Wellington arrived a few minutes after that hour, he was refused admission."

A writer in the *New Monthly Magazine* (1824) observes: "The nights of meeting fall upon every Wednesday during the season. This is selection with a vengeance, the very quintessence of aristocracy. Three-fourths even of the nobility knock in vain for admission. Into this *sanctum sanctorum*, of course, the sons of commerce never think of intruding on the sacred Wednesday evenings; and yet into this very 'blue chamber,' in the absence of the six necromancers, have the votaries of trade contrived to intrude themselves."

Mr. T. Raikes tells us in his "Journal" that the celebrated *diplomatiste*, the Princess Lieven, was the only foreign lady who was ever admitted into the exclusive circle of the lady patronesses of this select society, into the *tracasseries* of which establishment she entered very cordially, though her manner, tinctured at times with a certain degree of *hauteur*, made her many enemies.

"At the present time," writes Captain Gronow, in 1862, "one can hardly conceive the importance which was attached to getting admission to 'Almack's,' the seventh heaven of the fashionable world. Of the three hundred officers of the Foot Guards, not more than half a dozen were honoured with vouchers of admission to this exclusive temple of the *beau monde*, the gates of which were guarded by lady patronesses, whose smiles or frowns consigned men and women to happiness or despair as the case might be. These 'lady patronesses,' in 1813, were the Ladies Castlereagh, Jersey, Cowper, and Sefton, Mrs. Drummond Burrell, afterwards Lady Willoughby d'Eresby, the Princess Esterhazy, and the Princess Lieven.

"The most popular amongst these *grandes dames*," he adds, "was unquestionably Lady Cowper, now Lady Palmerston. Lady Jersey's bearing, on the contrary, was that of a theatrical tragedy queen; and whilst attempting the sublime, she frequently made herself simply ridiculous, being inconceivably rude, and in her manner often ill-bred. Lady Sefton was kind and amiable, Madame de Lieven haughty and exclusive, Princess Esterhazy was a *bon enfant*, Lady Castlereagh and Mrs. Burrell *de très grandes dames*.

" Many diplomatic arts, much finesse, and a host of intrigues, were set in motion to get an invitation to 'Almack's.' Very often persons whose rank and fortunes entitled them to the *entrée* anywhere, were excluded by the cliqueism of the lady patronesses; for the female government of 'Almack's' was a pure despotism, and subject to all the caprices of despotic rule: it is needless to add that, like every other despotism, it was not innocent of abuses. The fair ladies who ruled supreme over this little dancing and gossiping world, issued a solemn proclamation that no gentleman should appear at the assemblies without being dressed in knee-breeches, white cravat, and *chapeau bras*. On one occasion, the Duke of Wellington was about to ascend the staircase of the ball-room, dressed in black trousers, when the vigilant Mr. Willis, the guardian of the establishment, stepped forward and said, 'Your Grace cannot be admitted in trousers;' whereupon the Duke, who had a great respect for orders and regulations, quietly walked away.

"In 1814, the dances at 'Almack's' were Scotch reels and the old English country dance; and the orchestra, being from Edinburgh, was conducted by the then celebrated Neil Gow. It was not until 1815 that Lady Jersey introduced from Paris the favourite quadrille, which has so long remained popular. I recollect the persons who formed the first quadrille that was ever danced at 'Almack's:' they were Lady Jersey, Lady Harriet Butler, Lady Susan Ryder, and Miss Montgomery; the men being the Count St. Aldegonde, Mr. Montgomery, Mr. Montague, and Charles Standish. The 'mazy waltz' was also brought to us about this time; but there were comparatively few who at first ventured to whirl round the *salons* of 'Almack's;' in course of time Lord Palmerston might, however, have been seen describing an infinite number of circles with Madame de Lieven. Baron de Neumann was frequently seen perpetually turning with the Princess Esterhazy; and, in course of time, the waltzing mania, having turned the heads of society generally, descended to their feet, and the waltz was practised in the morning in certain noble mansions in London with unparalleled assiduity."

Mr. T. Raikes thus commemorates the arrival of the German waltz in England:—"No event ever produced so great a sensation in English society as the introduction of the German waltz in 1813. Up to that time the English country dance, Scotch steps, and an occasional Highland reel, formed the school of the dancing-master, and the evening recreation of the British youth, even in the first circles. But peace was drawing near, foreigners were arriving, and the taste for Continental customs and manners became the order of the day. The young Duke of Devonshire, as the 'magnus Apollo' of the drawing-rooms in London, was at the head of these innovations; and when the *kitchen* and country dance became exploded at Devonshire House, it could not long be expected to maintain its footing even in the less celebrated assemblies. In London, fashion is or was then everything. Old and young returned to school, and the mornings which had been dedicated to lounging in the Park, were now absorbed at home in practising the figures of a French quadrille, or whirling a chair round the room, to learn the step and measure of

persevered in spite of all the prejudices which were marshalled against them, every night the waltz was called, and new votaries, though slowly, were added to their train. Still the opposition party did not relax in their efforts, sarcastic **rem**arks flew about, and pasquinades were written **to deter** young ladies from such a recreation.

"The waltz, however, struggled successfully through all its difficulties; Flahault, who was *la fleur des pois* in Paris, came over to captivate Miss Mercer, and with a host of others drove the prudes

LORD WORCESTER.   LADY JERSEY.   CLANRONALD MACDONALD.   LADY WORCESTER.

THE FIRST QUADRILLE DANCED AT "ALMACK'S." (*From Gronow's "Reminiscences."*)

the German waltz. Lame and impotent were the first efforts, but the inspiring effect of the music, and the not less inspiring airs of the foreigners, soon rendered the English ladies enthusiastic performers. What scenes have we witnessed in those days at 'Almack's,' &c.! What fear and trembling in the *débutantes* at the commencement of a waltz, what giddiness and confusion at the end!

"It was perhaps owing to this latter circumstance that so violent an opposition soon arose to this new recreation on the score of morality.

"The anti-waltzing party took the alarm, cried it down, mothers forbade it, and every ball-room became a scene of feud and contention; the waltzers continued their operations, but their ranks were not filled with so many recruits as they expected. The foreigners, however, were not idle in forming their *élèves;* Baron Tripp, Neumann, St. Aldegonde, &c.,

into their entrenchments; and when the Emperor Alexander was seen waltzing round the room at 'Almack's,' with his tight uniform and numerous decorations, they surrendered at discretion."

The author of "Memoirs of the Times of George IV." favours us with the following curious comments on quadrilles, then (1811) newly exhibited in England:—"We had much waltzing and quadrilling, the last of which is certainly very abominable. I am not prude enough to be offended with waltzing, in which I can see no other harm than that it disorders the stomach, and sometimes makes people look very ridiculous; but after all, moralists, with the Duchess of Gordon at their head, who never had a moral in her life, exclaim dreadfully against it. Nay, I am told that these magical wheelings have already roused poor Lord Dartmouth from his grave to suppress them. Alas! after all, people set about it as gravely as a company of dervises, and seem to be paying adoration to Pluto rather than to Cupid. But the quadrilles I can by no means endure; for till ladies and gentlemen have joints at their ankles, which is impossible, it is

In July, 1821, a splendid ball was given here in honour of the coronation of George IV. by the special Ambassador from France, the Duc de Grammont. The King himself was present, attended by some of his royal brothers, the Duke

THE BALL-ROOM, WILLIS'S ROOMS.

worse than impudent to make such exhibitions, more particularly in a place where there are public ballets every Tuesday and Saturday. When people dance to be looked at, they surely should dance to perfection. Even the Duchess of Bedford, who is the Angiolini of the group, would make an indifferent *figurante* at the opera; and the principal male dancer, Mr. North, reminds one of a gibbeted malefactor, moved to and fro by the winds, but from no personal exertion."

of Wellington, and a numerous circle of courtiers. "Whatever French taste, directed by a Grammont, could do," writes Mr. Rush in his "Court of London," "to render the night agreeable, was witnessed. His suite of young gentlemen from Paris stood ready to receive the British fair on their approach to the rooms, and from baskets of flowers presented them with rich bouquets. Each lady thus entered the ball-room with one in her hand; and a thousand posies of sweet flowers displayed their hues, and exhaled their fragrance as the dancing commenced."

Here, from 1808 to 1810, Mrs. Billington, Mr. Braham, and Signor Naldi gave concerts, in rivalry with Madame Catalini at Hanover Square Rooms. In 1839 Master Bassle, a youth only thirteen years of age, appeared here in an extraordinary mnemonic performance; and in 1844 the rooms were taken by Mr. Charles Kemble, for the purpose of giving his readings from Shakespeare. In 1851, while the Great Exhibition was attracting its thousands, Thackeray here first appeared in public as a lecturer, taking as his subject "The English Humorists." Mr. Tom Taylor tells us an anecdote which belongs to his very first evening:—"Among the most conspicuous of the literary ladies at this gathering was Miss Brontë, the authoress of 'Jane Eyre.' She had never before seen the author of 'Vanity Fair,' though the second edition of her own celebrated novel was dedicated to him by her, with the assurance that she regarded him 'as the social regenerator of his day—as the very master of that working corps who would restore to rectitude the warped state of things.' Mrs. Gaskell tells us that, when the lecture was over, the lecturer descended from the platform, and making his way towards her, frankly asked her for her opinion. 'This,' adds Miss Brontë's biographer, 'she mentioned to me not many days afterwards, adding remarks almost identical with those which I subsequently read in "Villette," where a similar action on the part of M. Paul Emanuel is related.' The remarks of this singular woman on Thackeray and his writings, and her accounts of other interviews with him, will be found scattered about Mrs. Gaskell's biography of her."

As far back as 1840 it was pretty evident that "Almack's" was on the decline; as a writer in the *Quarterly Review* of that time puts it, there was "a clear proof that the palmy days of exclusiveness are gone by in England; and," he adds, "though it is obviously impossible to prevent any given number of persons from congregating and re-establishing an oligarchy, we are quite sure that the attempt would be ineffectual." Such an attempt, made in 1882, proved quite abortive.

Opposite Willis's Rooms are the auction-rooms of Messrs. Christie and Manson, still celebrated as ever for sales of pictures and articles of *vertu*. The sale-rooms of Messrs. Christie, as stated in a previous chapter, were originally in Pall Mall, but were removed hither in 1823. The eldest son of him who raised the firm to its lofty position, and who subsequently was himself its principal, was Mr. James Christie, no less distinguished as the scholar

and the gentleman than as an auctioneer. His first literary production was a disquisition upon Etruscan vases, a subject suggested to him through his intimacy with the collection of the famous Townley Marbles. Works of a similar character followed at different times; and, without entering into particulars, it will be sufficient to transcribe the opinion of the author of a memoir in the *Gentleman's Magazine*, "that the originality of his discoveries is not less conspicuous than the taste and talent with which he explains them." To this we may add, from the same eloquent tribute to his memory, that it will not seem surprising to find that such a man "raised the business he followed to the dignity of a profession. In pictures, in sculpture, in *vertu*, his taste was undisputed, and his judgment deferred to, as founded on the purest models and the most accredited standard. If to these advantages we add that fine moral feeling and that inherent love of truth which formed the basis of his character, and which would never permit him for any advantage to himself or others to violate their obligations, we may then have some means of judging how in his hands business became an honourable calling, and how that which to many is only secular, by him was dignified into a virtuous application of time and talents." This, the best of auctioneers, if we may credit the portrait here drawn of him, died in 1831.

The prices realised in these rooms for books, pictures, prints, old china, and other curiosities and antiquities, have almost always been high, though they have varied according to the direction taken by each passing mania of the day. It is stated that a pair of Sèvres china vases, for which in 1874 Lord Dudley gave £6,000 at Christie's, were not worth more than as many hundreds. It appears that a rival commission for this was given by one of the Rothschilds. A story is also told of a nobleman who sent an agent to a sale here with directions to buy a certain picture. The work was knocked down for a very large sum. "Well," said his lordship a few days after the sale, "did you bring the picture home?" "No," said the steward, "it fetched an enormous price, I did not think it worth the money, so I did not buy it." "Sir," said his lordship, "I did not say anything about the price; I told you to buy the picture." Similarly, these two agents of china-loving millionaires were told to buy the vases, and it is a good thing for one of the purchasers that both of them were not guided by the story of the noble lord, who, by the way, finished his rebuke to the steward with the remark, "Sir, it was your duty to buy that picture if you and your opponent had remained bidding for it until Doomsday."

Among the most important sales that have taken place here of late years were those of the art treasures belonging to Mr. Charles Dickens, and removed hither from his residence at Gad's Hill, near Rochester, where he died ; and the works of art, *virtu*, pictures, &c., belonging to the Duke of Hamilton, and brought from Hamilton Palace, which were sold here in 1882.

It may be interesting to record here the fact that the first book-auction in England, of which there is any record, was held in 1676, when the library of Dr. Searnan was brought to the hammer. Prefixed to the catalogue there is an address to the reader, saying, " Though it has been unusual in England to make sale of books by auction, yet it hath been practised in other countries to advantage." For general purposes this mode of sale was scarcely known till 1700.

In this street was born, in 1749, Mrs. Charlotte Smith, well known as a poet and a novelist. She was the daughter of Nicholas Turner, Esq., of Bignor Park, Sussex. She was the author of "The Old Manor House," "Rural Walks," and other works which enjoyed a wonderful popularity near the close of the last century. She died in October, 1806, at the age of fifty-seven.

At the beginning of 1847 the future Emperor of the French, then known as Prince Louis Napoleon, and an exile, took up his abode at No. 1*c*, on the north side of King Street, which bears on its front a tablet commemorating the fact. There he amused himself by collecting his books, portfolios, and family portraits, and made it his regular home. He was elected an honorary member of the Army and Navy Club, where he spent much of his spare time, rode in Hyde Park constantly, and frequented "Crockford's" in the evening. Here he entertained his friends quietly and unostentatiously, living quite a retired life in his "furnished apartments;" and it is pleasant news to learn, on the authority of Mr. B. Jerrold, that here the Prince made some clever sketches of decorations for Lady Combermere's and Lady Londonderry's stalls at the great military bazaar for the benefit of the Irish, which was held in the barracks of the Life Guards. Louis Napoleon was still living here in the following spring, when he served as one of 150,000 special constables who had been sworn in to keep order in anticipation of a Chartist rising. And here, too, he was residing when summoned to Paris a few months later by the events of the Revolution, which speedily raised him to the presidential chair, and ultimately to the imperial throne. When he entered London in 1855 along with his bride, the Empress Eugenie, he was seen to point out to her

with interest and pleasure the street in which he had spent those months of weary waiting, as, amid the cheering of the crowds, the *cortége* drove slowly up St. James's Street.

At one corner of King Street, in the year 1832, a large saloon, nearly 200 feet in length, was built for Mr. Crockford, and opened by him as the St. James's Bazaar. It was not, however, successful in attracting visitors. Here were exhibited, in 1841, three dioramic *tableaux* of the second obsequies of the great Napoleon in Paris ; and in 1844 the first exhibition of decorative works for the New Houses of Parliament was held here.

Two main thoroughfares connect King Street on the north with Jermyn Street—namely, Duke Street and Bury Street. In the former, on the 12th of February, 1781, was born Edward Burtenshaw Sugden, Lord Chancellor of Ireland, and subsequently of England also, and one of the most consummate lawyers of the nineteenth century. His father was a fashionable hairdresser and wig-maker ; and it is said—we know not with how much of truth—that the future occupant of the woolsack and "keeper of Her Majesty's conscience," as a boy, often held the bridles of the horses of customers who stopped to make their purchases at the shop of Mr. Richard Sugden. On one occasion, later in life, on the Sussex hustings, when reproached with his being the son of a barber, Mr. Sugden made the brave and noble reply, "The gentleman before me asks me if I remember that I am the son of a tradesman ? Yes; I remember it, and know it, and am proud of it. But the difference between my assailant and myself is, that I, being a barber's son, have raised myself to the position of a barrister, while he, if he had been born like me, would doubtless have remained a barber's son, and perhaps a barber, all his life." As it was, he netted in middle life an income of twenty thousand a year, and no doubt was a great loser in money by accepting a seat upon the judicial bench. It was late in life that he took a peerage, his patent as Lord St. Leonard's being dated 1st of March, 1852, certain obstacles to its acceptance being then removed. His lordship died in January, 1875, having reached the good old age of ninety-four. His will was afterwards the subject of litigation, the result of which was to establish, under certain conditions, the validity of a formal declaration of a testator's intentions, if satisfactorily proved and corroborated, as equivalent to a written will, where that will was known to exist, but was accidentally lost.

In this street Edmund Burke was living in 1795 when his hopes and parental pride were raised to the highest pitch by the election of his only son,

Richard, in his own room, as M.P. for Malton. These hopes, however, were destined to be speedily and rudely cast down, for no sooner had the father and son returned thither from Yorkshire than the latter was seized with a fatal illness, and died a week later at Brompton. The aged statesman was never himself again, and he survived the heavy blow only just two years.

At No. 10, now called Sussex Chambers, was formerly the Association of the Friends of Poland, over which the late Lord Dudley Coutts Stuart so long presided. This association was founded in 1832, for the purpose of diffusing information about Poland, of relieving poor Polish refugees, and of educating their children. The building, now the head-quarters of the Catholic Union of Great Britain, is, or once was, a very fine mansion, with a noble staircase, ornamental ceilings, and doors of the finest mahogany. It has below it large cellars and vaults, which, tradition says, went under Pall Mall and St. James's Park, and led to the Houses of Parliament. This, however, must be a fiction. There may, perhaps, be more truth in the story that the house was once occupied for a time by Oliver Cromwell.

Bury (or, more properly, Berry) Street, being so named after its original builder, being mainly let out as "apartments for bachelors," has had the honour of accommodating some distinguished residents; among others, Sir Richard Steele and Dean Swift, George Crabbe and Thomas Moore. Swift, as we learn from his writings, occupied a first-floor set of rooms, for which he paid eight shillings a week rent, "plaguy dear," as he remarks; but it is as well that he did not live here in our own day, and in the "season," or we fear that he would have found himself far more heavily rented.

Here, upon his marriage, in September, 1707, "Captain" (afterwards Sir Richard) Steele, the wit and essayist, took for his lady a house, "the third door from Germain [Jermyn] Street, left hand of Berry [Bury] Street." But it is clear, from autograph letters still to be seen at the British Museum, that the rent of this nuptial house, so sacred to "Prue," and to the tenderness and endearments of the honeymoon, was not paid until the landlord had put in an execution upon Steele's furniture. He appears soon after this to have migrated to Bloomsbury Square, where the same fate befell his establishment. Steele and "Prue" were married, in all probability, about the 7th of September in the above-mentioned year. "There are traces," writes Thackeray, "of a 'tiff' between them in the middle of the next month; she being as prudish and fidgety as he was impassioned and reckless."

Swift shared his lodgings here with his "Stella," Hester Johnson. Five doors off lived the rival lady, who flattered him and made love to him so outrageously, and in the end died for hopeless love of him—his "Vanessa." Thackeray tells us that Mrs. Vanhomrigh, "Vanessa's" mother, was the widow of a Dutch merchant who had held some lucrative posts in the time of King William. The family settled in London in Anne's reign, and had a house in Bury Street—"a street," he adds, "made notable by such residents as Steele and Swift, and in our own times by Moore and Crabbe." In one of his letters Swift describes his lodging in detail: he has "the first floor, a dining-room and bed-chamber, at eight shillings a week." He often lounged in upon the Vanhomrighs. In his journal to Stella, he writes: "I am so hot and lazy after my morning's walk that I loitered at Mrs. Vanhomrigh's, where my best gown and my periwig were, and, out of mere listlessness, dine there very often: so I did to-day."

On coming up to London from Trowbridge, late in life, George Crabbe took lodgings in this street, to be near Rogers and some other literary friends. Whilst here, he was a frequent visitor at Holland House, at Mr. Murray's, in Albemarle Street, and at Lansdowne House, from the doors of which he had been repulsed by its former owner, Lord Shelburne. At Holland House he made the acquaintance of Thomas Campbell, and Tommy Moore, and Brougham, and Sylvester Douglas, and the Smiths of the "Rejected Addresses," and Sydney Smith, and Ugo Foscolo. He writes in his "diary" on his return, "This visit to London has been indeed a rich one. I had new things to see, and was, perhaps, something of a novelty myself. Mr. Rogers introduced me to almost every man he is acquainted with; and in this number were comprehended all I was previously very desirous to obtain a knowledge of." It is only fair to add that by all that the quiet country parson-poet saw in the gay world of London he seems to have been quite unaltered, and that he returned to Trowbridge and his parochial duties with his head unturned and his kind heart unchanged.

At the corner of Ryder Street and Duke Street for many years lived William Yarrell, the naturalist, the author of "British Fishes," "British Birds," &c. He followed the trade of a news-agent. In 1849 he was elected a vice-president of the Linnæan Society. He died in 1856. His collections of British fishes, and the specimens illustrative of his papers in the "Transactions" of the Linnæan Society, were secured by the trustees of the British Museum at the sale of Mr. Yarrell's effects.

York Street, a short thoroughfare extending from the north side of St. James's Square to Jermyn Street, was the first street in London paved for foot-passengers. Strype, in his edition of Stow, describes it as "a broad street coming out of St. James's Square;" but, he adds, "the greatest part is taken up by the garden walls of the late Duke of Ormond's house on the one side, and on the other by the house inhabited by the Lord Cornwallis." On the eastern side of this street stood, till the present year, St. James's Chapel, a dull and poor-looking chapel-of-ease to the parish church. It was formerly occupied by Josiah Wedgwood, as a show-room for his pottery and porcelain from Etruria, in Staffordshire. In previous time this had been the residence of the Spanish ambassador, the chapel being used as a Roman Catholic place of worship under the ambassador's wing. It was subsequently used by Dissenting congregations, and from 1866 down to the time of its demolition the Rev. Stopford Brooke officiated here.

At No. 8 in this street were formerly the offices of the Charity Commission,* now located at Gwydyr House, Whitehall. The endowed charities amounted, in 1786, according to returns then made to Parliament under the Gilbert Act, to £528,710 a year. A Committee of the House of Commons, moved for by Mr. Brougham in 1816, recommended an inquiry into their condition. The first commission for this purpose was appointed by the Crown, under an Act of 1818, and further commissions of inquiry were issued and prosecuted under that and several subsequent Acts, until 1837. During many years after this time, numerous ineffectual proposals were made, in and out of Parliament, for the establishment of some jurisdiction for the permanent superintendence and control of these endowments. In 1853, an Act for the better administration of charitable trusts was, however, obtained, appointing commissioners and inspectors, but with the very minimum of power which could be given without rendering the commission altogether nugatory. Beyond a veto on suits by any one but the Attorney-General, the commissioners had only powers of inquiry, of advice, and of rendering assistance in a few cases in which trustees might seek it. Under the above Act the Lord Chancellor, in 1854, appointed official trustees of charity funds. In 1855, another Act empowered the Board to apportion parish charities under £30 a year; but with regard to new schemes, its operations were still subordinate, not only to Chancery, but to the County Courts. An Act

passed in 1860 for the first time gave the commissioners judicial power over charities of £50 a year, and like power, with the consent of the trustees, over larger charities; but being judicial, they can only be called into operation at the suit of persons interested in each case. Under the jurisdiction thus given, the Charity Commission has aided in establishing improved schemes in several cases; but a public department, which Parliament did not at its outset place even as high as a County Court, and which has ever since remained in the same position, cannot be expected to exercise influence enough with the public to originate and carry out any enlarged principles of administration on a subject in which so many individual and local prejudices are to be encountered. The Education Commissioners have proposed to vest the control of charities in a committee of the Privy Council, which might be governed less by technical and narrow rules than by an enlightened public opinion.

Abutting on York Street is Ormond Yard, so called after the Duke of Ormond, who suffered so severely in the royal cause during the Civil War. Mr. P. Cunningham reminds us that "the gallant Earl of Ossory" was his son, and the beautiful Countess of Chesterfield, of De Grammont's "Memoirs," his daughter, and that his grandson and heir was attainted in 1715 for his share in the rebellion of that year.

Jermyn Street, which runs parallel with Piccadilly on the north side of St. James's Square, and extends from St. James's Street to the Haymarket, was named from Henry Jermyn, Earl of St. Albans. This nobleman's residence, called St. Albans House, was on the south side of the street, and its site was afterwards occupied by part of Ormond House, of which we have already spoken. Like many other staunch loyalists, the Earl of St. Albans was little remembered by Charles II. He was, however, an attendant at court, and one of his Majesty's companions in his gay hours. On one of these occasions a stranger came with an importunate suit for an office of great value just vacant. The King, by way of joke, desired the Earl to personate him, and commanded the petitioner to be admitted. The gentleman, addressing himself to the supposed monarch, enumerated his services to the royal family, and hoped the grant of the place would not be deemed too great a reward. "By no means," answered the Earl, "and I am only sorry, that as soon as I heard of the vacancy, I conferred it on my faithful friend, the Earl of St. Albans," pointing to the King, "who constantly followed the fortunes both of my father and myself, and has hitherto gone unrewarded." Charles granted, for this joke, what the utmost real service would not have received. The Earl was supposed to have been privately married to the Queen Dowager, Henrietta Maria, who, as Pennant puts it, "ruled her first husband, *a king;* but the second, a *subject*, ruled her." The Earl died here in 1683.

In Jermyn Street, near the church, there was living, in the reign of Queen Anne, a Mrs. Howe, of whom, or rather of whose husband, we find an amusing account in Dr. W. King's "Anecdotes of

Church, Piccadilly (being so placed that she could not see him); and even frequented a coffee-house, from the window of which he could see his own wife at her meals. The strangest thing is, that the coffee-house keeper, supposing him to be an elderly bachelor, recommended to him the deserted lady and supposed widow as a wife. At the end of seventeen years, Mr. Howe sent to his wife an anonymous letter, begging her to be the next night, at a particular hour, in Birdcage Walk. On

BURY STREET. (*See page* 202.)

his Own Time." Her maiden name was Mallett; she was of a good family in the West of England, and married a Mr. Howe, who had a fortune of some £700 or £800 a year. Seven or eight years after his marriage, when he had two children, apparently without any reason he disappeared from his home in Jermyn Street, leading his wife to suppose that he had gone abroad. For seventeen years she heard no tidings of him, and, her two children having died, she removed into a smaller abode in Brewer Street, Golden Square. It appears that during all this long period Mr. Howe had gone no further away than Westminster, where he lived under an assumed name, and disguised in dress; that he constantly saw his wife at St. James's

repairing thither, the truant husband declared himself, and they lived happily together ever afterwards. It appears that the eccentric old gentleman was in the habit of even reading in the newspapers his wife's petition for a private Act of Parliament, entitling her and her children to a maintenance out of his estate; but that, in spite of this, he continued to keep up his incognito. The story is improbable, and would make the subject of a comedy.

At the Brunswick Hotel, in this street, Louis Napoleon took up his residence, under the assumed name of the Comte d'Arenenberg, on his escape from his captivity in the fortress of Ham, in May, 1846.

On the north side, extending through to the

south of Piccadilly, is the Museum of Practical Geology and Government School of Mines. It occupies an area of 70 feet by 153 feet, specially designed and built for its purposes by Mr. James Pennithorne, architect, at a cost of £30,000. The building comprises, on the ground storey, a spacious apartment having two galleries along its sides to give access to the cases with which the walls are lined. At the north and south ends are model-rooms, containing a gallery, and connected with the principal museum. The principal object of the Government School of Mines, which is engrafted on

TURKISH BATH, JERMYN STREET. (*See page* 206.)

hall, formed into three divisions by Doric columns, for the exhibition of building-stones, marbles, the heavier geological specimens, and works of art. Adjoining is a theatre for lectures upon scientific subjects, capable of accommodating upwards of 600 persons. There is also a library, librarian's apartments, and reception-room. On each side the entrance-hall is a staircase, joining in a central flight between Ionic columns, leading to the principal floor, containing the museum, a splendid the Museum of Practical Geology and Geological Survey, is to discipline the students thoroughly in the principles of those sciences upon which the successful operations of the miner and metallurgist depend. During the session, viz., from October to June, courses of lectures are delivered on chemistry, natural history, physics, mining, mineralogy, geology, applied mechanics, and metallurgy.

At No. 105, on the south side, is the Royal Society for the Prevention of Cruelty to Animals.

This institution, the only one having for its object the protection of dumb and defenceless animals, was founded in 1824, and is under the patronage of Her Majesty. The labours of this institution embrace the circulation of appropriate tracts, books, lectures, and sermons, and the prosecution of persons guilty of acts of cruelty to the brute creation.

At No. 76, on the same side of the street, is the London and Provincial Turkish Bath Company, which was established about the year 1860. Here, as in establishments of a similar kind which have sprung up in various parts of the United Kingdom, the plan of the old Roman bath is strictly followed. There is the Tepidarium, the Sudatorium (heated to a temperature of 120), and the Calidarium, in which the heat is exalted to 160 degrees. Next to this is the Lavatorium, in which the washing and shampooing process is carried on. *Apropos* of such baths, a writer in *Once a Week* has remarked that " the barbarian Turk has been the medium of keeping alive one of the most healthful practices of the ancients. There is scarcely a spot throughout the United Kingdom in which the remains of these very baths have not been disinterred and gazed at by the curious during the last half century. We turn up the flues, still blackened with the soot of fourteen centuries ago ; we find, as at Uriconium, the very furnaces, with the coal fuel close at hand ; and we know that the hot bath was not only used by the legionaries who held Britain, but by the civilised Britons themselves ; yet we must go all the way to the barbarian Turk for instruction upon one of the simplest and most effective methods of maintaining the public health."

In 1768 Dr. Hunter gave up his house in this street to his brother John, and took possession of one which he had built in Windmill Street, whence ultimately he moved, as we have noticed in a previous chapter, into Leicester Square.

Jermyn Street appears to have been at one time inhabited by artists. In 1782, at his rooms in this street, Mrs. Siddons gave sittings to Sherwin, for her portrait, in the character of the "Grecian Daughter," which was afterwards engraved ; the print from which, in consequence of a purse having been presented to Mrs. Siddons by gentlemen of the long robe, was dedicated to the Bar.

In this neighbourhood meets a Bohemian club called the " Century," composed of worshippers of the philosophy of Herbert Spencer, and other thinkers of the "advanced" school. The rest of the street is now mainly devoted to private family hotels, and to apartments for members of Parliament and aristocratic bachelors. A few years ago it was one of the head-quarters of gambling-houses.

In some papers in the *London Magazine* for 1773, signed " Harlequin," the whole of the neighbourhood of St. James's and Pall Mall, which we have described in this and the preceding chapters, is fictitiously traversed by a sprite, who peeps in at St. James's, at Carlton House, in Pall Mall, at " Boodle's," and at the "stately mansion of the Northumberlands, at Charing Cross." It is amusing, at the distance of a century or more, to note the scenes witnessed by " Harlequin." In St. James's Palace he saw the interior of the royal nursery, where " Madame Schulenberg was teaching the young Prince of Wales to play leap-frog," while his brother, the " Bishop of Osnaburg," was "riding a wooden horse called Hanover ; " and at Carlton House, Prince George and the Earl of Bute were standing in a bow window, while the Queen and the princess were engaged in working a flowered waistcoat for the simple and easy-going king!